Understanding the Psychology of

DIVERSITY

——— Second Edition ———

Understanding the Psychology of

DIVERSITY

—— Second Edition ——

Bruce Evan Blaine

St. John Fisher College, USA

Los Angeles | London | New Delhi
Singapore | Washington DC

Los Angeles | London | New Delhi
Singapore | Washington DC

FOR INFORMATION:

SAGE Publications, Inc.
2455 Teller Road
Thousand Oaks, California 91320
E-mail: order@sagepub.com

SAGE Publications Ltd.
1 Oliver's Yard
55 City Road
London EC1Y 1SP
United Kingdom

SAGE Publications India Pvt. Ltd.
B 1/I 1 Mohan Cooperative Industrial Area
Mathura Road, New Delhi 110 044
India

SAGE Publications Asia-Pacific Pte. Ltd.
3 Church Street
#10-04 Samsung Hub
Singapore 049483

Acquisitions Editor: Reid Hester
Associate Editor: Eve Oettinger
Editorial Assistant: Sarita Sarak
Production Editor: Laura Stewart
Copy Editor: Beth Hammond
Typesetter: C&M Digitals, Ltd.
Proofreader: Jeff Bryant
Indexer: Jennifer Pairan
Cover Designer: Anupama Krishan
Marketing Manager: Lisa Sheldon-Brown
Permissions Editor: Karen Ehrmann

Printed in the United States of America

Library of Congress Cataloging-in-Publication Data

Blaine, Bruce Evan.

Understanding the psychology of diversity / Bruce Evan Blaine. — 2nd ed.

p. cm.
Includes bibliographical references and index.

ISBN 978-1-4522-0333-1 (pbk.)

1. Prejudices. 2. Stereotypes (Social psychology) 3. Multiculturalism—Psychological aspects. I. Title.

HM1091.B54

2013 305.8001—dc23   2012016290

This book is printed on acid-free paper.

12 13 14 15 16 10 9 8 7 6 5 4 3 2 1

Brief Contents

Table of Contents

Preface

This Book's Purpose

The academic study of diversity has become a mainstay of undergraduate curricula. Diversity courses can be found in humanities as well as social science departments, in general education programs offered to first-year students as well as in disciplinary courses taken by majors. This type of college curricula seems to reflect a broader societal concern about teaching students how to understand the social and cultural differences in our communities. Indeed, liberally educated students *should* have some tools for thinking about diversity. That's where this book comes in.

Students can study diversity from many perspectives—college courses on diversity often reflect historical and sociological, as well as artistic and literary, voices and perspectives. However, if the study of diversity includes the need to understand the presence of, as well as the problems and issues associated with, social and cultural difference in our society, then psychology has much to offer. This book attempts to draw together a basic psychology of diversity for students in diversity-related courses that are taught within and outside of psychology departments. This book expands and improves on *The Psychology of Diversity: Perceiving and Experiencing Social Difference* (Blaine, 2000) by being a primary rather than a supplementary textbook, by expanding on the range of social differences covered, and by incorporating diversity-related social issues into the text. The book's level and language assumes no background in psychology among its readers, so that it will be a serviceable text for diversity courses that are taken by students with majors other than psychology. This book was not written as a psychology of prejudice text; nevertheless it covers enough of that material that the book could serve as a primary textbook in junior or senior level psychology courses on prejudice.

A note about striking a balance between the academic study of diversity and more personal responses to injustice and inequality is in order. When we study diversity, we confront the fact that social injustices exist. Too much emphasis on social injustices (e.g., where they originate, how they can be addressed) adds a political element to the book that may be intrusive. Avoiding social injustices altogether, however, intellectualizes problems and issues that students—particularly minority students—already face. It seems that a course on the Psychology of Diversity should provide a safe space for students to think about the moral implications of inequality. In writing this book I avoid explicit (but probably, given my own social and political attitudes, not implicit) polemic regarding social injustice and leave to both the instructor and student to strike their own balance between academic learning and social advocacy. However, Chapter 12 shows students that much has been learned about how to reduce inequality, intergroup conflict, and discrimination and provides instructors with a framework for advocacy/social action projects and discussions.

This Book's Organization

The book's 12 chapters could be divided, for the purposes of organizing a course, into 3 units. Chapters 1 through 4 comprise a "Basic Concepts in a Psychological Study of Diversity" unit. These chapters give student readers a toolbox of concepts and processes for understanding social difference in general, including dimensions and definitions of diversity (Chapter 1); social categorization, stereotypes, and stereotyping (Chapter 2); self-fulfilling prophecy and stereotypic communication (Chapter 3); and prejudice, and how anxiety, self-esteem, and projecting a public image influence prejudicial reactions to others (Chapter 4). Chapters 5 through 9 constitute a unit that might be termed "Stereotypes and Prejudice Toward Specific Groups" and that puts to use the general concepts and processes learned in prior chapters. These chapters consider racial stereotypes and racism (Chapter 5); gender stereotypes and sexism (Chapter 6); obesity stereotypes and weightism (Chapter 7); classism and homosexism (Chapter 8); and age stereotypes and ageism (Chapter 9). The final three chapters address "Further Topics in a Psychological Study of Diversity," including social stigma and the consequences of and responses to stigma (Chapters 10 and 11), and methods for responding to inequality (Chapter 12).

The book also includes 25 Diversity Issues—short (1-2 page) content set-asides that address practical issues and problems associated with diversity and responses to diversity. Collectively, the Diversity Issues provide a social issues flavor to the text, and questions posed to the student readers encourage them to make connections between academic principles and applied issues and problems. Some of the Diversity Issues topics include Hate Speech, Using the N-Word, The Glass Ceiling and the Maternal Wall, The Gender Pay Gap, and the *Sesame Street* Effect.

How to Use This Book

Three pedagogical features are woven into this book, each coded with a symbol that will assist you in planning class discussions, assignments, and student projects. Here are some ideas for how to use each in your course.

DI Diversity Issues

This symbol identifies the short interludes, called Diversity Issues, to the main chapter story to cover practical problems and issues that relate to or illustrate chapter concepts. Minimally, each diversity issue can be the focus of a class discussion; you can use them to draw out students' experiences and views on that issue. They can also be expanded to lecture topics, if you are interested in pursuing them yourself or in following students' interest, by adding supportive readings, video, guest lecturer, or other resource. Diversity issues can also be the basis for writing assignments, such as an assignment in which students find and summarize a research article on the issue, or another in which students clip a newspaper or Internet news item related to the issue and present it in class. Finally, a diversity issue can be the starting point for student research projects. For example, students might make some controlled observations about when they hear the N-word used in conversations, as a means of finding out about the situational or social variables that influence its use.

? Making Connections

This symbol means that student readers are being asked questions whose goal is to get them to think more deeply about the concepts they have just read about, and to make connections between concepts and applications. The Making Connections questions also help students pause and review concepts just read before reading further. You can use these questions to stimulate discussion in class, develop short writing assignments, or as a focus for small group discussions. They can also be appropriated as essay questions on exams.

Online Resources and Web Exercises

This symbol indicates a website that is particularly well suited for applying or extending students' learning on chapter concepts. The URL is provided, along with a description of the site and directions for finding the intended content. Some of these references also include some type of learning task such as answering a question from the web materials or gathering some information to test or illustrate an idea. Web exercises can be easily turned into student assignments or, with a little technological assistance, web-based presentations of an issue discussed in class.

Finally, there are For Further Reading resources at the end of each chapter, following the key terms. Here classic or provocative readings are provided with a description of why it is good reading and what contribution the reading makes to the larger chapter learning objective. Some of these readings will be more accessible to the psychology major than to the nonmajor, but you can choose which to recommend—or add your own favorite extra readings—based on the background of your class.

What's New for the Second Edition?

In addition to updating research examples throughout the book, the second edition features the following improvements:

- Chapter 9 is all new and covers age stereotypes and ageism. The chapter focuses on stereotyping and prejudice associated with old age, including a section on the discrimination of older workers. This chapter also features Diversity Issues on elderspeak and retirement. The media stereotype material from the first edition Chapter 9 has been merged into other chapters as appropriate.

• Substantial changes were made to Chapter 8 to focus its content on stereotyping and prejudice associated with being poor or from a sexual minority group.

• New or expanded coverage of the following topics: the stereotype consistency and negation biases (Chapter 3); aversive prejudice, secondary prejudice, and prejudiced personality dimensions (Chapter 4); the Princeton Trilogy, colorism, stereotypes of Asian-Americans, and race and jury composition (Chapter 5); gender stereotypes, hostile and benevolent sexism, and gender differences in STEM (Science, Technology, Engineering, and Mathematics) disciplines (Chapter 6); weightism at work and in the media (Chapter 7); gaydar and religious fundamentalism as a predictor of sexual prejudice (Chapter 8); stigma by association, stigma and mindfulness, and stereotype threat (Chapter 10); visibility as a moderator of coping with stigma and the consequences of concealing stigma (Chapter 11); and imagined intergroup contact (Chapter 12).

• Nine new Diversity Issues appear in the second edition. Some of the provocative and timely issues covered in these pieces are foreign accents and stereotypes, the Birther movement, the Obama effect, Title IX and the discrimination of women in college athletics, the Occupy movement, and mental illness stigma.

• Forty-four new web resources accompany the chapters in this book. These web links with descriptions provide a major new pedagogical support for instructors.

• Each chapter offers a For Further Reading resource in the form of an *American Psychologist* article. Together, these articles provide a coherent set of supplementary readings for students to explore issues and policies associated with a major topic in each chapter.

Acknowledgments

SAGE Publications would like to acknowledge the following reviewers:

Mona M. Abo-Zena, Suffolk University

Jack Klegan, Florida International University

Stella G. Lopez, University of Texas at San Antonio

Rick Pongratz, Idaho State University

Nancy Small Reed, University of Central Florida

Introduction to the Psychology of Diversity

Each of us lives in a diverse social world. Although we are frequently unaware of it, our lives unfold within social contexts that are populated by people who are different—both from us and each other. The people who populate the situations in our day-to-day lives may differ in many ways, such as their ethnic identity, sex, cultural background, economic status, political affiliation, or religious belief. The specific dimensions of difference do not matter nearly as much as the fact that we think, feel, and behave within diverse social contexts. Two important ideas follow from the fact that we, as individuals, are perpetually embedded in diversity.

First, because individuals are literally part of the social contexts in which they behave, those *situations cannot be understood independently of the people in them.* Have you ever been amazed that you perceived a situation, such as a job interview, much differently than a friend? Perhaps you approached the interview with optimism and confidence, regarding it a potentially positive step in your career goals. Your friend, however, may have viewed the same scenario as threatening and bemoaning how it would never work out. This illustrates how social situations are, in vital part, constructed and maintained by people. We project our own attitudes, feelings, expectations, and fears onto the situations we encounter. Applied to our social contexts, this principle says that the differentness we perceive between ourselves and other people, or among other people, may be inaccurate. As we will learn in subsequent chapters in this book, there are times when we project too much social difference onto our contexts and the people in them. At other times, however, we underestimate the diversity around us. So, the diversity of our lives is partly a function of us—our individual ways of thinking and emotional needs.

Second, because people live and behave in diverse social contexts, then *individuals cannot be understood independently of the situations in which they act and interact.* Are you sometimes a different person, or do you show a different side of yourself, as your social setting changes? For example, do you display different table manners when eating with your friends at the café than during a holiday meal with the family? Do you think of yourself differently in those situations? If so, then you realize how we are, in vital part, social beings. Our behavior and identity are constructed and maintained by the situations in which we act and live. Likewise, our thoughts and actions flex with the situational norms we encounter. If we are interested in explaining who we are and why we behave the way we do, we must look to the social context for insight. The diversity of our social contexts is laden with informative clues to help us demystify our own behavior and confront our attitudes and beliefs.

In sum, if we are to fully understand the diversity of our classroom, community, or nation, we must appreciate that it is more than statistics about race and gender. Diversity and the individual are inextricably linked; therefore, the study of one must include the other. This book examines how we can better understand diversity by studying how the individual constructs it, and how we can better understand the individual by learning how she or he is defined and influenced by social diversity. These two principles of the psychology of diversity will be revisited and elaborated at the end of this chapter. First, we must consider what diversity is and examine some of the common ways that term is used.

Diversity Is Social Difference

What is diversity? According to the dictionary, **diversity** is the presence of difference. However, the most common usages of diversity refer to *social* difference, or differences among people. People can differ in so many ways; to appreciate the range and types of diversity in the United States, and to introduce the dimensions of diversity that are addressed in this book, let's develop a statistical snapshot of the social differences of Americans from the 2010 U. S. Census Bureau statistics and other recent national surveys. So that we can simultaneously appreciate how much (or little) research attention has been given various aspects of diversity in the social scientific research literature, we review these in order from the most-researched to the least-researched (See Figure 1.1 for a display of the research activity in each area).

Figure 1.1   Research Activity on Various Dimensions of Diversity From 1887 to the Present

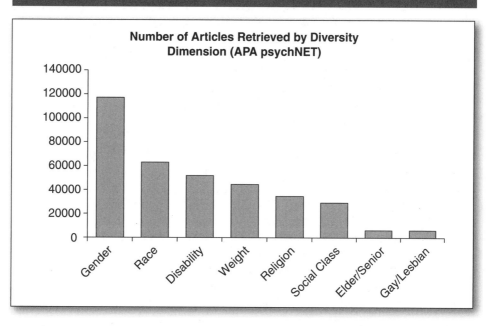

Gender

The study of gender, including related topics like sex roles and sex differences, is by far the most-researched aspect of diversity. Gender is a good case study for understanding that majority-group status is conferred by status and control over resources and not mere statistical majority. Figures from the 2010 U.S. Census show that females and males make up 51% and 49% of the U.S. population, respectively (Howden & Meyer, 2011). Put another way, there are about 97 males in America for every 100 females and, because women tend to live longer than men, they become more of a statistical majority as they age. Although, statistically speaking, women are a majority group, women have historically endured second-class status relative to men in many life domains. For example, even with legal protections against discrimination of women in the workplace, in 2011, a gender wage gap still existed such that women earn about 80 cents for every dollar earned by men (Hegewisch, Williams, & Henderson, 2011). We will take up gender diversity in Chapter 6.

Race

The second most-researched aspect of diversity involves race and other related topics such as racial identity and racism. Racial distinctions are based on physical and facial characteristics, skin color, and hair type and color that developed in response to particular geographic and climatic forces. The most common race labels are limited in that they combine color-based racial notions (e.g., White, Black) with ethnic and linguistic (e.g., Asian, Hispanic) elements. Moreover, many people now identify themselves on government surveys as biracial or multiethnic (e.g., having parents from different racial or ethnic groups). To deal with this complexity, the U.S. Census Bureau treats ethnic background and race as different concepts so that, for example, Hispanic people can identify themselves as White only, Black only, some other race, or even biracial. Measures of race and ethnic background (appropriately) defy simple snapshots of racial and ethnic diversity of Americans. Still, a general picture of who we are as Americans in racial-ethnic terms would be helpful.

In 2000, Whites constituted about 69% of the American population, with Black (about 12%) and Hispanic/Latino (about 12%) people comprising minority populations of about the same size. In 2010, 64% of Americans were White, 13% were Black, and 16% were Hispanic, with people from other racial categories (e.g., Asian, Native American, Pacific Islander) making up the remaining 7% of the population (Humes, Jones, & Ramirez, 2011). These figures indicate that Hispanics are now the largest minority group in the United States. Indeed, the total U.S. population grew by 27 million people in the last decade, and growth in the Hispanic population accounted for over half of that growth. In terms of racial identity, most Hispanic people consider themselves from one race, with about half of the Hispanics on the 2010 census listing their race as White. Most of the other half identified themselves as Black or "some other race," which was a catch-all category to include a variety of nationality-based responses (e.g., Mexican). In 2010, 3% of Americans identified themselves as biracial or multiracial, increasing from 2.5% in 2000. Although the absolute numbers of biracial Americans is small, this is a rapidly growing racial category. We will learn more about issues surrounding biracial identity in Chapters 2 and 4 (see also Diversity Issue 1.1 in this chapter).

About one in five Americans speaks a language at home other than English, and about one half of those people speak little or no English. Spanish is the most common language spoken in those homes where English is not, or rarely, spoken. Indeed, there are about 35 million first-language Spanish-speaking Americans (roughly the population of California), making Spanish literacy an increasingly important concern in government, business, and education. Look around your class: The changing nature of the American population is reflected in the make-up of your college or university student body. In 1990, about 20% of college students were non-White (9% Black, 6% Hispanic, 4% Asian). In 2008, just 18 years later, minority college students (14% Black, 12% Hispanic, 7% Asian) constituted 33% of the college population (National Center for Educational Statistics, 2008).

Disability

Disability takes many forms and includes any condition that affects individuals' vision, hearing, mobility, learning and memory, or communication ability. According to the Centers for Disease Control and Prevention (CDC), about 22% of American adults have some kind of disability, with roughly half of those people having a severe disability. Disability increases with age: About 38% of people over the age of 65 have some disability compared with 14% of adults between 18 and 44 (CDC, 2008). Disability rates tend to be slightly higher in women than in men, and higher in White and Black Americans compared with other minority groups. People with disabilities also have lower incomes and higher rates of living in poverty than do able-bodied people.

Weight

Body shape and size is a visible aspect of diversity. Research on the consequences of overweight and obesity for health, social opportunity, and well-being has exploded in the past several years. For evidence of that, look at Figure 1.1: In the first edition of this book (published in 2007), the number of articles retrieved from PsychNET on some aspect of weight was about 10,000, making weight the least-researched of the diversity dimensions pictured in Figure 1.1. Not even 10 years later, over 40,000 articles are available on some aspect of weight. Currently, about two out of every three American adults are overweight (having a body mass index, or BMI, over 25), and one in three is obese, having a BMI of 30 or more (Flegel, Carroll, Ogden, & Curtin, 2010). Obesity rates are higher among women than among men, among racial and ethnic minority groups than among Whites, and among lower income compared with middle- and high-income persons. Overweight/obesity is an important issue in a study of diversity for several reasons. First, body size informs self-image and self-esteem. Second, prejudice and discrimination against people because of their (heavy) weight is widespread and, unlike most other forms of discrimination, legal. Third, overweight and obesity are associated with tremendous loss of social status and opportunity. We will cover these topics and more in Chapter 7.

Religion

Americans are overwhelmingly Christian in religious affiliation or belief. Looking at Figure 1.2, if you combine Catholic and Protestant traditions, about 75% of Americans identify themselves as Christian. Jews constitute about 2%, and all other religions together about 7% of the American population. People who identify with no religious tradition are a sizable minority, constituting about 16% of the population. Although Christianity dominates the religious landscape, some religious minorities are growing at astounding rates. For example, in 1990, there were 1.5 million Muslims in the United States; by 2010 the number had increased to 2.6 million, and by 2030 over 6 million Muslims are expected to populate the American religious scene (Pew Forum, 2011). Religion occupies a more prominent role in the lives of Black compared with White Americans: About 80% of Blacks say religion is very important in their lives, compared with about 56% of White Americans. Black Americans also engage in more public (e.g., church attendance) and private (e.g., prayer) religious behavior than Whites do (Pew Forum, 2009). We will further consider religious diversity in Chapter 8.

Figure 1.2 Religious Preferences of Americans by Tradition (in Millions of Respondents and Percentage of Population)

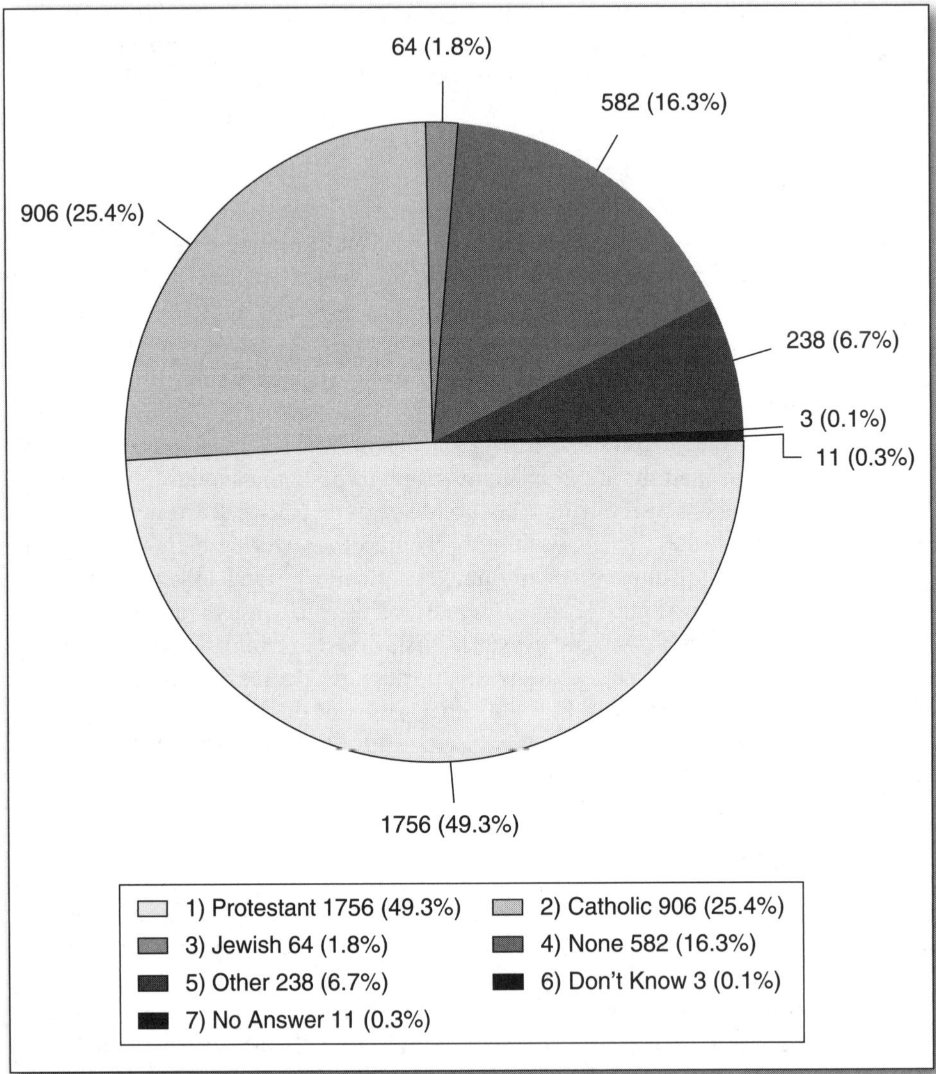
64 (1.8%)
582 (16.3%)
906 (25.4%)
238 (6.7%)
3 (0.1%)
11 (0.3%)
1756 (49.3%)
1) Protestant 1756 (49.3%)
2) Catholic 906 (25.4%)
3) Jewish 64 (1.8%)
4) None 582 (16.3%)
5) Other 238 (6.7%)
6) Don't Know 3 (0.1%)
7) No Answer 11 (0.3%)

SOURCE: Data from General Social Survey. Graph from Association of Religion Data Archives, http://thearda.com/. Used with permission.

Social Class

Social class, or socioeconomic status, refers to a marker that combines educational attainment and income. The median annual household income (the income level that divides the upper and lower halves of the population) for Americans in 2009 was

$49,777 (DeNavas-Walt, Proctor, & Smith, 2010). Household income, however, varied greatly by race: On average, White and Black households earned $51,861 and $32,584, respectively. As of 2009, poverty is defined as having an annual household income at or below $21,954 for a family of four, and 14% of all American families live in poverty. As with income, poverty status depends on one's race: 12% of White families live in poverty, compared with 26% of Black and 25% of Hispanic families. Most Americans (85%) have a high school education, and about one half (54%) of the population has some college education or a college degree (Crissey, 2009). Education, especially higher education, also varies sharply by race. Among White and Asian Americans, 31% and 50% respectively, earn a college degree or greater. Black (17%) and Hispanic (13%) Americans achieve a college degree or higher at much lower rates.

Age

Age diversity receives relatively little research attention, but that should change with the expected growth of the senior citizen population in the next 20 years. The median (or 50th percentile) age for the U.S. population is 36.5 years. The typical female is older than the typical male due to the longer life expectancy for women. For people born in the early 1990s, which includes many readers of this book, average life expectancy is 72 years for males and 79 years for females (Arias, 2011). The aging of the Baby Boom generation (those born between 1946 and 1964) means that in 2011, the first wave of Baby Boomers will turned 65. According to the U.S. Census Bureau, in 2010, 13% of the population was age 65 and older. In 2030, when the last wave of Baby Boomers reaches retirement age, 19% of all Americans will be 65 or older. The rapid growth of the senior citizen population has implications for eldercare, health care, and other issues. We will consider age-related stereotypes and agism in Chapter 9.

Sexual Orientation

Estimates vary of the percentage of LGBT (a term including lesbian, gay male, bisexual, and transgendered) individuals in the population due to two factors: the reluctance of some people to disclose their sexual orientation on a survey, and the error inherent in small sample surveys. The most recent and best data on the percentages of LGBT Americans come from the National Survey of Sexual Health and Behavior, a survey of 5,965 randomly selected Americans from age 14 to 94. Regarding homosexual identity, about 3% of male and 9% of female adolescents identify themselves as gay or bisexual. Among adults, 7% of men and 5% of women identify as either gay or bisexual (Herbenick, Reese, Schick, Sanders, Dodge, & Fortenberry, 2010). Same-sex sexual behavior is somewhat more common than homosexual identity: Among adults ages 40 to 49, 10% to 15% of men and 10% to 12% of women report having participated in same-sex oral sex in their lifetimes (Herbenick et al., 2010). Sexual diversity is noteworthy because, relative to gender and race, it is an invisible status and this greatly affects whether one is a target of gay-related prejudice and how one copes with prejudice.

> **?** Do visible differences matter more to us than invisible differences? Why?
>
> Electoral politics are color-coded: talk about what you think a red-state versus a blue-state voter is like.

Making Sense of Diversity

These statistics offer a glimpse of the extent of social differences around us. But how do we make sense of this diversity? When we talk about diversity, *how* do we talk about it? Do we regard diversity as a good thing or a bad thing, as something to be preserved and celebrated, or something to be overcome? Is diversity more of a political or a social word? Diversity can be approached from several intellectual perspectives, each imparting a different meaning to the concept. Before introducing a psychological perspective on diversity, let's clarify what is meant by diversity from demographic, political, ideological, and social justice perspectives.

Diversity as a Demographic Concern

A common use of diversity involves the range or proportion of social differences that are represented in a group of people, organization, or situation. When used in this way—often in concert with social statistics—the term reflects demographic concerns. To understand the nature of social differences, and how they differ from individual differences, try this exercise. The next time you attend the class for which you are reading this, look around and consider the many ways that the people in that class differ. Physically, they have different dimensions, such as weight and height, and characteristics, such as hair color and style. Psychologically, they have varying levels of self-confidence and anxiety. Intellectually, they differ in their verbal ability and intelligence. Finally, the students in your class probably differ in the social categories or groupings of which they represent, such as sex, ethnicity, cultural background, and religion. Notice how the first three (physical, psychological, and intellectual) are examples of *individual* differences—each student probably differs from every other student on that dimension. Social differences, however, refer to groupings or categories of individuals such as male and female; Catholic, Jewish, or Protestant; or single, divorced, or married. People are *socially* different when they associate with, or are members of, different social categories. Demographers, as scientists of vital and social statistics, study diversity using social categories.

Social categories are also useful and informative tools for a psychological study of diversity. They help us organize and remember other information about people, operating something like computer files in which social information is arranged and stored. As a result, when an individual's social category is brought to mind, that related information—such as our attitudes, beliefs, and expectations about people in that category—becomes very accessible. Try this free association task. What images or thoughts come to mind when you think of the social category *poor*? If you imagine a person who was lacking in intelligence or motivation to make something of himself, dressed in shabby clothes, and living in the bad section of town, you begin to see how social categories are rich with information about a person's characteristics and behavior, and how the concept of diversity is influenced by the kind of information we associate with dimensions of social difference.

Social categories are also useful for describing people: That is, we commonly identify others by their social characteristics. In describing a person to a friend you might say, "You know, she's Hispanic, an engineering major, and a Sigma Tau. . . ." How many social categories are employed in that description? Compared to descriptions of others that cite individual differences, such as their height, optimism, and grade point average, descriptions that involve *social* differences are more available and informative. Social identification is not limited to our thinking about other people; we also identify ourselves in social terms. If asked to describe yourself, you would likely use many social terms such as Asian American, female, Catholic, or Republican. Because we identify ourselves in social terms, we are conscious of the beliefs and assumptions that other people typically associate with those categories.

Psychologists and demographers, therefore, share a common interest in social categories. But whereas demographers analyze social statistics, psychologists are interested in how social differences relate to individual behavior. Clearly, dimensions of social difference are important to our thinking about ourselves and other people. The significance of social differences, however, goes beyond the mere fact that we think of people in terms of their social groups. Social categories are laden with a great deal of information that influences how we perceive and experience our social world.

Diversity as a Political Concern

Sometimes the term diversity refers to specific dimensions of social difference that typically include sex, race, ethnicity, and to a lesser extent, physical disability. This meaning may stem from the 1978 Supreme Court *Bakke* decision in which diversity was viewed as a goal that could justify admitting students to a university based on their race. If so, diversity in a political perspective refers to particular social groups who have experienced disadvantage and discrimination (i.e., women, Blacks, Hispanics, and other ethnic minority groups). To have a diverse corporation or university, for example, is to include (or not exclude) members of historically disadvantaged social groups. This definition, however, fails to acknowledge that many social groups other than women and racial minorities have experienced injustice in our society, including gays and lesbians, the poor, released convicts, Muslims and Jews, and obese people.

This conceptualization—that diversity is the presence of people from historically disadvantaged social groups or categories—has political overtones and is limiting to a psychological study of diversity in two ways. First, recall that one of the principles of this book is that we construct diversity through our perceptions, beliefs, expectations, and behavior toward people based on social dimensions. But if diversity is linked predominantly to women and ethnic minorities, then the range of social difference (or *important* social difference) is preset for us by a particular legal definition of diversity. Although the motives for including members of historically disadvantaged groups in our schools and businesses are noble, this political meaning of diversity restricts the actual diversity of our social environment.

Second, the political usage of diversity focuses too much attention on social differences that are visible. Although some social differences are visible, others are not so obvious. For example, can you tell which of your classmates is learning disabled, Jewish, or gay? Perhaps you *think* you can based on their behavior or appearance, but in fact, those judgments are probably not very accurate. From a psychological standpoint, diversity need not be limited to visible dimensions of social difference. Indeed, whether our social differences are visible or hidden from others is an important factor in understanding their influence on our psychological and social adjustment.

In sum, a psychological approach to diversity includes obvious dimensions of social difference as well as those which are less apparent or even unobservable. Psychological and political approaches to diversity, however, share an important feature—the recognition that there is a greater psychological burden associated with being a member of some social categories than others and some of this burden *is* attributable to past oppression and injustice.

Diversity as an Ideological Concern

Thus far we have considered that the concept of diversity is both a demographic and political concern. If social difference is a fact of life in our schools, communities, and nation, why is the concept of diversity such a controversial and divisive topic? The controversy that surrounds the term diversity is due to a third meaning that incorporates qualities that *should* be present in a diverse society. The qualities that should accompany social diversity are subjective and, as a result, open to debate and controversy. Not surprisingly, people take different positions on why diversity is valuable or desirable. Ideological perspectives on diversity tend to be one of three types: the melting pot, multiculturalism, and color-blindness.

The Melting Pot

For decades, the United States has taken great pride in the America-as-melting-pot idea, and its prominent symbol, the Statue of Liberty. Emma Lazarus's poem, mounted on the base of Lady Liberty, illustrates the melting pot:

> . . . Give me your tired, your poor,
> Your huddled masses yearning to breathe free,
> The wretched refuse of your teeming shore,
> Send these, the homeless, tempest-tost to me,
> I lift my lamp beside the golden door!

Emma Lazarus, 1883

People who use the term diversity in this way tend to believe that a diverse society should be one where all people are welcome, where social differences are accepted and understood, and where people with social differences relate harmoniously. In the film *Manhattan Murder Mystery*, when a gentlemanly neighbor is suspected of murdering his wife, Larry (Woody Allen) retorts: "So? New York is a melting pot." This parody is nevertheless instructive: The **melting pot** ideal involves the acceptance of others' difference if they are (or perceived to be) otherwise devoted to the majority group values and goals, such as working hard and being a responsible citizen. This melting pot view of diversity is reflected in an essay by Edgar Beckham, who coordinates Wesleyan University's Campus Diversity Initiative: "How unfortunate, especially in a democracy, that we fail to note how insistently diversity also points to unity." Beckham (1997) argues that diversity requires a unifying context in which social differences among people can work together for the benefit of everyone. So the melting pot embodies a vision of a school, community, or nation in which differences among people—especially those that relate to ethnicity and cultural heritage—are blended into a single social and cultural product.

Multiculturalism

Multiculturalism is the name given to beliefs or ideals that promote the recognition, appreciation, celebration, and preservation of social difference. People who espouse multiculturalism value the preservation of the separate voices, cultures, and traditions that comprise our communities and nation. A patchwork quilt, rather than a melting pot, provides a helpful metaphor for appreciating multiculturalism. In fact, quilts and quilting projects are used by educators to teach diversity concepts in elementary school-aged children. A song written by Lauren Mayer, and part of the *Second Grade Rocks!* educational curriculum, expresses this idea:

> We are pieces of a quilt of many colors
>
> See, how we blend together in harmony
>
> And each piece is not complete without the others
>
> Stitching a quilt made of you and me.
>
> Music & lyrics by Lauren Mayer, © 2004

In multicultural approaches to diversity, patches of people, each with a distinct cultural or national heritage, become sewn into a large social quilt. The patches are connected to each other, perhaps by a common commitment to some overarching value such as democracy or freedom. In the spirit of the metaphor and the values surrounding multiculturalism, the quilt preserves the uniqueness of social and cultural groups while at the same time uniting them for a superordinate purpose. In short, melting pot ideals hold that social differences can, and should, be blended in a harmonious way. Multiculturalism also values unity, but in a way that preserves and even capitalizes on our social differences.

Color-Blindness

As an ideology, **color-blindness** attempts to consider people strictly as individuals, ignoring or de-emphasizing racial or ethnic group membership. In short, race should not matter in the way people are treated. This aspect of color-blindness reveals that it is an ideology held by the racial majority about, or toward, racial minority persons. Also inherent in color-blindness is an assimilationist hope: that people from racial minority groups will downplay their racial and ethnic differences and adapt to mainstream norms (Wolsko, Park, & Judd, 2006). Color-blindness need not be antithetical to diversity: Indeed, proponents of color-blindness believe that racial diversity in communities, businesses, and schools is a valuable goal, but it should be achieved by making decisions based on factors other than race. Although true color-blindness is an ideal where race is irrelevant to life outcomes (e.g., income, housing, health), critics of color-blindness argue that race *is* relevant because of the persistence of racial discrimination in society.

Melting pot, multiculturalist, and color-blindness notions of diversity have different implications for individuals from minority groups. In melting pot and color-blind ideologies, racial and ethnic minorities gain acceptance to the extent that they assimilate and adopt majority group customs. In a multicultural society, minority groups' culture and customs are accepted and preserved by the majority group. Which ideology is better for minorities? The research is mixed: Some work shows that multiculturalism is threatening to Whites and contributes to prejudice against minorities (Morrison, Plaut, & Ybarra, 2010; Plaut, Garnett, Buffardi, & Sanchez-Burks, 2011). Other research finds that multiculturalism decreases, and color-blindness increases, minorities' perception of bias against their group (Plaut, Thomas, & Goren, 2009; Gutierrez & Unzueta, 2010).

Regardless of whether you believe that melting pot, multicultural, or color-blindness ideals are possible or even desirable, we must acknowledge that diversity is often used in a manner that conflates description and ideology—what is and what should be. With regard to diversity, the three ideologies described above are statements of what some people feel *should* be in a socially diverse environment. We will approach our study of diversity regarding it neither as inherently desirable nor undesirable, but simply as an important characteristic of our social world.

Diversity and Concern for Social Justice

Diversity is not something that is inherently good or bad, but many dimensions of social difference are associated with inequality and disadvantage. Therefore, diversity is also a concern of individuals who value and strive for social justice. Social justice exists when all the groups of people in a society are afforded the same rights and opportunities and when their life outcomes are not unfairly constrained by prejudice and discrimination. As the diversity of a community increases, so does the potential for some groups of people to be disadvantaged relative to other groups. In a socially just community, the accomplishments and well-being of some people are not won at the expense of others.

We know that America is a diverse society, but how socially just are we? Much data suggest that although all Americans enjoy similar rights and opportunities, not all realize comparable outcomes. Here are a few examples that highlight the divergent life outcomes of Whites compared with racial and ethnic minority individuals and the wealthy compared with the poor (U.S. Census Bureau, 2010). All U.S. citizens are entitled to free public education through grade 12, but not all of them get it. In 2009, 92% of Whites had earned a high school diploma, but only 84% and 62% of Blacks and Hispanics, respectively. In principle, all people should have access to health care, if not from their employer, then from a government health care program such as Medicaid. In 2009, however, 16% of White, 21% of Black, and 32% of Hispanic individuals had no health insurance. Even for people with insurance, racial disparities in health outcomes are common. For example, Blacks with diabetes were less likely to be screened for, or receive, hemoglobin testing than Whites with the illness, and five times more likely than Whites to have a leg amputated due to the complications of diabetes (Sack, 2008). We will consider racial discrimination in health care in Chapter 5.

In a socially just society, people will not be victimized because of their group membership. However, according to Bureau of Justice data from 2009, Blacks are about 50% more likely to be a crime victim, and about three times more likely to be a victim of a robbery, than Whites are (Truman & Rand, 2010). Although Blacks are about 12% of the U.S. population, they are about 50% of those arrested for crimes, and even though twice as many Whites as Blacks are arrested for crimes, White and Black individuals are imprisoned in equal numbers. These statistics paint an unsettling image. In a nation devoted to its citizens' life, liberty, and pursuit of happiness, racial and ethnic minorities and poor people have less of these than White and wealthy people do.

Psychologists have long approached the study of diversity with an underlying concern for identifying, explaining, and correcting social injustice. For example, Kenneth and Mamie Clark's (1940) work showing that Black children preferred to play with White than with Black dolls was instrumental in the Supreme Court's 1954 decision declaring that racially segregated schools were unconstitutional. Psychologists' concern for social justice is also evident in the way research on stereotyping and prejudice has been conducted. The great majority of research articles on stereotypes and stereotyping (numbering in the tens of thousands) have examined Whites' beliefs and preconceptions about Blacks, while only a relative handful of articles have examined Blacks' stereotypes of Whites. When stereotyping processes should be the same in both directions, and thus equally understandable from either group's perspective— why does this research bias exist? Stereotypes held by empowered, majority group members—like Whites and males—are much more problematic because stereotypes can cause, support, and justify discrimination of minority group individuals. Because leadership positions in business and government have traditionally been, and continue to be, disproportionately held by White people, their stereotypic beliefs about Blacks have the potential to become institutionalized and contribute to institutional forms of discrimination. So psychologists have combined their basic research questions (e.g., What are the processes that lead to stereotyping?) with concerns for understanding and potentially addressing social injustice. As a final bit of evidence for the social justice agenda of psychologists, consider the mission statements of the two national psychological societies in the United States. The stated purpose of the American Psychology Association is to "advance psychology as a science and profession and as a means of promoting health, education, *and human welfare*" (italics added). Likewise, the mission of the Association for Psychological Science is to "promote, protect, and advance the interests of scientifically oriented psychology in research, application, teaching, and *the improvement of human welfare*" (italics added).

> **?**
>
> Diversity is accused of buzzword or PC status, according to many.
>
> What is meant by that characterization? What meaning of the term *diversity* is being dismissed with these labels?

Let's pause and sum up. A psychological study of diversity shares with demographers and policy makers an interest in social categories and historically disadvantaged groups. However, the most prominent theme in a psychological study of diversity is the concern with social justice. So, as we proceed through the chapters of this book, we will strive to gain a psychological understanding of diversity *and* acknowledge the social injustices faced by people from various social groups. At the end of the book (Chapter 12), we will focus directly on interventions and strategies for reducing prejudice and promoting social equality and harmony. This book must also address two shortcomings in the psychological research on social difference. First, research attention to diversity has been dominated by a small number of dimensions: gender and, to a lesser extent, race and disability (see Figure 1.1). Race and gender affect our thinking about others more than other social categories do; this may explain the greater research activity on those dimensions of diversity. The research priorities displayed in Figure 1.1 may also reflect broader societal efforts, and the psychological research involved in those efforts, to extend equal rights all based on gender and race. Still, there are many other dimensions of diversity and social injustices that affect the members of those groups that students of the psychology of diversity must confront. Second, psychological research favors finding differences between groups of people over similarities between, and differences within, groups of people (Jones, 1994). For example, tens of thousands of studies document the (relatively few) psychological differences between men and women. This same research obscures, however, both the many ways that men and women are alike as well as the diversity within the populations of men and women. A psychology of diversity must therefore accentuate shared qualities between, and diversity within, groups of people. The goals of a psychological study of diversity are listed in Figure 1.3.

Figure 1.3 The Goals of a Psychological Study of Diversity

A psychological study of diversity must:

- Examine how diversity shapes our own identities and behavior.
- Examine how we shape the diversity of our social worlds.
- Confront a wide range of diversity dimensions, not just those that are associated with historical disadvantage.
- Recognize the social injustice that attends many dimensions of diversity, and use our scientific knowledge to respond to injustice.
- Recognize not just social differences, but also the diversity within, and similarities between, groups of people.

The Psychology of Diversity: A Conceptual Framework

A psychology of diversity considers how individuals' thoughts, feelings, and behavior are intertwined with their diverse social environments. At the beginning of this chapter, I introduced two principles that form a framework for a psychological study of diversity. First, social difference is constructed and maintained by individuals, and second, social difference exerts influence on individuals. Let us consider further the interdependence of the individual and his or her social context.

Diversity Is Socially Constructed

The Individual Is a Social Perceiver

As individuals living in a social world, we confront and process volumes of social information each day. From others' skin color to facial characteristics, from their clothing preferences to political attitudes, we sift through, organize, and make sense of countless pieces of social information. Although we can be very fast and efficient in the way we process these data, psychological researchers have demonstrated that we commonly make mistakes and exhibit inaccuracies in our thinking about other people and our social world. These tendencies and errors have consequences for our conclusions and judgments about our social world and the people who comprise it. We tend to rely on information that is most available in our memory banks to help us make judgments about other people, and this information leads us to make mistakes in judging the diversity of our social environments. Consider this: What proportion of your college or university student population is made of physically disabled individuals? Do you have to guess? On what information will you base your guess? Most of us have rather infrequent interactions with disabled individuals and tend not to notice them around campus. Based on our own interactions with and memory for disabled students, we would probably underestimate their numbers in the student population. In sum, the extent of diversity that we perceive in our schools, organizations, and communities is influenced by our natural limitations and biases in dealing with an overwhelming amount of social information.

Our attention and memory for social information tends to be organized by social categories, which, in turn, can distort differences and obscure similarities between members of different categories. Information about the characteristics of, for example, women and men are organized and stored in different memory structures. Although there are advantages to storing social information in this way, separating male and female information in memory leads to an overemphasis of the differences between men and women as well as an underappreciation of the ways that men and women are the same. The popular *Men Are From Venus, Women Are From Mars* books and videos suggest that the differences between men and women are vast and inexplicable (Gray, 1992). Psychological theory and research helps us see, however, that gender diversity—the extent to which men and women are different—is distorted by our use of social categories.

The Individual Is a Social Actor

Not only are we social perceivers, we also act within our social contexts in ways that have implications for diversity. We typically bring into our interactions with other people a set of beliefs and expectations about them. These expectations can function in two ways: guiding the way we act toward other people and influencing the way others react to us. Here's an example. Psychological studies have demonstrated that most of us feel tension and uncertainty in interactions with physically disabled people. These feelings may stem from the belief that handicapped individuals have special needs with which we are uncomfortable or unfamiliar. Our beliefs about disabled people may lead us to avoid them, or keep our interactions with them brief and superficial, thereby contributing to their differentness from us. Moreover, our suspicious and avoidant actions actually contribute to, rather than ameliorate, their marginalization and dependence on others. In other words, our behavior often sends signals to other people about their differentness and how they are expected to act, leading them to live up to (or, more commonly, down to) those expectations. In this way, our behavior toward others actually alters the extent of difference in our social environment.

Finally, our actions toward socially different others are also driven by our feelings about ourselves. We have discussed how we think of ourselves in terms of our social categories and affiliations. These social identities are value-laden; we are proud of being, for example, Jewish, Latino, or female. Because we are emotionally invested in our social categories and memberships, we want them to compare favorably with other social groups. The desire to have our social group look good compared to others invariably guides us to behave in ways that create or enhance differences between us. In short, the diversity we perceive in our schools or communities may result in part from our needs to feel good about our own social groups.

Diversity Is a Social Influence

To study how the individual and the social context are interdependent, we must recognize that our behavior is influenced by a variety of social forces, one of which is our differentness from others. Therefore, we not only perceive social difference in our environments, many of us *experience* diversity too. We are aware that we are different from other people in many ways, such as in our skin color, family background, and religious beliefs. This experience is psychologically important because being different from others influences the way we think and feel about ourselves and interact with other people.

Influence on Identity

Psychologists have learned that our identities—whom we regard ourselves as—incorporate the impressions and beliefs others hold regarding us. The experience of diversity acknowledges that we live among people who, themselves, are constructors of their social world. In other words, other people categorize *you* based on dimensions of social difference (just as you tend to do to them). Other people may not know you personally, but as a member of some (often visibly apparent) social group about which they have prior knowledge, you are known to them to some degree. The *you* that is known to other people, and based largely on your social group affiliation, may differ sharply from how you view yourself. The discrepancy between our identities and the way other people identify us has profound implications for our psychological well-being and social adjustment. Imagine a disabled individual who views herself in the following terms: intelligent, Italian American, athletic, Republican, and outgoing, but is viewed by others primarily in terms of her disability. How frustrating it must be to realize that other people think of you as disabled (and the negative qualities associated with being disabled) when you do not think of yourself in that way, or when disabled is just one (and perhaps a relatively unimportant) part of who you are. One's social identities, and the beliefs and assumptions that other people associate with those identities, have important implications for one's psychological identity and well-being. In sum, a psychological appreciation of diversity must include an understanding of the experience of being different from others.

Influence on Behavior

The experience of diversity extends beyond how we identify ourselves and includes how we behave. Just as our actions toward others that are guided by category-based expectations have implications for the perception of diversity, others' behavior toward us follows *their* beliefs and expectations about us and influences how we experience a diverse world. Others' beliefs and expectations about the traits and behaviors of the members of a social group comprise a role—a script for conducting oneself in the ongoing drama of life. However, social roles are a double-edged sword. On one hand they are comfortable contexts in which to live because playing the expected role brings the approval of others. On the other hand, social roles are limiting; they constrain what a member of a social group should be or do. For example, there is still a strong collective belief in this society that women are best suited for roles that involve nurturant, supportive, and helpful behavior. Not surprisingly, women greatly outnumber men in such occupations as elementary school teacher, nurse, and secretary. Adopting this female role in one's behavior is associated with opportunities in those vocational areas, as well as a cultural stamp of approval at playing the woman role appropriately, but also place women at an economic disadvantage. You can see, then, how our behavior is not ours alone, but is shaped by cultural forces that stem directly from social differences.

Summary

- Diversity is difference based on one's sex, sexual orientation, race and ethnicity, national background, income and education level, first language, religion, and appearance—and these are just the major categories of social difference!

- A psychological study of diversity must consider how social categories are tools for viewing and evaluating other people; that diversity is not limited to historically disadvantaged or visible groups; that diversity is an escapable and value-neutral aspect of our daily living; and that a concern for social justice must accompany the study of social difference.

- The psychology of diversity is based on two principles. One, through our thoughts, judgments, and actions, we shape and distort the raw material of objective social differences. Two, the diverse social contexts in which we live shape our identities and actions.

DI | Diversity Issue 1.1: Does White + Black = Black?

President Obama has a White mother and a Black father, making him the most famous biracial or multiracial person in America. And yet, most people think of Barack Obama as Black rather than biracial. Indeed, he was hailed in the media as the first Black president of the United States. In *Dreams of My Father*, President Obama tells of his conscious decision to think of himself as a Black American (Obama, 2004). How do you think of people who are of mixed-race background? Do you think of a biracial person in terms of one race and, if so, which one? Researchers Destiny Peery and Galen Bodenhausen (2008) examined this question by having White people look at racially ambiguous faces that either were or were not paired with information about the biracial/bicultural background of the person. What did they find? Compared with the no-information condition, when participants were given information about the biracial background of the person, they reflexively categorized the face as Black rather than White. However, when asked for more thoughtful, deliberate responses, the participants acknowledged the person's biracial identity. This study suggests that Whites automatically categorize multiracial people into minority categories, but also that knowing another person is from a mixed-race background helps White perceivers think about people in multiracial/multiethnic terms.

? Consider your own racial and ethnic background. Who were your parents and grandparents, in terms of their country of origin, language, race, and religion? Does your identity reflect that multicultural background?

> **?** If you have a multiracial or multiethnic identity, does your identity reflect a melt-
> **•** ing pot, multicultural, or color-blind model of diversity? In other words, are your
> racial identities mixed together to form a unique cultural product (you), are there
> elements of each heritage preserved and existing side-by-side in you, or do you
> not think of yourself in terms of racial or ethnic categories at all?

KEY TERMS

Diversity   2

Melting Pot   11

Multiculturalism   11

Color-blindness   12

FOR FURTHER READING

Boatright-Horowitz, S. L., & Soeung, S. (2009). Teaching White privilege to White students can
  mean saying good-bye to positive student evaluations. *American Psychologist, 64*(6), 574–575.
  doi: 10.1037/a0016593
  This article discusses the consequences of trying to confront racism, particularly White students' racial attitudes, in the classroom for students' evaluations of their course and teacher.

Online Resources

United States Census Bureau

http://www.census.gov/

  A great site to appreciate the diversity of Americans. From the main page follow the "People
& Households/American Community Survey" link. The American Community Survey is an
annual look at Americans' income, education, race and ethnicity, disability, and more.

United States Census Bureau 2011 Statistical Abstract

http://www.census.gov/compendia/statab/hist_stats.html

  The U. S. Census Bureau's Statistical Abstract shows historical data: current and past census
figures for demographics and many other variables. This site allows one to appreciate changes in
American diversity across time.

Centers for Disease Control and Prevention

http://www.cdc.gov/

  This site is excellent for finding basic prevalence statistics on diversity dimensions such as
obesity and disability, and also how those dimensions relate to health. From the main CDC page,
use the index to find pages on overweight/obesity (under O) and disability and health (under D).

National Center for Healthcare Statistics

http://www.cdc.gov/nchs/

For those interested in seeing how health-related outcomes are related to disability, obesity status, or demographic variables. From the main page, use the index to find research on disability and health (under D), then continue on to "more data and statistics."

National Center for Education Statistics

http://nces.ed.gov/

For those interested in seeing how educational outcomes vary by gender or race. From the main page, go to Tables/Figures, then Search Tables/Figures. Select a year and type in "gender" to get a feast of educational data for males and females.

National Survey of Sexual Health and Behavior

http://www.nationalsexstudy.indiana.edu/

Findings from a large representative survey of Americans' sexual behaviors, conducted in 2010, including data on same-sex identity and behavior.

United States Department of Health and Human Services Poverty Guidelines

http://aspe.hhs.gov/poverty/index.shtml#latest

For the latest definitions, measurement, and data on poverty.

The U.S. Census Bureau also has a poverty section:

http://www.census.gov/hhes/www/poverty/poverty.html

American Religion Data Archive

http://www.thearda.com/

A site with membership statistics of religious denominations in the United States. ARDA also provides learning modules for studying social issues that are related to religion in America (e.g., Evangelicalism, science, and homosexuality).

The Pluralism Project

http://pluralism.org/index.php

This site, through advocacy, resources, and research, enables people to explore the diversity of religions and faith traditions in the United States. From the home page, go to "America's Many Religions." Pick a religion to find links to statistics, news, essays, and multimedia presentations.

American Psychological Association

http://www.apa.org/

A national organization of academic and practicing professional psychologists. A good place to learn what psychologists do and how they do it.

Association for Psychological Science

http://www.psychologicalscience.org/

A national organization of psychology more devoted to the scientific and research than to the professional aspects of psychology.

2

Categorization and Stereotyping ❖

Cognitive Processes That Shape Perceived Diversity

Our study of diversity must begin with how we think about people who are different from ourselves. Two cognitive processes—categorization and stereotyping—frame our study of social thinking. Social categorization and stereotyping help shape the social world we perceive. This chapter will consider social categorization and stereotyping in turn, followed by a discussion of their implications for understanding people who are socially different from ourselves.

Social Categorization

How many people will you interact with, encounter, see, think about, or imagine today? Think about it for a minute—the number is probably several hundred people, or higher, for a typical day. Each of those individuals has a particular age, body shape, race or ethnicity, appearance, hair style, and language. If you were to take notice, you would likely find that they also differ in their income, political orientation, religion, health status, and many other ways. We obviously cannot possibly remember the distinctive qualities of even a small fraction of the people we encounter. So what happens to all that social information? Making sense of the diversity around us involves a great deal of information processing, often more thinking than we have time for or care to do. To ease this information processing burden, we employ categories, because thinking about categories of people (e.g., rich, middle-professional class, middle-working class, and poor people) requires less attention and less memory resources than trying to remember individual characteristics. **Social categorization** involves thinking about people primarily as members of social groups rather than as individuals. Social categories organize and economize our thinking about other people, especially those who are different from ourselves. In the following pages, we must address two fundamental questions about social categorization. First, how do we decide which category (or categories) to use when people can be categorized in many different ways? Second, how does social categorization affect our thinking about other people? We acknowledged above that social categories are beneficial for at least one reason—they help us economize on our everyday thinking about people. In what ways, however, do social categories influence our perceptions of others?

Think of someone you know well, such as a roommate or friend. Make a mental list of the possible social categories to which this person could be assigned. Most people are part of many social groups; some are easily visible, others are not. We have considered why social categorization is fundamental to social information processing, but how do we select the social categories? Or do they select themselves?

Primary Categories

Age, sex, and race are regarded by psychologists as **primary social categories**. Primary categorizations occur first and fastest when we consider other people. We notice, too quickly to be able to think about it, other peoples' age, sex, and race before noticing other categorizations that might apply to them. Researchers measured subjects' brainwave activity in the part of the brain devoted to attention as they simultaneously presented pictures of Black and White male and female targets. The race of the targets was noticed in about one tenth of a second, and subjects noticed the targets' sex only slightly slower. Other research suggests that we make age-based categorizations nearly as quickly (Brewer & Lui, 1989). This means that primary categorization is **automatic**—that is, it is spontaneous, unreflective, and uncontrollable.

The fact that we categorize people in terms of their race, sex, and age in a fraction of a second indicates that primary social categorization should be connected to areas of the brain that control automatic processing of stimuli. The amygdala is a part of the brain that processes and evaluates inputs with emotional significance, and indeed the amygdala has been linked to the processing of social information (Adolphs, 2009). Researcher Elizabeth Phelps and her colleagues had White participants view unfamiliar

Black and White faces while measuring the activation of their amygdalas through functional MRI, or fMRI technology (Phelps et al., 2000). They found greater amygdala activation when participants viewed Black compared with White faces, and this activation was correlated with a more conventional measure of implicit (or automatic) racial bias. The amygdala was not active when participants viewed familiar faces, however, suggesting that the amygdala plays a role in vigilance and evaluating stimuli that are unusual or potentially threatening.

The social categories race, sex, and age are similar in several respects, and this may shed light on why they are primary categories. As David Schneider (2004) points out, each of these categories has physical markers that are visible and easily identified. Skin color and facial features help us identify race. Body shape and stature enable sex categorizations. Finally, hair color and skin type help distinguish older from younger people. Physical similarities among people may also lead us to believe that the members of that group share internal qualities too, such as common traits, abilities, or backgrounds. This essentialist thinking can lead us to confuse category with cause. For example, many people regard men and women as *inherently* different, beyond their obvious physical differences, and the assumed essences of men and women, respectively, are used to explain differences in the behavior of men and women. Are these assumed differences accurate? We will address that later in this chapter.

Beyond Primary Categorization

Although categorizing people by their race, sex, and age occurs automatically in our social thinking, many other dimensions of diversity—some much more important to us than primary differences—are available to further organize and simplify our social worlds. Question: How do we decide what category, from among the many available, to use to think about someone? Answer: Beyond the primary categories, whatever characteristic of that person commands or occupies our attention is likely to inform our social categorization. Psychological researchers have found that categorization is driven by attention. The more we attend to an aspect of a person—such as one's weight, race, or physical disability—the more likely it is that we will categorize that individual with similar people we have noticed in the past (Smith & Zarate, 1992). Following this attention principle, social categorization can occur because of a distinctive feature (e.g., wheelchair user), because a situation highlights a category (e.g., at work you may think in terms of employee versus customer), or because a category is associated with a perceived threat to our values (e.g., Muslims, for many American Christians). Let's consider the factors that guide our attention and social categorization in turn.

Perceptual Similarity

People who appear to be similar in some respect tend to be grouped together in our minds. The primary categories mentioned above share many similar features, but even beyond those fundamental categories, the principle of perceptual similarity guides our thinking about people. For example, people with a physical disability can be thought of as a group even if those people are otherwise quite different.

Distinctive features activate categories for two reasons. First, people who share a distinctive characteristic tend to be associated in memory, even if they are different in many other ways. When we see, for example, a person walking with the assistance of a cane or walker, we recall other similar people we have encountered. Because of their association in memory, we tend to think of those people as a group. Second, information about salient categories is immediately available to the perceiver compared to other, less salient categories. It is easier for us to notice and remember other information about people with disabilities than, for example, gay men and lesbians because, unlike sexual orientation, physical disabilities themselves are salient and memorable. Some common, distinctive social categories include sex, race, and ethnicity (to the extent that it is perceptually salient, such as through language differences), as well as physical disability, obesity, economic status, and age.

The perceptual salience of a characteristic is partly due to the situation in which it is encountered. Shelley Taylor and her colleagues have found that **solo status**, such as being the only woman on a committee or the only Asian student in a class, commands others' attention (Taylor, Fiske, Etcoff, & Ruderman, 1978). In one study, participants watched a group of six students discuss a topic; the groups consisted of each possible distribution of men and women (e.g., six men, no women; five men, one woman, etc.). Participants then evaluated the contributions of a given group member. The results showed that the significance attributed to a group member's comments was inversely proportional to the size of their minority group. In other words, as people become more noticeable in a group, acquiring more solo status, their actions stand out and acquire greater importance in perceivers' eyes. This occurs even when the quantity of the member's contribution to the group remains the same across the various group types. Other research shows that evaluations of minority or solo status individuals are more exaggerated (Taylor & Fiske, 1978). We will take up solo status again in Chapter 6 when we learn about how females deal with solo status. In sum, distinctive attributes—whether that distinctiveness is inherent or situationally enhanced—is a basis for social categorization.

How do dress codes and uniform policies in schools or workplaces relate to solo status?

Do tattoos and piercings, through which people express their individuality, make them (ironically) more likely to be categorized by others?

Accessibility

Our social thinking is also governed by categories that are accessible. We are more likely to group people by frequently used categories, or categories that have just recently been used, than categories we rarely use. If we are accustomed to thinking about people in terms of a certain dimension, we will tend to activate these categories to deal with new or unknown social situations, thus adding to their accessibility.

In a demonstration of the influence of accessible social categories on social perception, researchers primed the category *women* or *Chinese* (or no category) by presenting one of these words for very short durations to study participants via computer (Macrae, Bodenhausen, & Milne, 1995). After the priming task, participants viewed a videotape (ostensibly to rate the tape) of a Chinese woman reading. Thus, participants' impressions of the person in the tape could be based on either social category: her sex or her ethnicity. In a final task, participants identified computer-presented trait words manipulated to include some that were typical of the social categories women and Chinese. The results were striking. Those participants who were primed with the category woman were faster in recognizing the women-typical traits, but slower in recognizing the Chinese-typical traits, than were the participants who had no social category prime. Parallel findings occurred for those who were primed with the Chinese category. They more quickly responded to Chinese-typical words, and more slowly to women-typical words, than did people with no category prime.

This study makes two important points. First, when more than one social category can be used to think about someone, *accessible* social categories—ones that we have recently used—take precedence. Second, when an accessible social category is appropriated to process social information, other relevant categories are inhibited—that is, they become less helpful than if we had no social category to work with. Here we see another aspect of the efficiency of social categories: When one is activated for use, others are deactivated until the social information processing is complete.

Perceived Threat

Earlier we learned that the amygdala processes social information that is unfamiliar or threatening. A third factor that guides social categorization is whether a person is perceived as potentially threatening. Research by Saul Miller and his colleagues demonstrates that when we perceive potential threat or harm in another person, we are much more likely to categorize that person as a member of an outgroup (Miller, Maner, & Becker, 2010). **In-groups** and **out-groups** refer to social groups or categories of which we are, and are not, a member, respectively. In one study, these researchers had White participants categorize the race of White and Black faces as quickly and accurately as possible. The faces were selected to have either angry or happy expressions. The researchers hypothesized that, for typical White participants, angry Black males would be the most threatening and therefore should be most quickly categorized as an out-group member. As they predicted, participants correctly categorized the race of the angry Black male faces in just under 500 milliseconds (or one-half second), faster than any other type of face. Happy White female faces were the least threatening, and indeed participants were slowest in categorizing those faces.

> **?** List three of your in-groups. Now list some out-groups—groups of which you are not a member. Is it harder to identify your out-groups? Why?

To sum up, our social categorizations are not random. Some categories select themselves by virtue of their visual distinctiveness; others because of their frequent use. Categorization also occurs when we want to define ourselves as different from people who are unfamiliar and threatening. Armed with some basic knowledge about social categorization, let us further examine how social categories influence the diversity we perceive in our social world.

What Do Social Categories Do?

Social Categories Economize Our Social Thinking

What if you kept your e-mails in one large file on your computer or phone? Finding an e-mail from a particular person or on a specific topic would necessarily involve looking through the whole list, a laborious task if they happen to be near the bottom! Obviously a categorization system with folders and subfolders makes storing and locating any individual e-mail much easier. The same principle operates in dealing with social information. Placing people in categories facilitates efficient social information processing, enabling us to combine individuals who have a similar quality or status into a group. As a result, thinking about groups of people requires fewer cognitive resources than thinking about individuals, leaving us better equipped to face the many other demands on our cognitive resources.

Researchers did a series of experiments designed to examine the cognitive efficiency of social categories (Macrae, Milne, & Bodenhausen, 1994). They had participants form an impression of a hypothetical person while doing a simultaneous cognitive task. The researchers reasoned that if social categories conserve cognitive resources, then people who are allowed or encouraged to use them in an impression-formation task should have more resources available to do other things. In one study, participants were shown a list of 10 traits (presented one by one on a computer) that described a hypothetical person named John. The traits included those typical of, for example, an artist (e.g., creative, temperamental) or a doctor (e.g., responsible, caring). Some of the participants were assigned to see an appropriate social category label (artist or doctor) appear above the trait words; others did not see the category label. While they were doing this impression-formation task, participants were also listening to a tape-recorded, factual lecture on Indonesian geography. After the tasks were complete, participants were given a 20-item multiple-choice test on the facts in the audiotaped lecture. The results confirmed the researchers' idea: Those who formed their impressions of John with the assistance of an explicit social category scored significantly better on the test of the lecture facts than those who did not have a category made available to them. In short, using a social category made the trait task easier and left those people with more resources for listening to and remembering the lecture.

A follow-up study showed that this influence of social categories on the performance of a simultaneous cognitive task was not merely intentional—an effect that participants thought should occur so they behaved accordingly. In a similar study, Macrae and his colleagues primed the social category word, by flashing it for merely a fraction of a second on the computer, and then presented the trait (Macrae et al., 1994). Still, participants who formed impressions of Jim with the aid of a social category (albeit one that they did not recognize!) performed better on a simultaneous but unrelated cognitive task compared to those who did not receive a social category prime. Together, these studies demonstrate the ability of social categories to economize cognitive resources, such as attention and memory, and make them available for other needs.

Social Categories Guide Social Judgments

It is well established that social categories, and the beliefs that we associate with them, influence our thinking about people from other groups (Hamilton & Sherman, 1994). Social category–based beliefs set up expectations for people from a particular group, and much research shows that these expectations influence our perceptions and judgments of people based on their group membership.

For example, researchers investigated the effects of class-based categorization on judgments of a child's academic performance (Baron, Albright, & Malloy, 1995). They had participants watch a video tape of a girl playing near her home and in a neighborhood playground. In the low social class condition, the home and playground were urban and run down; in the high social class condition, the home and playground were spacious, well kept, and obviously exclusive. Participants also watched a (bogus) tape of the child taking an intelligence test. The results showed that social class affected the ratings of the child's academic ability, but only when they had no information about the child's academic ability. Participants who had categorized the child as from a low socioeconomic background evaluated her test performance more negatively than those who believed she was an upper middle-class student. However, this social categorization effect did not occur when the participants were given information about the child's academic abilities. This study shows how categorization affects the way we think about people but also suggests that the influence of social categories, as a basis for judgments of others, may be overridden by other, more relevant information.

In another study, participants studied some information about a basketball player and then listened to a taped radio broadcast of an actual basketball game involving the player (Stone, Perry, & Darley, 1997). After the broadcast, participants rated the attributes and performance of the player. The information about the player, however, was manipulated in two ways. Participants were led to believe that the player was either Black or White (social information) and that he possessed either low or high athletic ability (individual information). The results revealed that participants' ratings of the player were influenced only by the social information. Those who believed the player was Black rated him as having higher physical and basketball ability than did participants who believed he was White. However, the White player was attributed with more effort than the Black player. This study also demonstrates the power of social categories to influence our perceptions of individuals and suggests that individualistic (and seemingly more accurate) information can be overridden by social categorical information.

The influence of social categories over our thinking about socially different people cannot be separated from the beliefs and knowledge we associate with a particular group of people. In the study described above, a simple social category can determine whether we see an athletic performance as due to athletic ability or effort (Stone et al., 1997). This influence of social categories, however, depends on the association of particular traits and abilities with a social category. In other words, we perceive athletic ability in the performance of a Black athlete not just because we think of him as Black, but also because we associate certain traits with the members of his group. This leads us to the second basic cognitive process through which we order and understand our social worlds: the stereotype.

Stereotyping

Categories help economize our cognitive resources, but they also help organize knowledge and experience with people from other social groups. When we categorize people based on a group membership, we risk discarding a great deal of individual information. We recover some of this information by developing a general description, called a stereotype, of the people in a social category and associating it in memory with that category. A **stereotype** is a set of beliefs about the members of a social group and usually consists of personality traits, behaviors, and motives. Stereotypes are also assumed to be overgeneralized beliefs about people from social groups (Allport, 1954). That is, when we stereotype people we apply a set of beliefs that represent the summary qualities of a group to *individuals* from that social group. These group-based beliefs do not provide very accurate information for understanding individual group members.

To learn how social categories and stereotypes are linked in memory, try this: What traits and behaviors come to mind when I say professor? Intelligent? Absentminded? You likely have little trouble accessing a general description of a typical professor because that stereotypical information is closely associated with the category *professor* in your mind. In addition to personal traits, that stereotype probably carries information about professors' education, income, and perhaps their social and political attitudes. In terms of our e-mail folder metaphor, stereotypes are essentially brief summaries of the contents of a folder. They provide a general idea of what is in the folder and save us the work of sifting through every individual element for that information.

As with social categorization, some stereotyping occurs automatically (Devine & Sharp, 2009). That is, the association between some social categories and the traits and beliefs we associate with those categories is so well learned that stereotyping occurs unintentionally. Mahzarin Banaji and Curtis Hardin (1996) had participants view words that were either related to females (e.g., mother, nurse), males (e.g., father, doctor), or unrelated to gender, followed by a gender pronoun (e.g., him, her). The words were displayed on a computer screen for about two tenths of a second, too quickly for participants to actually read the words. Following these words, a gendered pronoun appeared (e.g., him, her) and participants had to decide whether the pronoun was male or female by pressing a computer key. Participants made faster associations between male words and pronouns, and female words and pronouns, than between gender-inconsistent words and pronouns. Thus, even though the participants were unaware of the connections they were making, their responses showed that gendered descriptors (stereotypic traits) and the appropriate gender pronouns (social category) were connected in their memory. Moreover, automatic stereotyping occurred even when participants declared, via questionnaire, that they did not hold gender stereotypes.

Is automatic stereotyping inevitable? No, a variety of conditions can get in the way of the automatic activation of a stereotype when we are exposed to someone from a stereotyped group (Devine & Sharp, 2009). First, even though it occurs outside of our control, automatic stereotyping still takes cognitive resources like attention. Numerous experiments show that perceivers who are made cognitively busy by having mental tasks to do engage in less stereotyping than perceivers with a full complement of attention (Gilbert & Hixon, 1991). In other words, a member of a stereotyped group must have our attention for stereotypes about his or her group to be activated in us. Second, the context in which we perceive or interact with a person from a stereotyped group affects how much we stereotype that person. For example, participants were more biased against an Asian target when the target was seen in a classroom context compared to a basketball court; the opposite pattern of bias occurred when the target was Black (Barden, Maddux, Petty, & Brewer, 2004). In that study, seeing an out-group member in a stereotype-inconsistent situation prevented the stereotyping that occurred when the Asian target was seen in a classroom context.

Other research shows that the goal of an interracial interaction also changes the stereotyping that occurs in that situation. In one study, White participants interacted with a Black partner under one of three conditions: They were instructed to evaluate their partner (and thus have superior status relative to their partner), get along with him or her (and have equal status), or be evaluated by their partner (and have inferior status) (Richeson & Ambady, 2001). Race stereotyping in the White participants occurred less in the equal and inferior status, than in the superior status, interactions. Here we see how interaction goals can undercut stereotyping, a topic we will consider at greater length in Chapter 12. Third, automatic stereotypes can be inhibited if we are motivated to avoid them. Motivation to avoid stereotyping another person may occur because the individual values fair-mindedness (Moskovitz, Salomon, & Taylor,

2000), has been instructed by an authority to not stereotype (Lowery, Hardin, & Sinclair, 2001), or wants to make a good impression on the person (Sinclair & Kunda, 1999). In summary, stereotyping can occur spontaneously when confronted with someone from an out-group, but automatic stereotyping can also be brought under our conscious control with the proper motivation and practice. Our ability to overcome well-learned and unconscious biases, and the techniques that help us think in less stereotypic ways, will be considered again in Chapter 12.

Where Do Stereotypes Come From?

Thus far we have learned about the *processes* of stereotyping—how and why we stereotype other people. Let's shift our focus now to stereotype *content*—the characteristics that we associate with people from other social groups. Below we will consider some general rules that apply to the content of stereotypes, regardless of the specific group, followed by a discussion of where stereotype content comes from. In later chapters, we will confront the content of our stereotypes of specific groups based on race (Chapter 5), gender (Chapter 6), weight (Chapter 7), sexual orientation (Chapter 8), and age (Chapter 9).

Generally, the content of stereotypes is marked by two qualities. First, stereotypic beliefs tend to be dispositional; that is, they inform us about the inner qualities of individuals based merely on their group membership. Given that we cannot readily see an individual's personality traits or abilities, stereotyping is potentially valuable and advantageous in social interactions. The problem is that behavior is caused by *both* inner, dispositional and outer, situational factors. Thus, stereotypes are over informed by dispositional information and inherently inaccurate.

Second, the evaluative content of stereotypes tends to be negative. Research demonstrates that our stereotypes of many social groups—including Blacks, women, poor and unemployed people, gays and lesbians, people with physical and mental disabilities, and overweight people—are predominantly composed of negatively valued qualities (Allon, 1982; Brigham, 1974; Eagly & Mladinic, 1989; Farina, Sherman, & Allen, 1968; Furnham, 1982a; Gibbons, Sawin, & Gibbons, 1979; Herek, 1984). There are exceptions to this *stereotypes are negative* rule, but even people we positively stereotype (e.g., Asian Americans are intelligent) are limited by the narrowness and uniformity of those positive beliefs (see Diversity Issue 2.2 to think more about positive stereotypes). In sum, the dispositional assumptions inherent in stereotyping are negative, inaccurate, and are applied uniformly to each individual in that social category. Moreover, the negative traits and emotions associated with stereotyping form the basis for prejudice, a topic to be addressed in Chapter 4.

? When does a stereotype go from being a useful cognitive strategy to being prejudicial and unfair? Can you draw a clear separation between the two?

Operating together, social categorization and stereotyping influence our under-standing of the social differences that surround us, but where do our stereotypes come from? Stereotypic beliefs are derived from personal exposure to people from other social groups, our attention to the covariation of unusual events and people, and are learned from family and other cultural conduits.

Personal Exposure

When we know little about the members of another group, we rely on personal contact with or observations of them to inform our beliefs about the whole group (Rothbart, Dawes, & Park, 1984). Our observations of and experiences with socially different people contribute to stereotypes in two ways.

First, our stereotypic beliefs are informed by the social roles that we observe group members occupy. For example, we might observe that many more women than men are elementary school teachers and nurses. As a result we may assume that women as a group are nurturant and helpful, erroneously believing that women's association with these roles reflects a correspondent inner quality (Eagly & Steffen, 1984). In fact, social roles are more likely assigned by society rather than chosen by the individual, so the behaviors we observe of the members of a social group in a given role do not nec-essarily reflect their personalities or personal preferences.

Second, our stereotypes are likely to include beliefs that help us explain others' disadvantage or misfortune. Psychologists have demonstrated that belief in a just world—where people generally get what they deserve—is a common way of thinking about others (Lerner, 1980). In light of **just world belief,** when other people experience misfortune or tragedy, it is easier to hold them responsible for their plight than to admit that bad things can happen to undeserving people. Accordingly, when we observe a group of people who face disadvantage, we tend to suppose that they have an attribute or inner flaw that somehow caused their regrettable situation. For example, rather than being seen as victims of broader economic forces such as unemployment, poor people are stereotyped as lazy and unmotivated, dispositions that cause their disadvantage (Furnham & Gunter, 1984).

Distinctive Individuals and Behaviors

Our stereotypes would be more accurate if they represented the attributes of the most typical group members. The problem is that typical group members are neither noticeable nor memorable. In fact, it is the unusual individual that grabs our attention. Atypical group members stand out; their behavior and appearance are vivid and memorable. Hence, their attributes and actions exert disproportionate influence on our thinking about all the members of that social category (Rothbart, Fulero, Jensen, Howard, & Birrel, 1978). This influence is compounded when the social group itself is relatively small or unusual. Research on the **illusory correlation** demonstrates that the co-occurrence of an unusual behavior *and* a distinctive social category is particularly influential, leading us to erroneously believe that the two things are related (Hamilton & Gifford, 1976). Illusory correlations contribute to our stereotypes, causing them to reflect more unusual behavior or attributes than is warranted. As an example of illusory correlation, consider the drag queens who often march in gay rights parades and demonstrations. Cross-dressing is an unusual behavior that coincidentally occurs with the social category *gay*. The rarity of that combination of occurrences sparks an assumption that they are related, contributing to the stereotypical (and erroneous) notion that gay men are transvestites or, more generally, sexual perverts.

In one study, participants read a series of sentences that described positive and negative behaviors exhibited by hypothetical members of a majority (Group A) or a minority (Group B) (Johnson & Mullen, 1994). In a following task administered by a computer, participants read the sentences again, but this time the group information was omitted. After deciding whether the behavior was one that was described earlier as being committed by a majority or minority group member, they pressed a key to communicate their decision. The results revealed that participants over attributed negative actions to minority group actors, and they were faster in making these decisions compared to the other pairs of information (positive act by a minority actor, any act by a majority actor). Thus, stereotypes can arise when we erroneously connect unusual (and often negative) behaviors with unusual groups.

Socialization

Finally, cultures and societies invest in collective views of social groups, called **cultural stereotypes**. For example, beliefs about overweight people are much different (and more negative) in the United States compared to Mexico (Crandall & Martinez, 1996). Our stereotypic beliefs, in turn, are socialized by the steady influence of family members and television, two important conduits of cultural influence. Because children admire and imitate their parents, they accept parents' social attitudes rather uncritically. Parents' stereotypes are communicated to their children in many subtle ways, as in the kind of playmates that meet with their approval, warnings about neighborhoods to avoid, or casual use of racial or ethnic epithets in the home.

Cultural stereotypes tend to be learned early in life and rehearsed often. This is particularly true for people whose cultural education is limited to what is on TV or who otherwise have few opportunities to socialize with people from different ethnic, cultural, or economic backgrounds. When stereotypes are instilled early in life and go essentially unchallenged into adolescence and adulthood, they become what psychologists call dominant responses. That is, recalling well-learned, stereotypic beliefs tend to be the first response to encountering socially different people. Researcher Alan Lambert and his colleagues (2003) suggest that, as dominant responses, stereotypes are more likely to influence our thinking and behavior in public than in private situations. Public situations (e.g., shopping malls) require more cognitive resources from us; there are more things going on and more to notice, remember, and decide. In an effort to do more economical social thinking then, we tend to fall back on well-learned, stereotypic responses toward others. Indeed, much other research shows that when our cognitive resources are limited, we are more likely to stereotype other people (see Bodenhausen, 1990, for a clever illustration).

What roles do older people typically occupy? What traits do we assume fit those roles? Notice how your beliefs about older people as a group develop as you see them in situations.

Stereotypes Persist, but Why?

Psychologists have long regarded stereotyping to be part of a significant social problem (Allport, 1954). This is not only because stereotypic beliefs tend to be negative and dispositional. Once established, stereotypes are also difficult to change. Therefore, the influence of stereotypes on our thinking about, and behavior toward, other people can subtly contribute to prejudice and discrimination of people who are socially different than ourselves. Let us consider a few of the reasons for the persistence of stereotypes.

Stereotypes Possess a Kernel of Truth

Stereotypes persist because they seem to be accurate. Actually, most stereotypes *do* have an element of accuracy in them. For example, we tend to stereotype women as emotional relative to men. Research demonstrates that, compared to men, women *are* more attentive and sensitive to nonverbal expressions (Eagly, 1987). Are stereotypes generally accurate? The accuracy of a stereotype can be assessed in two ways (Judd & Park, 1993). First, we can examine how much we believe out-group members have a given trait with the extent to which they actually possess the trait. For example, we tend to stereotype Asian Americans as math whizzes, but are they as intelligent in math as we believe they are? If so, then our stereotype of Asian Americans (at least regarding beliefs about math ability) is accurate. Second, we can examine our beliefs about how prevalent a trait is among out-group members with the actual proportion of out-group members who possess that trait. For example, given our stereotypes of Asian Americans' math ability, we may believe that 60% of Asian students are math or computer science majors. If that proportion is actually reflected among Asian American students, then our stereotype (again, regarding that trait) is accurate.

Lee Jussim and his colleagues reviewed studies that tested the accuracy of stereotypes (Jussim, Cain, Crawford, Harber, & Cohen, 2009). Their review found that most people accurately judged differences between racial- or ethnic-based in-groups and out-groups based on their racial stereotypes. Similar accuracy was found in people's use of their gender stereotypes to make judgments about the differences between males and females. Furthermore, when inaccuracies occurred, they took the form of exaggerations of true group differences no more or less than underestimations of group differences. Other work suggests that stereotype accuracy may be more prevalent among minority, compared to majority, group individuals perhaps because people from minority groups have more to lose if they misjudge the actions of majority group people (Ryan, 1996). In that study, Black and White college students' perceptions of their own and the others' group were measured in the two ways described above.

On the first measure of accuracy, the results showed that Blacks were more accurate in their beliefs about Whites compared to the accuracy of Whites' beliefs about Blacks. On the second measure, Blacks judgments about the proportion of Whites who possessed a stereotypic trait were more accurate than Whites' judgments about the proportion of Blacks who possessed stereotypic traits.

Stereotypes Confirm Themselves

A second explanation for the resistance of stereotypes to change is due to our tendency to confirm rather than disconfirm stereotypical expectations about other groups (Rothbart, Evans, & Fulero, 1979). Because much stereotypic thinking is automatic and conserves cognitive resources, we selectively attend to evidence that supports our stereotypes. By contrast, attending to evidence that our stereotypes are inaccurate or misapplied requires thoughtful and deliberate action, which few of us are motivated to do.

In a demonstration of the tendency for stereotypes to confirm themselves, researchers presented study participants with a photograph of a woman who was known (through pretesting) to be a typical-looking member of the category *older woman* (Brewer, Dull, & Lui, 1981). After viewing the photograph, participants were presented with statements about the woman that were either stereotype-consistent (e.g., "she likes to knit"), stereotype-inconsistent (e.g., "she is politically active"), or of mixed content (e.g., "she walks with a cane and runs her own business"). Using a computer to present the statements, the researchers measured how long it took participants to process each statement. After the computer portion of the study, participants' memory for the statements was also tested. The results showed statements that were consistent with participants' stereotype of older women were processed in less time than stereotype-inconsistent statements and were easily recalled. Stereotype-inconsistent statements were processed slowly, but were also remembered well by participants. Participants' ability to remember stereotype-inconsistent statements, however, may have been due to the extra time they spent studying the statements. Statements with mixed content (e.g., an old woman trait and a young woman trait) were processed slowly and not well remembered.

This research demonstrates that recognition and memory is better for information that is consistent with our stereotypes compared to information that is contradictory or only partly relevant to our stereotypes. Could this occur because people are aware of, and therefore act out, what *should* happen when their stereotypes are activated? Not according to recent research on implicit stereotyping (Banaji, Hardin, & Rothman, 1993). That is, when our stereotypes are activated without our knowledge—such as through the use of a subliminal prime—we still tend to recognize and recall stereotype-consistent rather than inconsistent information.

Stereotypes also resist disconfirmation because of the way we explain the behavior of people from other groups. John Seta and his colleagues (2003) had participants read about one of two targets: a minister who displayed stereotype-inconsistent (e.g., molested a teenager) or consistent behavior (e.g., volunteered to help a human-itarian organization). Then they read about and rated the behavior of the other target. When participants encountered the stereotype-inconsistent person first, they saw the normal minister's behavior as more due to his personality (e.g., he is a giving person by nature) than when they were not exposed to the deviant minister. This research, and the other studies that supported it, shows that when we encounter a person who does not fit our stereotype of that group—say, a gay male athlete—we reinforce our stereotype by seeing more stereotype-consistent behavior in more typical group members. To sum up, our memory for and reasoning about other people's behavior is biased toward reaffirming stereotypical beliefs.

Stereotypes Diversify Through Subtypes

As we just learned, people who don't fit our stereotype can be disregarded as *exceptions to the rule* by focusing more on the behavior of typical, stereotype-confirming group members. But what do we do when we are chronically confronted with indi-viduals who do not fit our stereotype for that group? As encounters with stereotype-inconsistent people increase, we realize that social categories may be too broad and inclusive, and hence are error prone. In those situations, **subtyping** helps preserve the stereotype of the general category while incorporating new social information by grouping stereotype-inconsistent individuals together into a new subcategory of the original category. For example, as we become more aware of women in business man-agement roles, we will think of them as a subgroup of the general group *women* and modify our general stereotype to accommodate the differentness of the subgroup.

Patricia Devine and her colleague had White students list abilities and charac-teristics they associated with the group Blacks, as well as for several common sub-grouping of Black individuals, including streetwise, ghetto, welfare, athlete, and businessman Blacks (Devine & Baker, 1991). Their interest was not only in the traits associated with each of these subtypes, but also with how distinctive (or non-over-lapping) the subtypes were. Subtypes are likely to be most useful for accommodating atypical examples of a category if they are distinct from each other and the larger category. Their results indicated that the athlete and businessman subtypes of Blacks were the most clear and distinctive. That is, the traits associated with the athlete (physical qualities and athleticism) and businessman (well-dressed, ambitious, intel-ligent) subtypes differed from each other and, further, were not reflected in the overall stereotype of Blacks.

These findings suggest that subtypes not only help organize social information that is too diverse for one category to handle, they do so in a way that doesn't require alteration of the stereotype associated with that category. Because Black business-men are organized independently of Blacks in general, the positive traits associated with Black businessmen are not incorporated into the (largely negative) stereotype of Blacks. With respect to perceiving the social world, then, subtyping is a mixed blessing. Although subtyping does extend and diversify a social category, essentially allowing more difference to exist within a social group, it also protects our general (superordinate) stereotypic beliefs from change by creating new and separate cognitive groups for individuals who do not fit the stereotype.

 ? Review a bit: How do stereotypes perpetuate themselves?

Consequences of Social Categorization and Stereotyping for Perceiving Diversity

Although they are valuable information processing tools, social categories and stereotypes shape the diversity we perceive in our social surroundings. The very process of sorting people into categories constrains the possible ways that people can differ to group characteristics. Thus, the diversity we perceive in our surroundings is partially dependent on the complexity of our categorization systems. Simplistic, reductionistic categorizations contribute to a less diverse world than categorizations featuring an array of general and subordinate social groupings. They require fewer cognitive resources but may also lead to difficulties in our interactions with members of other groups. The process of categorization, therefore, must balance the need to distill an overwhelming amount of social information with the need to have an accurate picture of our social world and the people in it.

Still, diversity also exists *within* social categories. Even if we believed the world was composed of two categories of people (us and them), we could still find diversity in the members of the other group. As is explained below, we fail to recognize and appreciate this kind of social difference. Moreover, the true diversity within other social groups is dulled by stereotypical thinking. Operating in concert, social categorization and stereotyping have several specific implications for the social difference we perceive around us.

We Believe Groups Are More Different Than They Are

A natural consequence of categorizing objects into groups is to emphasize the distinctiveness of those groups. You will agree that a categorization system must maintain clear distinctions between categories to function efficiently. This cognitive tendency leads to a bias in our social thinking—we overestimate the difference between social groups. This bias has been documented in many studies that involve judgments of physical and social objects. In one study, children viewed pictures of three boys and three girls and assigned trait words to describe each picture (Doise, Deschamps, & Meyer, 1978). Half of the children (determined randomly) were told in advance that they would be rating pictures of boys and girls, thereby increasing the salience of that social category for those participants. Compared to the children who were *not* thinking about a boy/girl categorization, the participants who *were* described boys and girls as being more different. That is, fewer common traits were used to describe boys and girls in the children who were encouraged to categorize the photos by gender. This study shows that our perception of members of other social groups is influenced by the mere act of categorization. Applied to our own social contexts, this research suggests that some of the difference we perceive between ourselves and individuals from other social groups is spurious or manufactured, yet (as we will see in a later chapter) we behave toward those people as if those differences were genuine.

We Believe Individuals *Within* Groups Are More Similar Than They Are

A second consequence of thinking about people in terms of their group identification is that we tend to gloss over how different members of a social group actually are. Just as papers and notes placed into a file folder become more indistinguishable, social categorization causes us to overestimate the similarity of people in a social group. This bias is most evident when thinking about *out*-groups, groups of which we are not a member. Termed the **out-group homogeneity effect**, it means we tend to think that they (members of an out-group) are all alike, but we (members of our own group, or *in*-group) are a collective of relatively unique individuals.

There are good explanations for why we attribute more similarity to members of out-groups than is warranted. First, we categorize individuals based on a distinctive or salient characteristic. If people share a distinctive feature, we assume that they also share other qualities (Taylor et al., 1978). Secondly, we interact more with in-group, compared to out-group, members, providing us with more frequent reminders about the differences among individuals in our own group. As a result of the out-group homogeneity effect combined with our stereotype of that group, we tend to view the members of an out-group as all alike and in negative terms. These perceptions are fertile ground for prejudicial reactions such as resentment, fear, and avoidance.

In an examination of the out-group homogeneity effect, Bernadette Park and her colleagues recruited business and engineering majors to list as many types or kinds of business and engineering majors as they could (Park, Ryan, & Judd, 1992). In other words, they looked at how diverse (or homogenous) people saw their own group and a relevant out-group by measuring the subtypes that they generated for each. As they expected, people generated more subgroups for their in-group than the out-group. When this difference was held constant, the out-group homogeneity effect disappeared. In other words, the tendency to see out-group individuals as more homogenous than we see our own group members is driven by the number of subcategories we have at our disposal to know them. In another study, Park et al. (1992) manipulated the use of subgroups by having some participants sort out-group members into subgroups before measuring their perceptions of out-group individuals. The participants who were forced to sort out-group members into a variety of subcategories rated them as more variable than participants who did not do the sorting exercise.

This research discussed above shows that we have more complex cognitive structures (involving more subgroupings or types) for in-groups than we do for out-groups. One implication of this relative ignorance about who *they* are is that we might be highly influenced by evaluative information about out-group individuals. Researchers tested this idea by having participants evaluate a (bogus) application to law school under the pretext that researchers were interested in which information was most diagnostic of law school performance (Linville & Jones, 1980). The application, however, was manipulated to be from a Black or White applicant, and to have either weak or strong credentials. The participants (who were White) who reviewed the strong application rated the Black applicant as more intelligent, motivated, and likable than the White applicant. Those who reviewed the weak application had the opposite reaction: They rated the Black applicant as *less* intelligent, motivated, and likable than the White applicant. In other words, White participants' perceptions of a Black job applicant were more influenced by a single piece of evaluative information than their views of a White applicant were, and this effect can be attributed to the less developed knowledge we possess about out-group, compared with in-group, individuals.

We Explain Their Behavior Differently Than Ours

The categorization of others and ourselves into different social groups, and the application of stereotypes to out-group individuals, causes us to offer very different explanations for each others' actions. The results of many studies show our tendency to commit the **ultimate attribution error** (Pettigrew, 1979). That is, when explaining the behavior of out-group individuals, we tend to cite inner, dispositional causes, but when we explain our own actions, or those of a fellow in-group member, we cite situational, circumstantial factors. In one such study, participants who were employed attributed others' unemployment to laziness, whereas the unemployed individuals *themselves* externalized their plight by citing the belief that immigrants were taking all the jobs (Furnham, 1982b). This research indicates that we judge the behavior of out-group individuals more harshly than we do our own group's actions. Interestingly, our judgment of out-group members' behavior is lessened when we are socially similar in some way. For example, an employed person would be less likely to blame an unemployed individual for his own plight if he recognized that they attended the same church.

The ultimate attribution error has implications for our perceptions of diversity. Attributing the actions of socially different others to their personalities, rather than to situational factors, buttresses our stereotypic beliefs. Further, if their behavior is believed to be due to inner attributes, there is no reason to expect that they will change. This assumption affords our stereotypes predictability and additional resistance to disconfirmation.

> What is the price to our social perceptions of using stereotypes? What errors or biases are we likely to make when we use stereotypes? Are these biases serious or trivial?

Summary

The social diversity around us is sharply distilled by our perceptions about groups and their members. Although social categorization and stereotyping simplify and lend order to one's social world, they exaggerate and maintain differences between groups of people. They also promote thinking about others in more negative than positive terms and attribute their behavior to unchanging inner qualities. Although few of us willingly adopt and use social categories and stereotypes, the extent to which they are acquired through socialization and cognitive necessity have real consequences for the social world we perceive. Inevitably, these beliefs are acted out in our behavior, causing us to *actively* construct diversity in ways that extend beyond the cognitive processes covered in this chapter. This idea will be examined in Chapter 3.

DI Diversity Issue 2.1: Hypodescent

In Chapter 1 we learned that 3% of Americans identify themselves as biracial or multiracial. How do we categorize people who are members of two (or more) racial groups? How do multiracial people (e.g., Black-White, Asian-White) challenge our traditional social categories? **Hypodescent** refers to the historical practice of identifying mixed-race people by their socially subordinate parent group (Hickman, 1997).

In a simple test of whether hypodescent is still used to categorize biracial individuals, Arnold Ho and his colleagues had participants rate Black-White and Asian-White targets with questions like: Imagine a child with two Black grandparents and two White grandparents. To what extent would a person consider the child Black or White? Participants used a 1 = *completely Black* to 7 = *completely White* rating scale, with 4 indicating equally Black and White (Ho, Sidanius, Levin, & Banaji, 2011). The results showed that both half Black and half Asian targets were seen as more minority than White. A second study required participants to look at family tree diagrams on a computer (like the one shown below) and decide, as quickly as possible, whether the grandchild was White or minority by the press of a key. Showing the influence of hypodescent, participants in the study were more likely to categorize the child as a minority if at least one grandparent was minority than when no grandparents were minority. Furthermore, Ho and his colleagues found that it took more evidence of Whiteness for a Black-White, compared with an Asian-White, child to be considered White.

(Continued)

(Continued)

Figure 2.1   Family Tree Diagram (Ho, Sidanius, Levin, & Banji, 2011). Permission granted.

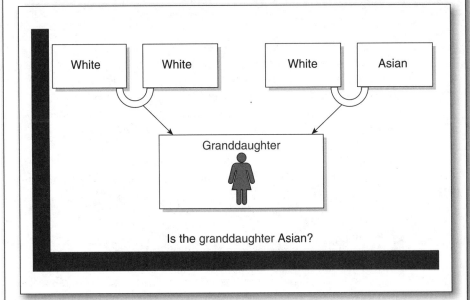

Is the granddaughter Asian?

SOURCE: "Evidence for hypodescent and racial hierarchy in the categorization and perception of biracial individuals," by A. Ho, J. Sidanius, D. Levin, and M. Banaji, 2011, *Journal of Personality and Social Psychology, 100,* p. 492–506. Copyright 2011 by the American Psychological Association. Used with permission.

? • Based on physical features you may suspect, but not know, that a person is biracial, does that uncertainty affect your thinking about who they are? Do you feel an impulse to categorize people that are racially ambiguous?

DI   Diversity Issue 2.2: Positive Stereotypes: Asian Americans as the Model Minority

Most stereotypes are negative—that is, they contain more negative than positive beliefs and assumptions. Asian Americans are among the few groups that are positively stereotyped. Asian Americans have been referred to as the **model minority** because of their (perceived) industriousness and value placed on academic and career achievement. Asian American students do score slightly higher than comparable White students on standardized tests (Kao, 1995). Other research, however, shows that Asians earn less than Whites with the same level of education (Kim & Park, 2008). Although the model minority label is more myth than fact, the stereotype nevertheless puts pressure on Asian Americans to live up to the high educational and occupational expectations held for members of their group. Cheryan and Bodenhausen (2000) selected Asian students for whom math was very important, and, before giving them the math test, made some of them aware of the high expectations Whites held about their group. Under these conditions, the positively stereotyped participants scored worse on the math test than those who were not aware of the positive stereotype about their group. A recent survey of Asians found that endorsement of the positive stereotype held about their group (e.g., agreeing, for example, with the statement "Most Asians are smart") was associated with more physical and psychological distress and less willingness to seek professional help (Gupta, Szymanski, & Leong, 2011).

The website Asian Nation has a page on the model minority image of Asians. See the WWW. resources that accompany this chapter.

? What other groups are positively stereotyped? What are the positive traits and beliefs attributed to the members of those groups?

? Interview someone from a positively stereotyped group and find out how he or she experiences the stereotype. Are there particular circumstances in which the stereotype has benefits? Drawbacks?

KEY TERMS

Social categorization   22

Primary social categories   22

Automatic categorization   22

Solo status   24

In-group   25

Out-group   25

Stereotype   28

Just world belief   31

Illusory correlation   31

Cultural stereotypes   32

Subtyping   35

Out-group homogeneity effect   37

Ultimate attribution error   38

Hypodescent   39

Model minority   40

FOR FURTHER READING

Fassinger, R. E. (2008). Workplace diversity and public policy: Challenges and opportunities for psychology. *American Psychologist, 63*(4), 252–268. doi: 10.1037/0003-066X.63.4.252
This article discusses barriers to greater diversity in the American workplace.

Online Resources

Native Nevada Classroom

http://www.unr.edu/nnap/NT/i-8_9.htm

An interesting site for learning about stereotypes about Native Americans. From the home page go to Nevada Tribes and then to Stereotyping of Native Americans.

Links About Stereotyping of Arabs and Muslims

http://www.muhajabah.com/anti-arab.htm

A large archive of news stories detailing stereotypes and stereotyping of Arab and Muslim people in the U.S.

Asian Nation

http://www.asian-nation.org/model-minority.shtml

A site on Asian American diversity with research, statistics, news, and resources for better understanding issues surrounding Asian diversity in the United States. From the home page, go to Ethnic Groups from the list on the left to see how diverse the Asian American population is. To study anti-Asian violence or the Model Minority stereotype, go to the Issues page and then to links for each of those topics.

Stereotypes of Blacks, Mexicans, Asians, gays, and blondes

http://www.youtube.com/watch?v=cOZd11Mcej4

A short and compelling video showing how stereotypes oversimplify diversity and disparage out-group members.

The Authentic History Center

http://www.authentichistory.com/

This site displays images from American popular culture and reveals the stereotyping inherent in popular cultural images in our history. From the home page, go to the Diversity link in the left panel. Explore stereotyping in the popular images of members of various groups (the pages for Native Americans, Blacks, and Asian Americans are the best).

3

Stereotypes Expressed

Social Processes
That Shape Diversity

Chapter 2 centered on thinking and processing information about people based on their social group. We learned of the many ways that social categories and stereotypes distort our thinking about out-groups and the inferences we make about people from those groups. However, it does not appear that categorical and stereotypic thinking (expressed only to ourselves) is bad. By definition, unexpressed stereotypic judgments of others cannot contribute to inequality and discrimination. We might make an academic distinction between stereotypes that are never expressed as harmless and those that are expressed as potentially damaging and discriminatory. Such a distinction would be trivial because, in fact, most of our stereotypes are difficult *not* to express. Once we give our stereotypes expression—in a conversation with someone, in a joke or story told to a friend, or in our interactions with other people—stereotypes cease to be merely private, and harmless, cognitive machinations.

Therefore, this chapter considers how stereotypes are expressed in our behavior and language as well as the social consequences of that expression. For example, do our stereotypic beliefs about the elderly lead us to behave differently toward them, and in turn, lead them to unwittingly confirm that stereotype? Does telling an insulting joke about gays to a friend change your behavior toward gay people? Does watching sexist portrayals of women on TV influence viewers' behavior toward women? If so, then, as social psychologist William Swann (1985) has noted, we become architects of our own social realities when we express stereotypic beliefs and expectations about people based on their group membership. The main lesson of this chapter is this: Stereotypes, often operating through our own behavior, have the power to create, maintain, and distort the diversity that we perceive around us.

The Self-Fulfilling Prophecy

In a clever study from 1964, researchers gave teams of two and three students in an experimental psychology course a rat to care for (Rosenthal & Lawson, 1964). Upon receiving their animal, the students were told either that their rat had been bred for brightness or bred for dullness. In reality, the rats were indistinguishable; Rosenthal and Lawson were interested in the effect of students' *expectations* about their rat's ability to perform a series of eight Skinner-box learning tasks. Remarkably, the bright rats performed better on seven of the eight learning tasks than the so-called dull rats. How did this happen? Somehow, the students' expectations for their rats ended up influencing their rats' behavior.

Now, imagine this happening with people instead of rats. A **self-fulfilling prophecy** occurs when our expectations for an individual's personality or behavior cause that person to act in ways that confirm our expectations for them (Merton, 1948). Hence, our prophecy (in the form of our expectations, assumptions, or beliefs for that person) is self-fulfilling—through our own actions we bring out in her or him what we expected in the first place. Research evidence for the self-fulfilling prophecy is abundant; the effect has been documented in general social interactions between researchers and research participants and between teachers and students (Brophy & Good, 1974; Jamieson, Lydon, Stewart, & Zanna, 1987; Jones, 1986; Rosenthal, 1974).

In the classic demonstration of the self-fulfilling prophecy modeled on the rat study described above, Robert Rosenthal and Lenore Jacobson (1968) led elementary school teachers to believe that some of their students had been identified through testing as *late bloomers*, students whose academic promise was just now expected to develop. These students, however, were selected randomly and thus were no more (or less) promising than the other students. After 8 months, the students who had been labeled as late bloomers were viewed more positively by their teachers than the average students. Amazingly, the late bloomers improved in the classroom, too; their IQ and standardized test scores improved significantly over the academic year. Many other studies have added support to this basic relationship: Teachers' expectations for a student's aptitude predict actual change in the student's performance in the expected direction (Brophy & Good, 1974; Cooper & Tom, 1984).

This research gained national prominence and became a rallying point for people concerned that teachers' expectations—informed by stereotypes—undermined the educational opportunities of broad classes of students, such as females, racial and ethnic minority students, and students from lower economic classes (Wineburg, 1987). However, two points help temper our interpretations of the early research on the self-fulfilling prophecy. First, although much research documents a relationship between teachers' expectations for students' ability and students' performance, in many studies the size of that relationship is small (Jussim, Eccles, & Madon, 1996; Jussim & Harber, 2005). Second, the fact that teachers' expectations for students predict student classroom performance does not necessarily mean that the self-fulfilling prophecy is operating—there are other explanations for the link between what teachers expect and how students perform in school (Jussim et al., 1996). Let's consider them.

How Are Teachers' Expectations Related to Students' Achievement?

Self-Fulfilling Prophecy

The tendency for teachers' positive expectations for students to be related to students' positive classroom performance (and negative expectations with negative performance) can be explained in three ways, as illustrated in Figure 3.1. First, the relationship could be due to the self-fulfilling prophecy. That is, teachers' positive expectations for a student (or a group of students) could lead them to pay more attention to those students in the classroom, offer more help on assignments, or be more encouraging in responding to their comments. Conversely, teachers who hold negative impressions and expectations for students might call on them less in class, give them less time to answer a question, or point out more deficiencies than strengths in their work. These behaviors could in turn produce (the expected) improvements or decrements in students' school achievement.

Do teachers really tip their hand about students they regard highly (or not so highly)? Much research says yes. In one study, teachers were videotaped talking about real students about whom they held high, or low, expectations (Babad, Berneiri, & Rosenthal, 1991). Study participants then viewed short (10-second) clips of the teacher's face while talking, but with the sound turned down. Amazingly, participants were able to correctly identify whether the teacher was talking about a liked or disliked student. This study shows that our expectations and liking for others leak through to our behavior in the form of identifiable facial expressions. Other studies show that women and minority students report more negative classroom experiences and interactions with professors and teachers than do male, majority-group students (Allen & Niss, 1990; Steele, 1997).

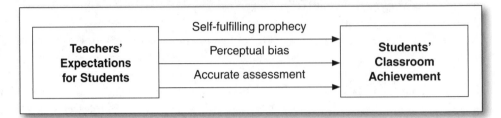

Figure 3.1   How Are Teachers' Expectations for Students Related to Students' Classroom Achievement?

Perceptual Bias

The relationship between teachers' expectations and students' achievement can also be due to a bias in evaluating students' classroom behavior or work. We know from Chapter 2 that stereotypic beliefs seek confirmation and resist disconfirmation. Similarly, beliefs about an individual (without regard to their social group) can bias our perceptions of that person to support our initial beliefs. The perceptual bias explanation differs from the self-fulfilling prophecy in an important way. In the self-fulfilling prophecy, students' behavior actually changes in accordance with the expectations of the teacher. With **perceptual bias**, teachers' expectations are not transmitted to students' behavior, but operate in evaluating students' work in expectation-consistent ways. Thus, although teachers' perceptual biases do not alter the extent or nature of social differences in a classroom (as the self-fulfilling prophecy does), they are no less unfair or discriminatory to students.

A great deal of research supports the existence of perceptual biases in attention to, memory for, and explanations of others' behavior. For example, when we are presented with information about an individual that is open to interpretation, we will selectively attend to the information that is consistent with our preconceptions of that person (Hilton & von Hippel, 1990). Our memory for others' characteristics can be shaped by current beliefs about them. In one study, researchers acquainted participants with the traits and behaviors of a hypothetical woman (Snyder & Cantor, 1979). Some of Jane's traits portrayed her as extroverted; others described her as introverted. Later, participants were asked to describe Jane's suitability to be either a saleswoman or a librarian. Participants who were considering her as a saleswoman recalled more of her extroverted qualities than those considering her as a librarian; likewise, thinking of Jane as a librarian led participants to remember her introverted traits.

In a similar study, male student participants had a get-acquainted telephone conversation with a female student who (having been given a bogus picture of her) they believed was either obese or normal weight (Snyder & Haugen, 1995). After having the conversation, participants gave their impression of their phone partner by rating her personality. The participants who believed their partner was obese formed more negative impressions of her and disliked her more than the participants who believed they were conversing with a normal weight partner. Both of these studies demonstrate the power of stereotype-based beliefs and expectations (e.g., librarians are introverts, fat people are lazy) on our perceptions and impressions of other people.

Finally, the tendency for us to cite dispositional (e.g., personality) more than situational (e.g., circumstances) factors when explaining others' behavior is itself an expression of an underlying perceptual bias (Gilbert & Malone, 1995). When we observe people, their actions and speech are much more salient than their situations. Thus, perceptually speaking, others' behavior seems to come from *them*, not their circumstances.

How could these perceptual biases in attention, memory, and explanation account for the relationship between teachers' expectations and students' behavior? A teacher with negative expectations for a student could attend more to the mistakes, than the strong points, of that student's project. Low expectations for a student may prompt a teacher to recall less class participation than actually occurred. Similarly, a student who misses an exam may do so for a variety of reasons, both internal (she doesn't care about the course) or external (her mother is ill and requires care). However, the teacher is more likely to assume the former and refuse to grant a make-up exam. In each of these scenarios, the tendency for student behavior to reflect teachers' expectations is due wholly to the teacher's (mis)interpretations of student actions—not to any actual change in the student's behavior or ability.

Accurate Assessment

Finally, the relationship between teachers' expectations and student achievement could result from an accurate assessment of the student's abilities (Jussim, 1991). Teachers do not form arbitrary positive and negative impressions of students; rather, their expectations are likely rooted in the records, reports, or observations of the student's past achievement. For example, a student (or group of students) may be expected to do poorly in eleventh grade English because the teacher is aware that the student received a D in tenth grade English. If the student *did* underachieve in her class, as expected, it need not be due to her influence or bias, but to the fact that the teacher's expectations and the student's achievement were caused by the same factor: a poor record of past achievement. Researchers have found evidence that teachers' expectations for students sometimes correspond to students' classroom performance because their (teachers') expectations are accurate—they are based on knowledge of preexisting factors that affect students' achievement.

Accurate Assessment or Self-Fulfilling Prophecy? Research Evidence

The relationship between teachers' expectations and student achievement has long been assumed to be unfair and discriminatory (Wineburg, 1987). Two of the three explanations for this relationship discussed above—the self-fulfilling prophecy and perceptual bias—are unfair. But it is also possible that teachers' expectations *fairly* predict student achievement because those expectations are accurate. Therefore, it is important to determine how much of the effect of teacher expectations on student performance is accurate and fair and how much is unfair and discriminatory.

In two large-scale studies involving about 1,700 students in sixth grade math classes, Lee Jussim and his colleagues measured teachers' perceptions of students early in the academic year, students' achievement in math across the school year, and students' motivation for achievement in math (Jussim, 1989; Jussim & Eccles, 1992). They reasoned that the self-fulfilling prophecy would occur if teachers' expectations for students in the fall term were related to students' math grades in the spring term, after controlling for two factors: (a) students' prior math achievement (the ability they brought with them from fifth grade) and (b) students' motivation to do well in math.

The results found that teachers' expectations for students' achievement in the fall were strongly related to students' math grades in the spring. However, very little of this relationship was due to the self-fulfilling prophecy. Rather, about 70% to 80% of the effect of teachers' (positive or negative) expectations on students' math achievement was accurate. Students who were known to be good at math based on their past grades were expected to do well—and they did. Likewise, students who were known to struggle with math were expected to do poorly—and they did. The small remainder of the total effect of teacher expectations on students (20%–30%) was due to the self-fulfilling prophecy (the researchers did not tease apart the self-fulfilling prophecy and perceptual bias in these studies).

? Teachers' expectations are associated with students' classroom achievement. Aside from the operation of the self-fulfilling prophecy, how can this occur?

Stereotypes and Expectations: Are Minority Students More Vulnerable to the Self-Fulfilling Prophecy?

The research summarized above shows that the self-fulfilling prophecy is real and operates in classrooms across the country, but the size of the effect is small. The small overall magnitude of the self-fulfilling prophecy found in these studies, however, may indicate that teachers' expectations are self-fulfilling for some students, or groups of students, and not for others. Students from minority, disadvantaged, or stereotyped groups are particularly vulnerable to the self-fulfilling prophecy because teachers' expectations for them may be affected by their stereotypic beliefs about the members of that group, and these beliefs are often inaccurate. According to Jussim and his colleagues, inaccurate expectations possess greater potential to create self-fulfilling prophecies (Jussim et al., 1996). Are minority or otherwise disadvantaged students therefore more likely to be affected by teachers' expectations?

The studies of sixth graders described above were reanalyzed to test this question based on the students' sex, social class, and ethnicity (Jussim, 1989; Jussim & Eccles, 1992). In each of these social group comparisons, students' fifth grade math grades and motivation for math achievement were controlled to rule out the possibility that teachers' expectations and students' achievement were related because of the teachers' accurate assessment of students' math ability and motivation. The results revealed that teachers' expectations were unrelated to student grades among boys, but they were related among girls. High teacher expectations for math achievement were associated with higher math grades (and low expectations with low grades) in girls. What is this effect in practical terms? For the average female student in Jussim's studies, moving from the teacher with the most positive expectations to the teacher with the most negative expectations would result in just under a half letter grade drop (e.g., B to B−) in math class performance. Similar-sized results were observed when comparing students of low and high socioeconomic status (SES). Students from lower socioeconomic backgrounds were most vulnerable to self-fulfilling prophecies—low teacher expectations were associated with low math test scores (and high expectations with high scores). Finally, Black, compared to White, students were more influenced by teacher expectations in the same manner. The size of the self-fulfilling prophecy was larger than observed in female and low SES students. Moving from a teacher with the most positive, to one with the most negative, expectations would result in a letter-and-a-half grade drop (e.g., B+ to C) in math class performance for the typical Black student in Jussim's studies.

Other research tested the effects of teachers' sex, social class, and ethnic stereotypes on students' math achievement by studying over 1,900 seventh grade students in math classes (Madon et al., 1998). Madon and her colleagues found that teachers' judgments of boys' and girls' classroom *performance* was based on accurate assessment of boys' versus girls' math abilities. However, teachers' judgments of boys' and girls' classroom *effort* were informed by an inaccurate stereotypic belief that, in general, girls try harder than boys in school. Teachers' judgments of low SES and ethnic minority students' math effort and achievement were almost entirely based on accurate information: Students whom teachers judged as high math achievers were those students who had a past record of high motivation and achievement for math. In other words, although teachers see differences in the achievement of girls versus boys, poor versus middle-class students, and ethnic minority versus White students, these judgments largely correspond to actual differences between those groups. Teachers' stereotypes about students from minority or disadvantaged groups have little or no effect on those students' classroom achievement.

> **?** Why would stereotypes drive teachers' estimation of students' effort in school but not their assessment of the students' grades? If your professor had low expectations for your effort in this course, how would it affect you?

Moderators of the Self-Fulfilling Prophecy

In the original self-fulfilling prophecy experiment, Rosenthal and Jacobson (1968) gave teachers either positive or no expectations about their students' abilities because it would have been unethical to give teachers negative expectations about their students. Nevertheless, positive and negative expectations for another person's behavior may have different effects. Which do you think would be a more powerful influence on your school behavior: having a teacher who believes you are bright and capable of the most challenging work, or one who believes you are not very smart and are not likely to achieve much? This moderator of the self-fulfilling prophecy was evaluated by Stephanie Madon and her colleagues in over 1,500 elementary and junior high school students and their teachers (Madon, Jussim, & Eccles, 1997).

The researchers first compared the teachers' perceptions of their students' ability with the students' actual ability based, for example, on the students' grades from the previous year. Teachers who expected more out of their students than their prior grades suggested they would achieve were said to have positive expectations, whereas teachers who expected less out of their students than their prior grades forecast for them were said to have negative expectations. The results showed that teachers' positive expectations influenced students' math test scores more than teachers' negative expectations. The size of the effect of having a teacher who believes you are capable of more than your past grades would suggest is considerable. Compared with teachers who had neutral expectations, students whose teachers had positive expectations for them scored about four points higher (a little less than 1 standard deviation, for the statistically savvy reader) on a standardized math test.

A second moderator tested by Madon and her colleagues (1997) was whether teachers' expectations affected high- and low-achieving students differently. Poor students—that is, students who receive below average grades and scores—may be more susceptible to the self-fulfilling prophecy for two reasons. First, poor students may have low motivation for school achievement. If so, they may be energized and focused by a teacher with positive expectations for them, and their work may exceed the level predicted by their past performance. Second, poor students are often uncertain of their abilities and have little confidence in what they are able to achieve in school. If so, they may be more influenced than more confident students by teachers with clear, positive expectations for them. The results showed that, as reasoned above, positive teacher expectations led to higher scores on a standardized math test than would have been predicted by the students' prior grades. However, this effect was much larger among low-achieving students. Low-achieving students, whose teachers had positive expectations for them, scored about three points higher on a standardized math test than the same students whose teachers had neutral expectations. This self-fulfilling prophecy was much smaller (roughly a one point effect) in high-achieving students, and this was not due to the fact that high-achieving students have less room to improve.

? Teachers' positive expectations for students are more likely to form a self-fulfilling prophecy than their negative expectations, and this influences low-achieving more than high-achieving students. Based on this principle, what would you recommend teachers do in the classroom to use the self-fulfilling prophecy to students' benefit?

A third moderator of self-fulfilling prophecy effects in the classroom is how much personal information a teacher has about a student. Teachers who know their students well have much more experience on which to base an expectation for the student's performance. Lacking that individualistic information, teachers are more vulnerable to rely on stereotypes about the student's group to form expectations. To test this, researchers had teachers watch a video of a boy or girl student doing some gymnastics exercises in a physical education class (Chalabaev, Sarrazin, Trouilloud, & Jussim, 2009). Unbeknownst to the teachers, the boys' and girls' gymnastic demonstrations had been rated the same by expert judges. After viewing the video, the teachers were then asked to predict how the student would do in the gymnastics test at the end of the 10-week gymnastics period. Teachers predicted better performances for boys than girls. Because true gender differences in gymnastic skill had been controlled, and lacking any other individuating information about the students, the teacher-participants in this study used stereotype-based expectations.

A second study was done to see if teachers' real class interactions with their students provide information that makes them less reliant on stereotypes when forming expectations for their students. At the beginning of a 10-week gymnastics unit, teachers watched their students' initial skills test on videotape. The teachers then gave their expectations for their students' final performances. In this study, however, teachers had been interacting with the students in class for 3 months prior. Based presumably on their knowledge of their individual students' athletic abilities, teachers expected equal performances from boy and girl students. In the end, girls ended up outperforming boys in the unit, but this study shows that with the benefit of many class interactions, teachers' expectations for their students' performance (though inaccurate) were not based on gender stereotypes.

Do the Effects of the Self-Fulfilling Prophecy Accumulate Over Time?

The research on the self-fulfilling prophecy reviewed above is based on cross-sectional research, which provides a picture of the direction and size of the self-fulfilling prophecy at one point in time. This research shows that when glimpsed at a particular slice of time, such as a standardized testing session at school, the self-fulfilling prophecy is small in magnitude. However, our expectations for others' behavior can *accumulate* by being repetitively communicated (as a teacher does over many weeks of class) or expressed by consistent multiple sources (such as parents' combined expectations for their children's behavior). Recent research tested the possibility that accumulated expectations are more powerful shapers of others' behavior than expectations expressed at any given point in time (Madon, Guyll, Spoth, & Willard, 2004).

Madon and her colleagues studied to what extent alcohol use among 115 teenagers was a self-fulfilling prophecy produced by their parents' inaccurate beliefs and expectations regarding their alcohol use. First, they measured the teens' actual alcohol use and other variables, such as their friends' level of drinking, the perceived availability of alcohol, and the rewards they associated with drinking. To show a self-fulfilling prophecy, the teens' drinking behavior 12 months later would have to be related to their parents' beliefs about their alcohol use beyond what would be predicted by the background factors mentioned above. This fascinating study showed that mothers' (more than fathers') inaccurate overestimation of their children's drinking (e.g., my son/daughter probably drinks more than he/she should) was associated with greater drinking among the teens than the prior behaviors, such as past drinking, would have predicted. However, when *both* parents overestimated their teen's drinking, the self-fulfilling prophecy was even larger; this effect was termed **synergistic accumulation**. In other words, when inaccurate beliefs about teens' behavior accumulate—in this case across parents—they form a more potent force for evoking the expected (and, in this case, feared) behavior. In contrast with research on teacher–student interaction, where the positive expectations of teachers form a more powerful self-fulfilling prophecy, in this study, parents' negative expectations for their teens were more self-fulfilling than their positive expectations. In short, inaccurate expectations about other people that accumulate across perceivers or time form a stronger self-fulfilling prophecy than the effect of those expectations in a single perceiver or at a particular time.

Summary Thoughts on the Self-Fulfilling Prophecy

Overall, several large-scale studies of elementary school and junior high school students provide little evidence that the self-fulfilling prophecy is a serious problem in the classroom. To be sure, students *do* conform to their teachers' expectations for them. However, this seems to occur not because teachers' expectations are a self-fulfilling prophecy, but because teachers have largely accurate expectations for their students' ability and achievement. The self-fulfilling nature of teachers' beliefs and expectations for students tends to shape students' behavior more if the students are members of minority groups or have low academic ability, but the size of these effects are also modest. However, the effect of accumulated expectations reveals the potential power of the self-fulfilling prophecy to shape behavior among members of minority and disadvantaged groups. Members of many stereotyped groups (e.g., overweight and obese people) face consistent negative expectations for their character and behavior from family members, peers, teachers, and coworkers. The accumulation of these shared beliefs and expectations undoubtedly means that perceivers (typically majority group members) create some of the diversity that we observe around us through the operation of the self-fulfilling prophecy.

But since the self-fulfilling prophecy always unfolds in the context of social interaction, the *perceived* individual also has a role in the confirmation of the perceivers' beliefs. Mark Snyder and Julie Haugen (1995) proposed that a basic need to be liked and accepted may lead us to confirm others' expectations for us by acting out their prophecy for us. Matching others' assumptions about us with responses that confirm those assumptions contributes to smooth and enjoyable interactions (e.g., he seems to assume I'm a liberal, so I'll discuss some liberal issues to keep his interest). They tested this by having *perceiver* students engage in a get-acquainted phone interaction with a target partner. Prior to the conversation, the partner was given instructions to pursue either a smooth and pleasing interaction or to gain accurate information about his or her partner; there was also a no-instruction condition. Additionally, one half of the perceivers were led to believe their partner was overweight, giving those perceivers negative and stereotypical expectations for their partners' behavior. The study showed that a self-fulfilling prophecy occurred in typical (no-instruction) situations and when the target was trying to produce a smooth interaction. Only when targets were trying to get accurate impressions of their perceiver-partners did they avoid fulfilling the negative expectations of their partners.

This research reveals two insights about the self-fulfilling prophecy and its implications for minority group individuals. First, the self-fulfilling prophecy arises in interactions when one or both people are trying to be accepted or liked by the other. Almost by definition, members of minority groups are more likely to face situations where they must engender acceptance from majority-group members, and as a result they become vulnerable to fulfilling others' stereotypical beliefs about them. Second, the self-fulfilling prophecy can be eliminated by efforts to understand and know, rather than please, other people. This insight can be put to practical use in social contexts involving high- and low-status groups (such as parent–child interaction) by fostering mutual understanding rather than one group's approval of the other.

Stereotypes Expressed in Language and Communication

As we learned with the self-fulfilling prophecy, our stereotypic beliefs can exaggerate, or even create, diversity around us by changing our behavior toward out-group members. This section deals with how stereotypes are expressed in our communication with and about out-group members. It is a well-established fact in the psychological research literature that we express our stereotypical beliefs and assumptions in our communication about and to people who are socially different than ourselves. In a classic demonstration of this, male participants had a get-acquainted telephone conversation with a female who they believed (because the researchers provided a bogus picture of the partner) was either attractive or unattractive (Snyder, Tanke, & Berscheid, 1977). Raters who were unaware of the partner's attractiveness listened to and evaluated the male participants' side of the contribution. The results showed that the males' ratings of their female partners were shaped by their stereotypic associations and beliefs about attractive and unattractive people. The attractive conversation partners were rated as more warm, outgoing, poised, and sociable than the unattractive partners. More importantly, males' stereotypes of their partners leaked into their behavior and were noticed by the raters. Men who conversed with women whom they believed were attractive displayed more social skill, warmth, interest in the partner, and humor than men who conversed with unattractive partners. This study demonstrates how stereotypes not only guide our perceptions of others, but also change the way we behave toward other people.

In a similar study, participants had a series of short phone conversations with a partner after first learning that the partner scored high or low on a loneliness questionnaire; this information was intended to activate participants' stereotype of lonely people (Rotenberg, Gruman, & Ariganello, 2002). The participants' contributions to the conversation were taped and analyzed by listeners who were not aware of the stereotype condition. When conversing with a partner whom they believed was lonely, the participants' communications were less sociable, warm, and friendly than the communications of people who believed their partner was normal. Thus, participants' stereotypic assumptions about lonely people were reflected in the way they talked to their lonely partners. Moreover, participants' stereotypic communication was observed even when the partner was instructed (unbeknown to the participant) to converse in a way that was inconsistent with the loneliness stereotype—in other words, to deliberately talk in an outgoing and friendly way. This is an amazing finding because it illustrates again how much our stereotypes resist change. Stereotypes don't just bias what we say to out-group members. Stereotypes also inhibit our ability to really listen to other people, especially when those people say things that contradict our preconceived beliefs about them.

> **?**
>
> How might these stereotypic conversation principles play out in a dating situation, when you're trying to impress him/her, and vice versa? Do we stereotype our dating partners and, if so, how might these stereotypes affect the relationship down the road?

Talking About Out-Group Members: Stereotypic Biases

Other research shows that when we talk *about*, rather than *to*, individuals from other social groups we tend to emphasize stereotypic characteristics of that group, refer to them as all alike, and subtly derogate the group (Ruscher, 1998). These communication tendencies exist despite communicators' insistence that they are not prejudiced toward the out-group. Why? Recall from Chapter 2 that well-learned cultural stereotypes emerge in our behavior spontaneously and unintentionally. Stereotypes influence our choice of words and verbal expression when talking about people from other social groups, even when we don't recognize our negative feelings about that group.

Researchers in one study had pairs of participants talk about a hypothetical person who was described as alcoholic and about whom they were given a list of characteristics (Ruscher & Hammer, 1994). Half of the characteristics were consistent with the alcoholic stereotype (e.g., forgetful, disagreeable), and half were stereotype-inconsistent traits (e.g., motivated, successful). After forming impressions of the target person together, the two participants shared their impressions on videotape. The participants made more references to, and spent more time talking about, characteristics of the person that were consistent (compared to inconsistent) with the stereotype associated with his group. This conversational pattern was not due to forgetting the stereotype-inconsistent traits; a test of participants' memory after the discussion showed that they recalled both types of traits equally well. Other research finds this pattern when people talk about physically disabled and Black individuals (Ruscher, 1998).

So, stereotypes are reflected in our communication patterns. Stereotypic expression is evident not just in the terms we select to describe out-group members, but also in the linguistic structure of those terms. Researchers have found that when we describe the expected or typical actions of out-group members, we use abstract terms, but when we describe their unexpected or atypical actions we use concrete terms (Maass, Milesi, Zabbini, & Stahlberg, 1995). For example, imagine observing a male or female student giving an eloquent solution to a problem posed in your math class. Researchers find that people will use abstract terms such as intelligent to describe the expected action (males being good in math), and concrete terms such as *she answered the question* to describe the unexpected action (females being good at math). This pattern is called the **linguistic intergroup bias**, and is similar to the ultimate attribution error discussed in Chapter 2.

The linguistic intergroup bias reflects, in our communication, the dispositional nature of stereotypic thinking. Abstract descriptions tie the typical behaviors of out-group members to underlying, unchanging qualities, and this lends stability to our stereotypes. Alternatively, when we observe a behavior that is atypical of an out-group member, we can isolate that action through concrete descriptive terms and avoid having to confront the inaccuracy of our stereotypic beliefs. Talking about out-group individuals also makes the members of that group seem more similar. This occurs when we liken the person we are talking about to other members of that group we are familiar with, such as through past experience or media exposure. Ruscher and her colleagues found that when pairs of participants talked about a hypothetical out-group individual (Joe), their conversation included more exemplars—examples of other members of that group who had similar qualities—when Joe's out-group was emphasized than when it was not (Ruscher & Hammer, 1994).

Another intergroup linguistic bias is the **negation bias**. If you wished to refer to an out-group person as unintelligent, what term would you use—stupid or not smart? Researchers believe that we are more likely to use negated terms (e.g., not smart) when referring to a person's behavior that is not consistent with our stereotype of his or her group, and more likely to use affirmative terms (e.g., stupid) when referring to stereotypical behaviors (Beukeboom, Finkenauer, & Wigboldus, 2010). In a study designed to test the negation bias, participants read sentences that described a stereotype-consistent (e.g., the soccer hooligan shouted at the waiter) or inconsistent (e.g., the nurse shouted at the waiter) behavior. They then rated the applicability of two different descriptions of the behavior (e.g., he is not nice and he is rude) on a 7-point scale. Affirmations were rated as more applicable for stereotype-consistent behaviors and negations were seen as more appropriate responses to stereotype-inconsistent actions (Beukeboom et al., 2010). A follow-up study showed that the negation bias has consequences for the impression we make on other people. Reflecting the self-fulfilling prophecy discussed earlier, referring to someone's positive behavior using a negation (e.g., not bad rather than good) subtly transmits negative stereotypic beliefs to out-group members.

Other research measured the imperative verbs used by men and women instructors to teach the Heimlich maneuver to either a man or woman student (Duval & Ruscher, 1994). The researchers reasoned that the number of imperative verbs (e.g., grab him around here, pull up like this) used in a lesson was an indication of how simply the task was taught to the student. The results showed that men teaching women used significantly more imperative verb statements than when men taught other men (or when women taught anyone). This suggests the operation of a stereotype: Men may see women as slightly less competent than males on tasks of physical skill or strength, and thus requiring a more detailed, authoritative lesson.

Stereotypes infect our communications with others—but why? Janet Ruscher and Laura Duval (1998) reason that when talking with other people stereotypes are a useful common denominator, a topic of conversation that most people understand and can agree with. As social common denominators, stereotypes expressed in our conversations with friends and acquaintances create consensus, good feelings, and cohesiveness among group members, albeit at the expense of out-group members. Conversation is also a good way to resolve uncertainty or ambiguity about our knowledge of people who are different than we are. A female Muslim student in a *hijab* (head scarf), for example, may prompt questions or speculations about Muslim women that take the form of "What is she like? What should I believe about them?" Conversations with friends about members of unknown out-groups can help fill in knowledge and expectations.

The Social Transmission of Stereotypes

Remember the party game where the first person in a chain privately tells a story to the second person, and each subsequent person must change one element in his or her transmission of the story? The fun is hearing the last person in the chain tell a story so absurd that it couldn't possibly have come from the original—but it did. Yoshihisa Kashima (2000) investigated whether people repeat more stereotype-consistent than stereotype-inconsistent content when they relate a story about a person. In that study, subjects were told a story about a man and woman, asked to remember it, and then tell it to another person. The story was transmitted through a five-person chain, and the last people in the chain tended to repeat more stereotypical facts when those facts were central to the story. Other research shows that when people transmit stories about other people, the transmission process strips out stereotype-inconsistent content to render a story that reflects shared stereotypic beliefs (Lyons & Kashima, 2001).

The tendency to refer to out-group members in stereotypic terms is called the **stereotype consistency bias**. Much research shows that when people relate a story about an out-group member to a friend or fellow in-group member, stereotype-inconsistent details tend to be dropped from the story. In a study by Tim Kurz and Anthony Lyons (2009), subjects read a story about a person from impoverished socioeconomic circumstances. The story was created to have equal numbers of stereotype-consistent and inconsistent elements. Then participants rewrote the story for someone who, they were led to believe, was either middle-class (an in-group member) or poor/working-class (an out-group member) in their socioeconomic status. The findings revealed that when participants were communicating with in-group compared with out-group members, their story contained much more stereotype-consistent content.

This tendency to edit our stories about out-group members so that they reflect our stereotypes of their group is caused by wanting better communication with in-group members, not to having poor memory for stereotype-inconsistent details (Lyons & Kashima, 2003). We repeat stereotypical content when we talk about out-group members because stereotypes are shared knowledge—in other words, a kind of social common denominator. Focusing on shared knowledge when we talk about other people may make stories easier to tell and promote our listeners' comprehension of the story. Indeed, researchers have found that people are more likely to repeat a story expressing stereotypes about an out-group member when talking with a friend than a stranger and when they believe that their listeners are at least partly aware of the stereotype (Klein, Clark, & Lyons, 2010; Lyons and Kashima, 2003). And when the stereotype is believed to have broad acceptance, we transmit stereotypes in our communication even more. This work shows that when we believe other people endorse a stereotype, we more freely repeat negative, stereotypic beliefs in our conversations with other people. However, stereotypic beliefs that are repeated often enough in conversation, anecdotes, or jokes develop credibility and consensus. Ruscher and Duval (1998) found that listeners who merely overhear an unflattering, stereotype-laden story develop more stereotypic attitudes.

Research demonstrates that our communication to, and about, people from other social groups reflects the influence of stereotypes about those groups. We describe socially different others in stereotype-consistent terms, use references that liken them to other group members, and use derogative language with out-group members in stereotype-consistent ways. Why do we communicate in stereotypical terms when we have no wish or intention to be prejudiced? Two answers are plausible. First, we define and evaluate ourselves and our own groups by pointing to others (Allport, 1954). Thus, even when we harbor no dislike of people from other social groups, talking about them in stereotypic terms helps us understand who *we* are and why *our* group is valuable. This explanation is strengthened by research that shows that when our group identity is threatened, we respond defensively with enhanced levels of the intergroup linguistic bias than when we have no need to defend our social identity (Maass, Ceccarelli, & Rudin, 1996). Second, we hold stereotypic beliefs with varying certainty, depending on the group, because we often have little actual contact with individuals from other social groups. Thus, conversations with other individuals, especially in-group individuals, are ways to test the validity of our ideas and develop consensus for them (Ruscher, 1998).

Stereotypes Expressed on Television

Many minority groups (e.g., racial and ethnic minorities, women, older people, overweight people) are underrepresented on television, in movies, and in video games relative to their proportion of the population. For example, a survey of the top-grossing movies from 1990 to 2005 found that males outnumbered females by a ratio of 2.6 to 1. Furthermore, females tended to be younger and more attractive than males (Smith, Pieper, Granados, & Choueiti, 2010). Gender imbalance and stereotypical portrayals of women also are evident in primetime TV programming (Gerbner & Ozyegin 1997), TV news (Desmond & Danilewicz, 2010), and video games (Downs & Smith, 2010). The final section of this chapter considers how stereotypes are expressed in the media and the consequences of viewing men and women (and members of many other groups) in stereotypical terms.

According to the cultivation hypothesis, television cultivates perceptions of the world that reflect the content and assumptions of the programming (Gerbner, Gross, Morgan, & Signorielli, 1986). Today, the cultivation hypothesis must include movies and video games because, like TV, they also entertain us with stories and actors. The cultivation hypothesis holds that the more we watch (or in the case of video games, play), the more we come to see our own world like the on-screen social world. Furthermore, the media's influence on our views of the social world is cumulative and not the effect of particular programs or types of programming. It is the volume of television that we watch, rather than the particular shows, that is a better predictor of our understanding of diversity. Why? According to George Gerbner and his colleague (1997), TV homogenizes diverse worldviews and traditions into their lowest common elements—called the *mainstream*—and then injects this product repetitively into programs, both within and across program genres. It is mainstreaming that accounts for the same characters and storylines in all detective-genre shows (e.g., *CSI, Law & Order*) or the familiar story lines in most reality shows. Finally, and most importantly, cultural stereotypes of women, ethnic minorities, and other groups are prominent themes in this mainstream because (as we have learned) stereotypes are widely understood and, even if not personally espoused, constitute a common denominator that informs our communication about out-group members.

The empirical evidence for the cultivation hypothesis consists mainly in studies that test the effects of media portrayals of Blacks, women, and other minority groups on viewers' social attitudes. Here are some highlights from recent studies. For example, after viewing a crime story that was shown with a light-skinned or dark-skinned Black perpetrator, heavy viewers were more uncomfortable with the dark-skinned perpetrator and more likely to sympathize with the victim than were light viewers (Dixon & Maddox, 2005). Viewing Blacks in stereotypical roles (men as violent, women as promiscuous) caused Whites to hold more negative views of Blacks compared to Whites, but the stereotypical portrayals also undermined Whites' support for social policies that assist Blacks (Johnson, Olivo, Gibson, Reed, & Ashburn-Nardo, 2009). In video games, stereotypical female actors (who were suggestively dressed and engaged in high eye gaze) produced more negative attitudes in both men and women viewers than did actors whose roles and appearance challenged cultural stereotypes of women (Fox & Bailenson, 2009). Margie Donlon and her colleagues (2005) found that heavy TV viewing was associated with more negative images of older people *among older viewers themselves,* after controlling for the effects of education and other demographic variables that influence both TV viewing and stereotyping.

The mainstreaming of cultural stereotypes of women, Blacks, older people, and other minority groups across the TV/movie/video game landscape means that negative beliefs and assumptions about members of those groups will be rehearsed for us—in the context of programs that seem superficially different—as we engage with those media. In terms of Devine's concepts of the automatic and controlled aspects of prejudice (see Chapters 2 and 4), stereotypic images and portrayals will strengthen the automatic component of our prejudices—the component that operates spontaneously and that most of us want to suppress—especially among heavy TV viewers. In addition to its role as teacher, television contributes to reliance on stereotypes by restricting the visibility, or excluding completely, members of some social groups. This segregation in the on-screen world feeds the ignorance we may already harbor about those who are different than us. Recall that lack of exposure to or personal experience with members of other social groups means that we rely more heavily on stereotypes to guide our thinking about them. This problem is magnified among people whose cultural opportunities are monopolized by television, such as elderly or poor people.

In addition to shaping our perceptions of our social worlds, television representations and portrayals of minority group individuals also have the power to shape actual diversity by influencing the behavior of viewers, although very little research has tested that notion. In one study, female viewers who watched gender-stereotypical TV commercials were more likely to avoid leadership roles in a subsequent task and select subordinate roles instead, compared with women who watched nonstereotypic commercials (Davies, Spencer, & Steele, 2005). This study is consistent with the large body of work (discussed in Chapter 3) on the self-fulfilling prophecy, and it suggests that repetitive exposure to stereotypic messages about members of their own group, as might occur among heavy TV viewers, helps remind minority group individuals of others' expectations for them and their abilities.

Summary

In Chapter 2, we learned that stereotypes are beliefs about social groups and the people in them that consist of, at best, exaggerations of their actual attributes and, at worst, fabricated assumptions about them. If we could previously comfort ourselves with the thought that stereotypes don't hurt anybody, we now know better. Stereotypes shape our social world in direct and indirect ways. Their direct influence operates through the self-fulfilling prophecy, as others come to act out the roles that are scripted by our expectations for them. As out-group members' behavior conforms to our stereotypical expectations and expressions, diversity is shaped in two ways. First, actual differences between groups of people grow. If we believe elderly and younger people have different traits and we treat them differently, over time those groups of people will fulfill our expectations. Second, actual differences between and among members of out-groups will decrease. The more our behavior is directed by stereotypic thinking, the more we require out-group members to conform to an unbending set of expectations and traits.

As those prophecies fulfill themselves through our stereotypic expression, socially different others will actually become more similar.

The cognitive and social processes, discussed in Chapter 2 and earlier in this chapter, set up a dynamic of stereotyping and avoidance. In other words, as our thinking relies too heavily on social categories and stereotypes, we remain separated from people who are socially different than us. Physical separation, in turn, heightens the need to rely on stereotypes in our thinking about socially different others, closing a circle of segregation and ignorance that enhances social differences around us.

A more subtle and indirect action of stereotypes is how talking about people from other social groups affects us, which in turn shapes the nature of our social contexts. Research suggests that when we talk to our friends and acquaintances about socially different people—hearing our friends' beliefs and experiences alongside our own—our stereotypic beliefs become more extreme (Myers & Bishop, 1970). So, although we may believe that talking about others leads to more validity or accuracy of our beliefs, the effect of discussing socially different others likely leads to less accuracy. Stereotypes, distorted and strengthened by discussion and communication, eventually find their way into our behavior and our expectations for people from other social groups, where they contribute to the social differences we experience around us. In sum, although social categories and stereotypes are useful information-processing tools, they act on our behavior in ways that make actual contributions to the social difference around us.

DI Diversity Issue 3.1: Hate Speech

Hate speech is speech motivated, in whole or in part, by an offender's bias against an individual's or a group's race, religion, ethnic/national origin, gender, age, disability or sexual orientation (adapted from the definition of hate crime, developed at the 1998 International Association of Chiefs of Police Summit on Hate Crime in America). Studies of the prevalence of hate speech are few, but according to one study, over 50% of minority college students report having been the target of hate speech (Cowan & Hodge, 1996). Hate speech can be spoken (e.g., an American Nazi Party rally speech) or written (e.g., an antigay website). In several high-profile court decisions, hate speech has been granted protection under First Amendment rights to freedom of expression (Heumann & Church, 1997).

? Should hate speech be protected under all circumstances? Are there situations or conditions where you think hate speech goes beyond our constitutionally guaranteed freedom of expression?

Racial or ethnic slurs are a common type of hate speech. **Slurs** (also called **ethnophaulisms**) are derogatory references to a particular group or to some members of that group. Slurs can be based on a person's race or ethnicity, religion, language, nationality, sexual orientation, and disabled status. Brian Mullen and his colleagues' research shows that the more derogatory and simplistic (e.g., referring to all Asian people as Japs) slurs we associate with a group, the more likely we are to support exclusion of that group's members from our neighborhoods and workplaces (Mullen, 2001; Mullen & Rice, 2003). In other research, Jeff Greenberg and his colleagues arranged to have White subjects overhear an ethnic slur about a Black person giving a videotaped speech (Greenberg & Pyszczynski, 1985; Kirkland, Greenberg, & Pyszczynski, 1987). Compared to subjects who heard a race-irrelevant slur or no slur, the subjects who overheard the slur evaluated the Black person more negatively. In other words, slurs help represent a group's (perceived) essential characteristics in our minds. Hearing or using a slur activates those stereotypic beliefs and leads to discriminatory actions toward members of that group.

? What slurs are most common among students at your school? How do the slurs reflect the stereotype held about members of that group? How does hearing (or overhearing) a slur directed at you or your group affect you? Does it matter if the slur is only directed at your group and not you personally?

DI Diversity Issue 3.2: Using the N-Word

Nigger is widely regarded as the most violent, ugly, and destructive slur ever used to refer to members of a racial or any other minority group. The English word is traceable to Latin, French, and Spanish words for black (niger, nègre, and negro, respectively) and has traditionally been used among Whites to express deep contempt for Blacks. Beginning in the 1970s and continuing to the present, Black comedians and musicians—especially in the hip-hop and rap genres—tried to redefine nigger (and the derivative term nigga) into a positive and exclusive term of greeting. This more positive, edgy meaning has helped the N-word become part of the adolescent lexicon among both Blacks and Whites. Despite, or perhaps because of, its currency in the youth culture, cities such as Baltimore, Maryland, and Santa Clara, California, are taking legal steps to limit its use (Willoughby, 2003).

? What does the N-word mean to you? Does it have different meanings in different contexts? Is the N-word, like other hate speech, protected under First Amendment rights to freedom of expression? Because nigger symbolizes racism and oppression of Blacks in America, do you think Blacks are more entitled to use the N-word, or to say how others may use it?

DI Diversity Issue 3.3: The *Sesame Street* Effect

From its inception in 1968, *Sesame Street* has become the best-known, most-watched, and most-researched children's educational program. *Sesame Street* addresses pre-school children's cognitive and emotional needs by teaching kids intellectual skills (e.g., counting), emotional skills (e.g., learning to deal with anger), and helping behavior (e.g., sharing). *Sesame Street* features a diverse cast of character puppets, each with strengths and weaknesses, and the show tells stories that promote accep-tance of difference and affirmation of commonalities. Much research supports the existence of the *Sesame Street* effect: Watching *Sesame Street* is associated with more positive views of oneself and others, even after the effect of family variables (e.g., income, parents' education) are controlled. See the *Sesame Workshop* website (URL below) for summaries of the research that has evaluated the effects of their educational programs.

? How do the unique coloring and facial characteristics of the *Sesame Street* pup-
pets teach children about diversity? Why might this approach work better than creating more realistic minority puppets (e.g., with black and brown skin tones and appropriate hair color and type)?

Watch one of the *Sesame Workshop's* programs and take some notes on how the program teaches positive social attitudes. How do the producers change the characters and stories to target children of different ages and stages of development? http://www.sesamestreet.org/videos

DI Diversity Issue 3.4: Accents

What comes to mind when you meet someone, exchange small talk, and hear a Southern accent in the other person's English? A Northeastern/Boston accent? A New York City/Brooklyn accent? A Texas/Southwest accent?

Accents are manners of pronunciation, and they carry much social information about a person. Preference for our own accent has been observed in infants as young as five months, suggesting that accents function much like primary social categories (see Chapter 2) in helping us sort the social world into us and them (Kinzler, Shutts, DeJesus, & Spelke, 2009). Much research shows that we view people who speak with an accent (other than our own) in negative terms compared to those who speak like us (Gluszek & Dovidio, 2010). We stereotype nonnative accented people as less intelligent and assign them lower status than us, especially when they are hard to understand (Bresnahan, Ohashi, Nebashi, Liu, & Shearman, 2002). Evidence of discrimination against people who speak accented English is wide-spread and, with the legal and social sanctions against race- and ethnicity-based discrimination, may be used by people to subtly (and legally) mistreat people with accents other than our own (Biernat & Dovidio, 2000; Lippi-Green, 1997).

? Are there accents that prompt positive stereotypes?

? How does a nonnative accent affect your impression of a teacher or other professional person? Could these impressions form a self-fulfilling prophecy?

KEY TERMS

Self-fulfilling prophecy   44

Perceptual bias   46

Synergistic accumulation   52

Linguistic intergroup bias   55

Negation bias   55

Stereotype consistency bias   56

Hate speech   60

Slurs/ethnophaulisms   60

Accents   62

FOR FURTHER READING

Rosenthal, R. (2002). Covert communications in classrooms, clinics, courtrooms, and cubicles. *American Psychologist, 57*, 839–849. http://psycnet.apa.org/journals/amp/57/11/839.pdf

This article includes an engaging history of Rosenthal's early research on expectancy effects as well as a clear explanation of how the self-fulfilling prophecy works in the classroom. Table 4 contains a great summary of how teachers convey their expectations to students and should create a lively discussion.

Online Resources

The Racial Slur Database
http://gyral.blackshell.com/names.html

Lists over 2,000 ethnic, racial, national, sexual, and religious slurs, their target group, and their derivation.

Media Awareness Network
http://www.media-awareness.ca/english/index.cfm

A Canadian site, but its coverage of stereotyping in the media includes American media examples. From the home page, go to Media Issues, then Media Stereotyping. Here you will find analysis and review of stereotypes in the media for a range of groups. Of particular interest is the section under Women & Girls on the economics of gender stereotyping.

Prejudice

Evaluating Social Difference

TOPICS COVERED IN THIS CHAPTER:

- How prejudice is expressed
- How self-esteem and prejudice are related
- How anxiety and prejudice are related
- How prejudice is related to our concerns about our public image

We not only think about and act on the diversity that surrounds us, as we learned in Chapters 2 and 3, we *feel* about it too. That is, we make sense of the social world not only by identifying and describing social differences but also by evaluating them. How good are *we*? Is my social group worthwhile? Are *we* better than *they* are? Evaluative judgments about groups of people are natural extensions of those we make about ourselves and other individuals. Like the social categories and stereotypes, these evaluative questions also help us understand and organize our social world. Prejudice arises within this process of evaluating people who are socially different than ourselves. In this chapter, we consider the general structure and expression of prejudice and the individual motivations and needs that fuel prejudice.

Prejudice: Basic Concepts

What Is Prejudice?

Prejudice is unjustified negative judgment of an individual based on his or her social group identity (Allport, 1954). There are three components to this definition of prejudice—let's clarify each in turn. First, what do we mean when we say that prejudice involves unjustified judgments or evaluations of others? Our feelings or evaluations of others, based on their social group, may be overgeneralized, such as regarding most or all Jewish businesspeople as scheming and dishonest. These negative categorical evaluations are unfair because they are applied indiscriminately to all the members of the group. In sum, prejudice is "thinking ill of others *without warrant*" (Allport, 1954, p. 6, italics added).

Second, prejudice involves negative, rather than positive, evaluations and judgments of others based on their group membership. Positive prejudice does exist, such as the feelings of respect and admiration we have about Nobel Prize winners or professional athletes. But positive prejudice is comparatively infrequent and is not considered to be a source of discrimination and disadvantage for members of those particular groups. The range of negative feelings encompassed by prejudice is considerable and includes dislike, resentment, and fear, as well as prejudiced actions such as avoidance, using ethnic slurs (or otherwise prejudiced epithets), discrimination, and physical confrontation.

Third, prejudice is a negative emotional response to an individual that is based primarily on his or her group identity. Therefore, prejudice can be based on any group label including such common groups as ethnicity, gender, social class, age, sexual orientation, religion, nationality or cultural identity, physical disability, or political affiliation. A proliferation of *-ism* terms, such as racism, agism, homosexism, or ethnocentrism, refers to prejudice against specific groups. Notice also that prejudice is not confined to people whose social group identity is visible; many important social categories, such as sexual orientation and religion, are invisible. Nevertheless, we develop biased and negative judgments about such people.

What Are the Components of Prejudice?

Prejudice involves negative feelings toward people based on their group membership or identity, whereas stereotyping involves negative beliefs and thoughts about such people. In other words, prejudice and stereotyping are not the same thing, but they often occur together. Given that most stereotypes are dominated by negative beliefs about out-group individuals, negative feelings toward those people can easily surface when thinking stereotypically. Stereotyping and prejudice are also alike in that both can be expressed unintentionally and deliberately. Patricia Devine (1989) was the first to investigate the automatic and controlled components of prejudice. The **automatic component of prejudice** originates from the same socialization process by which we acquire our stereotypes discussed in Chapter 2. It makes sense, then, that children display signs of automatic prejudice because they are passive and uncritical recipients of grown-ups' attitudes and biases. Evidence suggests that these internalized prejudices become automatic in children by around age 12 (Degner & Wentura, 2010). Devine reasoned that all people, regardless of their intention to be fair-minded and nonprejudiced, are aware of the stereotypes held about various groups. By internalizing these beliefs, we adopt negative emotional responses to those groups. These well-learned attitudes and responses operate automatically upon encountering a member of a disliked group. Like categorization (see Chapter 2), prejudice has a neurocognitive basis. Whereas categorization is controlled by the amygdala, where emotionally significant social information is processed, prejudice is associated with higher-level brain activity. Researchers have used functional MRI (fMRI) technology to show that the reasoning underlying in-group favoritism, wherein we advantage in-groups over out-groups on a variety of outcomes, occurs in the medial prefrontal cortex area of the brain (Volz, Kessler, & von Cramon, 2009). This area of the brain controls thinking about ourselves, both personal and social, and thus is important for understanding prejudice. By contrast, the **controlled component of prejudice** reflects *one's own* beliefs about people from other groups. Personal social beliefs—the controlled component of prejudice—are usually based on our personal experience with socially different people as well as larger social/ethical principles (e.g., humanitarianism) that we may adopt as adults. In short, the prejudicial impulses that most of us inherit from our socialization process are only part of the prejudice equation. Automatic prejudices can be overcome, through effort and diligence, with more positive, enlightened, and fair-minded beliefs about people from other groups.

To test these ideas, Devine (1989) had White participants who were identified as being low prejudiced or high prejudiced by nature list the traits and behaviors that were commonly associated with the category *Blacks*. Both low- and high-prejudiced participants had equal knowledge of the cultural stereotype of Blacks. In another study, she presented Black-stereotypic words (e.g., Blacks, Negroes, poor, lazy) on a screen so fast (less than one tenth of a second) that participants could not read the words, followed by a task in which participants evaluated a hypothetical target's behavior. Compared with participants who were exposed to neutral words, the participants who were exposed to the Black words, even though they did not consciously recognize those words, perceived more hostility in the target person's behavior. In a third study, low- and high-prejudiced White participants listed their personal thoughts and beliefs about Blacks (not, as in the first study, their knowledge of the cultural stereotype about Blacks). Compared with the high-prejudiced participants, those who were low in prejudice replaced their well-learned negative associations about Blacks with more positive, fair-minded beliefs. This research shows us that people do not realize the extent of their own prejudices because they are so well learned and operate outside of our awareness. However, because the automatic and controlled aspects of prejudice operate independently, those who want to avoid prejudice can do so through effort and by deliberately inhibiting their well-learned, automatic prejudices.

What Are the Conditions in Which Automatic Prejudice Is Expressed?

Researchers have discovered some of the circumstances that activate automatic prejudice. First, we express more unintended, automatic prejudice when we anticipate interacting with someone from another racial group, especially when that person is likely to have lower status than us. Researchers told White female participants that they would be having an interaction with either a Black or White partner and that they would play the role of either the superior or the subordinate in the interaction (Richeson & Ambady, 2003). In anticipation of this interaction, participants' *implicit* (a term synonymous with automatic) racial attitudes were measured. The participants who believed they would be playing the superior role to a Black subordinate revealed more prejudiced attitudes than did participants who anticipated being the subordinate in a mixed-race interaction. Implicit prejudice was not affected by the anticipation of same-race interactions.

Second, anger leads people to act out their prejudiced impulses compared with being in other emotional states. Researchers created bogus groups of people (labeled overestimators and underestimators) via answers to a personality test; in actuality, the groups were randomly determined (DeSteno, Dasgupta, Bartlett, & Cajdric, 2004). Then participants were randomly assigned to write about an event that made them angry, sad, or emotionally neutral. A subsequent measure of their automatic prejudice toward members of the other group revealed more negative attitudes but only among the angry subjects.

Third, prejudice is also expressed when our inner feelings and impulses toward socially different others are either insufficiently suppressed or sufficiently justified. According to the **justification–suppression model of prejudice**, the socialization process, in which parents, peers, television, and popular culture all have a role, equips us with negative attitudes and beliefs about people from various racial, ethnic, and religious groups (Crandall & Eshleman, 2003). As adults, we are aware that expressing prejudice is at least socially inappropriate and at worst illegal. Therefore, we learn how to inhibit and suppress our negative impulses so that they remain undetected. We suppress our prejudice by various means, including avoiding members of the disliked group, exerting control over our own thoughts, or simply denying that we are prejudiced. Prejudice, in this view, is a well-learned (to the point of being automatic) and natural response to social difference over which we learn to exert pragmatic control.

In addition to suppression, the expression of prejudice also depends on justification. When there is no pressure to cover up one's true beliefs, prejudice is more likely to be expressed when it can be made (to ourselves and others) more reasonable. Justifications are anything that we can use to make our expressed prejudice seem more logical and defensible. We justify our prejudiced impulses by citing a stereotypic belief as support for one's prejudice, revealing prejudices in the company of like-minded people, or arranging for a plausible alternative explanation for one's (admittedly) prejudiced actions. Another common justification for prejudice is to blame the victim—to observe, for example, that the disadvantaged plight of the poor is as much due to their own laziness as to societal discrimination. The strategic adoption of a blame-the-victim attitude, then, justifies and releases one's hidden negative attitudes toward the poor into expressed prejudicial behavior.

? How do stereotypes justify our prejudices? What situations inhibit or suppress prejudice?

Is There a Prejudiced Personality Type?

In the 1950s and 60s, psychologists invested a lot of energy in finding a prejudiced personality type. The earliest type was called the authoritarian personality and referred to someone characterized by generalized prejudice against out-groups and ethnocentrism (Adorno, Frenkel-Brunswik, Levinson & Sanford, 1950). However, the concept faltered because a valid and reliable measure of the authoritarian personality was never developed. Nevertheless, the appealing links between personality type and prejudice have persisted in the form of two personality profiles that have garnered the respect of researchers: right-wing authoritarianism and social dominance orientation (Altemeyer, 1998; Sidanius & Pratto, 1999). **Right-wing authoritarianism** describes a cluster of traits that values adherence to societal norms and traditions, deference to authorities who are seen as legitimate, and aggressiveness toward people who are seen as challenging those norms and authorities. **Social dominance orientation** describes a personality profile that values a hierarchical ordering of groups in society and a firm maintenance of that hierarchy. Much research documents that both right-wing authoritarianism and social dominance orientation strongly predict prejudice, even when the other is controlled (Altemeyer, 1998; Sidanius & Pratto, 1999).

Although right-wing authoritarianism (RWA) and social dominance orientation (SDO) are powerful predictors of prejudice, they have been criticized as not being personality traits but rather clusters of social beliefs that form two different ideologies for prejudice (Duckitt, 2001). Are there basic personality traits that predict RWA and SDO? Yes, according to Chris Sibley and John Duckitt, who synthesized the findings of a large number of studies and found evidence that two out of the so-called Big 5 personality traits were predictive of prejudice (Sibley & Duckitt, 2008). Openness to experience involves intellectual curiosity and an appreciation of diverse ideas and experience; agreeableness involves being compassionate and cooperative toward others (Costa & McCrae, 1992). People who score low on measures of openness to experience and agreeableness tend to hold prejudice toward a range of common out-groups including women, immigrants, homosexuals, and people with disabilities (Akrami, Ekehammar, & Bergh, 2011). Interestingly, low openness to experience was associated with prejudice through the RWA beliefs and low agreeableness predicted prejudice through SDO beliefs (Sibley & Duckitt, 2008). So, although there isn't a prejudice personality per se, there are basic personality traits that predispose people to develop beliefs that motivate and justify prejudice.

Summing up, prejudice involves negative evaluations of, and responses to, others based on their social group affiliation or identity. The raw material for prejudice is a mixture of particular personality traits and the beliefs and assumptions we acquire from society and other socializing agents about people who differ from us. But having negative impulses toward, for example, gay people doesn't mean that we will inevitably express anti-gay prejudice. The expression of prejudice depends on the interplay of automatic negative impulses we harbor toward others and the more thoughtful and fair-minded social beliefs and principles that most of us also espouse. We are able to suppress and weaken ingrained prejudices as well as rationalize and perpetuate them.

If we have the ability to suppress and even eliminate our prejudiced feelings, why—in a nation that has long valued equal rights and opportunity for all—hasn't prejudice been eliminated? Much evidence indicates that prejudice is alive and well in our schools, workplaces, and communities. In subsequent chapters, we will consider at length five prominent types of prejudice: racism (Chapter 5), sexism (Chapter 6), weight-based prejudice (Chapter 7), antigay prejudice (Chapter 8), and agism (Chapter 9). Before we get to those topics, we must first understand the psychological needs and motives that underlie *all* forms of prejudice. So, for the balance of this chapter, we will consider the extent to which we define and value ourselves in contrast with others, as well as the deep emotional needs that are satisfied by prejudicial behavior. In the next section, we will learn how our evaluations of our own and others' social groups are connected to the need to enhance and preserve feelings of self-esteem, the need to reduce social and existential anxiety, and the need to be seen by others (and to see ourselves) as fair-minded, nonprejudiced people.

Self-Esteem and Prejudice: Using Prejudice to Define and Defend Ourselves

The need for *self-esteem*—defined as perceptions of personal worthiness and competence—is fundamental to human nature. The need to protect and enhance self-esteem, therefore, motivates many of our behaviors, including prejudice. How does prejudice serve our self-esteem needs?

Prejudice Is Related to Maintaining a Positive Social Identity

Who are you? Try this exercise. List the terms, characteristics, or labels that are essentially descriptive of you on a piece of paper; list as many terms as you feel describe you. Are you finished? Recall from Chapter 1 that we can differ from others in many ways, both personal and social. Go through your list of self-descriptive words and indicate whether each is a personal or social quality. How much of your identity is based on personal characteristics? On social characteristics? According to **social identity theory**, we look to social categories and group memberships to help identify us, and we want these social affiliations to be as positive as possible. Our social identity can be derived from groups that are assigned to us (such as our race, gender, or perhaps religion) and acquired by us (such as our affiliations with clubs, teams, or organizations). Importantly, social identifications are a significant source of self-esteem (Luhtanen & Crocker, 1992).

Passive Social Identity Maintenance

According to social identity theory, we desire a positive social identity; we want to be associated with social groups that are worthwhile and valued. This desire causes us to passively affiliate with groups that succeed. Robert Cialdini and his fellow researchers found that students wore more team clothing and colors— identifying themselves with the school football team—after the team had won than when it lost (Cialdini et al., 1976). They also found that people distanced themselves from failing or disliked groups. Researchers called college students after their university team had either won or lost and asked them to describe the game. Students reflecting on a team loss used more *they* than *we* pronouns than those who described a victory (Cialdini et al., 1976). In other words, we desire to share a group's glory but avoid their disgrace. We therefore enhance our social identity by affiliating with groups when they succeed. Likewise, our social identity is protected when we distance ourselves from unsuccessful groups.

Active Social Identity Maintenance

We also actively pursue a positive social identity by forging comparisons between groups that boost, rather than threaten, our feelings of social worthiness. We create these favorable comparisons by selecting a lower status, less successful, or disliked group as a comparison for our group. For example, if Carol feels uncertainty about the value and integrity of her sorority, she can compare her sorority to another in a way that restores her pride. She can pick a struggling or disliked sorority as a ready-made comparison or strategically select a dimension on which her sorority outshines a rival.

A great deal of research supports the claim of social identity theory that, when given a chance, we create favorable comparisons with socially different others. Amazingly, this occurs even when the groups have little real significance. Many studies have been conducted in which participants were divided into two groups randomly and given arbitrary labels such as Red and Blue (see Brewer, 1979, for a review). In these studies, participants were asked to evaluate members of their own group and out-group members. Even though the social distinctions in these studies were artificial and little interaction took place among group members, participants exhibited a consistent preference for in-group, compared to out-group, individuals.

This tendency to evaluate people in one's own group more favorably than people in a comparison out-group is called **in-group bias**. The in-group bias is a well-established phenomenon and has been observed in a variety of real-world social groups (Furnham, 1982b; Kelly, 1988). Do these comparisons bolster social identity? Yes, according to research. Participants who are allowed to make favorable comparisons with out-groups experience increased self-esteem compared to those who are not (Lemyre & Smith, 1985; Oakes & Turner, 1980). In other words, even small or temporary advantages in the status or competence of your group compared to another group reflect positively on you, boosting your evaluations of yourself and your group.

Prejudice Is Related to Defending the Self

If in-group bias enhances self-esteem, then we would expect people with low levels of self-esteem to engage in the most in-group bias because they have the greatest self-esteem needs. Although this is intuitively sensible, it is actually people with *high* levels of self-esteem who exhibit the most in-group bias. A review of 37 in-group bias studies found that, overall, high self-esteem people exhibited more direct in-group bias than did low self-esteem people (Aberson, Healy, & Romero, 2000). Similarly, individuals in high status or successful groups exhibit more in-group bias than people in lower status, less successful groups (Mullen, Brown, & Smith, 1992; Sachdev & Bourhis, 1987). Why would people with high self-esteem be more prejudiced than those with lower levels of self-esteem? Compared with their low self-esteem counterparts, high self-esteem individuals feel more entitled to positive outcomes and believe their ideas and actions are competent. The entitlement, optimism, and certainty that are characteristic of high self-esteem people are also associated with externalizing blame for a negative outcome (it's their fault) and adopting negative attitudes toward the individuals and groups whom they believe are responsible.

In addition to those with naturally high levels of self-esteem, people who experience a threat to their self-esteem also tend to respond with prejudiced behavior as a defensive response. Steven Fein and Steven Spencer (1997) argue that prejudice helps reaffirm our self-images—our views of ourselves as good, worthwhile, and competent—when we suffer a blow to our ego. In one study, they gave participants an opportunity to affirm themselves by picking their most-valued quality from a list and writing why that quality was important to them. Some participants did not have this self-affirming opportunity. All participants then evaluated a job application from a person (allegedly a fellow student who was about to graduate) who was either a member of a negatively stereotyped group (Jewish) or a group about which there was no clear stereotype (Italian). The participants who were not able to self-affirm displayed prejudice by giving more negative evaluations to the Jewish than to the Italian job applicant. The participants who affirmed themselves, which temporarily boosted their self-esteem, displayed no such bias. A follow-up study randomly assigned participants to receive a short-term threat to their self-image (in the form of unfavorable feedback on an intelligence test) or not. Then participants read about and evaluated an individual whose biographical sketch was subtly altered to suggest that he was heterosexual or gay. The results of the study mirrored the first: Participants whose self-images had been threatened made more negative evaluations of the gay than the straight target. Participants whose self-images were not threatened did not display prejudice. A subsequent study showed that derogating a minority-group individual caused an increase in self-esteem, but this only occurred in participants whose self-images had been threatened. This important research establishes that prejudiced attitudes and behavior are a defensive response that restores temporarily threatened self-esteem.

Other research connects self-esteem to our views of out-groups and out-group individuals. Recall from Chapter 2 that stereotypes reduce perceived diversity in other groups and lead us to believe that *they* are all alike (or, the out-group homogeneity bias). When we are confronted with a deviant group member, such as a White rapper or a gay minister, our comfortable stereotypic assumptions are threatened. Laurie Rudman and her colleagues have shown that deviant members of groups—those who do not conform to our stereotype of that group—prompt backlash (Rudman, 1998). **Backlash** consists of social and economic punishments that we apply to social deviants, which here refers to group members who are perceived to violate the standards of character or behavior that are expected for members of that particular group. For example, research shows that atypical male and female job applicants (e.g., male applicant for nurse, female applicant for mechanic) prompt backlash in the form of lowered ratings of competence and likability compared with gender-typical applicants (Rudman & Glick, 1999, 2001). But how does backlash serve our self-esteem needs?

Rudman and Fairchild (2004) reason that backlash should occur only when the deviant out-group member poses some threat to our competence. They tested this by having male and female participants lose a computer game against a same-sex or opposite-sex partner that tested their knowledge in either a stereotypically masculine (football) or stereotypically feminine (children's development) domain. After the game, the participants were given the chance to help or sabotage their partner on a subsequent puzzle task by selecting which hints the partner would get in the task. What happened? Participants backlashed against deviant partners only: Women and men who won the test of football knowledge and child development, respectively, were deliberately given less helpful hints in their second task. This backlash effect did not occur, however, when participants lost to partners who did not violate gender stereotypes. Participants' self-esteem also improved when they sabotaged deviant partners but did not change (or went down) when they backlashed against nondeviant partners. Sabotaging someone who outperforms us in an area where we expect to be better also occurs across ethnic group lines (Phelan & Rudman, 2010). To sum up, threats to our identity and self-esteem arise when members of stereotyped out-groups violate our expectations for them. Backlash, which is an expression of prejudice, helps restore our self-esteem. The tendency for socially deviant others to threaten us also may relate to our need to have orderly and predictable social worlds, which is one function of social categories and stereotypes (see Chapter 2).

Threats to one's self-esteem can also occur when one's place in a comfortable social hierarchy is disturbed, which in turn produces prejudice similar to the backlash effect discussed above. People who are members of dominant, high-status groups (e.g., Whites, males) are said to have a social dominance orientation and are invested in maintaining their dominance over lower-status groups (Sidanius, 1993). Accordingly, they express more in-group bias and hold attitudes and support policies that protect the status of their group. Researchers studying 1,382 White Americans found that people with high, compared to low, social dominance orientation were much more likely to endorse prejudicial attitudes against Blacks (e.g., Blacks are dependent on welfare), and this prejudice was highest when White participants perceived that Blacks posed economic threats to their own group (Quist & Resendez, 2002).

Other research suggests that prejudice involves the defensive projection of our own (or our group's) most disliked or negative qualities on to other people (Newman, Caldwell, Chamberlin, & Griffin, 2005). Projection is defensive because it enables us to suppress the possibility that we might have negative qualities. Testing this idea, Leonard Newman and his colleagues created groups of three or four participants with information that they had similar personality profiles. The profiles were arranged to have three positive and two negative traits. The groups were instructed to discuss all the traits that comprised their profiles except one, arranged by researchers to be one of the negative traits; the groups were explicitly told not to discuss the negative trait.

After their discussion, the groups evaluated a different (target) group's behavior on the five traits. Interestingly, the target group was rated most negatively on the very trait that the participants had deliberately *avoided* discussing. This research suggests that identifying negative qualities in other groups, which may support prejudice against those groups, may result from our efforts to avoid recognizing the same qualities in ourselves.

Prejudice Is Related to Feeling Deprived

Finally, people who perceive that their group is getting the short end of the stick, compared with other groups, are prejudiced. That is, when your group is not receiving what you believe it should, what it has in the past, or what other groups are perceived to be receiving, a sense of **relative deprivation** ensues. Much research shows that the perception of relative deprivation is related to in-group bias (Bobo, 1988). One study surveyed White Americans who described themselves as either collectively deprived (compared to Black Americans), individually deprived (compared to other people), or satisfied with their circumstances on their attitudes toward Blacks (Vanneman & Pettigrew, 1972). Only those White participants who perceived that their group was deprived expressed negative attitudes toward Blacks.

Not surprisingly, research finds that we also evaluate socially different others negatively when we are in competition with them for some valued resource. This economic approach to prejudice is called **realistic group conflict** because dislike of out-groups often has a tangible, material basis. In some classic field experiments with boys at summer camp, Muzafer Sherif (1966) showed that when boys were divided up into teams for activities and camaraderie, the boys did show in-group bias but did not exhibit negative attitudes or actions toward the other team. However, when Sherif introduced competition between the groups for recognition, awards, and tokens of accomplishment, the boys became openly hostile and antagonistic toward the out-group members. Clearly, the boys felt threatened by the other team in the competitive situation. According to Sherif, group conflict results when a group's aims and purposes conflict with another group, such as concerning its desire and intentions for a limited resource. His research suggests that fear and anxiety contribute to negative evaluations of socially different people. Whether the boys were anxious about their ability to win the contests, of losing control of a resource, or of not getting what they felt they deserved, however, is difficult to determine from Sherif's research.

Researchers measured Israelis' attitudes toward Russian immigrants regarding whether the immigrants posed a realistic threat (e g., taking our jobs) or a symbolic threat (e.g., attacking our values), or provoked general anxiety in Israelis (Bizman & Yinon, 2001). They also measured participants' stereotype of, and prejudice toward, Russian immigrants. Perception of Russian immigrants as posing a realistic (economic) threat was the best predictor of Israelis' prejudice toward them, and this was most true for participants whose Israeli identity was important to them.

People from high-status, advantaged groups may perceive more deprivation and exhibit more in-group bias for two reasons. First, compared to people from low-status groups, they have loftier expectations and ambitions for their group. As a result, their actual circumstances, even if satisfactory at some absolute level, feel relatively disadvantaged. Second, people from groups that possess status, power, or some other valued resource are more sensitive to losing resources they currently have than those whose groups have never had such resources.

> **?** How does prejudice help shore up our insecurities and self-esteem? When we compare our group to an out-group in order to feel more competent, are we putting them down (engaging in out-group derogation) or building us up (engaging in in-group pride)? Is either any more or less prejudicial?

Anxiety and Prejudice: Using Prejudice to Reassure Ourselves

We have seen how prejudice is driven by a need to protect and enhance positive social identity, self-esteem, and personal feelings of entitlement. Threats we perceive in socially different individuals or out-groups can also arouse anxiety, tension, and fear. Research shows us that our prejudices are also a defensive response to anxiety and insecurity.

Managing Anxiety Through Social Identification

Many psychologists contend that all the fear and anxiety we experience in our day-to-day lives is, directly or indirectly, related to an underlying fear of death and the psychological vulnerability associated with our mortality (Greenberg, Pyszczynski, & Solomon, 1986). Indeed, many typical life events—such as sickness, accidents, broken relationships, and lost jobs—remind us that we are feeble beings and that bad things can happen to us unexpectedly and unjustly. According to **terror management theory**, the realization that we are insignificant creatures living in an unjust and often chaotic world terrorizes us (Greenberg et al., 1986). Social and cultural groups help us manage the terror associated with death and mortality by developing and maintaining systems of meaning or worldviews.

These systems of meaning provide answers to questions of existence and lend order, meaning, and permanence to life. Worldviews also provide roles for individuals to adopt, contributing to our perceptions of purpose and value. Worldviews are composed of values, beliefs, rituals, and concepts that are woven into a coherent system and, over time, consensually validated by a group of individuals. Some common worldviews include religious belief systems, environmentalism, and capitalism.

Researchers have shown that people who are able to affirm their cultural worldview, or defend it against threat, are less anxious than people who cannot affirm or defend their worldviews (Arndt, Greenberg, Solomon, Pyszczynski, & Simon, 1997). Thus, worldviews shield us from existential anxiety and despair. Moreover, because worldviews are developed and maintained *socially*, identification with groups of similarly believing others is important for dealing with our own sense of vulnerability and mortality. When one's worldview is shaken by an event or experience, people should respond with increased identification with the worldview and the individuals who affirm it. Research supports this expectation. In a classic study, psychologists (who were undetected) observed the behavior of a religious doomsday cult whose specific prediction for the end of the world proved to be incorrect (Festinger, Reicken, & Schachter, 1956). Instead of disbanding in embarrassment, the group's faith in their vision and cause was renewed.

In a more recent test of this notion, Christian participants completed a writing exercise in which they pondered their own death to temporarily heighten existential anxiety (Greenberg et al., 1990). Then they rated the likability of a hypothetical Christian person. Compared to those who did not do the anxiety-enhancing writing exercise, the participants who did do the writing exercise expressed more liking for the fellow Christian. This study shows that anxiety about death causes us to strengthen our social identifications. In terror management terms, worldview violators—people who threaten our core values—are predictable targets of prejudice. Joseph Hayes and his colleagues demonstrated this by having devout Christian female participants read an internet article describing how Muslims are gaining dominance in Nazareth, the presumed birthplace of Jesus Christ (Hayes, Schimel, & Williams, 2008). One half of the participants (randomly determined) read an additional piece of the article about how a plane load of Muslims on their way to Nazareth were killed (the annihilation condition); the other participants did not receive this information (the threat condition). In other words, the study presented participants with worldview violators (Muslims) and wanted to see how the tragic loss of life of those violators would affect the participants' views of Muslims. The study results showed that participants' liking for Muslims was higher in the annihilation condition (i.e., knowing that some Muslims had been killed en route to Nazareth) than in the threat condition. In other words, Christian participants displayed a lack of remorse when tragedy befell people they regarded as threatening to their values. This study is an example of how prejudice serves anxiety-management functions. Similarly, Batson (1975) found that when Christian believers were confronted with evidence contradicting their beliefs, they responded not with a more moderate position but with greater faith in their beliefs. Cultural worldviews serve vital functions: They order life, impart meaning, and protect us from life's uncertainties. Threats to our worldviews, therefore, are met with renewed identification with the supporting group and a defensive reaffirmation of the group's beliefs and values.

In summary, we are emotionally invested in social groups because the worldviews and values they support stabilize our lives and protect us from threats posed by a purposeless existence and death. As a result, we are selfishly interested in the validity of those beliefs to which we're committed and in finding a special role in the group. Perhaps it is not surprising that we habitually engage in in-group bias: Some of our social group identifications are deeply rooted in existential concerns.

Managing Anxiety Through Social Evaluation

In addition to coping with anxiety by reaffirming our faith in what we believe and our identification to those who share our beliefs, we also defend our worldviews through prejudice—by derogating others who hold different worldviews. For example, the typical Christian may find the Jewish worldview as foreign and potentially threatening because it does not recognize Jesus Christ as the Son of God. In the study described above,

Christians who were either temporarily death-anxious or not also evaluated a hypothetical Jewish individual (Greenberg et al., 1990). Christian participants who were acutely anxious about existential concerns evaluated the Jewish individual more negatively than the participants who were not anxious. In a similar study using different social groups, American students' death anxiety was made salient or not (using a writing exercise similar to the one described above) after reading an interview of a hypothetical person who expressed either pro-U.S. or anti-U.S. sentiment (Greenberg et al., 1990). Participants who were death-anxious expressed less liking for, and less agreement with, the anti-US interviewee than participants who were not anxious.

Other research tested the idea that anxiety causes a preference for stereotype-consistent members of out-groups, because they reaffirm what we believe about those groups. White participants were made to be anxious or not using a mortality salience writing exercise and then read and evaluated an essay by a Black or White writer who was made to be stereotype-consistent, stereotype-inconsistent, or neutral in his dress and language (Schimel et al., 1999). The participants who were existentially anxious expressed more liking for, and desire to meet, the stereotype-consistent Black person than the neutral or stereotype-inconsistent person. This bias did not occur among the participants who were not made to feel anxious. Similar findings occurred when participants, after being made to feel anxious or not, evaluated stereotype-consistent (e.g., female fashion writer, male sports writer) or inconsistent job applications (Schimel et al., 1999). The anxious participants responded more positively to the stereotype-reaffirming person than the stereotype-challenging person. This research demonstrates how anxiety leads us to reduce the diversity of our social worlds. When anxious and insecure, we see socially different others in more stereotypical terms and act in ways that preserve those stereotypes. Indeed, the very individuals who might prompt us to revise some of our prejudicial assumptions—stereotype-inconsistent people—are the most threatening and the likely targets of our prejudice.

Finally, existential anxiety and insecurity can produce prejudice by aggressing against members of other groups whose beliefs differ from, and challenge, our own. In a demonstration of this, researchers made participants anxious or not (through the mortality salience writing exercise) and then had them read an essay, allegedly written by another participant, that either supported or challenged their political views (McGregor et al., 1998). Subsequently, participants were given a chance to anonymously aggress against that person by spiking his or her food with hot sauce. Only when participants were anxious did they aggress, and the pattern was predictable according to terror management theory: Anxious participants were more aggressive toward the person who challenged, compared with the one who agreed with, their political views.

? Why does anxiety about our own mortality and vulnerability cause us to dislike, avoid, and aggress against socially different others? Does prejudice that springs from needs for self-esteem and prejudice that springs from needs for security feel different to the person who is the target of that prejudice?

Public Image and Prejudice:
Avoiding the Appearance of Prejudice

Having learned how prejudice serves needs for self-esteem and security, we now consider a third emotional factor in the expression of prejudice—the need to avoid being seen as prejudiced. Although prejudice is defined as holding negative attitudes and feelings toward other individuals based on their group membership, many studies find that participants rate both their group and the out-group positively (in absolute terms), with one's own group merely seen as *more* positive than the other group. Researchers have found, for example, that White students associate positive traits more quickly with the social category Whites than with Blacks, but Whites are not seen as any less negative than Blacks (Gaertner & McLaughlin, 1983). Is this pattern of social evaluation—we're both good but we're better—really prejudicial?

Marilyn Brewer (1999) notes that liking toward in-groups and hostility toward out-groups are not reciprocal responses. Prejudice, which involves biased evaluations of *us* and *them*, may just as easily result from more positive evaluations of *us* than *them* as from holding overt negative attitudes towards *them*. Although some expressions of prejudice are of this enlightened variety (we're better than them but they're still OK), Brewer contends that such victimless expressions of prejudice easily devolve into more hostile forms. Moreover, evaluative distinctions between groups of people are inevitably linked to unfair outcomes. That is, even if our evaluations of out-group members are less positive (but not objectively negative) than our self-evaluations, we will still divide resources in a preferential way. So, although others' groups may not be disliked, our preference for *us* will cause disadvantage for *them*.

Social psychologists have learned that expressions of prejudice have changed over the years due to changes in the cultural and political landscape. Prejudice is expressed differently in our present-day climate of civil rights, political correctness, and tolerance than it was in times past (Gaertner & Dovidio, 1986). **Modern prejudice** refers to any expression of prejudice that is subtle, easily justified, and hence, difficult to detect. Ambivalence lies at the heart of modern manifestations of prejudice. Most of us have well-intentioned social principles; we all want to believe that we are fair-minded people who support egalitarian ideals and would never deliberately act in a prejudiced manner. Nevertheless, we also have well-socialized and ingrained negative feelings about members of other social groups that are difficult to overcome or give up. These impulses can leak into our behavior, threatening the egalitarian principles with which we identify. All modern forms of prejudice, then, are concerned with maintaining one's public image as nonprejudiced and avoiding the psychological and social costs that are associated with being seen by others as prejudiced (e.g., guilt, others' disapproval).

In an early demonstration of modern prejudice, researchers asked White participants to evaluate their own group and Blacks (Sigall & Page, 1971). Half of the participants evaluated the groups via a questionnaire. Measured this way, participants' evaluations of Whites and Blacks were equally positive. The other half of the participants evaluated the groups while connected, via electrodes, to an imposing bank of equipment that they believed could detect their true inner attitudes and feelings. This measurement method, called the *bogus pipeline*, caused participants to respond more truthfully. Compared to the questionnaire respondents, the bogus pipeline participants evaluated Whites more positively and Blacks more negatively. Thus, this study shows that people can and do hide negative feelings about members of other social groups. Symbolic prejudice and aversive prejudice are two types of modern prejudice; we will consider each in turn.

Symbolic prejudice involves open dislike and derogation of individuals for reasons that are related *not* to group membership, but to the values attributed to those individuals (Sears, 1988). This modern form of prejudice is similar to the justification element of the justification–suppression model discussed earlier (Crandall & Eshleman, 2003). For example, if a nonracial reason can be found to justify one's negative feelings about a Latino political candidate ("He probably doesn't understand *my* concerns"), then one's prejudice can be freely expressed and, importantly, defended. Symbolic prejudice is reflected in research showing that Whites' negative feelings toward Blacks are justified by Whites' belief that many Blacks have not embraced the central American values of hard work and self-determination (Kinder & Sears, 1981). Based upon a set of traditional values rather than skin color or ethnicity, such prejudice appears less objectionable and is easier to justify and defend. In a series of studies, Crandall (1994) found that negative attitudes toward overweight people were related not to a general dislike of them but to the perception that overweight individuals repudiate the important American values of self-control and personal responsibility.

In **aversive prejudice**, people hold negative feelings about out-group members passively inherited from the surrounding culture, while simultaneously affirming egalitarian values and cultivating a self-image as fair-minded (Gaertner & Dovidio, 1986). People with aversive prejudice have negative feelings about out-group members that reflect anxiety, discomfort, and fear rather than the overt hostility that is characteristic of regressive or *old fashioned* forms of prejudice. As a result, aversive prejudice should be associated with subtle forms of discrimination like social distancing when interacting with a member of a disliked out-group. In a creative test of this idea, Philip Goff, Claude Steele, and Paul Davies (2008) had White male students engage in a conversation with two partners (one White, one Black) on one of two topics (love and relationships or racial profiling). Goff reasoned that White participants would find it threatening to their nonprejudiced self-image to talk about racial profiling, especially with a Black partner. To compensate for this threat, participants were expected to place more physical distance between themselves and their Black partner than between themselves and their White partner. Social distancing was measured by asking participants to arrange three chairs so that they could have a comfortable conversation. The findings (see Figure 4.1) revealed that participants sat farther away from their Black partners when they anticipated discussing a racial compared with a nonracial topic. Even within the racial profiling discussion condition, participants sat farther away from Black than White partners. The study also showed that the more threatened participants felt as being seen as racist by others, the more distance they placed between themselves and their Black partners. This distancing displayed in this study is subtle— a little over an inch between White participants and Black partners depending on the

Figure 4.1 Average Distance (Inches) Placed Between Conversation Partners' Chairs for Two Different Conversation Topics

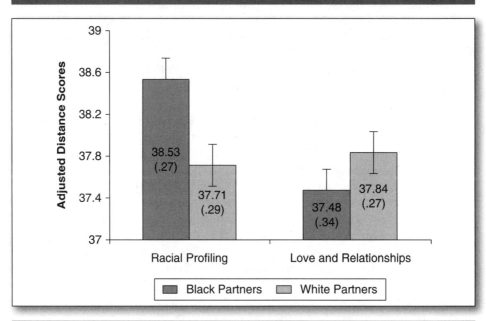

SOURCE: "The space between us: Stereotype threat and distance in interracial context," by P. Goff, C. Steele, & P. Davies, 2008, *Journal of Personality and Social Psychology, 94*, pp. 91–107. Copyright 2008 by APA. Reprinted with permission.

conversation topic. But that's the point: Aversive prejudice manifests itself in subtle, hard-to-detect behavior, which also is most easy to rationalize in the service of one's (nonprejudiced) self-image.

Finally, modern prejudice also arises when our stereotype about a group is inconsistent with our personal beliefs about that group (Devine, 1989). Stereotypes, as we have learned, are socialized through family, media, and cultural influences and, therefore, are well learned and operate automatically. As a result, stereotypic thoughts, judgments, and actions are often difficult to inhibit and become the default response whenever we are exposed to an out-group member. Our personal beliefs about a social group, however, may be more positive and informed than the stereotype with which we have been instilled. What's more, personal beliefs are more thoughtful and controllable. The automatic nature of stereotypes and the controllability of personal beliefs is an important distinction. It means that, even for individuals who espouse nonprejudiced ideals, one's immediate response to an out-group member is negative and stereotype driven. Thus, in terms of the automatic (stereotypes) and controlled (personal beliefs) components of prejudice, modern prejudice reflects the inability of people to *reprogram* their thinking about out-group members in a way that replaces stereotypic beliefs with personal beliefs (Monteith, Zuwerink, & Devine, 1994).

Well-learned prejudiced feelings can be inhibited through self-control and will-power, but that effort takes energy. In fact, researchers have found that exerting self-control depletes physical energy in the form of lowered glucose levels in the blood (Gailliot & Baumeister, 2007). Think of making yourself do something difficult—coping with stress, being nice to someone who is rude, or quitting smoking. Controlling and directing your own behavior requires physiological energy, and when our energy levels are low, self-control of any impulse becomes more difficult. Researcher Matthew Gailliot and his colleagues (2009) tested whether giving people a temporary energy boost would result in greater self-control over prejudiced impulses. College students participated in a study they were told was about food and personality. One half of the participants (randomly determined) was given a 14-ounce drink of lemonade sweetened with real sugar and having 140 calories; the other participants received the same drink with Splenda, a zero-calorie sugar substitute. Participants were then given the picture of an adult male (Sammy) who was described as gay, and they were asked to write for 5 minutes about events in a typical day for Sammy. After the writing task, participants' prejudice toward homosexuals was measured. Their essays were coded by independent raters (who were blind to the sugar condition the participants were in) for the number of derogatory statements in the essays. Here's what they found: Participants with low levels of prejudice toward gays made very few derogatory statements in their essays, and the sugar variable had no effect. Among highly prejudiced people, however, extra calories in the bloodstream improved self-control. Participants who got the sugary lemonade were far less derogatory of Sammy than those in the no-calorie lemonade group. This study highlights the important role of self-control in the inhibition of one's prejudicial impulses and the appearance of, and social costs associated with, being prejudiced.

> **?** How is the need to be seen by others as nonprejudiced related to self-esteem? Is modern prejudice, in its subtlety, any less unfair than overt expressions of prejudice?

Does being reminded of slavery and segregation make people more sympathetic to the plight of Blacks? Does recalling the Holocaust prompt more empathy for Jewish persons? Concepts we have covered in this chapter argue that knowledge of victim suffering—either current or past—*increases* rather than decreases prejudice toward members of that group, a phenomenon that has been termed **secondary prejudice** (Buruma, 2003). First, guilt is a common reaction when majority group members are made aware of injustices suffered by members of a minority group (e.g., gay, Muslim). Furthermore, others' suffering reminds us (majority group members) that we are part of the system that is (or has) caused their suffering. Reasoning from the perspective of modern prejudice, then, victim suffering and injustice is threatening to majority group members' self-images as nonprejudiced people and should motivate defensive prejudice. Secondly, suffering minority group members are worldview violators, in that they threaten our belief that the world is basically just and people generally get what they deserve. Reasoning from terror management theory, then, victim suffering should increase prejudice because we are motivated to punish worldview violators in order to defend our beliefs and values.

Researchers led by Roland Imhoff tested these ideas in a study of secondary anti-Semitism (Imhoff & Banse, 2009). They reasoned that people reminded of Jewish suffering as a consequence of the Holocaust should show more anti-Semitism under two important conditions: (1) whether they acknowledge the suffering at all and (2) if they are compelled to reveal their true attitudes toward Jews. The first condition is important because, for people in the majority group, it is tempting to disregard or deny injustices suffered by minority group members to avoid feeling the guilt associated with being part of the cause of the injustice. The second condition is important because people tend to present themselves as nonprejudiced if they can, even if they misrepresent their true attitudes. Researchers in this study used the bogus pipeline method described earlier, whereby people respond more truthfully to questions about their attitudes than they would on an attitude survey. Participants read about the violence and injustice perpetrated on Jews under the Nazi regime. One half of the participants (randomly determined) were reminded of the ongoing consequences of those actions for today's Jews; the other participants were reminded that those events had no consequences for today's Jews. All participants then answered questions designed to measure anti-Semitism. Some of the participants responded to a measure of anti-Semitism in the bogus pipeline condition (where they should be more truthful about their true attitudes); others responded to the same questions via a questionnaire (control condition).

The results (shown in Figure 4.2) reveal evidence of secondary prejudice. When participants were reminded about the ongoing consequences of the Holocaust for today's Jews and were compelled to tell the truth with the aid of the bogus pipeline technology, they reported more anti-Semitism. Participants in the control condition who were able to present themselves as nonprejudiced did just that. These findings remind us of the complexity and ambivalence inherent in modern forms of prejudice: People don't want to appear prejudiced or acknowledge that they might be partly responsible for others' suffering. But the need to maintain a nonprejudiced public image and defend our values, ironically, can increase prejudice and contribute to further inequality and suffering among minority group members.

In the next five chapters of this book we will consider the mountain of evidence that shows inequalities based on race (Chapter 5), sex (Chapter 6), weight (Chapter 7), sexual orientation (Chapter 8), and age (Chapter 9). We end our discussion of modern prejudice with this question: How do people maintain their nonprejudiced self-images in the face of all the evidence that prejudice, stereotyping, and discrimination are alive and well? One answer comes from Laurie O'Brien and her colleagues (2010) who propose that people don't have good ways to evaluate if *they* are prejudiced because there are no objective standards for diagnosing a bigot. Therefore, people compare themselves to widely-held representations of prejudiced people, and those representations—more often than not—come from media accounts of prejudice and portrayals of prejudiced people. O'Brien and her colleagues argue that our cultural conception of the bigot is overinformed by vivid, extreme events such as the murder of Matthew Shepard for being gay, the dragging death of James Byrd behind a pickup

Figure 4.2 Results From Imhoff and Banse (2009) Study on Secondary Prejudice

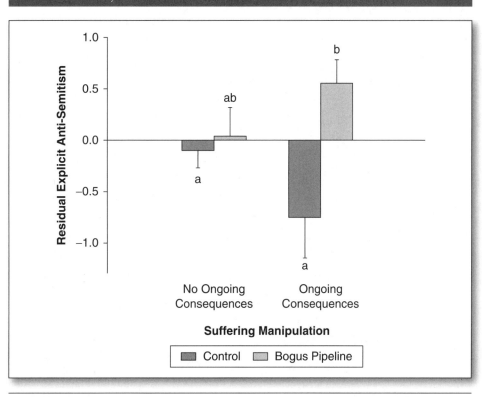

truck, Ku Klux Klan imagery, and other violent acts of bigotry. If we compare ourselves with these representations to calibrate our own level of prejudice, we will appear (to ourselves) as nonprejudiced.

Their research, for example, found that participants rated themselves as less prejudice after they perused descriptions of race-related DVD documentaries (e.g., *Politics of Hate,* a profile of David Duke, former Ku Klux Klan leader) than after perusing DVD titles that were not race-related (O'Brien et al., 2010). In another study, participants were told they would take a test identifying their own level of prejudice (threat condition) or personality type (control condition). Participants chose which kind of video they would like to watch while waiting for their score; videos were arranged so that some featured highly prejudiced people and others featured highly unprejudiced people. The findings showed that, compared with those in the control condition, participants in the threat condition were more likely to choose a video that featured highly prejudiced people. Those participants also reported that they were worried the prejudice test would confirm that, indeed, they held subtle prejudices. This research reveals one of the ways majority group members maintain nonprejudiced self-images—they strategically compare themselves with highly bigoted exemplars and, by comparison, feel good about themselves and their own level of prejudice.

Summary

We shape the social difference around us through social categories and stereotypes (Chapter 2) as well as through our own stereotypical actions (Chapter 3). In this chapter we learned how the active shaping of our social worlds stems from our own emotional needs. Three basic emotional needs—to enhance and protect our self-esteem, to minimize anxiety and fear, and to appear fair-minded to others—lead us to draw clear evaluative distinctions between *us* and *them*, especially when other groups pose a threat to our beliefs and resources. Prejudice, then, is much more a comment about who *we* are, as individuals and group members, than who *they* are.

DI Diversity Issue 4.1: Hate Crime

A **hate crime**, according to the Hate Crimes Statistics Act of 1990, occurs when a person is criminally victimized (e.g., assaulted) because of their race, religion, sexual orientation, or other aspect of their identity. Hate crimes require longer sentences be served than if the crime is committed without the *hate* dimension. According to the Department of Justice's Hate Crime statistics for 2009, 50% of all hate crimes victimize people because of their race. Hate crimes based on religious bias and sexual orientation bias constitute 19% and 18% of all hate crimes, respectively. What is the profile of the hate crime offender? Most (62%) hate crime offenders are White, their crime is most commonly simple assault, and they commit the crime against another person rather than a group of people or property. Most hate crime occurs in or around homes, but 10% of all hate crimes occur in schools and colleges.

? Is bullying another term for prejudice-motivated behavior at school? If not, how is bullying different from prejudice? Can bullying become hate crime? Go to http://www.stopbullyingnow.hrsa.gov/index.html to learn more about the definitions and warning signs of bullying.

DI Diversity Issue 4.2: The Birther Movement

The Birther Movement is the name given to the popular support around a group of related conspiracy theories regarding President Obama's citizenship and his eligibility to be President. The movement seems to have arisen out of reaction to then-Senator Barack Obama's victories in some important presidential primary elections over then-Senator

Hillary Clinton in the spring of 2008. The movement gained traction and drew the support of prominent elected public figures and was a nagging issue for the Obama Presidency for much of the next 3 years. A CNN/Opinion Research poll from the spring of 2011 showed that 25% of Americans, including 40% of Republican respondents, believed that President Obama either was not, or probably was not, born in the United States and therefore was not a U.S. citizen. Although President Obama released his long-form birth certificate to the press in April, 2011, *birthers* still maintain he has dual citizenship (and thus shouldn't be President) because his father was born in Kenya (http://articles.cnn.com/2011-04-27/politics/birthers.evidence_1_birther-movement-barack-obama-citizenship?_s=PM:POLITICS).

Take a look at some of the arguments, rhetoric, and people that support the birther movement at http://www.birthers.org/. Where do you see evidence of prejudice in the birther movement? Is the birther movement more racially (anti-black) or ethnic/religiously (anti-Muslim) motivated?

KEY TERMS

Prejudice   65

Automatic component
   of prejudice   66

Controlled component
   of prejudice   67

Justification–suppression
   model of prejudice   68

Right-wing authoritarianism   69

Social dominance orientation   69

Social identity theory   70

In-group bias   71

Backlash   72

Relative deprivation   74

Realistic group conflict   74

Terror management theory   75

Modern prejudice   78

Symbolic prejudice   79

Aversive prejudice   79

Secondary prejudice   81

Hate crime   84

FOR FURTHER READING

Greene, B. (2009). The use and abuse of religious beliefs in dividing and conquering between socially marginalized groups: The same-sex marriage debate. *American Psychologist, 64,* 698–709. doi: 10.1037/0003-066X.64.8.698

This article analyzes the role of religious beliefs in the same-sex marriage debate and prejudice against sexual minorities. Many concepts covered in this chapter can be discussed in the context of this article.

Online Resources

Understanding Prejudice
http://www.understandingprejudice.org/

This is a great site for prejudice-related material including many interactive pages such as a survey, slide tour, and more.

Implicit Association Test (IAT)
http://www.understandingprejudice.org/iat/

The IAT measures your implicit, or automatic, prejudice toward several common out-groups.

FBI Hate Crime Statistics
http://www2.fbi.gov/ucr/hc2009/index.html

For statistics on types of hate crime, victims, locations of hate crime, and more.

Stop Bullying.gov
http://www.stopbullyingnow.hrsa.gov/

A site full of resources for recognizing and opposing bullying. Bullying is a specific form of prejudice when bullying occurs because of the victim's (perceived or actual) group membership. By a wide margin, male gay students over female gay students are common targets of bullying and cyberbullying. Students can consider the motivations underlying prejudice covered in Chapter 4 in the context of the bullying of gay students.

The Birther Movement
http://www.birthers.org/

Look through the evidence and rhetoric of those who deny that Barack Obama is an American citizen. Go to The People, then Heroes to see the many prominent public figures who support the birther movement.

5

Understanding Race, Racial Stereotypes, and Racism

❖

TOPICS COVERED IN THIS CHAPTER:

- Race and ethnicity
- Stereotypes of Blacks, Hispanics, Asians, and Jews
- Racial discrimination in criminal justice and health care

We learned in Chapter 2 that race is a primary social category: We notice other people's race in a fraction of a second. Because primary categorization is automatic, our thinking about other people in terms of their race is unavoidable. Race-based categorization also makes racial stereotypes—the traits and abilities we associate with members of other racial groups—more accessible and more likely to influence our interaction with people from other racial groups. In this chapter, we first consider the concept of race and its limitations in our understanding of diversity, the related concept of ethnicity, and stereotyping and discrimination that is based on other people's race and/or ethnicity. We then discuss the content of stereotypes of four prominent racial/ethnic minority groups. Finally, we consider the discrimination of Blacks in the criminal justice and health care domains.

Race and Ethnicity

For most of us, the term **race** brings to mind a category of people who share the same skin color and associated physical qualities. Race was originally used to identify the lineage or *stock* of a group of people with similar physical characteristics (Banton, 1977; Jones, 1997). In the eighteenth century, race was used to classify people just as all other species had been classified (Bonham, Warshauer-Baker, & Collins, 2005). Gradually, however, race became more than just a way to summarize and distinguish diversity in external appearance. Race became an inner quality used as an explanation for differences in the behavior and character of people who looked different. In other words, race has become an evaluative term used to distinguish *us* from *them* and the main reason why *they* were different than *us*. Historically, our thinking about people of different races has been imbued with color references: African Americans with black, Hispanic Americans with brown, Asian Americans with yellow, and Americans of European heritage with white. Accordingly, to refer to a racial minority group in the United States is usually to refer to some non-White group of people.

The main problem with the race concept is that there is no biological basis for it (Helms, Jernigan, & Mascher, 2005). Scientists working on the Human Genome Project declare that all human beings are 99.9% the same, genetically speaking. All of the diversity we observe in the human race—in people's behavior, personality, and physical qualities—is determined by the remaining 0.1%. No genetic variations can be used to distinguish Whites from Blacks or Asians from Hispanics (Bonham et al., 2005). Even when we examine variability with the naked eye, we must acknowledge that there is more variability within so-called racial groups than there is between them (Zuckerman, 1990). For example, in many Latin American countries, the lightest-skinned people are indistinguishable from many Whites and the darkest-skinned indistinguishable from Blacks. If racial groupings are arbitrary and biologically mean-ingless, why do they persist? According to Jean Phinney (1996), the concept of race endures because, in general, we observe that people of color tend to be treated differ-ently than White people. When people from different racial groups are treated differ-ently or experience different life outcomes, it is very tempting to explain those differences by citing the obvious group difference (i.e., race) as the cause. Thus, race is a handy and compelling pseudo-explanation for a variety of social outcomes and expe-riences that, in our observation, vary by race.

In contrast to race, **ethnicity** refers to a cluster of nonphysical cultural character-istics such as one's national origin, language, and religion, as well as a sense of people-hood or the sharing of some cultural identity (Jones, 1997; Phinney, 1996). In the United States, an ethnic minority group is typically a group of people whose culture of origin is not Western European. Ethnic group labels are more specific, and therefore more accurate social constructs, than old-style racial groupings. For example, although they would share the racial label *Black*, African Americans and Caribbean Americans are ethnic groups with unique cultures, languages, and religious traditions. Although ethnic groupings are still somewhat arbitrary, ethnicity is a more useful construct than race because it is less reductionistic. In other words, if ethnicity has been substituted for race as our best explanation for why people who look different often act differently and have different life circumstances, the *cause* of diversity is at least no longer reduced to a single, changeless inner quality (e.g., they're different because they're Black). As a handy—but still simplistic—explanation for observed differences between groups of people, ethnicity is much preferable to race for capturing the multiplex circumstances that shape our personalities and behavior (e.g., they're different because they grew up in a different culture).

Racial Stereotypes

Studies of racial stereotypes have a long history in psychology and still are a major research focus among social psychologists. A search of the psychological research literature via *PsycNET* identifies over 2,200 articles on some aspect of race stereotypes or stereotyping. Most of these research articles, however, address White persons' attitudes and beliefs about Black people rather than Blacks' stereotypes of Whites: Why is this? White Americans' stereotypes about Blacks have the potential to be more destructive and discriminatory than Blacks' stereotypes about Whites because, as a group, White Americans have more economic and political power and control over resources than do Blacks (see Chapter 1). Understanding Whites' racial stereotyping, then, may be driven by a concern for social justice. It is also true that most stereotyping research is conducted at colleges and universities where White students (as study participants) outnumber Blacks. In the following pages, we examine the content of stereotypic beliefs about Blacks, Hispanics, Asians, and Jews and also consider some general principles governing the content of stereotypes.

Stereotypes of Blacks

When measuring racial stereotypes, researchers make a distinction between what traits people associate with members of a racial group and what traits they personally believe or endorse as true (Devine, 1989; Stangor & Schaller, 1996). A **cultural stereotype** is the set of traits and characteristics that people associate with a particular social group. Cultural stereotypes are beliefs about others held by consensus in cultural groups. Cultural stereotypes are transmitted through socializing agents (e.g., picked up from family and friends or learned through exposure to stereotypical portrayals in the media). As mentioned in Chapter 4, cultural stereotypes persist in part because they constitute a broadly understood and shared language for talking about people who differ from ourselves. Cultural stereotypes are, by definition, conservative: They preserve traditional knowledge about social groups and are passed from one generation to the next. As a result, cultural stereotypes should be slow to change.

Sufficient research has accumulated over several decades regarding White Americans' stereotypes of Blacks that it is possible to get a wide-angle look at how, if at all, Whites' racial stereotypes have changed over time. Several prominent studies are displayed in Table 5.1 that measured White students' cultural stereotypes of Blacks by asking them to select or list traits that they most associated with Blacks. For each study, the traits most commonly attributed to Blacks by White study participants are shown. As Table 5.1 illustrates, Whites' cultural stereotype of Blacks has changed noticeably in the past 70 years. Compared to the traits attributed to Blacks in the earliest studies (Gilbert, 1951; Katz & Braly, 1933), the most recent studies show that the content of Whites' stereotypes of Blacks is more positive. In addition, current research finds much less consensus around the stereotype that existed in the 1930s. In other words, Whites' views of Blacks have become not only more positive, but more varied and diverse. We must also recognize that people try to avoid expressing prejudice in their views, and thus these findings may represent the views that they are willing to report or acknowledge to themselves. Based on this research, two very negative traits—laziness and low intelligence—have apparently disappeared from White Americans' stereotypes of Blacks. However, have these stereotypical assumptions about Black individuals really disappeared, or have their expressions simply become more subtle and difficult to detect? As we will see, Whites' assumptions of Black students' ability and motivation figure prominently in the threat posed by cultural stereotypes to Black students in school and achievement settings, which we will discuss in Chapter 10.

Cultural stereotypes are often so well learned that they operate automatically. In one study of racial stereotyping, White participants' racial stereotypes were primed by displaying WHITE or BLACK on a computer screen for about two tenths of a second—in other words, too fast to be consciously recognized. Nevertheless, the short exposure to the prime word affected how well participants recognized trait words that followed the prime. The Black prime facilitated participants' recognition of negative (e.g., lazy) compared with positive (e.g., musical) Black stereotypical words, whereas

Table 5.1 The Most Common Traits in the Cultural Stereotype of Blacks From Six Prominent Studies Spanning Nearly 70 Years

Katz & Braly (1933)	Gilbert (1951)	Karlins, Coffman, & Walters (1969)	Dovidio & Gaertner (1986)	Devine & Elliot (1995)	Madon, et al. (2001) Study 1	Madon, et al. (2001) Study 2
Superstitious	Superstitious	Musical	Arrogant	Athletic	Musical	Listen to a lot of music
Lazy	Musical	Happy-go-lucky	Musical	Rhythmic	Loyal to family ties	Noisy
Happy-go-lucky	Lazy	Lazy	Very religious	Low intelligence	Loud	Athletic
Ignorant	Happy-go-lucky	Pleasure-loving	Pleasure-loving	Lazy	Tradition-loving	Have an attitude
Musical	Ignorant	Ostentatious	Aggressive	Poor	Very religious	Prejudiced
Ostentatious	Very religious		Materialistic	Loud	Aggressive	Sing and dance well

the White prime facilitated recognition of positive (e.g., ambitious) compared with negative (e.g., selfish) White stereotypical words (Wittenbrink, Judd, & Park, 1997). The participants in the study did not realize they were making stereotypical racial judgments; nevertheless, the social category Black was more strongly associated with negative, and White with positive, attributes in participants' memory.

In a more recent demonstration, researchers Gary Sherman and Gerald Clore (2009) measured participants' automatic associations between the colors white and black and words representing immorality (e.g., greed) and morality (e.g., honesty). The participants, who were mostly White, named colors faster when the associations were stereotype consistent (i.e., white paired with moral words, black paired with immoral words) than when they were stereotype inconsistent. This research shows that people make automatic associations between blackness and immorality. These hard-wired associations may be a residue of prior generations' stereotypes, but they also continue to inform Whites' beliefs about Blacks. Indeed, much evidence shows that Black men are stereotyped as threatening. In a demonstration of this, researchers presented participants with Black and White male faces on a computer for about one third of a second and measured attention to the faces (Trawalter, Todd, Baird, & Richeson, 2008). Participants attended more to Black than White faces. In a second study, however, the faces were selected to have averted eye gazes. In that study, participants did not distinguish between the Black and White faces. This is important: It indicates that it was the assumed threatening nature of the Black face, rather than the mere color, that caused greater attention. This conclusion is corroborated by the teddy bear effect, the name given to the phenomenon wherein observers rated the faces of Black chief executive officers (CEOs) as more baby faced than the faces of White CEOs (Livingston & Pearce, 2009). Further analysis found that baby-faced Black CEOs led more prestigious firms and earned higher salaries than mature-faced Black CEOs.

In a similar study, White participants looked at racially ambiguous faces that displayed angry or happy emotions (Hutchings & Haddock, 2008). Participants, particularly those high in implicit prejudice, tended to report that the angry faces were Black rather than White. These studies illustrate that automatic racial biases exist, reflecting deeply negative assumptions about Blacks and Black men, despite the apparent improvement in the content of Whites' stereotypes of Blacks summarized in Table 5.1.

Although negative trait associations with Blacks can occur automatically, when White people are asked about their **personal social beliefs**—in other words, the aspects of the cultural stereotype of Blacks that they themselves believe or espouse—they respond much more positively, especially if they value nonprejudiced ideals. Devine and Elliot (1995) asked White students to list the traits that they personally believed about Blacks as a group after first measuring their level of prejudice (e.g., holding negative attitudes and feelings about Blacks). The five traits listed by highly prejudiced subjects were athletic, rhythmic, hostile, lazy, and poor. Low-prejudice subjects listed kind, athletic, honest, straightforward, and musical. This research teaches two lessons: First, Whites' knowledge of traditional cultural beliefs about Blacks (which are largely negative) does not mean that they personally endorse those beliefs. They can have knowledge of the negative and traditional assumptions about Blacks *and* personally espouse positive beliefs. Second, although some people do personally endorse the negative cultural stereotype of Blacks, it is possible to revise those negative beliefs and adopt more positive and enlightened attitudes toward Blacks.

In Chapter 2 we learned that when a social category is too broad and inclusive, one response is to divide the category into relatively more accurate subtypes. There is evidence that White people subtype Blacks and that the traits associated with these subtypes differ. White college students described Blacks overall in the following terms: hostile, poor, dirty, athletic, negative personality, musical, unintelligent, and lazy (Devine & Baker, 1991). However, the participants' stereotypes of Blacks depended on which subtype they were associated with. Characteristics associated with the *streetwise, ghetto,* and *welfare* Black subtypes included having a negative personality, being unintelligent, and lazy. However, Black *athlete* and *businessman* subtypes were thought of in much more benign terms, including having a positive personality, being ambitious, and, in the case of Black businessman, being intelligent. In summary, Whites' stereotypes of Black people are generally negative, dominated by beliefs of laziness and low intelligence, while beliefs about particular subtypes of Blacks are more positive.

Beliefs about Blacks' intellectual inferiority are seen by many individuals as an inherent deficiency (Herrnstein & Murray, 1994). In fact, Black students do score lower on standardized tests of achievement than do White students. On a national achievement test, Black students' science scores were 49 points lower (on a 500-point scale) than were White students' scores (National Assessment of Educational Progress, 1996). Math test scores showed a similar difference: Black students scored an average of 27 points below White students (again, on a 500-point test scale). When reading proficiency was measured at the fourth, eighth, and twelfth grades, Black students read below, and White students above, the expected grade reading level. These findings need to be interpreted cautiously for two reasons. First, although White people may achieve more (on the average) than Black people in most studies, some studies show no race differences in achievement, and furthermore, the practical differences between the groups are small in magnitude (Loehlin, Lindzey, & Spuhler, 1975). Second, the differences observed *between* groups of Black and White individuals are dwarfed by the difference *within* those groups. The difference in intelligence between the lowest and highest scoring White students, for example, is much greater than the difference between the average White and Black student. Nevertheless, these statistics are often used as evidence that the stereotype of Blacks' intellectual inferiority is accurate. Recall from Chapter 2 that people who believe Blacks are not as smart as Whites will notice and remember statistics that seem to confirm the stereotype.

So, although school achievement differences between White and Black students are real, race cannot be an explanation for these differences because there is no known gene that contributes to intelligence or achievement. It is impossible for so-called racial groups to have different genetic equipment for achievement (Sternberg, Grigorenko, & Kidd, 2005). We must look *outside* of the person for possible explanations for the different school achievement levels of White compared with Black people. Two explanations are briefly discussed here: family support for school achievement and per-student spending on education. A national survey in the 1970s established that students' success in school was predicted by the level of their mother's and father's education, their parents' occupational status, and having an intact (presumably, a two-parent) family. In the intervening 30 years, all of those predictors of school success have declined in the Black population, whereas only the prevalence of intact families has declined for White individuals (Kuo & Hauser, 1995). Thus, Black students must overcome more obstacles to school achievement in the home than White students. Second, research suggests that Black children meet another set of inequalities when they enter school. Data from the 1996 National Assessment of Educational Progress national surveys shows that, compared to predominantly ethnic minority schools, schools with predominantly White students spent more per student on their education. This educational advantage remained when the economic differences between White and ethnic minority families were controlled. Even among equally poor school districts, more money is spent per student in White or predominantly White schools than in predominantly Black schools. To sum up, although some differences exist between the achievement levels of White and Black students, this cannot be explained by Blacks having lower intelligence than Whites. The achievement gap between average Black and White students is much more likely to result from the social and cultural contexts in which Black and White students, respectively, pursue school achievement.

Just as Whites' greater school achievement is often used as evidence of Blacks' lower intelligence—making Whites' stereotypes of Blacks seem correct—income disparities between Whites and Blacks help justify Whites' stereotype of Blacks as lazy. Recall from Chapter 1 that the median annual household income among Blacks is about 62% of that for Whites. Blacks are also unemployed and live in poverty at greater rates than Whites. Do these real differences in economic status between Blacks and Whites affect Whites' stereotypes of Blacks? Researchers surveyed over 1,100 White adults and found that as respondents' perceptions of Blacks' lower economic status (they're poor) increased, so did their belief that Blacks are, as a group, lazy (Brezina & Winder, 2003). This relationship was present even among Whites who understood that Blacks' lower economic status is partly due to structural forces (e.g., society's failure to provide good schools and jobs for many Americans). This research shows that typical Whites see Blacks' lower economic status as a kind of proof that Blacks are, in fact, lazy. These findings illustrate how racial stereotypes guide Whites' attention toward evidence that confirms their beliefs about Blacks. They also reveal the tautological (circular) reasoning that supports much of Whites' stereotypes of Blacks: A tautology occurs when a real difference is both the basis for an explanation and empirical proof of that explanation. In other words, Blacks' educational and economic achievements lag behind Whites because they are less intelligent and lazier than Whites, and the evidence for these conclusions is their poorer educational and economic achievements.

Finally, racial stereotypes are conventionally thought of as occurring *between* so-called racial groups (e.g., Whites' stereotypes of Blacks), and that such distinctions are based largely, if not entirely at times, on the differences in skin color between members of racial groups. However, skin color varies *within* racial groups too, and there is a long history that documents more negative assumptions and treatment of darker-skinned, compared to lighter-skinned, Blacks. **Colorism** refers to stereotyping and discrimination based on skin color that occurs within a racial group (Hunter, 2002). Although colorism can occur in any group, most of the research has investigated colorism among Blacks. Objective advantages accrue to lighter-, compared to darker-skinned, Blacks (Hughes & Hertel, 1990). Among Blacks, lighter skin is associated with having more education, higher income, and higher occupational status (Hunter, 2002). Indeed, the average difference between light-skinned and dark-skinned Blacks in socioeconomic status is equivalent to the average difference between Blacks and Whites on those outcomes. In an experimental test of colorism, Matthew Harrison and Kecia Thomas (2009) had participants, who were mostly White, review resumes of applicants for a marketing job in a hypothetical company. The resumes were systematically varied to reflect strong or weak qualifications (e.g., having a BA or MBA degree), and photos attached to the resumes manipulated the skin tone (light, medium, or dark skin) and gender of the applicant. After reading the resume, participants in the study gave recommendations for hiring the applicant. Compared to the dark-skinned applicant, participants gave higher ratings to the light-skinned applicant, and the preference was not trivial: Light-skinned applicants were rated nearly a full point higher (on a 7-point scale) than dark-skinned applicants. The preference given to light, compared to dark, skin applied equally to male and female applicants. Perhaps the most interesting finding in the study, however, had to do with the interaction of qualifications and skin tone. The more positive recommendations given to holders of an MBA degree compared to a BA degree only occurred among light-skinned applicants. Indeed, recommendations for the light-skinned BA-degreed applicant were substantially higher than the dark-skinned MBA-degreed applicant. In summary, negative stereotypes and outcomes based on color are just as significant within, as they are between, so-called racial groups.

Stereotypes of Hispanics

Comparatively little research has examined stereotypes about Hispanic individuals, but this work indicates that the cultural stereotype of Hispanics is negative and similar in content to the cultural stereotype of Blacks. For example, several studies find that Whites associate laziness, aggressiveness, cruelty, ignorance, and low intelligence with Hispanics (Fairchild & Cozens, 1981; Marin, 1984; Tomkiewicz & Adeyemi-Bello, 1997). As with Whites' stereotypes of Blacks, negative associations with Hispanics, particularly the belief that Hispanic people are less intelligent than Whites, are so well learned so that they operate automatically (Weyant, 2005). Nearly 50% of White respondents in a national survey believe that Hispanic people would prefer to be on welfare than work, an attitude that reflects a stereotype of Hispanics as lazy (General Social Survey, 1990). Other research finds that Hispanic characters in the media are portrayed as sexually promiscuous and given to criminal or antisocial behavior (Berg, 1990). According to Thomas Wilson's (1996) research, White American respondents to a large national survey regard Blacks and Hispanics as equally poor and unintelligent; however, Hispanics as a group are seen as somewhat less lazy, welfare dependent, and prone to violence than are Blacks. Recent research, which looked at changes in the cultural stereotype of Hispanics across a 10-year period, found that Americans' views of Hispanic people as poor, lazy, and unintelligent became more positive (actually, less negative) from 1990 to 2000. In contrast, only the stereotype of Blacks as lazy improved during that period (Weaver, 2005). In general, Whites view Hispanics in similar stereotypic terms as they view Blacks, but these beliefs are not as negative, and unlike beliefs about Blacks, the Hispanic stereotype among White Americans is growing less negative over time.

Stereotypes of Asians

In contrast to uniformly negative cultural stereotypes of Blacks and Hispanics, Asians are viewed with a mixture of benign and negative stereotypes. Recalling from Chapter 2, the *model minority* stereotype of Asians characterizes them as intelligent, industrious, quiet, family oriented, and being good in math and science (Osajima, 1988; Yee, 1992). This is the dominant stereotype of Asians in American culture and is reflected in media portrayals of Asians. Researchers analyzed television advertisements and found that Asians, compared with Blacks and Hispanics, were much more likely to be shown in professional occupations, in the workplace, and selling products such as financial services, internet services, and computers (Paek & Shah, 2003).

In contrast to the model minority stereotype, another more negative set of views is also associated with Asian people. The *yellow peril* stereotype, as it is often called, characterizes Asians as timid, sly, conforming, untrustworthy, and fit for common labor such as doing laundry (Suzuki, 1989). The mixed content of Whites' stereotypes of Asians is part of a general pattern that has been observed in stereotypes of other groups, according to the **stereotype content model** (Fiske, Cuddy, Glick, & Xu, 2002). The stereotype content model states that stereotypes about other groups often reflect two content dimensions: competence and sociability. Some groups are respected for their competence, high achievement, and status but disliked because they are not very friendly, lack warmth, and keep to themselves (e.g., Asians, Jews). Other groups are liked because of their approachability and warmth, but disrespected because of incompetence or ineptitude (e.g., elderly, disabled people). To see if Whites' stereotypes of Asians actually reflected these content dimensions, Monica Lin and her colleagues (2005) had students generate traits and behaviors they associated with Asians. These spontaneous responses were analyzed and found to organize into groups of competence-related beliefs (e.g., obsessed with competition, think they are smarter than everyone else) and sociability-related beliefs (e.g., dislike being the center of attention, socially awkward).

The association of both positive and negative traits with Asians displays a fundamental **ambivalence** in Whites' views of Asians (Kawai, 2005). To illustrate this ambivalence, Doris Chang and Stanley Sue (2003) gave school teachers descriptions of behavior problems in hypothetical Asian, Black, and White children. The behaviors attributed to the children were either aggressive (e.g., disruptive, talking out of turn, demanding attention, sulking) or anxious (e.g., excessive neatness, fear of making a mistake, worrying, clinging to adults). The teachers then evaluated the seriousness of the behavior problems and rated the child's typicality among his ethnic group. The teachers viewed the Asian student who exhibited anxious compared with aggressive behavior as more typical of all Asian students. (Incidentally, aggressive behavior was viewed as most typical of Black students.) Although classroom behavior problems of the anxious type were seen as stereotypically Asian by the teacher subjects, this problem behavior was also rated as less serious and more due to cultural factors than aggressive behavior (Chang & Sue, 2003). This study fits nicely with the stereotype content model described earlier. It suggests that teachers see problem behaviors in their Asian students not in their competitiveness (which is valued and admired) but in their social anxiousness and timidity (which is disliked). Even so, anxiety-related (or stereotypically Asian) behavior problems are still seen as less serious than aggressive (or stereotypically Black) school behaviors.

Other researchers have tried to understand this ambivalence—attributing positive qualities to, but also disliking, Asian Americans—by focusing on how Asian Americans might threaten the welfare of other groups (Maddux, Galinsky, Cuddy, & Polifroni, 2008). Maddux and his colleagues hypothesized that the perceived intelligence and high achievement of Asian Americans threaten the security of members of other ethnic groups. The thinking goes: In tough economic times, when good jobs are hard to find, Asians may have an advantage because of their (presumed) ability and work ethic. So, although majority group members attribute positive qualities to Asians, they may also resent Asians because those very qualities lead to preferential treatment in the employment marketplace. In a role-play experiment, White student participants were told to imagine that they were assigned a partner for a large and important project in their chemistry class. Participants were randomly assigned to receive either an Asian (e.g., Yoshi) or Black (e.g., Jamal) partner for the project (Maddux, et al., 2008). Theoretically, being assigned a Black, compared with an Asian, partner in a chemistry class should pose a threat to the security of the White participant because of (positive) stereotypical beliefs about Asians' aptitude for science. Postexperimental measures revealed that participants' attitudes and feelings toward Asian Americans were much more negative in the threat than in the nonthreat condition. Moreover, when researchers controlled for the threat felt by participants, the relationship between holding both a positive stereotype *and* negative feelings toward Asian Americans disappeared. In other words, threat projected onto Asians, particularly during hard economic times, helps explain the ambivalence among Whites about Asian Americans.

David Butz and Kumar Yogeeswaran (2011) tested this same idea in a different way. They had White participants read and think about one of three editorial articles. One article detailed threatening economic conditions (e.g., unemployment, housing industry collapse, national debt), the second detailed threatening environmental conditions (e.g., wildfires and storms due to climate change), and the third was a neutral article on national parks. Then participants' attitudes toward Asians and Blacks were measured. The findings, displayed in Figure 5.1, show that prejudice toward Asians increases when perceivers are threatened but only when the type of threat gives Asian Americans a perceived advantage. The positive aspects of the Asian stereotype (e.g., industrious and smart) increase in value under economic threat conditions and thus

Figure 5.1 Prejudice Toward Asian American and Black Targets Under Economic, Noneconomic, or No Threat Conditions

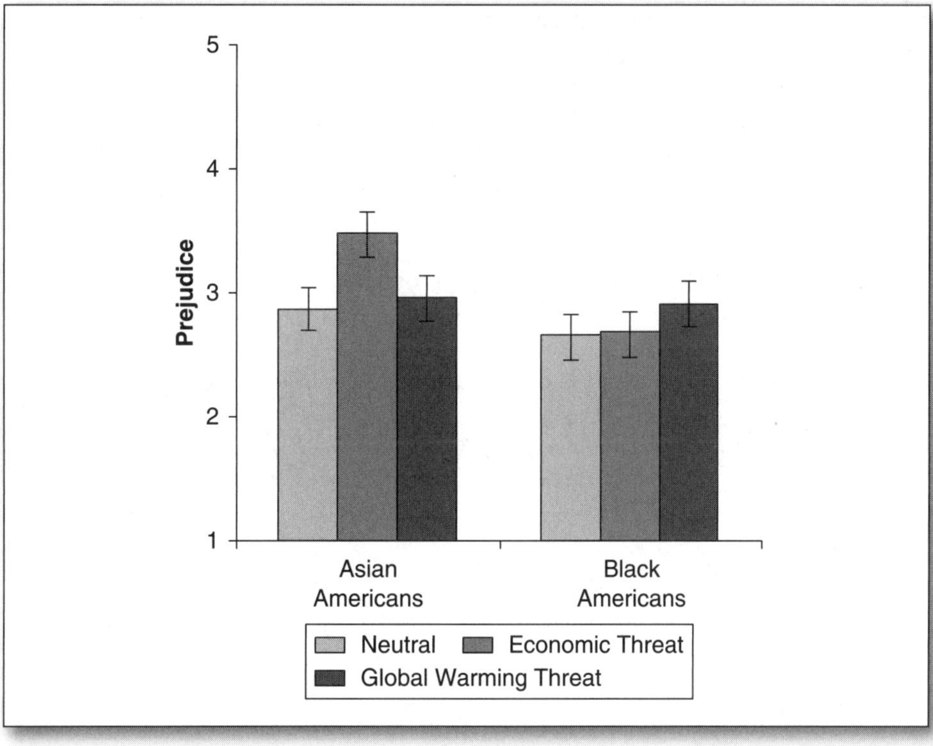

SOURCE: "A new threat in the air: Macrooeconomic threat increases prejudice against Asian American," by D. Butz and K. Yogeeswaran, 2011, *Journal of Experimental Social Psychology, 47*, pp. 22–27. Copyright 2011 by Elsevier. Used with permission.

threaten the (perceived) opportunities for non-Asians. The threat variable, however, had no effect on participants' attitudes toward Blacks, presumably because the stereotype held about Blacks does not include characteristics that would become more valuable when economic resources and opportunities are limited. This recent research has added considerably to our understanding of the ambivalence of the Asian American stereotype and underscores that being positively stereotyped, as Asians are, is very much a mixed blessing.

Stereotypes of Jews

Although the out-group status of Jews relative to non-Jews is based more on ethnic (e.g., shared religious and cultural background) than on racial (e.g., shared physical characteristics) grounds, Jewish people have long been referred to in racial terms. Perhaps this is due to the fact that Jews are, by tradition, physically descended from Abraham. Centuries of converts to Judaism have obscured that literal heritage, but a strong common-heritage identity remains even among nonreligious Jews. Stereotypes of Jews have long included a mix of positive and negative attributes. On the one hand, Jews are regarded as intelligent, shrewd, ambitious, successful, industrious, and loyal to family. On the other hand, Jews are associated with traits such as dishonesty, money loving, pushy, and ruthlessness (Allport, 1954; Quinley & Glock, 1979). In terms of the stereotype content model dimensions, these stereotypic associations suggest that Jews are respected for competence-related traits and disliked for sociability-related traits. However, research shows that fewer people endorse negative stereotypes of Jews now compared to 30 years ago (Smith, 1993). However, according to Thomas Wilson (1996),

Figure 5.2 A Cluster Analysis of Cultural Stereotypes of 23 Social Groups Along Dimensions of Competence (e.g., They're smart) and Warmth (e.g., They're nice to be around)

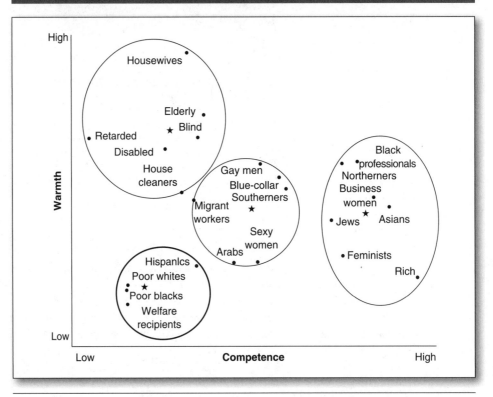

SOURCE: "A model of (often mixed) stereotype content: Competence and warmth respectively follow from perceived status and competition," by S. Fiske, A. Cuddy, P. Glick, and J. Xu, 2002, *Journal of Personality and Social Psychology, 82*, pp. 878–902. Copyright 2002 by American Psychological Association.

people who hold a positive stereotype of Jews (e.g., intelligent and high achieving) are not any more willing to interact with Jewish people than are people who hold a negative stereotype of Jews (e.g., dishonest and pushy). Thus, improving stereotypes does not mean that expressed prejudice and discrimination against Jews will also decline. The stereotypes of Jews' ambitiousness and achievement are potentially threatening to many non-Jewish Whites and, as we learned in Chapter 4, out-groups that threaten us often prompt prejudiced and discriminatory reactions.

Stereotype Content: Implications for Prejudice

We have considered the cultural stereotypes content of four prominent minority groups in the United States: Stereotypes of Blacks and Hispanics are uniformly negative, whereas stereotypes about Asians and Jews have a mix of admired and disliked attributes. Does stereotype content reflect any basic principles that apply to our stereotypes of *all* groups? Yes—the stereotype content model, introduced above, provides a basis for understanding the content of many stereotyped groups as well as predicting the type of prejudice that arises from particular stereotypes. According to that model, stereotype content reflects both competence and warmth dimensions and, as Figure 5.2 displays, our beliefs about people from other social groups vary widely along those basic evaluative dimensions (Fiske et al., 2002). Blacks and Hispanics are among a cluster of groups that are seen as having similarly low levels of competence and warmth. The research of Susan Fiske and her colleagues shows that these stereotypes are associated with *contemptuous prejudice*, marked by feelings of anger and resentment. Asians, Jews, and other groups are similarly stereotyped as being high in competence but low in warmth; such stereotypes are associated with *envious prejudice*. A third cluster features groups who are similarly stereotyped as not very competent but warm, such as disabled and elderly people. We tend to respond to members of these groups with *paternalistic prejudice*, which is marked by feelings of sympathy and pity. In a fourth cluster are social groups who are stereotyped as moderate on both dimensions—how do you think we respond to members of these groups?

This research also shows that our stereotypes of subgroups can differ on both evaluative dimensions. For example, women who are stereotyped as feminists (competent but cold) compared with housewives (very warm but not very competent) will prompt very different emotional and behavioral responses. Finally, the stereotype content model suggests that stereotypes of groups with which we have little contact and experience might be informed by the stereotypes of groups that are closest to that group on the warmth and competence dimensions. For example, I know migrant workers personally, but my stereotype of and feelings toward migrant workers will be influenced by my stereotype of the closest group to them. For me, the poor and Hispanic stereotypes would serve as the best approximation for what migrant workers are like (based largely on my memory of a few media images of migrant workers). And, until my personal experience could help differentiate migrant workers from poor people and Hispanics, my prejudices toward migrant workers (neither competence nor warmth) would reflect the content of those two proxy groups.

Racism

Racism is the term given to behavior that discriminates against people because of their race but especially when such discrimination becomes institutionalized in the policies and practices of organizations (Jones, 1997). To elaborate, if the rude treatment of Black compared to White customers is *racist*, then the practices and policies of the store (or chain of stores) that systematically treats Black customers worse than Whites are *racism*. Racism refers to behavior and actions, whether personal or institutionalized, that create a hierarchy of races—for example, that Whites are superior to Blacks, or that Asians are superior to Whites. Racial stereotypes (e.g., negative beliefs and assumptions about Blacks) and race prejudice (e.g., negative feelings toward Hispanics) are, technically speaking, not expressed in behavior and therefore not regarded as racism. However, as we learned in Chapters 2 through 4, stereotypes and prejudice inevitably find their way into our behavior. Accordingly, racial stereotypes and prejudice are common springboards for racism.

As with the research on stereotypes and stereotyping, most of the research on race-based discrimination examines Whites' discrimination of Blacks. By extension, racism research also measures Blacks' treatment at the hands of institutions that, though not White *per se*, represent the White establishment. The racism research literature is too large to attempt a comprehensive survey in one chapter (see For Further Reading below). Therefore, in the remaining pages of this chapter we briefly consider racism in two institutional contexts—the criminal justice system and health care system—by presenting some research examples and discussing how racism in each domain reflects expressed race stereotypes and prejudice.

Racism in the Criminal Justice System

There is much evidence that negative outcomes in the criminal justice system, from being arrested for a crime to sentencing, occur disproportionately to Blacks than Whites. For example, although Blacks make up about 12% of the U.S. population, the Uniform Crime Reporting Program arrest statistics (Federal Bureau of Investigations, 2004) reports that Blacks comprised 27% of all arrests, and 37% of the arrests for violent crime. If we suppose, for the sake of argument, that racism does not exist in law enforcement traditions and policies, how could we explain these much greater arrest rates of Black compared to White people? The most common explanation goes something like this: Blacks are by nature more aggressive and given to violence than Whites, and this causes them to run afoul of the law and be arrested at greater rates than Whites. What shall we make of this argument? First, there is no evidence that Blacks are inherently more aggressive than Whites. Research shows that the best demographic correlate of aggressiveness is gender (we will cover this in Chapter 6) and that, in general, aggressive behavior arises out of situations, not from one's personality or race. Second, this type of thinking illustrates the point raised at the beginning of this chapter: The concept of race, while not scientifically viable, is a handy pseudoexplanation for patterns of outcomes that might otherwise be seen as explicitly unfair. Indeed, when invoked as an explanation like this, race explains away, or at least minimizes, the threats posed by the seriousness of racism and the recognition of ourselves as part of a society that systematically discriminates against Blacks.

In 1999, four New York City police officers shot a Black man named Amadou Diallo 41 times in the lobby of his apartment building when he reached in his pocket for an object—the object turned out to be his wallet. This event followed a similar case in which officers sodomized a Black man with a plunger handle in a precinct bathroom, and prompted a national furor over police brutality and racism. In the scientific journals, psychologists began to probe the influence of race stereotypes on instantaneous shoot-or-don't shoot decisions.

In one study of the effect of race on responses to computer-presented armed and unarmed targets, participants played the role of police officers whose task was to react appropriately to a Black or White target that was holding either a weapon or a non-threatening object (e.g., a cell phone) (Greenwald, Oakes, & Hoffman, 2003). On half of the trials, the White target was a police officer and the Black target was the criminal; on the other half of the trials, the race and roles were switched. Participants were required to make the appropriate response (e.g., shoot the armed criminal, not shoot the unarmed criminal, warn the police officer) in under eight tenths of a second. The results of this interesting study showed that participants were less able to accurately distinguish a gun from a cell phone, and make the appropriate response, when the object was held by a Black compared with a White target. The participants were also more likely to shoot at a Black target than a White target, regardless of the target's role (police officer or criminal). In other words, the cultural stereotype of Blacks as aggressive and violent operated spontaneously to bias pseudo—police officers against the Black targets in potentially dire ways.

In a similar study, researchers found that although undergraduate student participants were initially more likely to shoot unarmed Black than White targets, with practice they eliminated this bias (Plant, Peruche, & Butz, 2005). An important question concerns whether a race bias resulting in more mistaken shootings of Black than White people exists in police officers. Ashby Plant and her colleagues (2005) had police officers serve as participants in a computer-simulated exercise as described above in which they were presented with Black or White targets who were either armed or unarmed. As with the student participants, the police officers were more likely to shoot the unarmed target when he was Black than when he was White. Their study showed that the officers had different criteria for shooting their gun at Black and White suspects; for the Black suspects, less evidence of threat was needed for them to shoot than when faced with a White suspect. This race bias, however, was eliminated over time as the officers made efforts to apply the same criteria for shooting at White and Black suspects.

These studies, taken together, suggest two conclusions. First, in situations where police officers must decide if a suspect is committing a crime or is armed and dangerous, cultural stereotypes about Blacks (e.g., Black men are aggressive) influence those decisions even when the officers making the decisions do not personally espouse those beliefs. Indeed, the amount of bias research subjects demonstrate in shooting unarmed

Black targets is positively related to their attributing *to Americans in general* (not to themselves) beliefs that Blacks are dangerous and aggressive (Correll, Park, Judd, & Wittenbrink, 2002). In other words, mere awareness (not personal espousal) of negative beliefs about Blacks is enough to bias people's judgments. When tainted by race stereotypes, the split-second decisions often required of police officers can result in tragic endings. Second, automatic race biases that discriminate against Blacks can be overcome. As discussed earlier in this chapter, people can replace negative assumptions about Blacks (or any other negatively stereotyped group) with more positive and enlightened personal beliefs. With effort and practice, fair-minded beliefs about Blacks will exert more influence over our behavior and reduce or eliminate race biases.

Let's now consider racism in another aspect of the criminal justice system—jury composition, verdicts, and sentencing recommendations. National statistics show that 3.1% of Black males, compared to less than 0.5% of White males, are in state or federal prison (U.S. Department of Justice, 2007). According to the U.S. Bureau of Justice statistics, Black males are incarcerated at a rate that is 6.5 times higher than White males, and 2.5 times higher than that of Hispanic males. Although women are a small minority of the incarcerated population, race disparities also exist among incarcerated females: Three Black women are incarcerated for every one White woman. One factor that contributes to race disparities in the incarcerated population is that juries may be selected that discriminate against Black defendants. Samuel Sommers and Michael Norton have studied how race affects jury selection by examining the process of peremptory challenges (Sommers & Norton, 2008). When prosecuting and defense attorneys are interviewing potential jurors for a trial, each is allowed a certain number of peremptory challenges—which allow an attorney to excuse a potential juror from the pool of potential jurors without justification. Because peremptory challenges allow attorneys to exclude potential jurors who may be biased, this practice is defended by its ability to impanel fairer juries. However, research shows that most challenges against Black jurors are made by the prosecutors, whereas most challenges against White jurors are made by the defense. This pattern seems to reflect beliefs that White jurors are less inclined to be sympathetic toward Black defendants. To better isolate the effect of juror race on peremptory challenges, Sommers and his colleague had study participants, including college students, law students, and attorneys, assume the role of a prosecutor in evaluating two potential jurors (Sommers & Norton, 2008). The jurors were described with characteristics that would typically raise red flags with the prosecution (e.g., a journalist who had written about police misconduct). The race of the jurors was manipulated, however, so that some participants (randomly determined) saw juror 1 as White and juror 2 as Black, and the other participants saw juror 1 as Black and juror 2 as White. The results showed that participants were more likely to recommend using a peremptory challenge against the Black, compared to the White, juror. Strikingly, this preference was strongest among the attorney participants. When asked to explain their decisions, participants used reasons other than race that also made sense with the case they were trying.

Race discrimination in jury composition sets the stage for race bias to emerge in juries' verdicts. Much research documents the biasing effect of a defendant's race on jury deliberations and verdicts—but how does this occur? One source of bias concerns the effect of inadmissible evidence, such as prior convictions, on jurors' judgments. Studies find that the mere knowledge that such evidence (which usually is damaging to a defendant's case) exists leads jurors to become surer about the guilt of a Black defendant but doesn't affect the jury's views of a White defendant (Johnson, Whitestone, Jackson, & Gatto, 1995).

A second source of bias consists of the match between the defendant's race and the crime of which he is accused. Racial stereotypes link Blacks with crimes such as assault, assault on a police officer, and grand theft auto; stereotypically White crimes, on the other hand, include embezzlement, fraud, and rape (Sunnafrank & Fontes, 1983). Researchers tested the idea that jurors would judge a defendant more guilty when he committed a stereotype-consistent, compared with a stereotype-inconsistent, crime (Jones and Kaplan, 2003). Participants read case summary materials (based on an actual case) in which a White or Black defendant was charged with either grand theft auto or vehicular manslaughter. Participants then rendered a verdict and attributed the defendant's behavior to either internal (personality) or external (circumstances) causes; they also gave a sentence recommendation. The results showed that defendant race/crime type congruence mattered: Guilty verdicts and internal attributions were significantly higher in the White defendant/vehicular manslaughter and Black defendant/grand theft auto conditions than in the noncongruent conditions. Black defendants were given harsher sentences than White defendants for grand theft auto, but White defendants were not given longer sentences than Blacks when both committed vehicular manslaughter.

Sentencing recommendations can also be racially biased. In one test of this idea, students acting as jurors read the trial summary (including the trial testimony) from an actual case in which a White police officer was killed during a robbery (Dovidio, Smith, Donnella, & Gaertner, 1997). Jurors considered the trial summary believing that the defendant was either Black or White. The Black defendant was significantly more likely to be recommended for the death penalty than the White defendant, but this overt racism only occurred among subjects who scored high on a measure of racism. Among the low-racism subjects, the sentencing bias depended on the race of one's fellow jurors. When a Black juror recommended the death penalty, White subjects recommended the death penalty more for the Black than the White defendant. This race bias did not occur when a White juror took the same position. This study shows the subtlety of modern expressions of racism: A Black juror who recommends the death penalty provides, for anxious White jurors who don't want to be seen as racists, a safe rationalization for their own racially biased attitudes.

The potential *direct* influence of race on the sentencing recommendations of actual juries (as opposed to mock juries composed of student research participants) has decreased thanks to laws that limit discretion in sentencing. Nevertheless, the defendant's race can and does have subtle, *indirect* influences on sentencing recommendations. For example, Irene Blair and her colleagues (2004) examined the cases of 100 Black and 116 White inmates, coding each case for several variables (e.g., sentence length, seriousness of crime, type of crime, prior convictions, etc.). Photographs of the inmates were also rated on how much each had Black facial features. The results showed that the seriousness of the crime and additional offenses were the best predictors of the inmates' sentence length; the inmates' race was not a factor in their sentence length. However, having Black facial features did predict sentence length beyond the effects just mentioned. So, there was no difference *between* Black and White inmates' sentences (when they were equated on crime seriousness and other variables) but race affected sentencing *within* each racial group. This study shows that, for both Black and White criminals, looking Black means getting a longer sentence.

Racism in the Health Care System

Much evidence indicates that Blacks and Hispanics perceive discrimination in the health care system (Lillie-Blanton, Brodie, Rowland, Altman, & McIntosh, 2000). The *perception* that the health care system is racially biased, independent of whether it actually is, is important because people who perceive that discrimination exists use health care services and fill prescriptions less frequently, which results in poorer health among minority than White people (Fiscella, Franks, Doescher, & Saver, 2002; Van Houtven et al., 2005). Aside from users' perceptions of the fairness of the health care system and its indirect effects on health, overwhelming evidence shows that the American health care system delivers poorer quality health care to Blacks than to Whites. For example, research on the treatment of heart disease has concluded that Blacks received poorer quality treatment than Whites (Ford & Cooper, 1995; Schulman et al., 1999). Angioplasty and coronary bypass procedures are both proven to lower death rates among people with heart disease. However, White patients are about twice as likely to have an angioplasty procedure and two or three times more likely to have a bypass procedure than Black patients. Do these differences reflect racism? Perhaps White patients have more serious heart disease than Blacks when they enter the hospital, and this, rather than racial bias, explains the treatment differences? Research shows the reverse is true: Black patients enter the health care system with more serious forms of heart disease, making the treatment differences even more unfair. Perhaps Blacks have less access to hospitals where these procedures are performed? They may, but Blacks receive poorer cardiac care than Whites even in full-service hospitals (Ford & Cooper, 1995).

Recent research shows that physicians' implicit racial biases are directly related to the delivery of poorer quality health care to Black, compared to White, patients. In one study, 287 physicians completed explicit and implicit measures of racial bias (Green et al., 2007). The physician participants were then asked to study the medical case of a patient admitted to the emergency department of a hospital with chest pain; the race of the male patient was experimentally manipulated by researchers. The point of the study was to see how readily physicians recommended thrombolysis—an appropriate and effective treatment for the symptoms presented by the patient. Based on explicit measure of racial prejudice, physicians did not show a preference for White patients, whereas the implicit measure revealed a strong preference for White patients. Compared with physicians with low levels of implicit race bias, those with high levels were much less likely to recommend thrombolysis when the patient was Black and much more likely when the patient was White. Louis Penner and his colleagues have found that physicians' implicit prejudice leaks into their interactions with patients, resulting in less satisfying care given to their patients (Penner et al., 2010). They asked Black patients of a community health clinic to evaluate a medical consultation with the physician. Previously, the physicians who serve the clinic had completed explicit and implicit measures of race prejudice. The findings revealed that physicians with explicit prejudice involved the patient less in the consultation and decision making. However, patients were most dissatisfied with physicians who had high implicit, but low explicit, race prejudice. In other words, physicians' implicit prejudice had subtle, negative consequences for the quality of primary care received by the patients.

Similar findings occur with regard to cancer care. Recent research examined over 14,000 people who were at risk for, or had been diagnosed with, early-stage lung cancer (Lathan, Neville, & Earle, 2006). They found that Blacks were less likely than Whites to have the tests that identify lung cancer and, once diagnosed, were less likely than Whites to be recommended for surgery or to actually have the surgery. Other research examined the breast cancer care received by Black and White women with similar access to health care and found that the 5-year survival rates were 77% and 84% for Black and White women, respectively (Yood et al., 1999). Finally, a recent review combined the findings of more than 100 published tests of race differences in health care, combining all types of illness, and found that Blacks consistently received lower quality health care than Whites (Institute of Medicine of the National Academies, 2003). These findings are strengthened by the fact that researchers controlled for participants' income, education, insurance status, and other variables before testing for race differences.

Racism in the health care system is made worse by the fact that racial minority status *itself* is detrimental to health, owing to the negative stereotypes faced by Blacks in all areas of life. Rodney Clark and his colleagues (1999) argue that racism is experienced by Blacks as stressful. What is stress? Stress is the perception that you don't have sufficient resources to meet the demands placed upon you by particular tasks or circumstances. Chronic stress—stress that you experience consistently, even at low levels—raises blood pressure (increasing the risk of cardiovascular illness) and injects stress hormones into the blood (increasing the risk of infectious illness). For Blacks, racism is a chronic stressor. The awareness that racial stereotyping and discrimination occur in stores, workplaces, and schools places demands on Blacks that White people never have to deal with. These demands often involve working harder to avoid confirming others' beliefs about Blacks (that they're not as intelligent or competent as Whites). In short, racial stereotypes and discrimination chronically threaten Blacks, and this threat has physiological and health consequences.

In one demonstration of this, Black women who scored high on a measure of perceived racism experienced greater increases in blood pressure in anticipation of a common stressor than women who had low perceived racism scores, and this was particularly true for those with few friends or other social supports (Clark, 2006). Other research shows that Blacks have higher rates of hypertension (chronically high blood pressure) than Whites and racism-related stress is associated with high blood pressure (Clark, 2000). In a longitudinal study of 684 Black families, perceived racism predicted later alcohol use in both the parents and children (Gibbons, Gerrard, Cleveland, Wills, & Brody, 2004). This research suggests that the chronic stress of facing racial stereotyping and discrimination can lead to unhealthy stress-coping behaviors such as drinking or smoking.

Summary

Institutional racism occurs in the systematic preferences and advantages afforded to Whites compared with Blacks in criminal justice and health care outcomes. Racism, as illustrated above, can be sustained in organizations without the explicit endorsement of individuals in the organization; this is the legacy of negative stereotypes about Blacks that continue to be passed from generation to generation and repeated in conversations, jokes, and media portrayals of Blacks. Indeed, organizations like the health care system can discriminate against Blacks even when the system includes fair-minded people. Negative cultural stereotypes that influence our behavior without our awareness can be unlearned and replaced with more positive (and accurate) beliefs about people from other racial and ethnic groups. We will discuss the principles and methods of reducing racism and other forms of prejudice in Chapter 12.

Diversity Issue 5.1: Affirmative Action: Confronting Institutional Racism *and* Perpetuating Stereotypes of Incompetence?

Enacted in 1965 during the Civil Rights Era of American history, **affirmative action** was intended to promote equal opportunity for Blacks in college admissions and the workplace. However, the *affirmative action principle* has been carried out in myriad ways (see Crosby & Cordova, 1996, for full discussion). Laws were passed to tailor affirmative action to changing social conditions, and guidelines were established to make employers and universities more accountable to the principle. Today, affirmative action is perceived as a principle that gives preference to Blacks in hiring and college admissions, and this perception has negative implications for how recipients of affirmative action are viewed. Many studies demonstrate that affirmation action recipients are seen as less competent and qualified than other applicants and as having received preferential treatment (Heilman, Block, & Lucas, 1992; Kravitz & Platania, 1993).

Although affirmative action recipients are stereotyped as incompetent and seen as the beneficiaries of race-based favoritism, these negative attitudes and feelings toward (generally Black) recipients of affirmative action are expressed in more subtle ways. In one study, insurance company managers studied the educational and work background and job performance information of a recently hired (fictional) employee (Heilman, Block, & Stathatos, 1997). The job performance information was manipulated to indicate that the employee had achieved either clear or mixed success; in some cases no job performance information was given to the subjects. Additionally, the employee was identified as being hired under an affirmative action program or not. The results showed that the managers evaluated the employee hired under affirmative action less positively than the other employee but only when her record was not clearly successful. In other words, when the employee's accomplishments were so-so or not available for review, the managers rated the affirmative action employee as less competent, deserving of a lower salary, and a recipient of more special treatment than the other employee. This study shows that the stereotype of incompetence associated with affirmative action recipients negatively biases managers' interpretations of the performance record of an affirmative action employee, except when the performance record was obviously above reproach.

The affirmative action stereotype is not applied uniformly to all affirmative action–eligible groups: Blacks are accorded the most negative perceptions associated with affirmation action status (Clayton, 1992, 1996). Other research validates the finding that Audrey Murrell and her colleagues found—that affirmative action programs that benefited Black individuals compared with members of other disadvantaged groups (e.g., women) were least likely to be supported by others (Murrell, Dietz-Uhler, Dovidio, Gaertner, & Drout, 1994). Moreover, people hold more negative attitudes toward Blacks than any other group that benefits from affirmative action while still voicing their support for affirmative action in principle (Clayton, 1992).

Stereotypes about affirmative action recipients affect our attitudes toward groups of people as well as to individuals. Participants in one study read a positive description of a new immigrant group to Canada (people from Suriname) that included references to Surinamers being "good job prospects," "active in many different kinds of job," and "contributing tax revenues" (Maio & Esses, 1998). In one condition, the immigrant group was described as eligible for affirmative action programs; in the other condition no such status was mentioned. Participants who read the affirmative action–eligible description viewed Surinamers as less competent and having poorer job skills and reported more negative overall attitudes toward them than participants for whom affirmative action was not mentioned. Also, participants were less supportive of Surinamers' immigration and of *immigration in general* when the immigrant group was described as affirmative action eligible.

This research suggests that recipients of affirmative action may be scapegoats. When people are unhappy or frustrated by circumstances and cannot correct or control their situations themselves, research shows they often vent their hostilities against out-group individuals who are believed to be contributing to or causing the stressful situation (Allport, 1954). These targets for displaced hostility are called **scapegoats**. Scapegoats tend to be members of relatively powerless social groups—like immigrants—who cannot defend themselves against the unfair actions of the majority. Affirmative action may heighten majority-group members' fears that they are not receiving their fair share of resources and opportunities. These fears are then taken out on the blameless but also relatively powerless recipients of affirmative action in the form of prejudice and discrimination.

(Continued)

(Continued)

In symbolic forms of racism, negative feelings about Blacks are disguised and expressed as opposition to policies that would assist Blacks. Opposition to affirmative action, then, can be defended on purely ideological grounds—that it violates principles of fairness. Nosworthy and his colleagues (1995) found that opposition to affirmative action doesn't have to be based on negative stereotypes about groups, such as Blacks, who benefit from affirmative action; it can be justified by *defending a fairness principle.* This respectable position, if it resulted in a weakening of affirmative action practices, would nevertheless discriminate Blacks and other affirmative action-eligible groups. Hence, racism occurs in the shadow of principled, seemingly nonracist attitudes.

? In the 40 years since its inception, has affirmative action finally *leveled the play-ing field* for Blacks (and other affirmative action-eligible minorities) in hiring and college admissions? What evidence do you have that it has or has not?

? Do you support affirmative action in some situations or for some cases and not support it in other situations? What are those qualifying circumstances? Why do they matter to you?

? Are all immigrants to the United States, regardless of their race, in some way affected by the affirmative action stereotype? Explain your thoughts.

DI   Diversity Issue 5.2: The Obama Effect

The election of President Obama in November of 2008 was heralded by many as historic, not just because he was the first Black President of the United States but also because of the hoped-for positive impact his election would have on race relations in the United States. In psychological terms, President Obama was seen as a positive and counter-stereotypic exemplar and exposure to him should reduce implicit anti-Black attitudes and feelings. The **Obama effect** was originally demonstrated amid the presidential cam-paign, when it was likely that then-Senator Barack Obama would become the Democratic nominee for President. Researchers found markedly lower levels of implicit race prejudice in samples of students tested during the primary campaign than similar samples who were tested during the Bush presidency (Plant et al., 2009). Follow up research showed that this reduction in implicit prejudice was partly due to the effect of Obama as a positive Black exemplar (Columb & Plant, 2011). Based, however, on Implicit Association Test scores on hundreds of thousands of people who took the online test at the Project Implicit site from September 2006 to May 2009, implicit racial attitudes have not changed as a result of Barack Obama's election (Schmidt & Nosek, 2010). After his election to President, however, exposure to Obama increased symbolic expressions of prejudice (Lybarger & Monteith, 2011). Recall symbolic racism occurs when people discriminate against Blacks citing nonracial reasons for their actions. Accordingly, Eric Knowles and his colleagues found that implicit prejudice was associated with opposition to Obama's plan for health care reform (Knowles, Lowery, & Schaumberg, 2010). In a study of Black and White students 1 year after the election, racial prejudice predicted poorer evaluations of Obama's job performance in White, but not Black, participants (Hehman, Gaertner, & Dovidio, 2011). Furthermore, participants' negative views of Obama's performance were explained by how American they thought Obama was. This study nicely shows how negative evaluations of President Obama that are rooted in racial prejudice are justified by referring to nonracial factors.

DI   Diversity Issue 5.3: White Privilege and White Guilt

We typically refer to racism as involving disadvantage to the members of a racial minority group (e.g., being stereotyped, experiencing discrimination) and believe that racism must be addressed by eliminating disadvantages for Blacks, Hispanics, and other racial minority persons. However, racism can also be seen as something that grants advantage to Whites. **White privilege** is the state of having advantage and opportunity because of one's White skin color (McIntosh, 1989). Think about some of the advantages of being White that Whites rarely notice but nevertheless improve their day-to-day lives. For example, on job interviews, Whites are likely to be interviewed and evaluated by another White person. Black and Hispanic job seekers, on the other hand, must face the likely prospect of being interviewed and evaluated by someone who does not share their ethnic background.

? What assumptions will be made about you, if you are White, by other White people? Considering that these assumptions will not be made about Black or Hispanic people, how are you advantaged by your skin color and those traits that are believed to be associated with your skin color?

? To the White readers: How does thinking about these privileges make you feel?

Research shows that the social and material advantages conferred on Whites by their skin color produces guilt. Janet Swim and Deborah Miller (1999) found that guilt about being White, and thus being identified with a group that has been the agent of racial and ethnic discrimination, was related to support for affirmative action. Over several studies, which included adults of all ages and from varying backgrounds, Swim and her colleagues found that **White guilt** was associated with negative evaluations of one's (White) racial group, greater awareness of the privileges of being White compared to Black, and greater recognition that Blacks experience discrimination. Could these other attitudes, and not White guilt, explain Whites' support of affirmative action? No, because when the researchers controlled for participants' guilt about being White, the relationship

(Continued)

(Continued)

between White privilege and support for affirmative action disappeared. When White guilt was held statistically constant, the relationship between recognition of Blacks' experience of discrimination and support for affirmative action also disappeared. So, Whites' guilt about the advantages of being White and about being part of a discriminatory society appears to be an important explanation for positive, supportive attitudes toward affirmative action. Interestingly, White guilt is only associated with support for compensatory affirmative action, not programs that simply increase opportunities and equality for Blacks in general (Iyer, Leach, & Crosby, 2002). This subtle difference suggests that self-interest trumps other interest: Whites may be more concerned with assuaging their guilt through a simplistic fix (e.g., monetary restitution for the effects of slavery) than with the difficult work of making life better for members of racial and ethnic minority groups.

? To the White students: What is your response to the very real benefits you realize from racial inequality? In what ways do Whites try to rationalize their race-based guilt and privilege?

? For an online reprint of McIntosh's essay, including her *backpack* of advantages of being White, go to: http://www.learntoquestion.com/class/log/archives/print/000442.html.

KEY TERMS

Race   88

Ethnicity   88

Cultural stereotype   89

Personal social beliefs   91

Colorism   93

Stereotype
    content model   95

Ambivalence   95

Racism   100

Affirmative action   106

Scapegoats   107

Obama effect   108

White privilege   109

White guilt   109

FOR FURTHER READING

Markus, H. (2008). Pride, prejudice, and ambivalence: Toward a unified theory of race and ethnicity. *American Psychologist, 63*, 651–670. doi: 10.1037/0003-066X.63.8.651

This article integrates the concepts of race and ethnicity by characterizing them as cultural projects rather than fixed, internal qualities. For Markus, race and ethnicity are things that people create rather than things people are.

Online Resources

Racial Profiling Data Collection Resource Center
http://www.racialprofilinganalysis.neu.edu/index.php
> Learn how communities study racial profiling and what they are finding.

Project Implicit
https://implicit.harvard.edu/implicit/
> Take the Implicit Association Test (IAT) and learn about research using the IAT.

The Racial Slur Database
http://www.rsdb.org/
> This is a vast lexicon of racial and ethnic slurs and their explanations or origins.

American Association for Affirmative Action
http://www.affirmativeaction.org/
> Go to the Resources page of this site for affirmative action program guidelines and links to important legislation affecting the fair treatment of minority group individuals in the workplace.

The Obama Effect
http://hypemovie.com/
http://www.slate.com/articles/news_and_politics/crime/2011/10/the_obama_effect_a_surprising_new_theory_for_the_continuing_crim.html
http://www.nytimes.com/2009/01/23/education/23gap.html
> Here are some sites presenting diverging views on the Obama effect in different domains.

American Psychological Association (APA)
http://www.apa.org/topics/race/index.aspx
> In the APA site, go to Psychology Topics and then to Race for recent news events involving race and other resources.

Anti-Defamation League
http://www.adl.org/
> The Anti-Defamation League (ADL) is an organization that fights racism of any type but, in particular, anti-Semitism. The ADL is an authority on the internet culture of hateful speech and ideology; of particular interest is the Internet Rumor page, where the ADL keeps track of, and debunks, e-rumors that inappropriately accuse organizations of racism.

Affirmative Action and Diversity Project
http://aad.english.ucsb.edu
The Affirmative Action and Diversity Project website is an excellent resource for learning more about affirmative action (**AA**). Its material represents all ideological and political perspectives on affirmation action—from pro-AA to anti-AA. To extend your study of racism concepts, check out the listings for *reverse racism* and *race blindness*.

Understanding Gender Stereotypes and Sexism

TOPICS COVERED IN THIS CHAPTER:

- Gender stereotypes and gender bias
- Hostile and benevolent forms of sexism
- Explanations for sex differences

Having discussed race as a tool for parsing diversity, we now consider an equally useful primary social category: sex. Sex-based and race-based categorizations are similar in three basic ways. First, we notice others' sex almost as quickly as we notice their race (in less than one second). Noticing and categorizing people by their biological sex, like race, occurs reflexively. Second, like race differences, male*ness* and female*ness* are rooted in different sets of physical characteristics that are visible and easily distinguished. Very few people cannot be identified as either male or female, and that quality makes sex-based categories useful tools for organizing our social worlds. Third, as with race, the physical differences between men and women have come to represent inner qualities and essences.

A good illustration of this principle is the best-selling book *Men Are From Mars, Women Are From Venus* (Gray, 1992), which offers practical advice on how to overcome the significant differences between men and women to make better relationships. The *Mars and Venus* metaphor suggests men and women are alien species who, with no common language, struggle to communicate with each other. But are the assumed differences between men and women merely a convenient way to *explain* the different life circumstances that men and women realize, similar to what we learned with race? In this chapter, we examine the content of gender stereotypes and discuss the ambivalent nature of attitudes toward women. Second, we evaluate whether the presumed differences between men and women are actual or perceived. Third, we review some explanations for why stereotypical beliefs about gender differences (e.g., that men are logical and women are emotional) arise and persist. A brief clarification of terms will be useful here. **Sex**, as a social category, refers to one's biological sex (male or female) and is genetically determined. **Gender** refers to the traits and abilities associated with males and females. Your gender is determined by your socialization in, and identification with, the cultural meanings of male and female. For most people, sex and gender are heavily overlapping. Biological males tend to be raised as boys and identify themselves as males, which includes, to some extent, embracing the traits associated with maleness. Likewise with biological females, most of whom are socialized and self-identify as females.

Gender Stereotypes

Gender stereotypes are a much-researched topic by psychologists. A search of the psychological research literature via *PsycNET* identifies over 1,100 articles on some aspect of gender stereotypes or stereotyping, most of which address attitudes and beliefs about women. Stereotypes held about women, especially among men, have the potential to be more discriminatory than women's beliefs about men. Thus, as we saw with racial stereotyping and racism, social justice concerns also shape research on gender stereotypes. In the following pages, we examine the stereotypic differences between men and women by looking at the content of cultural gender stereotypes. We also review research that tests those stereotypic assumptions—in other words, men and women are *believed* to be different, but in what ways (if any) are they *actually* different?

Displayed in Table 6.1 are some of the attributes that make up our **gender stereotypes**. These are generally agreed-upon ways of thinking about men and women and define what is masculine and feminine. Your personal beliefs about what men and women, as groups of people, are like or what constitutes masculinity and femininity may differ from the stereotypes in Table 6.1. Still, most people know these cultural gender stereotypes, and many of these stereotypical beliefs and assumptions are commonly repeated in media portrayals of men and women.

What is immediately apparent about the content of gender stereotypes is how different men and women are believed to be. Stereotypically speaking, men act and women relate. That is, the positive aspects of gender stereotypes hold that masculinity is associated with strength and agency, whereas femininity is associated with sociability and nurturance. These themes of strength and sociability are also reflected

Table 6.1 Traits in the Cultural Stereotype of Men and Women

Men		Women	
Positive Traits	Negative Traits	Positive Traits	Negative Traits
Independent	Egotistical	Helpful	Spineless
Self-confident	Hostile	Aware of others' feelings	Gullible
Competitive	Cynical	Warm to others	Servile
Stands up under pressure	Arrogant	Gentle	Subordinates self to others
Active	Boastful	Emotional	Whining
Makes decisions easily	Greedy	Devoted to others	Complaining
Never gives up easily	Dictatorial	Kind	Nagging
Feels superior	Unprincipled	Understanding	Fussy

SOURCE: "Negative and positive components of psychological masculinity and femininity and their relationships to self-reports of neurotic and acting-out behaviors" by J. Spence, R. Helmreich, and C. Holohan, 1979, *Journal of Personality and Social Psychology, 37*, pp. 1673–1682. Copyright 1979 by American Psychological Association.

in the negative aspects of gender stereotypes where we see less-valued expressions of both strength (e.g., hostile, dictatorial) and sociability (e.g., gullible, subordinate). We consider two important aspects of stereotypes of women: the valuing of masculine traits over feminine traits and the ambivalent nature of stereotypical attitudes toward women.

Recall from our discussion of the stereotype content model in Chapter 5 that the content of stereotypes about other groups reflects two prominent underlying dimensions: competence and warmth. According to Susan Fiske and her colleagues, those two basic dimensions account for as much as 85% of the variance in people's impressions of other groups (Fiske, Cuddy, & Glick, 2007). Let's now consider gender stereotypes along those content dimensions. Thomas Eckes (2002) had participants rate 17 subgroups of women on how each was generally viewed in society on warmth and competence evaluative dimensions. The findings, displayed in Figure 6.1, show a striking pattern. Stereotypes of subgroups of women were in one of two clusters: either high in warmth and low in competence (e.g., housewife, secretary) or low in warmth and high in competence (e.g., career woman, feminist). The subgroup of *typical women* was in the first cluster. These findings show that stereotypes of women

Figure 6.1   Female Subgroups as They Are Placed Along the Warmth and Competence Dimensions of the Stereotype Content Model

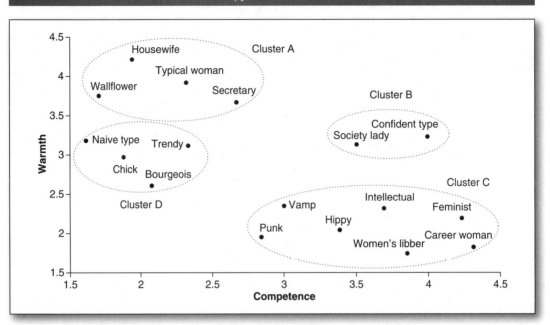

SOURCE: "Paternalistic and envious gender stereotypes: Testing predictions from the stereotype content model," by T. Eckes, 2002, *Sex Roles, 47*, pp. 99–114. Copyright 2002 by Springer. With kind permission from Springer Science+Business Media.

tend to take two forms: paternalistic stereotypes, where women are liked but not respected, and envious stereotypes, where women are respected but not liked. Susan Fiske (2010) observes that these stereotypes of women reflect the ambivalence that is also seen in the content of stereotypes of Blacks, Jews, and Asians as discussed in Chapter 5. Later in this chapter, we consider this ambivalence further as it is expressed in sexism.

Athleticism is a stereotypically masculine trait, but how are female athletes—a subgroup of women not part of the study described above—viewed in the context of the stereotype content model? Recent research suggests that female athletes are probably the target of envious stereotypes, where they are viewed as competent but not warm. Jennifer Pearson and her colleagues (2009) found that, compared with nonathletes, female athletes are much more likely to be academically oriented, and intellectual women are clearly stereotyped as high in competence and low in warmth. They reported data from the National Longitudinal Study of Adolescent Health, which showed that female high school athletes were more likely to take advanced-placement courses in language and science than their nonathletic counterparts.

Even a feminine-sounding voice is sufficient to activate gender stereotypes. In an interesting demonstration of this, male and female speakers posed as job applicants and were rated by evaluators on their warmth and competence (Ko, Judd, & Stapel, 2009). The speakers were selected based on their voices having been determined by independent raters as stereotypically masculine or feminine (for their gender). The results showed that feminine-sounding voices lowered the competence attributed to the applicants, and this effect held regardless of the gender of the speaker. A feminine-sounding voice, however, had no effect on perceived warmth. What is noteworthy about the findings, however, is that the effect of a feminine-sounding voice on the perceivers' judgments of competence overcame a host of individual information in the form of a job resume. That is, despite having information about the individual (e.g., his or her education, experience, and interests) on which to base one's judgments of competence, evaluators were more swayed by cues to femininity in their voices. This study shows how ingrained and powerful gender stereotypes can be in shaping our evaluations of others—even males who sound feminine. We now turn to the problem of the systematic preference of men and masculinity over women and femininity.

Gender Bias

The problem with gender stereotypes is not merely that women and men are presumed to be different; it is that men's qualities are more positively valued than women's qualities. Look again at the list of attributes in Table 6.1. In our culture, independence is valued over dependence, logic over intuition and emotionality, and assertiveness over interpersonal sensitivity. Gender stereotyping is a social problem because it is associated with **gender bias**—the tendency to value men and masculine traits over women and feminine traits. Let's examine some evidence for the claim that men are perceived as better, more competent, and more valuable people than women.

In the classic demonstration of gender bias, Philip Goldberg (1968) gathered published writings from a variety of professional fields and condensed them into a series of essays, such as would be generated by a student on an exam. He then had participants read and evaluate the essays, which were labeled with a fictitious male (John McKay) or female (Joan McKay) student's name. The results showed that the same writing was evaluated more favorably when it bore a man's, compared to a woman's, name. Other demonstrations of gender bias have found that men's success is attributed to their ability, but women's success is attributed to the ease of the task (Feather & Simon, 1975).

Gender bias is subtly communicated to children in many forms, such as in the form of coloring book and cereal box character depictions. Researchers coded the content of coloring books purchased from a random sample of stores for gender-biased characterizations (Fitzpatrick & McPherson, 2010). They found that females constituted just 41% of all characters. Furthermore, characters that were shown doing stereotypically feminine things (e.g., cooking, sewing) were overwhelmingly female. The characterizations on cereal boxes are similarly gender biased: In a comprehensive analysis of cereal boxes, female characters were much more likely than males to be shown as a child rather than as an adult, and in passive rather than active roles (Black, Marola, Littman, Chrisler, & Neace, 2009).

Gender bias depends on what men and women are being evaluated for. For example, in one study, equally qualified men and women applicants called about jobs that were traditionally masculine (e.g., security guard) or feminine (e.g., receptionist). The supervisors on the other end of the line tended to discourage or disqualify women who were interested in *men's* jobs and men who were interested in *women's* jobs (Levinson, 1975). In that study, the mere voices of men and women callers were sufficient to activate stereotypes, as discussed earlier, which then guided potential employers' behavior toward men and women in stereotype-consistent ways. A survey of male managers found that, compared to male employees, females were seen as less competent and motivated (Gungor & Biernat, 2009; Rosen & Jerdee, 1978). Because gender bias is driven by stereotypes of men and women, it is less likely to occur when people have other information (besides an individual's sex) with which to evaluate someone (Swim, Borgida, Maruyama, & Myers, 1989). Thus, gender stereotypes lead to more positive evaluations of men than women. However, gender bias sometimes favors women, although this *advantage* is only gained in traditionally feminine tasks, abilities, or jobs. Recent research finds that women who hold gender stereotype–inconsistent jobs—being a female police chief, for example—are held to higher competence standards. That is, when women in male-dominated jobs make mistakes, they are punished more in the form of lowered ratings of competence than women in traditionally feminine occupations (Brescoll, Dawson, & Uhlmann, 2010). As if to add insult to injury, when men succeed in traditionally feminine occupations, they are judged as less competent (Heilman & Wallen, 2010). Together these studies characterize the strong cultural bias against women and female-stereotypic occupations.

Gender bias is also evidenced by the fact that women's physical and psychological differences from men (notice that men are the standard) are often cast in terms of disease or disorder, and these *deficiencies* are then treated (Tavris, 1992). For example, premenstrual syndrome (PMS) describes the hormone-related mood changes that women allegedly experience each month. Research demonstrates, however, that only a small minority of women (about 5%) experience severe enough PMS symptoms to see a physician. Further, PMS seems to be, in part, a self-fulfilling prophecy. That is, women *report* experiencing PMS more regularly than is evidenced by physiological measures taken on them, suggesting that many women have internalized stereotypic expectations about them. PMS, then, is as much (perhaps more) a social belief about women as it is a physiological fact and provides a tidy explanation for women's supposed moodiness and emotionality.

Women's perceived psychological differences from men are also framed as disorders. The clinical category *self-defeating personality disorder* and the similar pop-psychology concept of *codependency* feature symptoms that are thinly veiled extensions of the female stereotype: sacrificing one's own interests for others, overinvolvement in others' lives and problems, and taking too much responsibility for relationship problems. According to psychologist Carol Tavris (1992), these *disorders* reflect the institutionalized devaluing of feminine attributes. They provide a respected clinical justification for the *deficiencies* of women and also demonstrate that standards of mental health and adjustment are more masculine than feminine.

Finally, gender bias is subtly communicated in graphical displays of data. If you wanted to display some data in a bar graph for male and female samples—say, the average number of friends on Facebook—how would you present the data? Peter Hegarty and his colleagues have found evidence of gender bias in graphs, whereby males' data is consistently presented above or to the left of females' data, and to viewers these positions tend to signify greater importance (Hegarty & Buechel, 2006). One such study asked undergraduate students to state a hypothesis predicting a gender difference in a social behavior (e.g., Women have more credit cards than men) and then draw a bar graph showing results that supported the hypothesis (Hegarty, Lemieux, & McQueen, 2010). Sixty-eight percent (68%) of the graphs put males' data to the left of females', and this finding was emphasized by the fact that most of the participants were females. A second study showed participants—again, mostly women—a bar graph of achievement test data by gender but varied whether males' or females' data were on the left side (in other words, held the *important* position). Later, participants were asked to reproduce the graph from memory. Most of the participants recalled the graph correctly, but a large minority switched the order of the bars in their recall. Of those cases, participants were far more likely to switch if they had viewed the *females-on-the-left* graph originally. This shows again a bias in favor the males' data having the prominent position in a graph. It also shows that stereotype-consistent graphs (with men on the left) are recalled more accurately than stereotype-inconsistent graphs.

In summary, gender stereotypes reveal a cultural bias in which men and masculine traits and skills are valued more than women and feminine traits and skills. This gender bias results in a pattern of bias or discrimination against women that extends to many areas of life.

Ambivalent Attitudes Toward Women

Although prejudice has been regarded as holding negative attitudes toward members of another group, we learned in Chapter 5, and also earlier in this chapter, that prejudice sometimes reflects ambivalence—or the presence of positive and negative attitudes. Earlier we learned that stereotypes of women are ambivalent in that women tend to be viewed either as warm but not competent or as competent but not warm. Ambivalence toward women can also be understood in terms of hostile and benevolent forms of sexism. According to Peter Glick and Susan Fiske (1997, 2001), **hostile sexism** regards women as inferior to men, assigns women to traditional and subordinate roles, considers women as sexual objects, and believes that women are ultimately interested in dominating and controlling men. Hostile sexists tend to support traditional gender role arrangements (e.g., wife as mother and homemaker, husband as wage earner) and tend to be openly derogatory of feminist ideals. **Benevolent sexism**, on the other hand, regards women as refined objects to be idolized, protected, and cared for. When Tom Cruise's character in the famous scene from *Jerry Maguire* confesses "You complete me" to his girlfriend (played by Renee Zellweger), he is expressing a benevolent stereotype of women. Benevolent sexists tend to romanticize women's sexuality, rather than see it as threatening. They also regard women as emotionally weaker but morally superior and deserving of adoration and sacrifice from men.

Benevolent sexism doesn't sound like prejudice, does it? Actually, hostile and benevolent stereotypes both assume (albeit in different terms) women are weaker and inferior to men, and therefore, both stereotypes enforce *patriarchy*—a social system in which men have more power, status, and resources than women. Indeed, in a study of gender stereotyping and discrimination in 19 countries, Peter Glick and his colleagues (2000) found that *both* hostile and benevolent stereotypes of women were associated with fewer women in management and professional occupations, as well as shorter life expectancy, less education, and lower purchasing power among women than men. This research also showed that across the 19 countries studied men consistently endorsed hostile sexist attitudes more than women, but (remarkably) men and women endorsed benevolent sexist attitudes in equal measure.

Why would women endorse stereotypic attitudes that are limiting and discriminatory to themselves? Glick and Fiske (2001) suggest that men's benevolent stereotypes of women don't feel oppressive or unfair and are not recognized as sexist. Indeed, many women may find such attitudes flattering and attractive. Another explanation involves the tendency for men who hold both hostile and benevolent stereotypes of women to subtype women into more polarized groups (e.g., *devoted mom* or *radical feminist*). Women therefore might never come to see the connection between—indeed, the complementary nature of—hostile and benevolent stereotypes. Julia Becker (2010) found that women endorsed hostile sexist attitudes when they were thinking about particular subgroups of women (e.g., career women, feminists) but endorsed benevolent sexism when they identified with more traditional subgroups such as housewives. These findings are consistent with the distinction between paternalistic and envious stereotypes of women discussed earlier. Finally, women may not recognize benevolent stereotypes as sexist because men may subtly use benevolent attitudes (e.g., I'm going to take care of you) to reward women for occupying traditional gender roles. Similarly, researchers have found that supervisors who displayed benevolent sexism in their treatment of female job applicants were liked more than those who displayed hostile sexism (Good & Rudman, 2010). This suggests that benevolent, but not hostile, sexism is tolerated and even approved even though it is just as limiting to women than hostile forms of sexism. A final explanation for the persistence and social approval around benevolent sexism concerns the fact that traditional roles for women reinforce the status quo, whereas nontraditional roles unsettle and threaten the status quo (Lau, Kay, & Spencer, 2008). Grace Lau and her colleagues randomly assigned Canadian male participants to system-threat or no system-threat conditions by having them either read an article criticizing the sociopolitical system in Canada or a control article. After the reading, participants were allowed to declare their romantic interest in a series of women whose profiles were engineered to reflect characteristics of benevolent or hostile gender stereotypes. The participants were more attracted to the benevolent-stereotypic women when their national worldview was threatened than when it was not threatened. This study suggests, then, that benevolent sexism reinforces traditional sex role stereotypes in the service of sociocultural status quo maintenance.

To sum up, modern forms of sexism are ambivalent, treating women both as inferior objects to be controlled and as treasured objects to be protected. However, both hostile and benevolent stereotypes discriminate against women because both characterize women as objects and insist on women occupying traditional, subordinate roles. Illustrating the subtlety of modern sexism, benevolent sex stereotypes are endorsed by women as much as men.

Stereotypic Gender Differences: Actual or Perceived?

We have considered the ways men and women are believed to be different, in the form of gender stereotypes, and some consequences of gender stereotyping for the discrimination of women. In Chapter 2, we learned that stereotypes usually have some *kernel of truth* as Allport (1954) called it, but this actual difference is unfairly distorted or generalized. Let's now examine whether some of the gender differences discussed above have any factual basis.

Intellectual Differences

Stereotypically, women are regarded as having better verbal ability than men. That is, they supposedly are better readers, have better language skills, and are more interested in art and literature than men. Is it true that women are more verbally skilled than men? In 1950, girls *did* outscore boys on tests of verbal skill, but by 1980, boys and girls were equal (Feingold, 1988). Other researchers reviewed over 160 studies, which compared men and women on various verbal skills and tasks and found small differences, with women higher than men (Hyde & Linn, 1988). A parallel, but reverse, gender difference is in the area of quantitative ability. Stereotypically, men are presumed to have a better *head for numbers*, to be more logical, and to be more interested in math and science domains than women. Does this difference in ability really exist? An early review of the literature showed that girls had closed the presumed *math gap* that existed for decades (Hyde, Fennema, & Lamon, 1990). The most recent examination of gender differences in mathematical ability consists of a meta-analysis of 242 studies representing over 1.2 million participants (Lindberg, Hyde, Petersen, & Linn, 2010). The results from all these studies combined indicated no overall gender difference in math ability. Although boys and girls, and men and women, do not differ in math ability *on average*, math scores are more variable in men than in women. In other words, there are more extremely high and low scorers among males than among females. This is one of the reasons cited for females' underrepresentation in science, technology, engineering, and math (STEM) fields. For example, if extremely high Graduate Record Examination (GRE)-quantitative scores are a prerequisite for quantitative and scientific careers, then there are more males with those high scores to choose from than females. Stephen Ceci and Wendy Williams (2010) argue, however, that although this may be a factor, it cannot explain all of the underrepresentation of females in math-intensive fields. What are some of the other possible reasons? The possibility that women are discriminated against in STEM fields has little research support (Ceci & Williams, 2010). One compelling explanation lies in the interests of girls and boys in math-intensive fields and the career choices those interests promote. According to Ceci and Williams, comparably math-talented girls and boys differ in their interest in quantitative careers, with boys more interested in engineering and other math-intensive fields and girls more interested in careers that incorporate social interaction such as medicine and law. Finally, compared to math-talented boys, equivalent math-talented girls also have higher verbal/language abilities, and that edge opens up other challenging career options for females that may compete with, and win out over, math-intensive careers (Ceci & Williams, 2010).

Psychological Differences

Gender stereotypes refer not only to differences in intellectual abilities and competence but also to psychological differences. Research evidence suggests that women and men differ in four general domains of behavior: helpfulness, aggressiveness, gullibility, and sexual attitudes and behavior. The first three are discussed below; the fourth is included in the discussion of evolutionary psychology at the end of the chapter.

Helpfulness and Empathy

Most people (including women) perceive women as more empathic and helpful than men and more sensitive to the feelings and needs of others than men are. Much research data establish that men and women do behave differently in the areas of helpfulness (Eagly & Crowley, 1986). Studies that measure *heroic* helping—assisting someone in dire need or distress—show that men help more than women. However, studies that measure mundane expressions of help find the opposite: Women are more likely than men to do favors, express concern, or provide support to someone in need. Thus, the direction of sex differences in helpfulness depends on the kind of helping observed.

Both large surveys and smaller experimental studies show that women respond with more empathy than men to a needy individual (Batson et al., 1996; Eisenberg & Lennon, 1983). Compared to men, when women talk, they relate more personal experiences and show more support (Eagly, 1987). Another dimension of empathy involves sensitivity to nonverbal behavior; in this area, researchers have found a reliable gender difference. Women are more attuned to subtle nonverbal cues in others' behavior and better at interpreting nonverbal behavior than men are (Hall, 1978).

Aggressiveness

In general, research shows men to be more aggressive than women (Eagly & Steffen, 1986; Hyde, 1984). However, stereotypic beliefs about men being more aggressive than women are, in part, an artifact of research that compares men and women on *physical* expressions of aggression. Surely, men are far more likely than women to commit violent crimes, such as murder, robbery, and assault. When aggression is measured in other ways, however, the stereotype that *men are more aggressive than women* is not as accurate. Some studies find that boys and girls and men and women do not differ in their use of verbal aggression such as name-calling and insults (Osterman et al., 1998; White & Kowalski, 1994). Gender differences in aggression also disappear in responses to provocation and in older people (Bettencourt & Miller, 1996). Finally, Karin Osterman and her colleagues (1998) found *more* indirect or relational aggression in girls than in boys. Relational aggression includes social exclusion (e.g., ignoring or shunning others), spreading rumors or lying about others, and passive aggression (e.g., being aggressively uncooperative or unhelpful toward others). The tendency for boys to exhibit more physical aggression than girls and girls to exhibit more relational aggression than boys has even been observed in preschool-aged children (Ostrov & Keating, 2004).

Furthermore, gender differences in aggressiveness are often based on responses to surveys or questionnaires. Could these differences really be due to the way men, compared to women, present themselves to researchers and pollsters? Research does point to bias in questions designed to measure aggressive attitudes (Zur, 1989). When questions are posed in confrontational *us or them* terms, men affirm them more than women, but men and women are equally supportive of questions that frame aggression in humanitarian terms (e.g., *liberating oppressed people*). Thus, perhaps some of the differences we observe between men and women in aggressiveness are not innate but are responses to society's different expectations for men and women.

Gullibility

Popular stereotypes of women are that they are easily influenced and susceptible to persuasive appeals and claims. Some studies have shown females to be more easily influenced, while others provide no evidence of such a gender difference (Eagly, 1987; Eagly & Carli, 1981). When the results are summed up, women appear to be slightly more gullible and conforming than men. These gender differences also depend on factors such as the type of appeal made or whether the pressure is exerted by a group or an individual.

Carol Tavris (1992) has suggested that comparing men and women on measures of gullibility and susceptibility to influence is a subtle expression of gender bias. Indeed, asking the question "Are women more easily influenced than men?" raises the specter of another *deficiency* in women, which needs to be studied and explained. One might conduct the same studies to learn "Are men less trusting than women?" Surely, lacking the ability to trust another person is just as deficient as being easily influenced. Thus, gender bias, in the form of how research questions are asked, could have subtle effects on gender differences research.

To sum up, in comparison to the many ways that women and men *could* differ, reliably demonstrated gender differences are few in number and small in magnitude. As reviewed above, women and men are not different in intellectual domains, but they do differ in several psychosocial areas. To what extent, then, are gender stereotypes accurate summaries of the ways that men and women really differ? Janet Swim (1994) investigated the accuracy of gender stereotypes by comparing participants' perceptions of gender differences with more objective meta-analytic reviews of the research (reviews which quantitatively summarize many studies on the same topic). The results showed that participants accurately estimated gender differences in some behaviors and underestimated gender differences in other behaviors. Moreover, participants' responses were biased by favoritism toward women. In other words, all participants were more accurate in estimating positive female attributes than all other types of attributes. Also, participants' responses reflected in-group bias. That is, women perceived greater gender differences in nonverbal behavior (a women's *specialty*) than men did, whereas men estimated greater gender differences on leadership ability (a man's *specialty*) than women did. This study suggests that our gender stereotypes have some factual basis and may not be gross exaggerations of the truth. Are the psychological differences reviewed above reflective of a man's and woman's personality? Or could gender differences be a natural response to differing social and environmental forces facing women and men? Next we discuss how gender differences are explained.

Googling *dumb blonde jokes* delivers over 1 million hits; here is a sample site: http://www.humorsphere.com/sms/blonde_jokes.htm. Do a simple research project: Visit some dumb blonde joke sites and find the percentage of the jokes that refer to a dumb blonde woman, a dumb blonde man, or a dumb blonde person (if no gendered pronouns are used).

- What are the results of your research? What do you think they mean?
- Do dumb blonde jokes illustrate hostile or benevolent sexism? Explain.
- What other attributes in the cultural stereotype of women (besides intelligence) are conveyed in dumb blonde jokes?

Explaining Gender Differences

One of the most common questions posed by students in introductory psychology courses is, "Why are men and women different?" We now know that there are two sets of gender differences: those that are widely believed but not factual (e.g., men are better at math than women) and differences that are both believed and factual (e.g., men are more physically aggressive than women). To the extent that research has documented real gender differences, where did they come from? We will consider explanations for each set of gender differences below, starting with why we regard men and women as different in domains where they are clearly the same.

Gender Stereotypes Shape Perceived and Actual Diversity

Let's reprise the lessons of Chapters 2 and 3, respectively, by acknowledging that gender stereotypes shape both the differences we perceive, as well as actual differences, between men and women. The great similarities between men and women on most intellectual and psychological traits mean that the few gender differences are more unexpected, noticeable, and memorable. These noteworthy differences skew our assumptions about men and women in general so that we believe they are more different than they are. Moreover, there is a publication bias against research that finds that groups of people do not differ. Therefore, we hear more about the few studies that find some evidence of a gender difference than the (much larger number of) studies that are conducted but find nothing. Even when faced with some studies that find gender differences and others that do not—we react differently to them. That is, because we prefer to have our stereotypes supported, rather than threatened, we are more inclined to believe research that is consistent, rather than inconsistent, with our beliefs. These explanations, applications of concepts learned in Chapter 2, show that stereotypic beliefs about men and women's intellectual abilities persist because they seem to have more factual support than they do. However, it is our stereotypes that guide us to notice and remember supportive instances and research studies. Finally, gender stereotypes create their own supportive evidence in the form of self-fulfilling prophecies. The classic demonstration of this occurred in a study by Mark Zanna and Susan Pack (1975) in which female participants had an interaction with a male partner who was either attractive or not and who was believed to hold either progressive or traditional views about women's roles. In the *desirable partner* conditions, participants' behavior subtly reflected their partner's expectations for them. Those women whose partner endorsed traditional sex stereotypes reported more traditional views of women themselves and acted in more stereotypical ways, compared to women with a progressive-thinking partner. In sum, gender stereotypes shape the evidence by which we evaluate gender differences and can even create stereotype-consistent evidence.

Girls and Boys Are Socialized Differently

The most prominent explanations for gender differences share the general notion that gender differences are acquired through exposure to one's social environment. One's immediate and broader social environment features many socializing agents, including parents and other caregivers, teachers, peers, and television. While they differ in their particular predictions, the two socialization models discussed below agree that the differences between men and women are not inherent but learned.

Gender Differences Arise Out of Social Interaction

One explanation for gender differences specifies that gender differences emerge when people interact with each other (Deaux & Major, 1987). The differences between men's and women's behavior that arise in interactions depend on two factors. First, we all have beliefs and expectations about the traits and abilities of men and women. The stronger our gender beliefs are, the more they will guide our interactions with members of the opposite sex in ways that confirm those very beliefs. Second, situations vary in the extent to which one's gender is relevant. The more *gendered* a situation is, the more active and influential our gender expectations will be in that situation. In short, this model characterizes gender beliefs as following the processes of a self-fulfilling prophecy while acknowledging that situations alone can activate our gender beliefs.

As an example, consider a male supervisor who must interview applicants for two positions: a manager and a secretary. Because the man subscribes to stereotypic beliefs about women's abilities and traits, he will bring these beliefs into all of his interviews. However, the situation—in this example, the position for which he is interviewing— will have an independent effect on his beliefs. Because of the gender-relevant nature of the secretary's role, those interviews will likely activate the supervisor's gender beliefs more than the gender-irrelevant interview situations. What does the social interaction model predict will happen in this scenario? The man will treat women differently (and more negatively) than men, especially in the gender-relevant situations. His treatment will also tend to alter how the female, but not the male, applicants respond. In effect, his beliefs combine with the situation to produce the expected gender difference.

Recognize that the gender difference described in this scene did not exist—or only potentially existed—*before* the supervisor and the applicants interacted. Thus, Kay Deaux and Brenda Major's (1987) *social interaction* model of gender differences makes an important point: Gender differences are, in part, context-dependent out-comes. Their model explains the process by which gender differences arise and what factors are important in that process but does not, however, explain the origin of gender beliefs.

Gender Differences Arise Out of Social Roles

Another perspective on the socialized nature of gender differences looks to the social roles traditionally occupied by men and women. According to Alice Eagly (1987), gender differences arise when societies assign different responsibilities and roles to men and women, and people make assumptions about the traits and abilities associated with those roles. As we discussed in Chapter 2, we often erroneously assume that men and women *choose* these different roles because they are inherently different types of people to begin with. Actually, the reverse is more accurate. Males and females start out very similar in their traits and abilities but *become* different partly as a result of being assigned or *guided into* different roles, interests, and occupations which, in turn, draw out different skills and behaviors. Thus, the gender diversity we observe around us is partially constructed by gender roles and role-appropriate behavior.

The roles traditionally occupied by men (e.g., livelihood provider) and women (e.g., childcare provider) in our society have given rise to general beliefs that women *relate*— they are nurturing, caring, relationship-oriented individuals—and men *act*—they are assertive, decisive doers. Gender differences arise, then, when girls and boys learn the skills and behaviors that are required by their respective social roles. To competently discharge their roles, girls need to learn nurturance, cooperativeness, and dependence, and boys need to learn assertiveness, ambition, and independence. If gender differences are created by society's assignment of men and women to different roles, would those differences change if the role assignments could be changed? One researcher compared the child-rearing behaviors of single men who were raising children with similar women and found the fathers to be as equally nurturing as the mothers (Risman, 1987). So, when men are placed in roles or situations where they are expected to be nurturing, they respond with nurturing behavior—just as women do!

Likewise, women's superior skill at interpreting nonverbal behavior is an adjustment necessitated (for women) by being in subordinate positions more than men (Snodgrass, 1985). People who tend to be in *follower* rather than *leader* roles (as women are) will naturally develop better skills at decoding and interpreting the actions and intentions of their boss or supervisor. However, the influence of these roles on our actions is the same for men and women. If *men* were consigned to subordinate, low-status jobs in which female supervisors were questioning their ability and motivation or relationships in which they were financially dependent on their wives, surely men would likely become adept at *reading* other people too.

This model of socialized gender differences differs in two ways from the previous one. First, it specifies where gender beliefs and expectations originate. Second, it says that gender differences are not constrained to social interactions but appear in a broader range of behavior and life contexts. Both models of socialized gender differences, however, have a similar promising message for addressing the gender differences that result in disadvantage for women. Gender differences can become less discriminatory to women if we rely less on gender stereotypes for information about women's and men's abilities. So, do men and women have inherent differences that lead them to choose different roles, or are their behavioral differences the result of adapting to roles that are assigned to them? Research indicates that the second of those two models is more accurate. In the following paragraphs, we will examine the influence of three prominent socialization agents on gender differences.

Family Influences on Gender Differences

Much of our behavior is learned by watching other people—a mode of learning that is especially important for children. Gender-appropriate behavior is modeled by parents, grandparents, and siblings in the typical home, and children are rewarded for reproducing the *appropriate* behavior. For example, boys learn very early that trucks, guns, and athletic gear are approved boy toys and girls understand that dolls, clothes, and dishes are girl things. Moreover, gender-inappropriate behavior is often disapproved by authority figures, as when a little boy dresses up in mom's clothes or when a little girl gets dirty playing with trucks outside. Most children also naturally strive to identify more with their same-sex than their opposite-sex parent, adding strength to gender-appropriate behavior patterns. So, to the extent girls learn that *their* activities are cooperative and nonaggressive and occur in the home, and boys learn that *their* activities involve competition and dominance and occur on the playing field, the seeds of gender-based advantage and disadvantage, opportunity and limitation, are already firmly rooted in the home. As suggested above, children also draw information about what women and men are like from observing their parents' and other adults' behavior in various social roles. In our society, at home men are providers and protectors whereas women occupy homemaker and child care roles. At work, men's roles involve power, decision making, and physical labor, whereas women's tend to entail helping, teaching, and supporting.

School Influences on Gender Differences

When children enter school, many already have clear notions about what boys and girls are like and do. These gender stereotypes are often supported and perpetuated in the schoolroom. According to the observational research of Barrie Thorne (1986), elementary schoolrooms and playgrounds are markedly segregated by sex. Observing hundreds of students in several grade levels at several elementary schools, Thorne found that principals and teachers commonly referred to students as boys and girls and often compared boys' and girls' behavior (e.g., the girls are ready; are the boys?). Classroom seating arrangements tended to be divided along gender lines, as did other activities such as lunch and walking in hallways. Teachers frequently divided classes into girl and boy teams for learning competitions, a highly questionable practice that makes social categorization based on gender explicit and sets up a battle of the sexes for teacher approval and grades.

School recreation also tends to be divided along gender lines. Playgrounds become divided into boys' and girls' territory, with girls' territory being closer to the school than boys' (Thorne, 1986). Further, boys tend to play with other boys in rougher, more competitive games than do girls (Maccoby, 1990). It is important to reiterate that although these behavioral differences may not be *caused* by school influences, school is a place where gender stereotypes are learned, rehearsed, and strengthened. Indeed, some of the gender segregation, such as the lunchroom seating patterns, reflected the *students'* preferences, showing that even children as young as 5 years old have already learned some lessons about how boys and girls differ, and these perceptions influence their behavior.

Gender stereotypes in school are also evident in the fields of study chosen by women and men. Although females and males score equally well on standardized math tests in elementary and middle school, men achieve more than women in math and engineering fields (Hyde et al., 1990). Nine out of ten jobs in engineering, math, and the physical sciences are held by men, and the women employed in those fields earn about 75% of what men earn in comparable jobs (Hewitt & Seymour, 1991, cited in Steele, 1997). In other words, until high school, males and females have equal math ability and comparable academic achievement in math and science. But during college years and beyond, men's math and science achievement outstrips women's. Why is this?

Claude Steele (1997) suggests that stereotypes about women's logical and mathematical deficiencies undercut the ambitions and accomplishments of women in math and science fields. In other words, women feel vulnerable in those domains and, as a result, they disidentify with math and science achievement. In other words, they stop believing that math and science fields hold promise for them and that their accomplishments in those areas will be appreciated. Steve Spencer and his colleagues (1999) tested this idea by giving men and women students a math test that was described as able (or not able) to show gender differences. The women who believed their math deficiency would not be detected scored just as well as men, but the women who felt vulnerable to the stereotype about being bad at math scored much worse than men. This study demonstrates that women's poorer performance in math-related domains is due to their vulnerability to stereotypical beliefs about women; when that vulnerability is eliminated, women achieve equally to men. It also shows the power of stereotypic beliefs to generate their own fulfillment. Because women are believed to lack math ability, they are not expected to do well by teachers and peers. These negative expectations bias instructors and guidance counselors against women, lead to diminished opportunities for women to demonstrate their competence, and contribute to the general *unfriendliness* of math and science domains for women. Given those circumstances, it is not surprising that women's achievement goes down.

To sum up, school is a social context that is organized around gender categorizations (by teachers, administrators, and other students), and naturally, gender stereotypes become part of that context. Our school experiences, from elementary school through college, reflect and perpetuate the gender stereotypes. Worse, stereotypes about males' and females' academic abilities, though untrue, can *become* true through the self-fulfilling prophecy.

Media Influences on Gender Differences

As we will discover in Chapter 9, children spend almost as much time watching television as they do at school. What does TV teach them about gender differences? Men outnumber women in the TV world, and in general, men's characters have more power, independence, intelligence, and courage than female characters do; women, however, are younger and more romantically available. Men are portrayed as experts about products, whereas women are product *users*. Men are bombarded by advertisements that appeal to their strength, competitiveness, and sense of adventure, whereas women typically view ads for cleaning, home care, and personal hygiene products. Stereotypic images and messages are worse in music lyrics and videos where men appear as sexually aggressive and rational, whereas women are sexually attractive, passive, and irrational (Freudinger & Almquist, 1978).

Clearly, the media constructs images of, and messages about, women and men that perpetuate gender stereotypes. These vivid, repetitive portrayals influence our attitudes and perceptions, especially if we watch television uncritically. Viewing the social world on TV leads us to believe that males and females are much more different than they actually are, and that these gender differences are inherent, rather than natural, responses to different social roles and circumstances.

Self-Construals

There is good evidence to indicate that the socializing effects of family, school, and media on men's and women's behavior may be mediated by the self-concept (Cross &

Madsen, 1997). That is, socializing agents probably exert their influence on behavior indirectly by forming the way men and women mentally represent—or construe—themselves. Researchers have identified two general types of self-construals: independent and interdependent. Independent self-construals feature a mental representation of oneself that is separate from one's representation of others. People with independent self-construals strive to preserve their autonomy and individuality in behavior (Markus & Kitayama, 1991). Interdependent self-construals, on the other hand, feature representations of oneself that are intertwined with one's thinking about other people. People with interdependent self-construals strive for connectedness with others.

These types of self-construals map easily on to gender differences wrought by traditional social roles—women's roles promote nurturing and cooperative behavior, and men's roles promote assertiveness and independence. It is very likely, then, that women develop interdependent self-construals and men independent self-construals. These fundamental cognitive differences between men and women influence a variety of behaviors (Cross & Madsen, 1997). For example, research shows that women are more likely to attend to, and remember, information about other people in an interaction than men are (Josephs, Markus, & Tafarodi, 1992). Women's self-esteem, compared to men's, is also more dependent on interpersonal outcomes, such as the reaction of a friend, than on achievement outcomes (Hodgins, Liebeskind, & Schwartz, 1996).

Recent research explores how females' self-construals are affected by being the target of benevolent and hostile sexism. Manuela Barreto and her colleagues (2010) had female participants read an article about the nature and prevalence of either hostile or benevolent sexism in society, an exercise that essentially primed one of those two ideas in participants' minds. Participants then described themselves by rating the importance of task (e.g., academic achievement) and relational (e.g., attentive, warm) qualities to their self-concepts. The results showed that benevolent sexism caused the participants to rate relational, compared to task, characteristics as more self-descriptive. A follow-up study examined what happens when women are confronted with benevolent sexism in the workplace, where task-oriented qualities like competence and achievement often predict success and professional advancement (Barreto, Ellemers, Piebinga, & Moya, 2010). Female participants worked on a project with a computer-networked partner. In the context of the project interaction, participants learned of their partner's attitudes toward women (either benevolent sexist or nonsexist, randomly determined). As in the first study, participants' task-related self-descriptions were measured. What they showed was that having a benevolent sexist, compared to a nonsexist, work partner lowered female participants' ratings of their task-related qualities, particularly when the participants believed they had to collaborate with the partner.

In a similar study, female participants were given job descriptions to read and evaluate. The descriptions included a subtle manipulation of the company's attitudes toward women, reflecting either hostile or benevolent sexism; again, participants' assignment to the sexism conditions was random (Dumont, Sarlet, & Dardenne, 2010). Following that exercise, participants were engaged in another, ostensibly unrelated, exercise on autobiographical memory, in which they had to list memories about themselves in which they felt incompetent or less smart than others. Exposure to benevolent sexism caused participants to remember an average of 11 memories of themselves as incompetent, whereas hostile sexism prompted only about six thoughts on average. Taken together, these studies show that women's self-construals—the way they think about themselves and their abilities—are shaped by being exposed to, or being a potential target of, sexism. Benevolent sexist attitudes have predictable effects: They cause women to think of themselves more in relational, and less in competence, terms. In this way, we are reminded of the power of stereotypes in shaping one's character and conduct, as discussed in Chapter 3. These studies suggest that women who are the targets of benevolent sexism at work will unwittingly conform to the expectations of the paternalistic stereotype that underlies benevolent sexism.

Social Selection of Gender Differences

Some of the differences between men and women can also be explained in evolutionary terms. Evolutionary psychology explains behavior by noting how it perpetuates the genes of the individuals who display that behavior. In evolutionary terms, behavior patterns arise and persist because they help people successfully adapt to changing natural and social conditions, hence securing their genetic contribution to future generations. Evolutionary explanations of gender differences are particularly compelling in the areas of sexual and courtship behavior (Archer, 1996). The basic prediction of an evolutionary model of gender differences in sexual attitudes and behavior is as follows. To maximize the perpetuation of their genes, males must aggressively pursue and mate with as many females as possible. Females, however, must carefully select, and remain with, a devoted and responsible mate to maximally perpetuate her genes. These cross-purposes are at the root of gender differences in sexual behavior, and much research evidence supports this general prediction (Buss, 1995). For example, men are more accepting of casual sex, take more initiative in sexual behavior, and engage in more casual sex than do women (Hendrick, Hendrick, Slapion-Foote, & Foote, 1985; Oliver & Hyde, 1993). Across very different cultures, men tend to be attracted to women for their youth and beauty, whereas women are attracted to men for their emotional stability, income, and ambition (Buss & Schmidt, 1993).

In addition to explaining gender differences in sexual attitudes and behavior, evolutionary psychology also addresses gender differences in domains that have been, until recently, thought to be due exclusively to socialization (Archer, 1996). For example, men's lower levels of nurturance, social connectedness, and emotional expressiveness have been traditionally attributed to their social roles and training. However, this difference can also be explained by noting the evolutionary advantage for males, who are in competition with other males for furthering their genes through liberal mating and procreation, to resist displaying signs of vulnerability, weakness, and excessive emotional attachments to others.

In summary, evolutionary psychology helps temper the longstanding claim that gender differences are largely socialized. However, as John Archer (1996) explains, the present array of gender differences probably reflects both influences of the natural selection and evolution of adaptive behaviors among men and women and the presence of socializing agents. He speculates that perhaps our tribal ancestors, observing the different patterns of behavior among men and women, gradually created traditions, rites, and myths to infuse those starkly evolved differences with meaning. If so, these social and cultural traditions would have begun to have their own effects on the behavior of men and women.

Summary

Gender stereotypes exaggerate the actual differences between men and women and imply that such differences stem from internal, unchanging qualities. In other words, they contribute to—rather than break down—the notion that men and women are inherently different. Compared to males, females' stereotypical attributes and abilities are negatively evaluated, leading to a pervasive gender bias in our culture. Stereotypic beliefs, even those that are positive, about women generate their own fulfillment and result in lower educational and career opportunities for women. Finally, the gender differences that have been reliably demonstrated can be explained by citing the different socialization of men and women and by understanding those differences as evolved and genetically adaptive behavior patterns.

DI Diversity Issue 6.1: The Gender Pay Gap

The payment people receive for their work is one objective measure of the value placed by society on that work and the people who do it. Historically, men have earned more than women for equivalent work, an outcome called the **gender pay gap**. As much as we believe equality between the sexes has been achieved through the Civil Rights and Women's Liberation movements, data reveal a persistent pay gap between men and women. According to the Institute for Women's Policy Research, an organization that tracks gender wage gap data, the ratio of men's to women's median weekly income in 2010 was 80.3. In other words, in 2010, women's earnings were about 80% of men's earnings (Hegewisch, Williams, & Henderson, 2011). The wage gap is larger when looking at annual earnings: In 2009, women's income was about 77% of men's income. The gender pay gap in annual income, which was around 60% in 1960, has steadily narrowed over the past 50 years. However, the rate of growth in women's compared to men's income has slowed in recent years. Between 1980 and 1994, the gap closed by 12 percentage points, but improved only an additional 5 percentage points in from 1995 to 2010. Hilary Lips's (2003) review of the gender pay gap evaluates numerous possible artifacts (i.e., explanations other than sex) for why men earn more than women. Let's briefly consider her analysis. Is the gender pay gap in part explained by women working at part-time jobs more than men, and thus earning less? No—when just full-time workers are analyzed, men still earn about $15,000 more per year on average than women. Is the gender pay gap simply the result of women choosing different (and lower paying) careers and occupations than men? To test this idea, Lips (2003) compared what men and women are paid in jobs that are dominated by women (see Table 6.2).

It is true that jobs traditionally occupied by women pay less than jobs traditionally occupied by men, but these data show that even in *female* (stereotypically speaking) occupations, women earn less than men. There are jobs in which women earn more than men, but the pay gap, favoring females, in those occupations is tiny. For example, special education teacher is the occupation where women outearn men the most, and women earn on average only 103% of males' earnings in that field. By comparison, in occupations where men outearn women the most (e.g., management, health, and medicine), women earn about 63% of men's salaries. The large gender pay gap in traditionally male-dominated occupations (e.g., construction worker, truck driver, physician, attorney) suggests that advice to women to pursue male-dominated careers to avoid gender discrimination is misplaced. Women will earn higher salaries in those fields than in female-dominated fields, but their work will be valued less than men's work (insofar as salaries indicate value). Indeed, Lips suggests that the gender pay gap reflects the devaluation of anything done by women more than the devaluation of particular occupations. Finally, the current gender pay gap does not seem to reflect slower-than-anticipated progress toward gender equality. In 1951, women earned 64 cents for every dollar a man earned; today, over 50 years later, women are earning just 80 cents for every dollar a man makes.

Table 6.2	The Five Most Female-Dominated Occupations, the Percentage of Female Workers, and the Percentage of Males' Pay Earned by Women in Each Occupation

Occupation	Percentage of Women in Occupation	Percentage of Men's Earnings Earned by Women
Bookkeepers/accounting clerks	92	94
Registered nurses	91	88
Financial records processing	91	92
Nursing aides/orderlies	89	90
Information clerks	88	81

SOURCE: "The gender pay gap: Concrete indicator of women's progress toward equality," by H. Lips, 2003, *Analyses of Social Issues and Public Policy, 3*, pp. 87–109. Copyright 2003 by Blackwell.

Another explanation for the gender pay gap focuses on different perceptions of **income entitlement** in men and women. Brenda Major and her colleagues (1984; see also Major, 1994) have found that women feel entitled to, and are satisfied with, lower pay than men for the same work. Researchers controlled job status and other

(Continued)

(Continued)

background variables in a study of pay entitlement in over 1,500 Canadian full-time workers (Desmarais & Curtis, 2001). On average, males felt entitled to an annual salary of $37,030 for their work; females felt deserving of $24,821. When the analysis equated male and female workers on age, educational attainment, years of experience on the job, occupational status, and number of subordinates, women ($27,111) still felt entitled to less pay than men ($31,718) felt they deserved. When the previous year's income was added to the group of control factors, however, the gender difference in salary entitlement disappeared. This shows that the salary people feel entitled to for the coming year is based strongly on their previous year's salary (which tends to be lower for women than for men). When those unequal comparisons are held constant, men's and women's salary entitlements do not differ. This conclusion was also reflected in the raise men and women felt entitled to: 34% of the women compared with 27% of the men believed they deserved a raise of at least $10,000.

? What do you think would happen if women were to overtake a traditionally male-dominated field? Would salary levels and occupational status decrease because the field was now associated more with women than men? Can you think of an example where this has happened?

? Discuss some of the following explanations offered for the gender difference in salary entitlement:

- Women value money less than men (Crosby, 1982).
- Women evaluate their work differently than men (Major, McFarlin, & Gagnon, 1984).
- Women compare their pay with other women rather than men (Bylsma & Major, 1994).

DI Diversity Issue 6.2: The Glass Ceiling and the Maternal Wall

Women are underrepresented at the highest levels of professions (e.g., tenured full professors in academia, upper-level managers or vice presidents in business)—a situation that has been called the **glass ceiling**. The glass ceiling metaphor suggests that invisible factors prevent women from advancing to the highest levels of their chosen occupation, but what are those factors? Here are several. First, gender stereotypes may lead personnel officers to assume that women don't possess the traits (e.g., aggressiveness) needed to succeed in higher status jobs (Eagly & Karau, 2002). Second, the qualifications of female job applicants have been shown by Biernat and Kobrynowicz (1997) to be evaluated in the context of other women (She has good management experience, for a woman) rather than all applicants, males included. Third, men tend to evaluate other men more positively than women. For example, research shows that even when men and women have done equally well on a task, women are held to a higher standard, and thus given lower evaluations than men (Foschi, 1996). Fourth, when men and women do equally well on a masculine task (e.g., a logic problem), men are seen as skillful and women as lucky (Deaux & Emswiller, 1974). Finally, compared with views of women in general, *professional women* as a subgroup are seen as more competent but less warm and likable. In terms of stereotype content, then, professional women are similar to rich people, Asians, and Jews—respected but resented (Fiske, Cuddy, Glick, & Xu, 2002). So, women face evaluative biases, especially in male-dominated organizations that help stall their upward occupational mobility.

Another set of factors that helps explain the glass ceiling effect is what happens in the workplace when women become mothers. Pregnancy and motherhood are associated with negative stereotypes and assumptions of questionable competence (Halpert, Wilson, & Hickman, 1993). Jane Halpert and her colleagues (1993) found that a female employee's work was evaluated more negatively when she was pregnant than when she was not pregnant, and this bias was greatest among male evaluators. When new mothers return to work, they face new stereotypic assumptions from their coworkers. In terms of the stereotype-content dimensions discussed in the Chapter 5, *businesswomen* or *careerwomen* tend to be seen as high in competence and low to moderate in warmth. Stereotypes of *working mothers* are low in competence and high in warmth. In other words, working moms are liked but not respected (Cuddy, Fiske, & Glick, 2004). Other groups that are similarly stereotyped include the elderly, the physically and mentally disabled, and housewives (Fiske et al., 2002). Amy Cuddy and her colleagues (2004) show that the loss of presumed competence in others' eyes is detrimental to workplace evaluations—participants in their studies are less willing to hire and promote working moms than childless women—and this discrimination is not offset by the extra warmth and likeability attributed to working moms. The collective impact of negative stereotyping and behavior toward working mothers on their occupational achievement is called the **maternal wall** (Williams, 2004). According to Joan Williams (2004), the stereotype associated with working mothers can have direct and indirect negative effects on performance evaluations. Assumptions of questionable competence and professional commitment can directly shape supervisors' views of working mothers' work. Anecdotal evidence also suggests that supervisors assume that out-of-office time is being spent on family responsibilities rather than working, which leads to a judgment that working mothers don't work as hard as childless women. Finally, working moms must work harder to overcome their supervisors' stereotypic assumptions about their competence and commitment, and this extra burden—not faced by childless women—may also help account for the glass ceiling effect.

? Do you think there is a *paternal wall*? Do new fathers face negative stereotypes in the workplace that interfere with their career achievement?

? Why or why not? Is it possible that men's careers *benefit* from fatherhood? Discuss.

? Are there other subgroups of women in the workplace who face negative stereotypes and obstacles to their occupational advancement? Discuss your thoughts or experiences.

DI Diversity Issue 6.3: Title IX and College Athletics

Title IX refers to a law enacted in 1972 that requires **gender equity** in all educational programs that receive federal funding. One of Title IX's more noteworthy effects was to reshape high school and college athletic opportunities and participation for women. Prior to Title IX, athletic opportunities for high school girls consisted of cheerleading and square dancing (http://www.titleix.info/10-Key-Areas-of-Title-IX/Athletics.aspx). Today, far more opportunities exist for female athletes in high school and college. Despite this progress, many believe that gender equity in athletics has not been achieved. For example, according to www.titleix.info, although women constitute 57% of the college population, only 37% of all money spent on athletics goes to women's athletics. An investigation into compliance with Title IX by the *New York Times* found evidence that colleges are using subterfuge to maintain an image of equity and not addressing actual inequities (Thomas, 2011). For example, some colleges exploit a loophole in the law that allows schools to count practice players, regardless of their gender, as team participants. This has led to the practice of allowing males to practice with female team members, and those males are counted under Title IX as females. Another tactic that schools use to boost the reported participation of females in team sports is to allow females to practice with the team, showing up (or not) as they like, with full knowledge that they lack to skill to make the team and compete. For example, in the 2009-2010 school year, the University of South Florida reported that their women's cross country team had 71 members (while the men's team had nine), but the number of female runners who actually ran races in meets was 28. Who were the others? They were runners who were allowed to show up at practices and run for fitness, but were not official team members.

To read Thomas's full article, and others of a series of investigative reports on gender equity (or lack thereof) in college athletics, go to: http://topics.nytimes.com/top/news/sports/series/gender_games/index.html?scp=1&sq=title%20ix&st=cse

? How is your school doing in complying with Title IX?

? What other areas of Title IX interest you? Pick one area, and learn if the ideals of Title IX have been achieved, or if not, why not?

KEY TERMS

FOR FURTHER READING

Glick, P., & Fiske, S. (2001). An ambivalent alliance: Hostile and benevolent sexism as complementary justifications for gender inequality. *American Psychologist, 56,* 109–118. doi: 10.1037/0003-066X.56.2.109

This is a short and engaging overview of research on ambivalent stereotypes of women and their relation to the discrimination of women; it is a fine article to read and discuss. The article also includes the Ambivalent Sexism Inventory, so you can assess your own hostile and benevolent sexism or just look at the test items to learn about the two types of sexism.

Cheung, F., & Halpern, D. (2010). Women at the top: Powerful leader define success as work + family in a culture of gender. *American Psychologist, 65,* 182–193. doi: 10.1037/a0017309

How do women leaders excel in their professions and manage family responsibilities at the same time? In this article, Cheung and Halpern present a model of leadership that emerges from their conversations with women executives that contrasts with traditional notions of leadership based on Western men.

Online Resources

Women's Media: Expert Advice for Working Women

http://www.womensmedia.com/new/Lips-Hilary-gender-wage-gap.shtml

Dr. Hilary Lips, the Director of the Center for Gender Studies at Radford University and the author of the article on the gender pay gap discussed in Diversity Issue 6.1, has a website that reviews and illustrates the findings from her study. It is worth visiting.

Institute for Women's Policy Research

http://www.iwpr.org/

This site has reports on policy issues that affect women. Reports on the gender pay gap can be found under Publications.

Title IX

http://www.titleix.info/

Under Ten Key Areas of Title IX on the home page, this site describes what Title IX was supposed to address, how gender equity has improved, and what work still needs to be done in that area to achieve gender equity.

Gender Stereotypes in Televised Sports

http://www.aafla.org/9arr/ResearchReports/ResearchReport2.htm

This article reports ways in which TV sports coverage reflects gender stereotypes.

Glass Ceiling Resource Center

http://www.glassceiling.com/

This site organizes news and podcasts on glass ceiling-related findings and reports.

7

Understanding Obesity Stereotypes and Weightism

Recall what we learned about social categories and categorizations in Chapter 2: The most useful categories are those that have clear criteria and nonoverlapping boundaries. Primary categorizations—identifying someone's race, sex, or age—are largely based on identifiable physical characteristics. Further, categorizing a person as male or female and, to an extent, young or old draws on aspects of body size and stature. That is, females tend to have differently shaped bodies than males; likewise, elderly people lose height and weight as they age. In short, body size is a visible aspect of human diversity that aids in primary categorization. In this chapter, we continue our study of the stereotypes and prejudice against members of specific groups to consider weight-based stereotyping and prejudice.

Before we turn to how obese people are stereotyped and discriminated and how they cope with this prejudice, we must have a brief lesson on how obesity is defined. The term *obese* refers to a specific population of people whose body mass index is 30 or greater (Centers for Disease Control, 2012). Body mass index is a measure of weight that is corrected for height and is the sole criterion for defining obesity. A body mass index of 30 is equivalent to a 5′4″ woman who weighs 175 pounds or a 5′10″, 205 pound man. These don't seem like morbidly large people, do they? By this body mass index criterion, about 30% of American adults and 11% of children are obese (Centers for Disease Control, 2012). Much of the public concern and news coverage of obesity in recent years has emphasized the *epidemic* nature of obesity. We need to think critically about this media message because it may indirectly contribute to prejudice against obese people. If epidemic means *widespread*, or affecting a large number of people, then yes, obesity is epidemic. If epidemic means *rapid spread*—which is implied in most news reports of obesity rates—then obesity is not epidemic, at least among typical people. Americans have been getting steadily heavier in the past 15 years at a modest rate of about half a pound per year. These small, cumulative weight gains have recently pushed a large group of overweight Americans just over the threshold dividing the obese from the merely overweight. So, although 30% of adults were technically obese in 2005, compared with 23% in 1991, that does not mean people suddenly gained a lot of weight. Research only shows dramatic weight increase among the heaviest Americans. In that relatively small group of adults, people are 25 to 30 pounds heavier today then they were in 1991.

It is important to distinguish between the clinical definition of obesity and its cultural meanings. Many millions of people are technically obese but healthy, whereas a small proportion of the obese population is morbidly fat and, as a result, has serious mobility problems and life-threatening health concerns. Nevertheless, these cases color what is believed about all people in this social category. Likewise, media coverage of obesity and its associated social issues draws disproportionately from the most extreme cases, and these stories help define the cultural stereotype for obese people. Before we learn about obesity stereotypes and stereotyping, a brief note on terminology is in order. In this chapter, we will use the term *obese* broadly, to refer to people who are significantly overweight (without regard to their body mass index or clinical classification) and are categorized by others, or self-categorized, into a negatively stereotyped social category. This is important because some people *feel* fat, and even though they may not be technically obese, they are nevertheless sensitive to obesity stereotypes.

Obesity Stereotypes

Weight-based categorizations and stereotyping go back to the classic work of Sheldon and his colleagues (1940), who posited three main body types, each associated with different personality characteristics. Endomorphic body shapes, which we now call plump or overweight, were believed to be associated with complacency and the love of physical comforts. Mesomorphic, or muscular, body types were associated with traits such as aggressiveness and love of adventure. Finally, ectomorphic, or thin, individuals were believed to be restrained and socially inhibited. A recent test of these stereotypic associations had participants look at silhouette drawings of each body type and rate them on a series of personality traits (Butler, Ryckman, Thornton, & Bouchard, 1993). Butler and his colleagues found that endomorphic (plump) body shapes were viewed most negatively. In that study, the traits more frequently associated with plump body types were introverted, insecure, and lazy.

Much research has established that obese individuals face very negative stereotypes about their abilities and character, including the beliefs that they are lazy, self-indulgent, unattractive, asexual, unhappy, lacking in self-esteem, socially inept, uncooperative, and intellectually slow (Allon, 1982; DeJong, 1993; Harris, 1990; Hebl & Heatherton, 1998; Madey & Ondrus, 1999). For example, Hiller (1981) had students write stories about hypothetical targets who were obese or thin. The results showed that students were more likely to write sad or negative stories about the obese targets and to characterize them as more unpleasant than the thin target. In another study examining the stereotypes of overweight people, participants rated overweight individuals as less active, attractive, intelligent, hardworking, popular, successful, and outgoing than normalweight persons (Harris, Harris, & Bochner, 1982). Other researchers placed personal ads in two metropolitan newspapers: One indicated that the woman who advertised was 50 pounds overweight; the other indicated that she had a history of substance addiction (Sitton & Blanchard, 1995). Fewer men responded to the ad for the overweight woman, suggesting that obesity is perceived as less desirable in a prospective date than substance abuse.

Obese stereotypes, like racial and gender stereotypes, operate at both automatic and controlled levels. Gayle Bessenoff and Jeff Sherman (2000) presented participants with pictures of thin and obese women flashed on a computer screen for less than one tenth of a second. Participants then made *word* or *nonword* judgments on a series of positive and negative traits or nonwords. Participants were faster in recognizing negative trait words when the words were preceded by the picture of an obese than a thin woman. In other words, images of obese people, even when presented for a fraction of a second, are linked in our minds with negative traits. This research made two other discoveries. First, automatic, or unconscious and uncontrollable, stereotyping of obese people was generally not related to participants' self-reports of attitudes toward obese people. This means that people try to display less negative attitudes than they actually hold toward the obese. Second, the more automatic (but not the more self-reported) prejudice participants had, the more they distanced themselves from an obese person in a subsequent interaction.

The Role of Weight Controllability in the Obese Stereotype

Stereotypic beliefs that obese people are lazy and gluttonous reflect a broader cultural belief that weight is controllable. The traditional reasoning goes like this: People can control their weight, so fat people must be doing something that makes them fat, like not exercising (lazy) or overeating (gluttonous). Therefore, fat people are to blame for their plight. Research by Christian Crandall has shown that attitudes and feelings toward obese people are grounded in traditional American values of personal responsibility, individualism, and self-discipline (Crandall, 1994). For example, people who hold negative attitudes toward obese people also tend to be socially and politically conservative: They endorse racist attitudes, support capital punishment, and espouse traditional sexual values (Crandall & Biernat, 1990). Perceptions that obese people are responsible for their weight moderates others' views of them. Participants in one study were given the opportunity to administer electric shocks (under the pretext of sending a message) to an obese person whose obesity was described as either controllable or uncontrollable (Vann, 1976). Longer shocks were given to the obese person who was believed to be responsible for his or her weight. Participants in another study gave more favorable ratings to an obese job applicant when his obesity was linked to a *hormonal imbalance* than when it was believed to be behaviorally caused (Rodin, Price, Sanchez, & McElligot, 1989). Finally, Crandall (1994) conducted an experiment in which participants heard either a persuasive message about the uncontrollability of weight or a non-weight-related control message, followed by a measure of attitudes toward obese persons. Relative to the control group, participants exposed to the "weight is uncontrollable" message liked overweight people more and viewed them as having more willpower. Therefore, beliefs about the nature of weight, specifically, how controllable it is, figure prominently in people's evaluation of and behavior toward obese individuals.

It is important to clarify that it is the *perceived* controllability of weight that shapes our views of obese people and our treatment of them. In *actual* terms, however, weight is far less controllable than we believe. Genetic influences on your body size and basic metabolic rate suggest that weight is not very controllable (Feitosa et al., 2000). Some people can overeat and not gain weight, whereas others cannot lose weight regardless of what they eat or do—these tendencies seem to be largely inherited. Additionally, dieting and weight loss programs are notoriously ineffective; over 90% of people who lose weight on a diet gain all or most of the weight back within a year (Jeffery, Epstein, & Wilson, 2000). If weight was controllable, then people should be able to lose weight effectively and at will, but permanent weight loss is rare. Such evidence tends to have little impact on the widespread belief that weight is controllable, and as a result, overweight people tend to be blamed for their own plight.

In recent years, the stereotype of obese people has increasingly included the notion that obese people are unhealthy. The growing prevalence of obesity in the United States, both in adults and children, and the health risks associated with obesity (e.g., Type II diabetes, heart disease, high blood pressure, stroke) have pushed obesity to the fore as a public and national health concern (Ernsberger & Koletsky, 1999). The belief that obese people are unhealthy is another negative aspect of an already negative and deeply discrediting stereotype, because it too assumes that obesity *causes* illness and thus the health problems associated with obesity are largely deserved. As with the physiology of weight, however, the obesity stereotype seriously misunderstands the relationship between obesity and health in two ways. First, there is no question that obese people have more health problems than thin people. However, with the exception of the obesity–Type II diabetes link, there is little solid evidence to show that obesity causes health problems such as heart disease and stroke (Ernsberger & Koletsky, 1999). What is more likely is that particular lifestyle factors (e.g., little exercise, high-fat diet, stress) cause both obesity and poor health outcomes. Second, exercise reduces the health risks associated with obesity even when no weight loss occurs. In other words, obese people who exercise improve their health prospects similar to what occurs with thin people, suggesting that it is fitness level, more than weight, that determines how healthy a person is.

> **?**
>
> Why is the perceived controllability of weight crucial in understanding prejudice against obese people? What other groups of people are thought to be responsible for their own disadvantage? How does the belief that, for example, poor people are poor because they don't work hard enough affect your attitudes toward them?

Obesity Stereotypes Depend on the Ethnicity of the Perceiver and the Target

Definitions of beauty and normative appearance standards vary by culture. Accordingly, attitudes toward obese people depend on the ethnicity of both the perceiver and the target. Michelle Hebl and Todd Heatherton (1998) had Black and White women rate photographs of women that varied in weight. The photographs were rated on attractiveness, intelligence, happiness, and other personality traits. Black participants only distinguished between thin and heavy targets on attractiveness (with thinner being regarded as more attractive). White participants, on the other hand, rated heavy women, especially White women, as less attractive, intelligent, successful, and happy than thin women. In another study, White participants scored higher than ethnic minority participants on a general measure of prejudice toward fat people, even after controlling for the participants' weight, age, and family income (Blaine, DiBlasi, & Connor, 2002). Michelle Hebl and her colleagues (2009) had Black and White female participants evaluate photos of Black and White target individuals that had been selected and photo engineered to vary in weight but be equivalent in other respects such as attractiveness. The findings revealed that White participants rated thin targets more positively than thin targets, but Black participants did not discriminate based on weight. Perhaps not surprisingly, the study found that Black participants were much less likely to value the importance of thinness compared with White participants. Among Black participants, the less value they placed on thinness, the more positively they viewed the heavy target individuals; this relationship did not occur among White participants.

Other research shows that Black and White women differ in the weight they define as overweight and at which they become dissatisfied with their own bodies. In a sample of 389 adult women, researchers found no differences among White, Black, and Hispanic participants in their body image discrepancy (the difference between their actual and ideal weights); all women, regardless of their ethnicity, wanted to weigh less than they did. However, White women reported body image dissatisfaction at a significantly lower weight—and at a weight that, technically speaking, wasn't even overweight—than did Black or Hispanic women (Fitzgibbon, Blackman, & Avellone, 2000). In sum, White women are subject to more pressure to be thin than women of other ethnic groups, and White women also hold negative stereotypic beliefs about obese women.

Weightism: Weight-Based Prejudice and Discrimination

Stereotypically, obesity combines beliefs about people with physical disabilities (e.g., unattractiveness, mobility problems, beliefs about dependence and inactivity) with the character flaws associated with other *controllable* behavioral deviations (e.g., alcoholism, homosexual orientation). In this way, obese people are the targets of two converging streams of stereotyping and prejudice. Because there are both physical/appearance and characterological aspects of obesity stereotypes, obese people are targets of widespread discrimination. Prejudice and discrimination against people because of their large size or extreme weight is called **weightism**. Weightism, or more specifically, weight-based discrimination, is a growing problem.

Weightism at School

Bias against obese students begins early in the educational process—antiobesity feelings and attitudes are present even in preschool children—and is expressed by classmates, teachers, admissions officers, and even parents. Children exhibit negative stereotypes and attitudes toward their heavy classmates, and the social rejection of obese students in school is common (Latner & Stunkard, 2003). In a classic study of weightism among school children, 600 students ranked pictures of children with various disabilities and physical traits by whom they would most like as a friend (Richardson, Goodman, Hastorf, & Dornbusch, 1961). Most students ranked the obese child last, as less desirable than an amputee, a student on crutches, a wheelchair-bound student, or someone with a disfigured face. Notice that none of these physical disabilities would be assumed to be the person's fault, as obesity is. Perceived controllability explains why physically disabled people (who did not cause their disability) provoke both negative feelings (e.g., tension, avoidance) and positive feelings (e.g., sympathy, pity) in others, whereas obesity prompts blame, hostility, and rejection (Weiner, Perry, & Magnuson, 1988).

In short, obese children are held in the lowest regard by their peers, and disliking for obese school children has not improved in the 50 years since that study. Other research shows that in addition to disliking obese students, grade school children believe that weight is controllable, and thus their obese classmates are more or less deserving of insults and rejection (Tiggemann & Anesbury, 2000). Weightism is directed more at girls than boys, and one study found that 96% of a sample of teenage girls who were overweight reported experiencing teasing, jokes, and mean names from peers at school (Neumark-Sztainer, Story, & Faibisch, 1998). Recent large-sample surveys of adolescents show that teasing, threats, and harassment of students because of their weight is commonplace, reflecting the lack of social constraints and prohibitions against weightism that curb other expressions of bias (e.g., racism). A high percentage of high school students report witnessing their heavy peers being avoided, ignored, or excluded from activities (Puhl, Luedicke, & Heuer, 2011). The victims of others' weightism are more often female than male, and feeling depressed and angry are common reactions to being a target of weight-based prejudice (Puhl & Luedicke, 2012).

Weightism also surfaces in the evaluation of high school students for college. One early study of over 2,000 students who applied for college found that obese students—females in particular—were less likely to be accepted to college than were thin applicants despite having comparable qualifications (Canning & Meyer, 1966). In more recent research, Robert Crosnoe analyzed data from the National Longitudinal Study of Adolescent Health and found that girls who were obese in high school were significantly less likely to attend college, but this relationship did not occur in boys (Crosnoe, 2007). Interestingly, obese girls were less likely to go to college if the rates of female obesity were low at their college of choice. This suggests that girls, but not boys, feel more obesity-related stigma. Further analysis showed that girls, much more than boys, internalize negative obesity stereotypes, engage in substance abuse, and disengage from academic pursuits. Together, these behaviors account for a good portion of the gap in college enrollment rates between obese females and males. Once in college, Christian Crandall (1991, 1995) found that compared with normalweight students, overweight and obese college students received less financial support for college from their parents. Once again, daughters were more likely to be discriminated against by their parents than sons, and in some of Crandall's studies, the antifat bias was observed only in daughters. This pattern of discrimination existed even after controlling for the parents' education level, income, and the number of children in the family who were attending college.

Weightism at Work

Obese people are subject to as much negative stereotypes in the workplace as they are in general. Because obese people as a group are believed to be lazy and undisciplined, the competence and skill of obese workers come under suspicion in the workplace. Weight-based discrimination in the workplace starts at the point of screening and interviewing applicants for employment. In a fascinating field experiment of weightism in hiring processes, researchers submitted application materials for actual job openings (Agerstrom & Rooth, 2011). The materials were matched in every respect except for the weight of the applicant, which was experimentally manipulated by a photograph. The outcome measure was whether the *applicant* received an interview invitation from the employer. Later, the employment managers who were sent the applications took the Implicit Association Test to measure implicit antifat prejudice. The findings of the study showed a strong bias against interviewing obese, relative to normalweight, job applicants. Moreover, this bias was best predicted by the employment managers' automatic, but not self-reported, weight-based prejudice. So, weightism at work probably begins with hiring practices that discriminate against overweight and obese applicants. The fact that these practices may be linked only to implicit, and not explicit, prejudice means that the bias is subtle and difficult to detect.

According to one review of studies about employees' perceptions of obese workers, obese workers are regarded as lazy, incompetent, unstable, and lacking self-discipline (Roehling, 1999). According to Patricia Roehling (1999), overweight and obese workers face discrimination at work for several reasons, including the perception among other employees that overweight people don't project the proper image, are viewed to be responsible for their weight, and will cost the organization more in terms of absenteeism and health care costs. Not surprisingly, obese employees tend to be paid less than thin employees, perhaps as much as 10% to 12% less, even when working at the same job (Loh, 1993). The economic cost of obesity is higher among female than male employees, and this reflects the fact that normative standards of weight and appearance are applied more to women than men. In 1992, obese women's net worth was about 40% less than comparable thin women, and these comparisons controlled for the women's health and other factors that could affect earning power. In 1998, the situation was worse: Obese women's economic worth and earning power were about 60% less than their thin counterpart (Institute for Social Research, 2000). Researchers isolated the wage penalty associated with being overweight and obese in a survey of over 12,000 Americans and found that, among men, overweight and obese employees earned between 1% and 3% less than their ideal-weight counterparts, controlling for background variables (Baum & Ford, 2004). The wage penalty was twice that size among women, illustrating the layering of sexism upon weightism in the workplace. The tendency for obese employees, particularly women, to be paid less than thin employees does not mean that their managers and supervisors are prejudiced. Rather, the obesity pay gap may reflect an accumulation of disadvantage in the form of subtle weightism experienced at home and throughout one's education. College students who have been neglected, discriminated against, or expected to underachieve at school do not enter the working world on the same footing as comparable thin students. Not surprisingly, obese people are also more likely to be passed over for promotions than thin employees (Register & Williams, 1990).

Another comprehensive review of workplace weightism concludes that obese workers were less likely to be promoted than their thin coworkers, despite having comparable qualifications and experience (Puhl & Heuer, 2009). Large national survey studies show that overweight and obese individuals were between 12 and 37 times more likely than ideal-weight individuals to report discrimination at work (Roehling, Roehling, & Pichler, 2007). In one study, participants who worked as supervisors evaluated several hypothetical candidates for promotion, each with a particular disability or health issue (e.g., obesity, diabetes, poor vision, depression). The supervisors evaluated the obese and depressed employees more negatively than the nondisabled employee. Moreover, supervisors' promotion recommendations for the workers were negatively correlated with the blame they attributed to each (Bordieri, Drehmer, & Taylor, 1997). This research once more illustrates the key role played by the perceived controllability of weight in others' treatment of obese persons.

A bias against promoting overweight and obese employees suggests that there should be very few obese chief executive officers (CEOs) and corporate executives. Patricia Roehling and her colleagues examined this issue by obtaining photographs of CEOs of Fortune 100 companies and having independent observers categorize them as normalweight, overweight, or obese (Roehling, Roehling, Vandlen, Blazek, & Guy, 2009). Based on their sample, they estimate that between 5% and 22% of all female, and between 45% and 61% of all male, CEOs are overweight. Given that about 67% of American adults are overweight, these data reflect far more weightism applied to women than to men. Their analysis, however, found that only about 5% of all CEOs were obese—compared to a population prevalence of about 33%—and this did not vary by gender. Even among the highly competent and compensated ranks of corporate executives, weightism limits opportunity, and this discrimination is applied more to female than to male executives.

Weightism in the Health Care System

According to a literature review by Rebecca Puhl and Chelsea Heuer (2009), many studies document more negative evaluations of obese compared with thin persons among all kinds of health care professionals, including physicians, nurses, medical students, and dietitians. This research evidence even includes experimental studies, where the causal effect of patient weight on health care attitudes and outcomes can be demonstrated. One study measured the implicit, or automatic, attitudes toward hypothetical obese and thin patients in 400 professionals (e.g., physicians, clinical psychologists) attending an obesity conference (Schwartz, Chambliss, Brownell, Blair, & Billington, 2003). These professionals exhibited both antifat (associating fat with negative words) and prothin (associating thin with positive word) biases. These physicians and mental health professionals—who, amazingly, had professional interests in obesity—endorsed the stereotype of obese people as being lazy, stupid, and worthless.

A similar study tested a sample of physicians, nutritionists, and pharmacists who also worked in positions involving obesity care and treatment (Teachman & Brownell, 2001). These professionals also displayed strong antiobese bias in their automatic attitudes but their self-reported attitudes reflected a pro-thin bias. Physicians in another survey were more likely to recommend weight loss treatment for female than for male patients with the same weight, suggesting that weightism is expressed more to women than to men (Anderson et al., 2001). Finally, surveys of nurses show no less stereotyping than one would expect from the general public. For example, in one study about 65% of the nurses surveyed believed that obesity can be prevented through self-control, and a majority believed obese people should be put on a diet when in the hospital (Maroney & Golub, 1992).

Prejudiced doctors and nurses directly affect the quality of health information and care available to obese persons. For example, weight management treatment options for overweight and obese patients are undermined by beliefs among medical professionals that the treatments are not effective or by higher than recommended weight-loss goals being set for obese patients (Thuan & Avignon, 2005). Two other forms of weightism indirectly influence the health care of obese people. First, some evidence indicates that obese people are denied health benefits because of their weight, must pay more than thinner people pay for the same coverage, or are fired because of their weight or their failure to lose weight (Rothblum, Brand, Miller, & Oetjen, 1990). This discrimination reveals stereotypic but largely erroneous beliefs that obese individuals are unhealthy and thus more likely to need health care services from employers than thin workers. Second, the subtle stereotypes and negative reactions obese people confront in their physicians and nurses lead many obese people to avoid or delay treatment, and this may occur more in obese women than men and more for some types of procedure (e.g., pelvic exams) than others (see Puhl & Heuer, 2009). Avoiding treatment, either because of the desire to avoid weightism at the doctor's office or to avoid unpleasant focus upon one's body, contributes indirectly to health problems among the obese.

Finally, does the experience of being a target of weight-based discrimination have negative effects on health, independent of physiological influences of obesity on health? Markus Schafer and Kenneth Ferraro (2011) tested this question in data from the National Survey of Midlife Development in the United States. They measured perceived weight discrimination at Time 1, along with a host of health status indicators. At Time 2 (10 years later), they measured health and disability. The point of the study was to see if perceived weightism could predict future decrements in health and disability at Time 2 when controlling for demographic and background variables, including one's health status at Time 1. The results showed that among both the overweight and obese, those who reported being targets of weight-based discrimination at Time 1, compared with those who did not, were much more likely to have decrements in health outcomes and disability 10 years later.

Weightism on Television

Rebecca Puhl and Chelsea Heuer (2009) reviewed the research on the visibility and representations of overweight and obese people on television, including entertainment, news, and advertising programming, and came to the following conclusions. First, overweight and obese characters are a very small minority in the television world, whereas they constitute two thirds of the real world population. Underrepresentation of overweight and obese characters is greater for females than males. When overweight characters appear on the screen, they also tend to play minor roles and be shown engaging in stereotypic behavior (Greenberg, Eastin, Hofshire, Lachlan, & Brownell, 2003). Second, obesity is deeply stigmatized on television; overweight and obese people are targets of others' antifat prejudice and discrimination. In one study, researchers coded the weight of female cast members in prime-time situation comedies from October 1996 and then examined the comments made to, and about, female cast members (Fouts & Burggraf, 1999, 2000). They found that the frequency of negative comments increased with the woman's weight, and 80% of these comments were followed by audience laughter. The same negative on-screen treatment has been observed against overweight and obese male characters, and that study also found that the male characters frequently made self-derogatory comments about their own weight or size, which prompted audience laughter (Fouts & Vaughan, 2002). Negative portrayals of overweight and obese characters exist in children's television programming too. Overweight characters tend to be shown as unattractive, unhappy, and engaged in eating and antisocial behaviors (Klein & Shiffman, 2005; Robinson, Callister, & Jankoski, 2008). Third, the negative and stigmatizing portrayals of overweight and obese characters on television affect viewers' attitudes. Particularly among children, research shows that viewing negative portrayals of overweight people shapes their own attitudes and feelings about overweight people (Harrison, 2000).

Chelsea Heuer and her colleagues (2011) analyzed the content of online news stories about obesity, and photographs accompanying the stories, for evidence of weightism. Perhaps not surprisingly, the majority of photographs accompanying news stories on obesity show overweight or obese people. However, those people are not portrayed in the same way as normalweight people shown in obesity news stories. Overweight, compared with normalweight, photographs were more likely to show the person's body, to be less clothed, and to be shown eating or drinking; they were also less likely to be portrayed as professional people or exercising (Heuer, McClure, & Puhl, 2011).

To summarize, discrimination against obese people begins in the early school years and occurs in many areas of life. Negative treatment of obese people may be justified, in the perceiver's mind, by the belief that obese people are fat by choice— through overeating and/or laziness—and thus the negative treatment is deserved. From the obese person's perspective, the accumulation of negative stereotyping, prejudice, and discrimination received takes a toll on their psychological well-being.

The Psychological and Social Consequences of Obesity

Weightism results in poorer psychological adjustment of obese compared with thin people, and much research attests that obese people have greater rates of depression than thin people (Friedman & Brownell, 1995). Obese people also have lower self-esteem, greater loneliness, and more personal dissatisfaction than thin people (Allon, 1982; Maddox, Back, & Liederman, 1968; Miller & Downey, 1999). Obese people evoke feelings of disgust, contempt, fear, and hostility in others, and these reactions interfere with normal social relations with them. In stereotypic beliefs that too easily become self-fulfilling prophecies, people regard obese individuals as too awkward, physically limited, or unattractive to participate fully in many social activities (Allon, 1982).

Chapters 10 and 11 will consider at length the topic of social stigma, or the experience of prejudice. For now, let's consider stigma as it applies to obese persons: How do obese individuals cope with weightism? Three concerns arise for obese people in their efforts to cope with others' stereotyping and prejudice. First, because others assume weight is controllable, obese people must deal with others blaming them for their own condition, whether that condition is loneliness, sickness, unemployability, or some other undesirable outcome. Second, because of the highly visible nature of obesity, obese people must manage the impact of their weight on interactions with others. Finally, as discussed earlier, weightism combines negative reactions based on obesity as a physical disability (e.g., slow moving, not athletic) with those based on obesity as a disorder of character (e.g., lazy, irresponsible, undisciplined). Given these underlying dimensions of obesity prejudice, several avenues of coping are open to overweight individuals.

Attributing Negative Outcomes to Prejudice

For Blacks, women, and most other members of negatively stereotyped groups who are not perceived as responsible for their minority status, attributing the discrimination they experience to others' prejudice helps protect against the sting of prejudice (Crocker & Major, 1989). Obese people, by contrast, face the assumption that they are responsible for their obesity, and hence their minority group status. Worse, obese people often internalize this belief—as the self-fulfilling prophecy predicts—and see themselves as at least somewhat deserving of others' negative treatment of them. As a result, obese people may not be able to attribute negative outcomes to prejudice as effectively as other minority group members. In an early demonstration of this, researchers asked obese and normalweight participants to express why they felt a confederate had behaved in a nasty manner toward them during an interaction (Rodin & Slochower, 1974). Whereas normalweight participants did not respond with any single explanation for the confederate's behavior, overweight participants overwhelmingly attributed the nasty behavior to their overweight condition. The authors posit that overweight individuals consistently use their weight to explain negative behavior toward them. More recently, Jennifer Crocker and her colleagues examined explanations made by obese women for their rejection for a date by a male peer (Crocker, Cornwell, & Major, 1993). The obese participants attributed the rejection almost solely to their weight and were unable to see the negative evaluation as reflecting poorly on the evaluator or to view him as prejudiced. Instead, they internalized the negative attitudes toward weight they perceived from their evaluator, resulting in increased depression and decreased self-esteem.

These studies suggest that for obese people attributing negative feedback to an evaluator's prejudice does not help them cope with weightism. Recall that obesity is assumed to be a controllable condition; because obese individuals themselves tend to agree with that assumption, they tend to see others' negative treatment of them as just and deserved. To examine the influence of belief in the controllability of overweight on reactions to negative experience, researchers had obese and normalweight women participate in a study they thought was about *dating relationships* (Amato & Crocker 1995). As a basis for forming initial impressions of each other as possible dating partners, they exchanged personal information with a (fictional) male in the next room. While the participants waited for their partner's response, they read a *surgeon general's* report on obesity. For half of the participants, the report characterized weight as controllable; for the other half, the report described the uncontrollable nature of weight. After this, the participants received either a negative ("I wouldn't be interested in dating you") or positive ("I would like to go out with you") response from the male partner. The results indicated that, more than any other group, overweight women who were led to believe that weight is uncontrollable attributed their rejection from a male to his obesity prejudice. In turn, these attributions protected their self-esteem from the threat of being turned down by a prospective dating partner. This research suggests that attributing negative outcomes to others' prejudice can be an effective strategy for coping with others' negative treatment but only when obese people reject the stereotypic belief that they are responsible for their own plight.

Devaluing Negative Outcome Dimensions

Devaluing a particular trait or ability on which obese people fare poorly is another strategy for coping with weightism. **Devaluing** involves strategically de-emphasizing the importance of a domain to one's self-concept and is often complemented by a corresponding selective valuing of an alternative domain on which one is likely to succeed (Miller & Myers, 1998). Obese individuals may devalue traits such as thinness or physical attractiveness, placing a higher value instead on areas where appearance is less important or irrelevant, such as intelligence or having a particular skill. Hebl and Heatherton (1998) found that obese Black women often devalue mainstream White ideals, including the importance placed on thinness for women. Devaluing has been shown to protect the identity and self-esteem of members of many negatively stereotyped groups, including obese persons (Crocker & Major, 1989; Schmader, Major, & Gramzow, 2001).

The psychological tactic of devaluing can be done with one's goals too. When a goal seems unlikely to be achieved because of stereotypic bias and discrimination based on one's weight, obese people may shift to an alternative goal that is perceived to be more attainable. For many adolescents, for example, peer group inclusion and popularity are a valued goal. Obese adolescents, however, may perceive popularity as unattainable and be forced to find alternative goals (Miller & Myers, 1998). Often, to rationalize the abandonment of the initial goal, that goal will become selectively devalued by the individual, simultaneously making the failure to reach it less devastating and the new, replacement goal more enticing.

Strategic Self-Presentation

Obese people may also cope with others' stereotyping and prejudice toward them through presenting themselves to, and interacting with, others in strategic ways. One such strategy is termed *heading off* (Miller & Myers, 1998). Heading off involves offering a verbal or nonverbal signal of friendliness at the first sign that another person may be engaging in weightism. For example, an overweight person may use humor, witty comebacks, or graciousness to set a positive tone for the interaction and thereby preempt insensitive comments from prejudiced others or uncomfortable focus on their weight. A similar strategy involves obese people compensating for the effect of others' stereotypes when interacting with them. Carol Miller and her colleagues (1995) had obese women engage in a phone conversation with a male partner who, one half of the participants were told, could see her; the other participants believed the partner could not see her. After the conversation, the telephone partners rated the obese women who thought they were visible as more socially skilled than the obese women who believed they were not visible. These results suggest that the women who believed their partner could see them had to deal with his potential stereotypes and prejudice against her because of her weight. Therefore, those participants compensated for their partner's assumed weightism by demonstrating finer social skills such as better conversational skills, more wit and humor, and more expressed interest in one's partner. In another example of compensating for weightism, researchers found that obese people display counter-stereotypical traits and behaviors to show others that they cannot be reduced to a stereotype and perhaps in an effort to actively change others' assumptions about what obese people are like (Myers & Rosen, 1999). This strategy has been shown to increase self-esteem among obese people. Compensating for others' prejudice is an attempt to regain some control over social interactions and opportunities that are constrained and limited by weightism.

Summary

Obese people—that is people who are categorized by others or categorize themselves based on their heavy weight or large size—are stereotyped in particularly negative terms and these stereotypes are applied more to women than men. Stereotypic beliefs about obese people reflect both physical disability and moral weakness. Prejudice against obese people, as well as how obese people cope with that prejudice, depends significantly on the perception that weight is controllable. Perhaps more than with members of other negatively stereotyped groups, obese people deal best with weightism expressed against them as they learn not to internalize the belief that their weight is controllable and that they are thus deserving of discrimination.

DI Diversity Issue 7.1: Lookism

Lookism refers to the positive stereotypes, prejudice, and preferential treatment accorded to physically attractive people or more generally to people whose appearance matches cultural values and priorities (e.g., blonde hair). Physical attractiveness is a culturally valued status and is associated with a well-defined set of beliefs called the *What is beautiful is good*, or physical attractiveness stereotype (Eagly, Ashmore, Makhijani, & Longo, 1991; Jackson, Sullivan, & Hodge, 1995). The traits associated with attractive people and the ways that they actually differ from average-looking people are presented in Table 7.1. As you can see, the physical attractiveness stereotype is composed almost entirely of positive traits and beliefs.

However, only in the domains of social skills and sociability is the stereotype accurate. Attractive people are believed to be more socially skilled than they are, but with this social poise also comes greater self-consciousness. Attractive people are also believed to be more sociable, and indeed, they tend to have more friends and be more well-liked than average-looking people. These actual advantages may be due to attractive people being given more attention and opportunities to learn social skills and make friends. In other words, the actual differences between attractive and average-looking people may be due to self-fulfilling prophecies, as attractive babies and children rise to others' expectations for them. However, our preference for facial beauty and physical attractiveness may also have evolved because it produced more attractive offspring in our primeval forbears. Research shows that people spontaneously attend to, and remember better, attractive, more than average-looking faces (Manor et al., 2005).

Table 7.1 Perceived and Actual Differences Between Attractive and Typical-Looking People

Attractive People Are Perceived as . . .	Attractive People Are Actually . . .
Sexually warmer or more responsive	More sexually experienced but not more responsive
More socially skilled	More socially confident and have better social skills, but also more self-conscious in public
More sociable, more dominant	More popular and have more friends
Mentally healthier, more intelligent, less modest	Less lonely but not mentally healthier overall
. . . than typical-looking people.	. . . than typical-looking people.

SOURCE: "Good-looking people are not what we think" by A. Feingold, 1992, *Psychological Bulletin, 111*, pp. 304–341. Copyright 2001 by Wiley.

? Where do you see evidence of lookism? Are there other aspects of lookism besides facial beauty, such as height, skin tone, or body build?

? The increasing ethnic and racial diversity in the United States suggests that the *ideal look* may be evolving away from Northern European characteristics (pale skin, blond hair, blue eyes) and accommodating more Southern European, Asian, and African qualities. What do you think?

DI Diversity Issue 7.2: Size Acceptance

Beliefs that obese people are morally weak—that is, that they are lazy, self-indulgent, and irresponsible—play a significant role in their discrimination in all areas of life. Some scholars who study the cultural and historical context of attitudes toward obese persons suggest that obesity prejudice shares a darker and unspoken goal with eugenics: the desire to improve the species by rooting out fat, which means rooting out sloth and self-indulgence, physical weakness and unattractiveness, and poor health and disease. Other scholars maintain that weightism is a new, socially acceptable form of racism. That is, given that obesity is more prevalent in Black and Hispanic portions of the U.S. population, antifat prejudice can be a subtle vehicle for racial prejudice. The **size acceptance** movement challenges the moral panic and judgment surrounding obesity, including the beliefs that weight is controllable and significant weight loss is achievable. The National Association to Advance Fat Acceptance (NAAFA) and the International Size Acceptance Association (ISAA) are two organizations that promote body size acceptance and *health at any size* among obese individuals. They also strive to educate the public about the uncontrollable nature of weight, the difficulty of weight loss, the psychological consequences that attend dieting, and the health dangers of weight cycling (repeated weight loss and regain).

Linda Bacon and her colleagues randomly assigned obese women who were chronic dieters to one of two interventions (Bacon, Stern, Van Loan, & Keim, 2005). The standard diet program consisted of restricted eating, nutritional education, and exercise; the health-at-any-size intervention emphasized body acceptance, internally controlled eating, and education to overcome physical barriers, become more assertive, and effect change in others and their environments. Over the 104 weeks from the start of the program to follow-up, the dieters lost weight and then regained it, whereas the health-at-any-size participants' weight didn't change. In other words, neither program reduced weight, although weight loss was a goal only in the dieting group. The most interesting results were on the health and psychological measures. The health-at-any-size participants, but not the dieters, experienced lowered cholesterol and blood pressure. The health-at-any-size participants also finished the program with less dietary restraint (an attitude that predicts diet failure and binge eating), greater body satisfaction, and higher self-esteem; these benefits did not occur in the dieting group. This study shows that physical and mental health can be improved in obese people without weight loss and the repressive psychology of dieting.

? Positive media portrayals of heavy characters help advance size acceptance ideals in the mainstream culture. What characters currently on television contradict cultural stereotypes of obese people?

KEY TERMS

FOR FURTHER READING

Mann, T., Tomiyama, J., Westling, E., Lew, A., Samuels, B., & Chatman, J. (2007). Medicare's search for effective obesity treatments: Diets are not the answer. *American Psychologist, 62*, 220–233. http://psycnet.apa.org/journals/amp/62/3/220.pdf

Consistent with stereotypes of obese people as overeaters is the assumption that they can lose weight with the proper amount of willpower and effort. This article, reviewing the effectiveness of dieting as a treatment for obesity, comes to quite different conclusions about whether significant weight loss is achievable through one's own efforts.

Online Resources

Rudd Center for Food Policy and Obesity

http://www.yaleruddcenter.org/

This site organizes news reports, research, and legislation surrounding obesity and food policy.

National Association to Advance Fat Acceptance (NAAFA)

http://www.naafa.org/

International Size Acceptance Association (ISAA)

http://www.size-acceptance.org/

Check out these size acceptance websites. What values do they promote? What position do they take on dieting and weight loss? What supports and resources do these organizations provide for obese people?

Understanding Moral Prejudice

Classism and Homosexism

In Chapter 7, we learned that stereotypes and prejudice against obese people have a moral dimension. The laziness attributed to obese individuals is a severely negative trait because it violates the Protestant (or Puritan) work ethic, a psychology of personal responsibility and religious piety that helped shape the American moral psyche (Weber, 1958). Even today the American dream involves the hope that people can start with nothing and, with hard work and determination, make something of themselves. Indeed, people who go from rags-to-riches by their own effort and ingenuity are celebrated as heroes more in the United States than in any other nation. In addition, religious faith is woven through this traditional American creed, and is reflected on our currency (In God We Trust) and in our national hymns ("God Bless America"). In this chapter, we look more closely at expressions of prejudice that are rooted in religious belief and ideology. We focus on two groups of people who face stereotypes and discrimination that are dominated with moral condemnation and judgment: poor people and homosexuals.

Stereotyping and Discrimination of Poor People

How many people live in poverty in the United States? It depends on how poverty is defined. According to the U.S. Census Bureau (2002), 9% to 11% of American families with two children (totaling over 30 million people) live below the *poverty line.* The poverty line consists of an annual income of $18,850 for a family of four, and this income level defines eligibility for government assistance for food and medical care. The cost of having the basic necessities of life in most American towns and cities, such as adequate shelter, food, utilities, transportation, and basic health care, greatly exceeds this income level. Therefore, many millions of families live in poverty—meaning that they are often hungry or cannot pay their rent or utility bills—whose income is above the official poverty line and who, as a result, do not qualify for government assistance programs.

The Content of the Stereotype of Poor People

What are our attitudes toward poor people? Research on perceptions of and behavior toward poor people in the psychological literature is scant. This underrepresentation in psychological research may reflect **classism**, which refers to negative stereotypes, feelings, and behavior toward poor people or people who are perceived to be economically impoverished. Scientists are not immune to classism: Research and clinical concern among psychologists and medical researchers have generally ignored poor people and the mental and physical health issues that arise with living in poverty (Larson, 1994; Lott, 2002). Early research in this area examined attributions for poverty—in other words, beliefs about what caused people to be poor. These studies found that people tend to attribute poverty more to personal factors (e.g., not working hard enough) than to structural factors (e.g., unemployment). This tendency to hold poor people responsible for their own plight is greater among Whites, people with conservative political values, and people who affirm the Protestant work ethic (Kluegel & Smith, 1986; Zucker & Weiner, 1993).

Cathy Cozzarelli and her colleagues surveyed college students' attitudes toward poor people and their explanations for poverty (Cozzarelli, Wilkinson, & Tagler, 2001). Participants rated typical poor and middle-class people on 38 traits and behaviors. Although the most prominent traits in the stereotypes of poor people were negative (see Table 8.1), when the researchers combined all the positive and negative traits together to create measures of positive and negative stereotyping, poor people were not seen in more negative than positive terms. Middle-class people, on the other hand, were; participants did more positive than negative stereotyping of middle-class persons. The prominent traits in the stereotype of poor people reveal, without too much interpretation, underlying beliefs that reflect the American creedal values discussed earlier. Poor people are seen as *capable* of work and self-sufficiency, but due to their lack of motivation and irresponsibility, reflected in beliefs about poor people abusing alcohol and producing too-large families, they do not achieve this status. They are also seen as being depressed and embarrassed, which may reflect the belief

Table 8.1 Most-Mentioned Traits in the Cultural Stereotype of Poor and Middle-Class People

Poor	Middle Class
Uneducated	Hardworking
Unmotivated	Capable
Depressed	Family oriented
Capable	Healthy
Embarrassed	Intelligent
Alcoholic	Responsible
Have too many children	Loving

SOURCE: Cozzarelli, C., Wilkinson, A., & Tagler, M. (2001). Attitudes towards the poor and attributions for poverty. *Journal of Social Issues, 57,* 207–227.

that the poor *know* they are failing to live up to cultural expectations. In sum, the stereotype of poor people in this study reflects an understanding of poverty as individually caused. Accordingly, poor people were rated very low on traits such as proud, happy, and responsible.

In research with about 1,500 participants in two studies, Bernice Lott and Susan Saxon (2002) found that participants rated a working-class person higher than a middle-class person on two clusters of negative traits: irresponsibility (insincere, lazy, stupid) and crude (harsh, incompetent, unfeminine, untidy). Other researchers measured participants' stereotypes of wage earners whose income varied from $10,000 to $190,000 per year (Johannesen-Schmidt & Eagly, 2002). Relative to their views of middle- and upper-income earners, participants viewed lower-income earners as being less intelligent and ambitious, less honest and warm, less likely to be faithful to their spouse, and spending less time at their job. Together, these stereotypic views reflect the underlying dimensions attributed to poverty-defined subgroups according to the stereotype content model. People view poor Blacks, poor Whites, and welfare recipients nearly identically—as having low levels of competence and warmth (Fiske et al., 2002).

Alongside this negative stereotype, people also endorsed positive traits (e.g., friendly, nice, loving) as descriptive of the poor. This apparent ambivalence may be evidence of subtypes of poor people. Researchers have found that people view poor women much more positively (or less negatively) than poor men (Cozzarelli, Tagler, & Wilkinson, 2002). In addition, although poor people are generally held responsible for the circumstances in which they live, impoverished women and men are held responsible for different outcomes. Specifically, women are held responsible for living in mother-only families and for having too many children, whereas men are held responsible for their own laziness and their failure to improve themselves and find work. There are other complexities to the stereotype of poor people: Poor elderly and children prompt more positive attitudes in others than poor people of working age, because they are seen as less responsible for their poverty (Gilens, 1996). The stereotype of poor people as responsible for their poverty may reflect Western, White, middle-class values. For example, university students from India tend to see poverty as being caused by structural forces more than by personal irresponsibility (Nasser, Singhal, & Abouchedid, 2005). Likewise, Black and Hispanic Americans attribute poverty more to structural problems than to the lack of personal effort (Hunt, 1996).

Another aspect of the cultural stereotype of poor people is that poverty is associated with racial minority status. Martin Gilens (1996) reports that Americans think about 50% of the poor people are Black; in reality Blacks constitute about 30% of Americans living in poverty. This (mis)impression of who is poor accounts for the similarity in the stereotypes of poor people and Blacks: Beliefs about laziness and intellectual competence figure prominently in perceptions of both social groups. The misunderstanding of the racial makeup of poor people has implications for societal efforts to relieve poverty. If poverty is perceived largely as a *Black problem*, it is more likely to be attributed to the laziness or inability of Blacks than if it is understood as a set of circumstances that affects adults and children of all ethnicities.

The most negative stereotypes, however, are held about people who receive government assistance, and indeed, a coherent subtype of poor people exists regarding the *welfare mother*. Women who receive government assistance are stereotyped as young, Black, never married women who are lazy and *cheat the system* by having children simply to increase their government benefits (Davis & Hagen, 1996). The intense disliking of so-called welfare mothers comes from a convergence of at least three overlapping and negatively stereotyped groups. First, welfare mothers are stereotyped as poor, and as young, capable, and employable, are held responsible for their poverty. Second, welfare mothers are also (mis)perceived as largely Black and thus negatively stereotyped in racial terms. Third, welfare mothers are seen as rejecting the value of the nuclear family and contributing, as with other *nontraditional* family arrangements such as gay marriages, to the erosion of moral values (Seccombe, James, & Walters, 1998). In terms of the stereotype content model introduced in Chapter 5, the content of the stereotypes of White poor people, Black poor people, and welfare recipients is remarkably consistent: All three groups are regarded as both low in warmth and competence (Fiske et al., 2002). According to Susan Fiske and her colleagues (2002), *no* group is regarded as less warm than poor and welfare-reliant people. Only one group is stereotyped as less competent than poor people—the mentally retarded—but stereotypes of them also reflect warmth, compassion, and sympathy. In sum, poor people, especially those of working age, are stereotyped as morally deficient and largely responsible for their own impoverished circumstances (Chafel, 1997).

The moral basis of stereotyping and prejudice against poor people suggests that religiousness among perceivers may predict classism. We will consider the relationship of religious belief to prejudice against homosexuals at length later in this chapter.

However, very little research has studied how religious belief predicts attitudes toward poor people and poverty. We might hypothesize that if religious believers tend to be more prejudiced against people who are perceived to have *chosen* their out-group status (e.g., gays, atheists) than people who have been assigned their minority status (e.g., Blacks, women), poor people may be seen by religious people, especially fundamentalist believers, as responsible for their own poverty. Moreover, the current popularity of the *prosperity gospel*—the belief that faithful followers of God are entitled to material blessing and riches—in many Protestant churches around the world suggests that poor people may be seen in some religious circles as lacking in faith and not worthy of God's blessing (see Hunt, 2000).

Discriminating Against Poor People

Classism not only involves holding negative stereotypes about poor people but also treats them differently because they are poor. In a review of how people behave toward the poor, Bernice Lott (2002) argues that classism is rooted in the power that economically advantaged people have to define and enforce their values and views of the world. Moral exclusion is the natural extension of stereotypes and judgments of poor people as morally inferior to middle- and upper-class people. **Moral exclusion** involves excluding, dehumanizing, and punishing people who are perceived to be indifferent or threatening to the empowered group's beliefs and values (Lott, 2002). Given what we have already learned about the stereotyping of poor people, it is hard to imagine another group of people that is as scorned and marginalized as poor people.

Moral exclusion is expressed, like institutional racism, in organizational policies and practices that are biased against poor people. For example, the public school system discriminates against poor children. Because public school is financed primarily through property taxes, poor children will likely go to schools that are supported by low-income taxpayers, which in turn will have less money for teacher training, computers, and academic supports than more affluent communities. The high cost of college education and shrinking federal tuition-assistance programs also discriminate against poor students and their families. Statistics show that the proportion of poor college students is declining annually (Hoyt, 1999). Finally, stereotypes of the poor affect how poor students are evaluated in school. In a classic demonstration of this, researchers had participants evaluate the academic abilities of either a poor or a middle-class fourth grade student (Darley & Gross, 1983). One half of the participants were allowed to view a videotape of the student being given an intellectual test; the other half did not see the testing. Relying solely on their stereotype of the academic abilities of poor students (in the no-test-viewing condition), participants rated the poor student's math and reading abilities slightly, but not significantly, beneath those of the middle-class student. When the participants had the opportunity to test their stereotype by watching the student in action, however, discrimination emerged. In the test-viewing condition, the poor student's math and reading levels were rated a full grade level below the middle-class student's ability. This study reminds us of the power of stereotypes to guide our minds toward stereotype-confirming, rather than disconfirming, information.

> **?** What things do middle-class college students take for granted that students from poor or low-income families might not have? How would these things affect college achievement?

The moral exclusion of poor people also occurs with regard to mental and physical health. Living in poverty means dealing with fewer resources and greater difficulties in nearly every life domain, and this is a recipe for stress. Linda Gallo and her colleagues (2009), summarizing a large research literature on the relationship between socioeconomic status and health, note that going down each rung on the economic ladder is strongly associated with increased risk of serious illnesses, as well as lowered life expectancy. They explain this relationship by finding that, relative to middle-class and wealthy people, poor people have less access to resources for dealing with negative life events and stress. Resources that allow middle-class people to cope with life stressors and negative events—such as extra money, time, social support, perceived control over one's life circumstances, and optimism about one's future—tend to be in short supply for poor people. This limited *reserve capacity*, as Gallo et al. (2009) has termed it, to buffer the effects of stress on one's physical and mental well-being, leaves poor people more vulnerable to illness. Not surprisingly, poor people, especially women and women with children, suffer higher rates of depression than middle-class individuals (Belle & Doucet, 2003). Depression is a common response to stress, but stress is also bad for your health. Depression is a risk factor for catching colds and upper respiratory infections and for developing coronary heart disease and cancer (Cohen, 1996; Frasure-Smith & Lesperance, 2005; Freeman, 2004). Family income at or around the poverty level is associated with health problems in children and death at earlier ages in elderly people (Schultz, Martire, Beach, & Scheier, 2000). As mentioned earlier, poor people tend to be underrepresented in clinical research (Larson, 1994). Similarly, the health issues that attend poverty, such as those common to developing nations, are underemphasized in the top medical journals (Horton, 2003). Finally, poor people are much less likely to have health insurance and, as a result, access to health care and prescription drugs. In 2002, about 15% of the American population had no health insurance, and most of those 44 million people lived in poverty (U.S. Census Bureau, 2002). To sum up, poor people are denied adequate educational and health outcomes; each of these areas of discrimination only further disadvantages and marginalizes poor people.

> **?** Together, educational attainment and health can be thought of as a springboard for middle-class achievement. How is obtaining the American dream dependent on being educated and healthy? We considered White privilege in Chapter 4: Is there such a thing as middle-class privilege, with a knapsack of assumed privileges that are not available to impoverished people?

Stereotyping and Discrimination of Gay Men and Lesbians

The first term to denote others' negative reactions to homosexuals was *homophobia*, which emerged in the late 1960s and early 1970s (Weinberg, 1972). Based on the Freudian concept of phobia, homophobia referred to the dislike and fear of homosexual persons. Although homophobic reactions—fear, disgust, and aversion—are still part of many people's responses to gay men or lesbians, the term *homophobia* does not capture the degree to which prejudice and discrimination based on sexual orientation are socialized and institutionalized. As an alternative, *homosexism* works better. If sexism is prejudice against people based on their biological sex or socialized gender, then homosexism adapts that focus to people based on their homosexual orientation. **Homosexism**, then, involves stereotyping, prejudice, and discrimination directed at people because of their homosexual orientation. This term is limited too because it excludes prejudice expressed against other nonheterosexual people such as bisexuals and transgendered individuals. To address this limitation scholars have offered the term **sexual prejudice** to include stereotyping, prejudice, and discrimination based on one's sexual identity or behavior. But given that prejudice and discrimination directed at gay men and lesbians comprise much of the problem of prejudice based on sexual identity or behavior, we will focus on those two groups and henceforth use homosexism in our discussion.

Stereotyping, as we learned in Chapter 2, begins with the process of categorization. Social categories such as race, gender, and age have numerous and obvious physical and perceptual cues that help us to rapidly and accurately categorize people from those groups. Regarding gay men and lesbians, does categorization only occur after we find out that someone is gay? The popular concept of **gaydar** suggests that people identify and categorize gays based on physical or perceptual cues, or at least they believe they can. Recent research, summarized in a fascinating article by David France (2007), has identified some physical characteristics that appear to vary reliably with sexual orientation. For example, hair-whorl patterns tend to grow in a counterclockwise direction among gay people and in a clockwise direction among heterosexuals. Hair-whorl pattern is believed to be genetically connected to handedness, and indeed, gay men and lesbians are much more likely to be left-handed than right-handed, compared with the handedness rates in the heterosexual population. Other evidence of biological differences between homosexual and heterosexual individuals occurs in the relative lengths of one's fingers. For most heterosexual males, the index finger is shorter than the ring finger; among gay males the opposite pattern occurs. Likewise, lesbian and heterosexual females' relative finger lengths are also reliably different.

The problem with the gaydar hypothesis—that people can accurately identify another person's sexual orientation from visual evidence alone—is that the accuracy of gaydar judgments cannot be objectively and strenuously tested in real life. Although we may strongly suspect that someone is gay, we rarely get feedback on those judgments. Worse, from a scientific perspective, is that we do not think to test the accuracy of our nonjudgments—those people who we do not suspect are gay, but really are. A study by Nicholas Rule and Nalini Ambady (2008) provided a rigorous test of gaydar.

Their study examined two questions: Could people accurately identify a person's sexual orientation merely from visual facial evidence, and how quickly could those categorizations be made? Rule and Ambady took hundreds of images of men's faces from online sites; in every case, the men publically self-defined as either homosexual or heterosexual. They then eliminated all pictures of men with facial hair, glasses, or piercings so that all faces were equally clear, and from that group, they randomly selected 45 gay and 45 straight pictures for the study. These pictures were presented to participants via computer for varying exposures ranging from 33 milliseconds (one third of a second) to 10 seconds, and participants were asked to categorize each face as either gay or straight. The results showed that accuracy rates ranged from 57% in the 50 millisecond (one-half second) condition to 62% in the 6,500 millisecond (6½ second) condition; these rates were significantly better than what would be expected if people were merely guessing. A follow-up study used candid pictures of gay or straight target people. This allowed the researchers to eliminate the possibility that people put up pictures of themselves that subtly present themselves as gay or straight. This study replicated the first study: Participants were able to identify gay and straight individuals from photographs beyond chance levels. Overall, Rule and Ambady's research provides evidence that gaydar has some scientific validity and that people can make accurate categorizations based on sexual orientation in less than a second.

The Content of Gay Stereotypes

Stereotypes of gay men and lesbians reflect the complex mixture of negative and positive attitudes that we have already learned are held toward other groups (e.g., Asians and Jews; see Chapter 5). In general, heterosexuals' attitudes toward homosexuals are negative, more negative for gay men than for lesbians, and seem to be based significantly on the perception that both gay men and lesbians engage in unnatural and immoral sexual behavior (Herek, 2000). Indeed, a sizable minority of Americans, around 40%, believes that homosexuality is an unacceptable, immoral lifestyle (Yang, 1997). This shows not merely the prevalence of negative attitudes toward gay persons but also the perception that the gay *lifestyle* is, at least to some extent, believed to be a matter of choice. We will discuss this key perception below. As with stereotypes of poor people, perceived immorality—in this case, sexual immorality—figures prominently in the judgment and rejection of homosexuals. As we will see, people who invest in conservative ideologies (e.g., fundamentalist religion), and for whom moral principles are clear and important, hold the most negative attitudes toward gays. Given the disliking and moral judgment of gay people prevalent in the broader culture, surveys show that most Americans are surprisingly willing to support some legal recognition and protections of gay men and lesbians, such as shared health benefits and civil unions (Herek, 2000).

Although cultural stereotypes of gay men, and to lesser extent lesbian women, revolve around the notion that to be gay is to engage in immoral sexual behavior, several other beliefs inform the gay cultural stereotype. First, the negative stereotype of gay men is shaped by the perceived association between homosexual (particularly male) sex and AIDS. In a survey of over 1,000 American adults, a large minority of respondents erroneously believed HIV/AIDS was more likely to be transmitted through homosexual than heterosexual sex (Herek, 2005). These are consistent with (also erroneous) perceptions that gay, compared with heterosexual, men are more sexually active and promiscuous.

A second belief, again applying much more to stereotypes of gay males than females, is the association between homosexuality and pedophilia. In 1970, over 70% of the respondents in a national attitude survey believed that homosexuals preyed on children for sexual gratification (Herek, 2006). Today, still one in five heterosexual men believes that gay men molest children; lesbians are much less likely to be connected to pedophilia. Does this stereotypic belief square with actual rates of sexual abuse of children among gay men? Physicians from a Denver children's hospital examined 269 cases of sexually abused children in which the abuser was known and found that in only two of the cases (or less than 1%) was the abuser a homosexual adult (described in Herek, 2006). In short, heterosexual adults are far more likely to perpetrate child sexual abuse than gay persons.

A third (again, mostly inaccurate) belief that shapes stereotypes of gay people is that homosexual men and women are HINKs—that is, having high income and no kids (Lind, 2004). Overall, same-sex households have no higher income than typical, mixed-sex households. However, the perception that gays are well-paid professionals, unencumbered with the responsibility of raising children, should lead to ambivalent reactions in others. Stereotypically speaking, successful single people should invite respect and admiration. The perceived abdication of child rearing among gay men and women, however, violates traditional gender role responsibilities and prompts judgment and resentment.

> **?** The stereotypic association of gay men with pedophilia is very likely shaped and sustained by vivid and memorable cases portrayed in the media. As an example, discuss the Catholic priest/child sexual abuse scandal. Do you assume that the alleged abusers are gay? Why? Does the reporting and media coverage of this affair subtly reinforce that belief?

Perceptions of gay men are moderate on both the warmth and competence dimensions of the stereotype content model described in Chapter 5; lesbians were not included in that research (Fiske et al., 2002). This neutral-content stereotype may indicate that people simply have neutral feelings about gays. It is much more likely, however, that the overall neutral (they're somewhat competent and somewhat warm) content suggests that people may hold both positive and negative views about gay men or divide gay men into smaller subgroups that are evaluated differently, which then leads to an overall but misleading emotionally neutral stereotype. There is evidence that people subtype gay men into at least two types: those who are effeminate and have female-stereotypic qualities (e.g., emotionally sensitive) and those who violate traditional sex roles for men (e.g., have sex with men; Madon, 1997). People like the first type of gay man better than the second. In another study, participants generated traits they associated with gay men and sorted those traits into gay male subtypes (Clausell & Fiske, 2005). Three subtypes of gay males emerged from the analysis. *Cross-dresser/ leather/biker gay men* were combined into a group and linked with traits such as makeup wearing and flamboyant. A second group consisted of *effeminate gay men,* who were described with traits such as dramatic and soft-spoken. The third subtype consisted of *artistic/straight-acting/masculine gay men.* Not surprisingly, the cross-dressing subgroup was rated low on both competence and warmth. Of the three subtypes, these individuals would be most likely to be perceived as threatening traditional male sex roles and being sexually active. The effeminate subtype was regarded as warm but not very competent, stereotype content that is similar to stereotypes held about disabled and elderly people. The artistic/straight-acting/masculine subtype of gay men was stereotyped as highly competent but cold, in much the same way as wealthy people and Jews are. The tendency for perceivers to layer opposite-sex stereotypes onto their perceptions of gay men and lesbians was demonstrated in an experiment in which participants were randomly assigned to rate a target person who was either male or female and characterized as either gay or straight (Blashill & Powlishta, 2009). The participants rated the target on a series of masculine (e.g., works with tools, dominant) or feminine (e.g., bakes cookies, appreciative) traits. The findings were striking: Participants stereotyped gay males as less masculine than heterosexual males, but also as less masculine than lesbians. Lesbians' masculinity was perceived as higher than that of heterosexual females, and nearly as high as heterosexual males. In summary, the overall stereotype of gay males is emotionally neutral, but only appears to be neutral because it combines several subtypes with very different emotional content.

As we have seen, stereotypes about obese (Chapter 7) and poor people rest on assumptions about the controllability of weight and one's economic circumstances, respectively. Similarly, assumptions about the nature of sexual orientation seem to be crucial for explaining homosexism (Haslam & Levy, 2006). As with weight and poverty, perceived control over one's sexuality is an important predictor of homosexism; people who hold negative attitudes toward gay men and lesbians tend to see homosexuality as controllable and changeable. Homosexists also tend to see homosexuality as an *either-or* status—that you're either gay or not. Finally, people who deny that homosexuality exists in every culture and throughout historical eras, seeing it rather as a modern *movement,* also express negative attitudes toward homosexual persons.

In addition to stereotypic beliefs, homosexism also includes negative emotional (homophobic) responses to gay people. Up until 1973, homosexuality was defined as a sexual perversion by the American Psychiatric Association. Attitudes toward gay people have become less negative and more tolerant over the subsequent 40 years. Because people are reluctant to admit to feeling disgust, fear, and aversion to homosexuals on questionnaires and surveys, other methods are necessary to study homosexist emotions. Amanda Mahaffey and her colleagues (2005) used startle eye blink response to study students' responses to homosexual individuals. Startle eye blink has been shown to increase in response to disturbing or feared stimuli (e.g., an accident victim) and decrease in response to comforting or nonthreatening stimuli (e.g., a floral arrangement).

Most importantly, startle eye blink is an uncontrollable response and thus is a more valid measure than a paper-and-pencil survey of people's true feelings about gay people. In this study, male participants completed a survey measure of homosexism, were fitted with electrodes that could detect small movements of the eyelid muscles, and were then presented with picture slides of nude or seminude men and women. The results showed that men who expressed homophobia on the survey showed greater startle blinks, indicating more negative emotional responses to the nude male images. A follow-up study in another sample of male participants used photos of nude gay, lesbian, and heterosexual couples. This study also found that self-reported homosexist attitudes were associated with more negative emotional responses to the nude male images. In both of these studies, however, homosexist participants also showed more negative emotional responses to the nude female and lesbian couple images. These findings suggest that homophobia in men overlaps somewhat with **erotophobia**, or fear and disgust with erotic activity (e.g., looking at pornography, engaging in oral or anal sex). These findings therefore reflect the belief that sex is important and central in the lives of gay men and lesbians and that gay sex is perceived as more erotic and immoral than heterosexual sex.

Other research suggests that homophobia is also related to feeling threatened by gays. Bonnie Moradi and her colleagues measured the psychological threat posed by gay and lesbian individuals by having heterosexual participants rate how much each of 30 personality traits described them presently and described themselves as a gay or lesbian person (Moradi, van den Berg, & Epting, 2006). Threat was defined as the difference between one's current identity and one's identity as an imagined gay person. Participants with high threat scores were more likely than low-threat participants to endorse antigay sentiments such as "I think homosexuals are disgusting." Highly threatened heterosexuals also used the antigay attitudes to reaffirm their own identities. This research shows that expressing negative attitudes and feelings toward gays is partly rooted in heterosexuals' need to enhance their self-esteem and public image, and this reprises the lessons of Chapter 4—that prejudice is often done to help us feel better about ourselves or look better to other people.

Religiousness and Homosexism

We have learned that stereotypes and prejudice toward some groups are rooted in beliefs that the members of those groups violate important moral principles. Poor people, and to a large extent obese people (see Chapter 7), are judged because of their laziness and self-indulgence; gays are judged because of their (perceived) immoral sexual preferences and behavior. Unlike targets of racial or gender-based prejudice, targets of moral prejudice are all seen as causing or maintaining their "problem." We now turn to the question of stereotyping and prejudice among religious people. If any subpopulation of people can be expected to internalize and value moral principles, it is religious believers. But what moral principles do religious people uphold, and how are they related to stereotyping and prejudice?

Early research defined two religious orientations, or ways of being religious (Allport & Ross, 1967). **Intrinsic religiousness** involves internalizing and living out the precepts of one's faith, as typically occurs in people whose faith is important to them. **Extrinsic religiousness** involves a pragmatic approach to religion; extrinsically religious people use religion for social or personal goals (e.g., having a group of friends with similar interests). **Fundamentalism** describes religious beliefs that are based on a literal reading of scriptures and are held with certainty and rigidity (Kirkpatrick, Hood, & Hartz, 1991). Fundamentalism, then, refers to how religious beliefs are formed and held rather than the content of those beliefs. Fundamentalist believers, whether they are Christian, Jewish, or Muslim, tend to be the most judgmental and militant of religious people (Altemeyer & Hunsberger, 1992; Kirkpatrick, 1993; McFarland, 1989).

Homosexuality is generally considered morally unacceptable in the doctrine and tradition of the major God religions. A literal reading of the few biblical statements about homosexuality condemns it as a perversion of true (hetero) sexuality and what are believed to be divinely ordained roles for man and woman. Thus, we would expect gays to be viewed more negatively than women, members of racial minority groups, and religious out-group members. Research generally supports this notion: Fundamentalist believers hold negative and discriminatory attitudes toward homosexuals (Kirkpatrick, 1993; McFarland, 1989). In fact, the association between fundamentalism and homosexism is several times greater than the association between extrinsic religiousness and racial prejudice. Negative responses to gay people have been observed among fundamentalist Christians, Jews, Muslims, and Hindus, which shows that moral prejudice—at least toward gay people—is much more driven by the rigidity and literalness of one's beliefs than by the content of the beliefs (Hunsberger, 1996).

Prejudice is also expressed in the social distance people try to maintain between themselves and members of disliked or negatively stereotyped groups. Participants in one such investigation gave social distance ratings for several subgroups of homosexuals (i.e., celibate gays, Christian celibate gays, sexually active gays) as well as other groups who are viewed in similarly negative moral terms (i.e., overeaters, liars, alcohol abusers). Participants expressed a desire to have moderate levels of social distance from gays in general but desired the greatest social distance from sexually active gay people (Fulton, Gorsuch, & Maynard, 1999). In fact, participants in general, but especially among fundamentalist participants, wished to have more distance between themselves and sexually active gays than between themselves and liars and alcoholics. These findings may reflect erotophobia—fear and hostility regarding gay expressions of sex—or the belief that being a sexually active gay person is more immoral and thus more deserving of exclusion, than being a celibate gay person. Mark Brandt and Christina Reyna (2010) found that fundamentalism is associated with prejudice against gay individuals in part because fundamental belief systems provide certainty regarding ideological questions, and prejudice against out-groups—particularly homosexuals—reinforces that certainty.

In an interesting test of homosexism as moral prejudice, Aubyn Fulton and his colleagues (1999) had participants respond to antigay statements that were either moral ("homosexuality is a perversion") or nonmoral ("a person's homosexuality should not be the basis for job discrimination") in nature. Fundamentalism was associated with greater endorsement of moral than nonmoral antigay statements, suggesting that perceived immorality in gay men and lesbians drives fundamentalist believers' judgment of them. In another study designed to look at the components of homosexism, Wayne Wilkinson (2004) measured four expressions of homosexism in a large sample of college students: a desire to avoid contact with gays, the immorality of homosexuality, intolerance for the gay rights movement, and belief in the gay stereotype. The participants' authoritarianism, a variable that correlates highly with fundamentalism, was associated with all four components of homosexism, but the largest association was with the immorality component.

Discrimination Against Gays

What are the consequences of these stereotypic beliefs and prejudiced feelings toward gays? In order to determine the causal effects of homosexual orientation on others' treatment of a job applicant, researchers sent undergraduate students into stores to pose as job applicants (Hebl, Foster, Mannix, & Dovidio, 2002). The students asked four standard questions to the manager (e.g., do you have any job openings? can I fill out an application?). Before entering the store, the participants donned a hat that read Gay and Proud (in the gay condition) or Texan and Proud (in the heterosexual, control condition). The participants did not know which hat they were wearing, preventing them from influencing the interactions with the store employees. Additionally, participants carried a tape recorder to record the interaction for later analysis. The results of this study revealed no formal discrimination of gays. That is, gay and straight job applicants received comparable responses about the availability of openings, and both types of applicants filled out job applications in equal rates. However, gay applicants were spoken to less, and for a shorter time, than were straight applicants. The gay applicants also perceived more negativity in the store managers than did the straight applicants. This study suggests that, although one's sexual orientation can be concealed with some effort, when it is revealed at work or when an employee is suspected of being gay, a pattern of interpersonal discrimination ensues that involves more social distancing, tension, and hostility between gay people and their coworkers. This finding meshes with other research discussed earlier on the content of stereotypes of gay men being low in warmth and the visceral aversive response people have to images of gay men and lesbians.

Discrimination of homosexuals is also institutionalized in policies that promote and protect social welfare (Lind, 2004). For example, in most states gay men and lesbians are barred from the status of legal marriage. As of early 2012, 7 states and the District of Columbia had legalized same-sex marriage, but 37 states still had statutes that defined marriage as between one man and one woman (National Council of State Legislatures, 2011). Indeed, under the administration of President George W. Bush, the U.S. Government spent hundreds of millions of dollars to encourage *healthy marriage* (read: heterosexual marriage) programs and promote heterosexual marriage in the context of *abstinence only* sex education programs (see Lind, 2004). These policies negatively affect gay couples' ability to receive benefits upon the death of their partner, prevent them from taking advantage of the tax laws that benefit married individuals, and are a big obstacle for couples hoping to adopt a child. Another institutional form of discrimination against gays involves how, if at all, gay people are counted in censuses of the population. Although the census records data on many aspects of social and cultural diversity, there is currently no item that measures sexual orientation. However, the 2010 Census was the first to record data about same-sex partners or same-sex spouses of the respondent (U.S. Census, 2010). Similarly, whereas in the 2000 census, the U.S. Census Bureau defined a *family* as involving two or more people who were related by birth, marriage, or adoption, the 2010 census included *residing together* in the definition of a family. This change, therefore, allowed unmarried gay couples to be recognized as families for the first time.

The cumulative effects of being negatively stereotyped, experiencing others' prejudiced and sometimes violent reactions, and facing the many ways in which gay men and lesbians are disenfranchised from the community are chronically stressful and impact the mental health and adjustment of gay persons. As applied to homosexual people, **minority stress** refers to the chronic experience of being stereotyped (e.g., disliked, feared, judged) and socially alienated (e.g., excluded from social institutions; Meyer, 2003). Minority stress is considered an extra layer of stress that simply adds to the typical relationship and work-related stress all people face. What evidence is there for minority stress and its consequences for gay people? Research shows that in the United States gay people are about twice as likely as heterosexuals to have experienced prejudice or discrimination in some form (Mays & Cochran, 2001). A literature review examining the effect of being a sexual minority on mental health concluded that, compared with equivalent heterosexual people, gay and lesbian individuals have higher rates of alcohol and tobacco use, suicide thoughts and attempts, and depression (Hatzenbeuler, 2009). As was the case with poor people, higher risk of depression, substance abuse, and suicide in gay and lesbian populations is due to the fewer resources gays have to deal with the stressors of being a target of prejudice. For example, many gay and lesbian adolescents feel isolated and cut off from social support and advocacy resources. The experience of antigay violence is not an unusual occurrence, according to surveys, and happens more to gay adolescents than gay adults (Herek, Gillis, & Cogan, 1999). Among the gay population, gay and lesbian youth are disproportionately targeted for abuse and harassment, such as being physically threatened, threatened with weapons, having their belongings stolen, or being the target of gay slurs and homophobic speech (see Meyer, 2003, for a review).

Discrimination against gay men and lesbians also occurs in subtle ways, such as being forced to listen to, or being the target of, antihomosexual slurs and jokes. Peter Silverschanz and his colleagues (2008) surveyed over 3,000 college students about their experience of being exposed or being the target of antihomosexual verbal harassment. They found that 57% of the gay respondents experienced at least some of this kind of harassment in the previous year, with gay males experiencing more gay bashing than females. In another study, researchers measured the level of social constraints in a study of over 100 adult lesbians. Social restraints referred to feeling alienated from their social networks and disapproval when talking about lesbian issues (Lewis, Derlega, Clarke, & Kuang, 2006). Participants who had high social constraints, or in other words experienced lesbian-related minority stress, also had higher levels of negative mood (e.g., depression, anxiety) and more frequent symptoms of physical illness or distress (e.g., common cold). Coping with the stereotyping and discrimination that is directed at gay men and lesbians exacts a price in terms of decreased psychological and physical well-being.

Summary

Let's sum up the main ideas of this chapter: Poor people and homosexuals face negative stereotypes that feature assumptions about their immorality and being personally responsible for their minority status. Members of both groups prompt negative emotional reactions in others, such as fear, disgust, and hostility. Both poor people and gays also face exclusion from mainstream society. Classism and homosexism are similar in that impoverished people and homosexuals face moral exclusion from others, an extension of stereotyping and prejudice that is not experienced by women or members of racial or ethnic minority groups.

> **DI** **Diversity Issue 8.1: Conversion Therapy**
>
> **Conversion therapy**, also called reparative therapy, is the name given to therapeutic efforts to turn gay people into heterosexuals. Conversion therapy is the centerpiece of a largely religious movement (see Exodus International below) to *save* gay men and lesbians from a life of shame, unhappiness, and sin. According to Gregory Herek (1999), a leading researcher on gay prejudice, advocates and practitioners of conversion therapy based their claims on a small research literature whose methods and conclusions have been repudiated by the mainstream psychological scientific community (e.g., American Psychiatric Association). For example, numerous studies have been published that report success in reducing a gay person's self-reported attraction to same-sex persons, such as might happen after being subjected to nausea-inducing drugs while viewing photos of same-sex nudes. Although many tests of conversion therapy report a reduction in homosexual attitudes or behavior among their participants, these behavior changes cannot be reliably attributed to the therapy, nor is it proof that homosexuality has been replaced by heterosexuality. Finally, it is probable that many of the success stories of conversion therapy occurred not among gay men or lesbians who *turned straight* but among bisexuals who were strongly motivated to pursue heterosexual relationships. Conversion therapy is based on a stereotypical view of homosexuality, one that sees being gay as confined largely to one's choice of sexual partners and behavior (Herek, 1999). Apart from what conversion therapy may accomplish (if anything) with regard to changing homosexual orientation, it also surely contributes to stereotypic and homophobic views of gay people. Conversion therapy ideology, and the prejudice that suffuses it, are likely to be felt most by gay adolescents living in conservative religious households or communities, where levels of homophobia and homosexism are already high.
>
> *(Continued)*

(Continued)

? Look through the Exodus International website (details below) and think about some of these questions:

- Who is this organization talking to?
- What subpopulation of people is likely to avail themselves of Exodus International's resources?
- Are there some positive resources offered on the site? What are they?
- What evidence of gay stereotyping do you find in the site's materials?

DI Diversity Issue 8.2: The Occupy Movement

The *occupy* movement began in New York City on September 17, 2011, as a protest against the greed and corruption of the economic elite, including both corporations and individuals, on the democratic process. The movement spawned occupy-type protests in hundreds of other cities in the United States. and around the world. The occupy movement uses the motto: "We are the other 99%" to draw attention to the growing disparity in wealth between the richest 1% and the rest of the population and the consequences of this disparity for average citizens. Although the occupy groups differ somewhat as to their aims and demands, they are all united in their demand for fairer distribution of wealth, reform in the banking industry, and less money in the political process. One way to define what the movement stands for is to ask its participants. The website *We Are the 99%* (see Online Resources below for link) contains hundreds of pages of profiles of occupy protesters, with compelling descriptions of what it means to them to be part of *the 99%*. Read some. As you can see, their stories tell of anxiety about what sort of society they are joining, about the exorbitant cost of higher education and health care, and whether they have a voice in their own future.

Discuss your thoughts about the occupy movement: Why has it prospered? Where is it headed? Has it been a force for improving democracy? Do you feel the effects of the gap between the wealth of the 1% and 99% in your life?

KEY TERMS

Classism   158

Moral exclusion   161

Homosexism   163

Sexual prejudice   163

Gaydar   163

Erotophobia   167

Intrinsic religiousness   167

Extrinsic religiousness   168

Fundamentalism   168

Minority stress   170

Conversion therapy   171

FOR FURTHER READING

Burks, D. (2011). Lesbian, gay, and bisexual victimization in the military: An unintended consequence of "Don't Ask, Don't Tell"? *American Psychologist, 66,* 604–613. doi: 10.1037/a0024609.
    Although "Don't ask, don't tell" (DADT) was officially repealed on September 20, 2011, this article traces the legacy of discrimination of LGBT military personnel under DADT.

Savin-Williams, R. (2006). Who's gay? Does it matter? *Current Directions in Psychological Science,15,* pp. 40–44. doi:10.1111/j.0963-7214.2006.00403.x
    This article addresses the difficulty of estimating who's gay due to the varying definitions of homosexuality and the consequences of those definitions for the life outcomes of gay people.

Online Resources

Class Action: Building Bridges Across the Class Divide
http://www.classism.org/
    This site is devoted to education and activism about class-based prejudice and discrimination.

Class Matters
http://www.classmatters.org/
    Class Matters organizes news and resources for exposing and confronting class-based prejudice and discrimination. Check out the section on *classist comments* to see how classism is implicit in our language.

Occupy Wall Street
http://occupywallst.org/

Occupy Together
http://www.occupytogether.org/

We Are the 99%
http://wearethe99percent.tumblr.com/
    These websites document the original *occupy* group (Occupy Wall Street) and contain news and resources for supporters and participants in other occupy movement groups.

Exodus International
http://exodusinternational.org/
    Exodus International is founded on the idea that homosexuality is immoral and incompatible with a relationship with Jesus Christ. They provide resources for gay individuals and their families who want to "reconcile their faith with their sexual behavior."

http://exodusinternational.org/2009/12/sexual-orientation-and-change
    The centerpiece of this ministry is conversion or reparative therapy.

OK Cupid/The Gaydar Test
http://www.okcupid.com/the-gaydar-test

    Based on what we have learned in this chapter, there is some scientific basis for people being able to identify who is gay at a better-than-chance rate. Although it lacks scientific credentials, this test presents you with pairs of photographs of real people (one gay, one straight) and asks you to identify the gay person.

National Council of State Legislatures, 2011. Same-Sex Marriage, Civil Unions, and Domestic Partnerships
http://www.ncsl.org/default.aspx?tabid=16430

U.S. Census FAQ, LGBT Fact Sheet
http://2010.census.gov/partners/pdf/factSheet_General_LGBT.pdf

Understanding Age Stereotypes and Ageism

TOPICS COVERED IN THIS CHAPTER:

- Stereotypes association with older people
- Age-related discrimination

As we learned in Chapter 1, America has a graying population. Presently, seniors (people age 65 and older) make up 13% of the population. By 2030, when the youngest members of the Baby Boomer generation reach retirement age, 19% of all Americans will be seniors (U.S. Census Bureau, 2010). The graying demographics of the U.S. population will focus more attention on issues facing older aged Americans. Research on **successful aging** is particularly applicable here: Successful aging is a concept that incorporates freedom from disease and disability, good cognitive and physical functioning, social connections, and productive activities. Data from large national surveys from 1998 to 2004 estimate that fewer than 12% of all older adults are aging successfully (McLaughlin, Connell, Heeringa, Li, & Roberts, 2010). This means that the large majority of older adults face challenges in their older years due to poor health, diminished cognitive ability, social isolation, and boredom. Even though age is one of the primary categories by which we organize our social world (see Chapter 2), the stereotyping and discrimination of older people has received only a fraction of the research attention that has been devoted to the understanding of race and gender-based prejudice. In this chapter, we explore how stereotyping, prejudice, and discrimination of older adults undermine successful aging.

Old Age Categorization and Stereotyping

Recall from Chapter 2 that age (along with race and gender) is a primary social category, meaning that age-based social categorizations are automatic, or made too quickly (under 1 second) to be thoughtful and deliberate (Brewer & Lui, 1989). As with race and gender, we rely on physical cues for categorizing people based on age. What physical characteristics do you associate with older or elderly people? Wrinkled skin, gray or white hair, and posture and movement variables can all assist rapid identification of people based on their (old) age. The labels we give to these social categories vary but include old people, elders, seniors, senior citizens, and the elderly. Categorization of people into old age groups supports **ageism**, which refers to attitudes and beliefs, feelings, and behavior toward people based on their old age. We will consider each of these aspects of ageism in turn.

Early research found that there was not a *one-size-fits-all* stereotype of older people; rather, people held stereotypes of subgroups of older people (Brewer, Dull, & Lui, 1981). These subgroups, and the stereotypes associated with them, were first examined by Daniel Schmidt and Susan Boland (1986). They generated a pool of 99 adjectives and traits that were used in the study by asking people for terms they use when they think about older adults. These traits were then given to participants who were instructed to sort them into groups based on the traits they associated with particular kinds, or subgroups, of older people. Participants' trait sorting varied widely; some used as few as two subgroups, while others identified as many as 17 different types of older people. These trait sorts were analyzed via a hierarchical clustering procedure that identifies the best structure of nonoverlapping groups of traits. The analysis in this study found that stereotypes of older people had three levels—general traits, positive versus negative subgroups, and individual traits within each subgroup. At the most superordinate level were traits that described all old people, regardless of their subgroup. These included gray haired, hard of hearing, balding, and poor eyesight; indeed, the only nonphysical trait in the overall stereotype of old people was *retired.* Participants identified 12 subtypes of older people, eight were negatively valued and four were positively valued. Mary Lee Hummert and her colleagues (1994) replicated Schmidt and Boland's (1986) study with a more age-diverse sample of participants. They found that older-age participants had more, and more varied, stereotypes of the elderly, whereas younger participants had relatively simple stereotypes of the elderly. When the findings of the two studies are combined, seven common stereotypes of old people emerged. Table 9.1 displays the stereotypes and their traits.

When people evaluate a variety of out-groups along the fundamental dimensions used by the stereotype content model, older people consistently are grouped with disabled and developmentally disabled/retarded people. Thus, general stereotypes of old people reflect low levels of competence and high levels of warmth (Cuddy & Fiske, 2002). Whereas views of the elderly's competence are low but not extremely low, very few groups get higher warmth ratings than the elderly. Accordingly, stereotypes of the elderly contain more traits that reflect warmth than competence. Amy Cuddy and her colleagues (2005) tested the malleability of the old age stereotype; in other words, does

Table 9.1	Representative Traits in the Stereotypes of Subgroups of Older People

Subgroup	Traits
Despondent	neglected, sad, afraid, lonely
Severely impaired	feeble, slow thinking, senile
Shrew/curmudgeon	ill-tempered, complaining, prejudiced, stubborn, nosy
Recluse	quiet, timid, live in past, set in ways
John Wayne conservative	proud, patriotic, wealthy, conservative, religious
Perfect grandparent	kind, generous, family oriented, wise
Golden Ager	intelligent, productive, healthy, independent

SOURCES:

Schmidt, D. F., & Boland, S. M. (1986). Structure of perceptions of older adults: Evidence for multiple stereotypes. *Psychology and Aging, 1*(3), 255–260.

Hummert, M., Garstka, T., Shaner, J., & Strahm, S. (1994). Stereotypes of the elderly held by young, middle-aged, and elderly adults. *Journal of Gerontology: Psychological Sciences, 49*, 240–249.

the *warm and incompetent* change if older people disconfirm the stereotype in some way? They had participants read a description of an elderly adult that incorporated the warm traits in the elderly stereotype. The description then included further material that manipulated the competence of the person: Participants (randomly determined) read either about the person's poor or excellent memory. After this exercise, participants rated the person on warmth and competence dimensions. Elderly targets who were described as low in competence were given higher warmth ratings compared with the highly competent (and a no competence information control) target. Interestingly, the competence manipulation did not change participants' ratings of the elderly target's competence. When the elderly target behaved in a stereotype-consistent manner (by being less competent than expected), participants rewarded the elderly person with higher warmth ratings. Cuddy et al. (2005) concluded that the positive dimension of the old age stereotype is malleable (old people can be more or less warm) but the negative dimension resists change (old people are always incompetent).

In an important review, Richard Posthuma and Michael Campion (2009) studied stereotypes of older people in the workplace by synthesizing findings from over 100 studies of age-related stereotyping at work. Based on their analysis, stereotypes of older workers have three strong themes. First, they are perceived as less motivated and competent at work. This meshes with the stereotype content model's conclusions—that older people are viewed as warm but not very competent—but in fact, there is little evidence that work performance declines with age (Posthuma & Campion, 2009). Some studies even show that, relative to younger people, older people are more productive at their jobs. Second, numerous studies show that older employees are also viewed as harder to train or retrain and are thus inherently less valuable as employees. This stereotypic assumption may reflect the low-competence stereotype but also reveals assumptions of older employees' inability to change, their likely shorter tenure with the company, and less potential for development. Third, older workers are perceived as more expensive employees because they have higher salaries and, due to declining health, use more health care benefits. This piece of the stereotype reflects the widespread, though exaggerated, assumption that old age and illness are correlated (Ruppel, Jenkins, Griffin, & Kizer, 2010). Although it would appear that stereotypes of older workers are uniformly negative, Postuma and Campion also found a lot of research evidence that older employees, compared with their younger-age counterparts, are viewed as more trustworthy, stable, sociable, and dependable. These perceptions reflect a warmer and more positive aspect of stereotypes of older workers. Another review of the research supports these conclusions. Anne Bal and her colleagues (2011) summarized studies on perceptions of older workers and found that older workers are viewed as less worthy of advancement and less interpersonally skilled but more reliable, compared to younger workers.

Another way to look at old age stereotypes is to examine how older people are perceived in various life domains they include, and that is what Anna Kornadt and Klaus Rothermund (2011) did. Their large-sample survey found that stereotypes of older people are clustered into eight independent domains, including physical and mental fitness, leisure activities, religion and spirituality, and work and employment. The most negative stereotypes were in three particular domains: friends and acquaintances, financial and money-related issues, and physical and mental fitness. Stereotypes were the most positive in the religion and spirituality domain. These findings show again the ambivalence of old age stereotypes: We hold very negative and positive attitudes toward older adults depending on the life domain being considered.

Finally, some research shows that old age stereotypes are just as prevalent in older as they are in younger adults. People tend to attribute memory lapses and other *senior moments* in older people to stable, dispositional causes, whereas the same behaviors in younger people are attributed to more changeable causes, (Erber, Szuchman, & Rothberg, 1990). Most notably, this attribution bias occurs in older, as well as younger, people. Mary Lee Hummert and her colleagues (2002) measured both implicit and explicit ageism in younger (average age = 22 years) and older (average age = 80 years) participants. Implicit ageism was measured with the Age Implicit Association Test (Age-IAT), in which participants responded as quickly as possible to positively and negatively valued traits that were paired with the words *old* and *young*. Explicit ageism was measured by having participants identify their attitudes toward older people on a thermometer where 0° and 99° represented cold and warm feelings, respectively. All participants, regardless of their age, showed implicit ageism, but negative age-related attitudes were notably higher among the older, compared with the younger, participants. Explicit attitudes among the old participants revealed bias in favor of younger people and bias against older people.

Interestingly, this proyoung/antiold bias was not observed among young participants. Elderly people who hold stereotypical views about their own-age peers seem to be stereotyping themselves. We know from Chapter 2 that stereotypes have the power to shape people's identity and behavior in stereotype-consistent ways. We will consider, a bit later in this chapter, if old age stereotypes are self-fulfilling.

Old age stereotypes are expressed in the representations and portrayals of older adults on television. Unlike the real world, the social world of television is not very age diverse. Although about 12% of the U.S. population is 65 years or older, only 2% of the TV characters are in that age group (Gerbner & Ozyegin, 1997). Jake Harwood (1995) counted the older (defined as age 60+) main and supporting characters on 40 of the most-watched TV programs in 1995. Out of a total of 490 characters, only 29 (or 6%) were older adults. He also found no older lead characters and very few older supporting characters in the most popular shows watched by children and young adults. These figures show that older adults are underrepresented on TV, especially on programs aimed at younger viewers.

In general, older characters are portrayed in negative and stereotypical terms—as dependent, lonely, disagreeable people who have various physical and mental limitations (Bishop & Krause, 1984; Gerbner, Gross, Signorielli, & Morgan, 1980; Montepare & Zebrowitz, 2002). Older characters are more than twice as likely to be shown with some disability—such as an illness, injury, or significant maladjustment—than are younger characters. And, compounding the gender discrimination on TV that was discussed previously, older women are more likely to be portrayed as *disabled* than are older men (Dail, 1988; Gerbner, 1997). However, not all types of programming have such an age bias. Older adults are more visible and positively portrayed on daytime serials (i.e., soap operas) than in prime-time shows (Cassata, Anderson, & Skill, 1980). Also, there are benevolent images of older people in TV advertisements in which older characters are seen as advisors, doting grandparents, high-income investors, and active retirees (Miller, Leyell, & Mazachek, 2004). In other words, we see the ambivalence of old age stereotypes on television too: Older people have a lot of negative, but some positive, qualities.

Two of the examples of older characters who are regular cast members on prime-time TV shows are on *The Simpsons,* a critically-acclaimed, prime-time animated comedy about a dysfunctional but endearing family of five and one of the longest-running shows in U.S. television history. Abe Simpson is the nursing home-bound father of Homer; he is typically portrayed as a senile and dependent individual who is a burdensome figure in his son's life. Mr. Burns (Homer's boss) is cast as a disagreeable, spiteful, miserly, and manipulative old man. *The Simpsons* cast of characters is age diverse, in a way that is roughly proportionate to the real world, but the older characters are portrayed in negative stereotypical terms.

Children are also underrepresented on TV, a surprising finding given that Saturday morning—and on some cable channels, all day every day—is devoted largely to children's programming. These shows, however, typically feature animal, puppet, cartoon, or adult characters. Thus programming designed for children portrays an odd cast of characters that largely excludes real children. Despite comprising about 19% of the U.S. population, children (ages 0 to 10) make up only 6% of the TV cast of characters. Adolescents are similarly underrepresented on TV, making up 10% of the real-world population but just 5% of the TV population (Gerbner, 1997). In summary, the television world is vastly less age diverse than the world in which we live. Senior citizens and youth are underrepresented on TV and, when they appear, have less important roles. Older adults, particularly older women characters, are portrayed in negative and stereotypical terms. These representations send an implicit message, especially to heavy TV viewers, that the *important* people in our world are men and women in the prime of life.

Old Age Prejudice

In addition to stereotypic attitudes and beliefs about older people, ageism also involves emotional reactions to the elderly. It is no surprise that prejudicial reactions to old people mirror the ambivalent stereotypes held about them. Susan Fiske and her colleagues (2002) found that pity was the most common emotion felt about the elderly; indeed, few groups prompt as much pity as the elderly. Pity is a typical response to people who, through no fault of their own, face difficult or diminished life circumstances. And indeed, the pity and sympathy we feel toward the elderly acknowledges difficulties such as declining health and loss of opportunities that plague elderly people but that are not seen as responsible for. In addition to being pitied, older people in general also prompt admiration in perceivers (Fiske et al., 2002). Of the subgroups of stereotyped older people in Table 9.1, which ones prompt pity and which ones prompt admiration? We admire older people particularly when we perceive that they have lived life on their own terms and achieved a sort of longitudinal form of success—having *done something* with their lives.

Old people also prompt a range of negative feelings in others, and chief among those is anxiety. Researchers have found that anxiety is a common response to older people among the young, and the main reasons seem to be that old people remind us what may, or likely will, happen to all of us eventually (Greenberg, Schimel, & Martens, 2002). The elderly remind us that youth and beauty will fade; that illness and disability, along with the social isolation they can cause, are likely; and that death is a certainty for everyone. As we learned in Chapter 4, anxiety and prejudice are closely linked, and much research in the terror management tradition shows that existential anxiety motivates all manner of prejudice. Researchers measured contact with, anxiety about, and behavior toward the elderly in a sample of students (Bousfield & Hutchison, 2010). They found that the more anxiety participants had, the less contact they had with older people. In addition, anxiety about older people predicted attitudes and behavior: Participants who reported more anxiety also attributed more negative characteristics to older people and reported less willingness to help the elderly. This study highlights the spiraling nature of ageism: Anxiety leads to avoidance and more stereotyping of the elderly, which in turn produces more ignorance and negative emotions.

Another explanation for the anxiety and threat posed by the elderly to younger people trades on the stereotypic beliefs that old people are sick and feeble and therefore more likely to catch and carry illnesses that can be caught by others (Bugental & Hehman, 2007). Indeed, anxiety and the fear of infection has been observed in response to people from groups (e.g., the obese) whose physical qualities are not even remotely related to illness let alone contagiousness (Park, Schaller, & Crandall, 2007). To test the relationship between concern with illness and ageism, Lesley Duncan and Mark Schaller (2009) measured participants' perceived vulnerability to disease and then exposed them to a slide show that raised the salience of germs (or, in the control condition, accidents) in the environment. Ageism was measured with the Age-IAT, a test of implicit prejudice mentioned frequently in past chapters. When participants were reminded that germs are ever present in the environment, their agist attitudes increased. And, consistent with the reasoning above, the greatest prejudice was observed in those participants who felt vulnerable to infectious illness.

Are Old Age Stereotypes Self-Fulfilling Prophecies?

We know from previous chapters that stereotypes can generate their own fulfillment. That is, under certain conditions stereotypes of students' ability, for example, undermine their academic performance and lead to the very outcome that was assumed by the stereotype. Do old age stereotypes shape the behavior of older people? To find out, Brad Meisner (2010) conducted a meta-analysis of studies that manipulated age stereotypes and measured behavior in older-age samples. In this sort of study, older participants typically were randomly assigned either to a set of old-age stereotypic stimuli (e.g., images or words) or control stimuli, followed by a measure of some behavior. In some studies, the stimuli reflected positive aspects of the old-age stereotype, whereas other studies had negative old-age stimuli. Typical dependent measures included memory tests, walking speed and other physical tests, and self-perceptions of age-stereotypic dimensions. Two important findings emerged from this quantitative review. First, both types of stereotypic content had self-fulfilling properties: Negative age-stereotypic stimuli produced negative effects on participants' behavior, and positive stimuli produced positive effects. Second, the impact of negative stimuli on behavior was much larger than the effect of positive age stereotypic stimuli. So, although the old age stereotype is a mix of positive (e.g., warm) and negative (e.g., incompetent) traits, negative traits have more power to shape elderly persons' behavior and self-concepts in stereotype-consistent ways.

How do negative old-age stereotypes become self-fulfilling? Richard Eibach and his colleagues (2010) suggest that feeling old helps explain how negative stereotypes get internalized by older people and change their behavior. In one study, older participants (average age = 55 years) read paper material that was arranged to be difficult to read (e.g., small type, low contrast) or easier to read. One half (randomly determined) of the participants were given an explanation for the lack of clarity (a photocopying problem); the others received no explanation. The dependent measure in the study was subjective age (How old do you feel?). Participants who did not have an explanation for their difficulty reading the material self-stereotyped and reported feeling almost 10 years older than the participants who had an explanation for the reading problem. In a second study, they found that older participants self-stereotyped in the *no explanation* condition but only after hearing negative, but not positive, age-stereotypic material.

Other researchers found that older people were particularly vulnerable to the threat imposed by negative age-related stereotypes if they were more educated (Hess, Hinson, & Hodges, 2009). In that work, older participants took a memory test that was described in one of two ways: as able to assess the impact of aging on memory (threat condition) or having had the age bias removed from the test (no threat). Participants who felt threatened by the old-age stereotype and who were the most educated did the worst. Hess and his colleagues argue that better educated senior citizens identify with their group membership more and therefore are more vulnerable to internalizing stereotypes about their group. In addition to greater affiliation with their in-group— older people—seniors with more education are also more likely to participate in groups and organizations such as senior citizens' interest groups, defined for the older adult demographic. According to Becca Levy's (2003) analysis, the more connections older adults have with these groups, the more they self-identify as old, become the target of old-age stereotypes, and internalize those stereotypes. Levy (2009) notes that unlike members of other negatively stereotyped groups (e.g., racial minorities, women, gay and lesbian individuals) who have the opportunity to gradually develop coping strategies throughout their lives, older adults don't become *old* until they reach a threshold defined by the broader culture (e.g., age 65, or retirement). As a result, they acquire their membership in a negatively stereotyped group rather abruptly and are not prepared to handle the negative stereotypes they suddenly face as members of that group. Moreover, the newly *old* bring with them the accumulation of negative attitudes and feelings toward the old they passively acquired throughout their lives. As new members of the group they stereotyped when they were younger, those stereotypes now apply to themselves, making self-stereotyping difficult to resist.

Discrimination of Older Workers

The Age Discrimination in Employment Act (ADEA), passed by the U.S. Congress in 1967, made age-based employment discrimination illegal. The ADEA was responding to engrained policies that reflected old-age stereotypes—older workers were assumed to have diminishing mental competence and physical ability—that led to discrimination of older workers. Prior to ADEA, many companies had mandatory retirement ages that pushed older workers into unemployment regardless of their ability to continue doing their jobs. These displaced older workers could spend years in unemployment, creating a class of discouraged workers with eroding skills. Also, people were living longer and healthier lives and thus were able to be productive past the arbitrary retirement ages of their employers. Although the ADEA has achieved successes, including eliminating mandatory retirement ages, there is plenty of evidence that age-based discrimination in the workplace persists. We review some of that evidence here.

The past several years, beginning with the collapse of the banking and financial sector in 2008, have seen massive layoffs of workers and the movement of American jobs to foreign labor markets. According to Vincent Roscigno (2010), who summarized the effects of this period on older workers, tenure (the amount of time a worker is employed at a company) has declined steadily for older workers. Indeed, annual displacement rates of workers age 55 and over have been the highest of all age groups since 2001. According to Roscigno (2010), layoffs of older workers are often preceded by a period of harassment, in which older workers are asked to take on more responsibilities or do tasks that younger employees are not asked to do. The workers' refusal, or legitimate inability, to perform such duties can be used to justify their dismissal. In this way, age-based discrimination is legitimized and rationalized, making it difficult to challenge in court. Nevertheless, the last few years have seen a rapid increase in the number of age discrimination suits filed under ADEA (Macnicol, 2006). Roscigno and his colleagues (2007) studied the wage loss and hardships associated with being laid off among older workers and found that termination of older workers just prior to crucial dates regarding their pension, when the company would be obligated to pay the full pension, was common. Many of these layoffs are engineered by citing *infractions*, or the refusal to perform particular (unreasonable) duties, as mentioned earlier. When older workers are pushed out of their jobs, in addition to the economic hardships they must deal with, they also face age discrimination in hiring practices. Because older workers are stereotyped as being resistant to change, difficult to train, and having physical limitations, younger workers (despite their inexperience) are given preference in hiring new workers. As a result, older workers take more temporary and part-time jobs to make ends meet than displaced younger workers. Additionally, older compared with younger job seekers spend much longer looking for work and respond to many more ads in order to get an interview than younger people (Bureau of Labor Statistics, 2009). And finally, older workers who experience forced displacement from their jobs are cut off from a network of workplace friends, colleagues, and coworkers that feels very much like a family and provides major social support resources.

As we stated earlier, the disproportionate layoffs of older workers, who are still productive and interested in working, mean that older workers attempt to reenter a job market that is already age biased. Numerous studies have been done that present participants acting as employers, or actual employers, with identical employment qualifications and materials of hypothetical job applicants that differ only in age and measure their willingness to hire the applicant. Frederick Morgeson and his colleagues (2008) reviewed these studies and made several conclusions. First, studies that have been done in laboratory settings (usually with college student participants) consistently find evidence of age discrimination: Participants evaluate younger, compared with older, applicants more positively even when they are equivalent in all other respects. Second, some of these studies also find that the evaluations of the applicant depend on the type of job they are applying for, such that older applicants may be discriminated against for *younger* jobs such as those in the fast food industry. Also, discrimination of older workers has been found to be mediated by the hirer's competence-related old age stereotypes (Krings, Sczesny, & Kluge, 2011). This shows the interdependence of stereotyping and discrimination: Well learned or situationally activated old-age stereotypes can produce discriminatory behaviors that might not have occurred in the absence of those stereotypes. The strength of laboratory studies (control over extraneous variables) is also their greatest weakness. Laboratory investigations of hiring scenarios lack ecological validity, meaning that the findings from these studies may not describe what happens in real-life interviews. For that reason, Morgeson, et al. (2008) also summarized hiring studies that were done in real employment settings, with store managers and other personnel professionals as participants. Some, but not all, of these studies reveal a bias against older workers. The presence of age discrimination in these studies depended on other variables, such as the type of job being interviewed for and the sex of the interviewer. However, some of those studies also found that older workers were viewed more favorably than younger workers on particular measures. Morgeson et al. (2008) concluded that factors like qualifications and past experience were much more determinant of hiring decisions than age.

Summary

Stereotypes of senior citizens and the elderly contain a mix of positive (warm, trustworthy) and negative (incompetent, feeble) traits, although negative traits tend to dominate the stereotype. Negative stereotypical subtypes of older people (e.g., the curmudgeon, the recluse) also outnumber positive subtypes (e.g., the perfect grandparent). The fundamental ambivalence that underlies our beliefs about older people is reflected in prejudicial reactions and discriminatory behavior in that old people prompt both pity and anxiety in us. In the workplace, older workers are also seen as more trustworthy and reliable than younger workers, but are discriminated against for their presumed declining mental and physical vitality. The aging of the American population should focus researchers' efforts to better understand ageism.

DI | **Diversity Issue 9.1: Elderspeak**

Do you talk differently to your elderly grandparent than to your friends? Communication with older adults is not only louder and slower, it is also less understandable and is perceived by older adults as patronizing (Ryan, Bourhis, & Knops, 1991). Presumably, this pattern of communication reflects stereotypic beliefs of the elderly as hard of hearing or dim-witted. According to Ruscher (2001), we tend to patronize, or talk down to, outgroup members whom we believe are less intelligent than us. Older adults are the most common target of patronizing speech, called **elderspeak**. Elderspeak features more basic vocabulary and simpler structure, a slower speech rate, and more pitch variations than typical conversational speech (Kemper, 1994; Ruscher, 2001). Participants in one study prepared to interview either an elderly or a middle-aged adult (Rodin & Langer, 1980). The participants who prepared for the elderly, compared with the middle-aged, interviewee chose questions from a master list that were simple and easy to answer, even when the interviewee was characterized as intellectually competent. In other words, the (intended) communication of the interviewer was guided by his or her stereotypic beliefs that old people, as a group, have diminished intellectual capacities. Much other research shows that people speak more slowly, repetitively, and simply to elderly people (Kemper, 1994; Rubin & Brown, 1975).

Does elderspeak have effects on the senior citizens with whom we interact? Monica Harris and her colleagues (1994) had subjects teach a lesson either to an elderly person or another student. Those teaching the elderly, compared with the college-aged, student were less friendly and more nervous and, among female teachers, taught less material. Later, other students watched the videotaped teaching session (without being told what condition the teacher was in) and took a test on the lesson material. The students who watched the elderly teachers scored worse on the test than those who watched the college-student teachers, even when the lesser amount of material taught in the lesson was accounted for. This study provides only indirect evidence of the negative effect of elderspeak because the responses of elderly individuals themselves were not measured. Still, if college students do more poorly when taught in *elderspeak*, we should expect similar underperformance among elderly people. Other research finds that elderspeak is perceived by elderly people as offensive and leads them to feel inadequate about their communication skills (Caporael, Lukaszewski, & Culbertson, 1983; Kemper, Othick, Gerhing, Gubarchuk, & Billington, 1998). However, elderspeak may not be experienced by older people as uniformly negative; depending on who is doing the speaking it may convey warmth or superiority (O'Connor & St. Pierre, 2004). Nevertheless, when nursing home staff were trained to avoid elderspeak with elderly residents, their communications were rated by the residents as more respectful and less controlling compared to the pretraining communications (Williams, Kemper, & Hummert, 2003).

In summary, elderspeak tends to be experienced negatively, especially by higher-functioning elderly people. The effects of being spoken to with obviously simpler and more deliberate speech may make older people acutely aware that they are viewed in negative stereotypic terms. This awareness, in members of other stereotyped groups, such as Blacks and women, has negative effects on both self-evaluations and behavior and makes them vulnerable to confirming the stereotype.

DI Diversity Issue 9.2: Retirement

For most of history, people worked until they were physically unable to work; there was no such thing as **retirement**. For much of the last century, however, pension plans, Social Security, and other worker provisions allowed workers to leave employment and begin a new stage of life called retirement that was not defined by one's relationship

(Continued)

(Continued)

to a company or professional identity. Researchers found that people who identified strongly with their professional roles both delayed retirement and had more difficult transition and adjustment to retirement (Adams & Beehr, 1998; Quick & Moen, 1998). Up until the ADEA legislation discussed earlier, workers faced mandatory retirement ages. Today, most workers are free to work, again, as long as their physical and mental abilities allow them to. So, what does it mean to be retired, and how has the concept of retirement changed?

Kenneth Schulz and Mo Wang (2011) have observed that retirement can take one of three forms: a decision-making process, an adjustment process, or a career-development process. In the first, workers actively disengage from work on their own schedule and put work-related identities permanently aside, while focusing on their connections to family, interests, and community activities. In this model, retirement is defined by the decision to retire, and it is a major, and often stressful, life event. In the second form, retirement is defined not by a decision to retire but by one's transition from work and adjustment to retirement. Retirement, then, is the process of adjusting to a life in which work and work identities no longer apply. This model is illustrated by those who use retirement to try new activities and identities, travel, or develop new skills. These sorts of retirees may not call themselves retired—for them, the focus is on the adjustment process rather than the status. The third form of retirement views it as a career change process rather than a career exit. For many, retirement is a new stage of a continuing career, with new professional challenges and growth. In this model, retired workers try to redesign their work lives to accommodate the greater freedom and leisure time they have in retirement. Workers who retire, only to find new challenges as writers, teachers, or consultants, reflect this understanding of retirement.

This decision-making model most characterized retirement for much of the last century, when most people worked their whole careers with the same one or two companies and generally chose when to retire. Economic recessions and large scale layoffs and downsizing in the past 10 years forced a new model of retirement—an adjustment process—on a whole generation of workers. In contrast with their parents, many of those workers were not ready to retire and did not decide to retire. Finally, many workers now use retirement (whether planned or forced) to strategically acquire new skills or get more education with the goal of transitioning to a new career.

? Which model best describes your father or mother's (or grandparent's) retirement? Explain how these different models of retirement depend on one's individual goals and values.

KEY TERMS

Successful aging   175

Ageism   176

Elderspeak   184

Retirement   185

FOR FURTHER READING

Karel, M. J., Gatz, M., & Smyer, M. A. (2011). Aging and mental health in the decade ahead: What psychologists need to know. *American Psychologist*. Advance online publication. doi: 10.1037/a0025393

This article examines the consequences of the aging Baby Boomer generation for mental health and health care policy.

Online Resources

U.S. Equal Employment Opportunity Commission (EEOC)
http://www.eeoc.gov/laws/statutes/adea.cfm

This section of the EEOC website presents information about the ADEA. Go to the Prohibited Practices page to see what forms of age-based discrimination are illegal under ADEA.

National Center for Victims of Crime
http://www.ncvc.org/ncvc/Main.aspx

Go to Resource Library, Statistics, and then Elder Victimization to see a lot of data and facts on how older people are victims of crime.

National Center on Elder Abuse
http://www.ncea.aoa.gov/ncearoot/Main_Site/index.aspx

Go to FAQ / Basics for information on types of elder abuse, risk factors, and typical abusers of elders.

10

Social Stigma: The Experience of Prejudice

❖

In prior chapters, our learning about the psychology of diversity has been from the perspective of the perceiver. That is, we have learned how *we* process social information, how *we* respond to people who are different than us, and why *we* are prejudiced. A psychological study of diversity, however, must also consider how social difference is experienced. In the next two chapters, we will consider the perspective of someone who *experiences* prejudice and ask questions like: What does it feel like to be stereotyped? How do people experience being the target of prejudice? And, how do people cope with the effects of prejudice and discrimination? People who are potentially or actually targets of others' stereotyping and prejudice are said to be stigmatized. In this chapter, we will consider some of the basic psychological elements involved in social stigma—the experience of stereotyping and prejudice.

Understanding Stigma: Basic Components

Social scientists have long been interested in the experience of being socially different—or stigmatized—and its implications for one's identity, mental health, and social adjustment (Goffman, 1963; Jones et al., 1984; Katz, 1981). Stigma is an ancient term that refers to a physical mark symbolic of some negative status. The modern psychological usage of stigma conveys this meaning in social terms. To be stigmatized is to possess an attribute or status that has negative social implications or prompts in others' stereotypic judgments, prejudice, or discrimination. Stigmatizing attributes include social statuses (e.g., being Black, gay, or poor), physical marks (e.g., obesity, blindness), and marks that are more characterological in nature (e.g., developmental disabilities, alcoholism). **Social stigma**, then, refers to the experience of being socially discredited or flawed by a personal trait or characteristic. Let's consider the basic theoretical components of social stigma.

Stigma Involves a Mismatch of Identities

The central concept for understanding stigma is identity—that summary of information that describes who you are. Take a few minutes and do the following exercise. On the left side of a page, describe yourself by listing terms that answer the question "Who are you?" On the right side of the page, list terms that answer the question "Who do people think you are?" When you have finished, continue reading.

The descriptors in the left column form your **actual identity,** or the *you* you know yourself to be. The terms in the right column make up your **virtual identity,** or the *you* other people believe you to be. Look at the terms that compose your actual and virtual identities: They are probably not the same. Compared with how you know yourself, do others know you in terms that are inaccurate, negative, or unfair? If so, you feel stigmatized. Stigma—the realization that you are not just different, but your difference is viewed negatively by others—involves an inconsistency between one's actual and virtual identities (Goffman, 1963). In the great majority of cases, stigma is associated with a virtual identity that is more negative and/or more simplistic than one's actual identity.

If stigma involves a discrepancy between others' views of you and your own views of you, could stigmatized individuals resolve the discrepancy by merely dismissing others' errant or prejudiced beliefs? That is easier said than done. A long history of thinking and research in psychology asserts that our identity is fundamentally social (Cooley, 1902; Mead, 1913). Understanding who we are is not just a simple matter of looking within ourselves. Part of our self-understanding comes from internalizing others' views of us. Researchers have found that matching our self-views with others' views of us is an important need, both in short-term interactions and long-term relationships (Swann, Hixon, & De La Ronde, 1992). When friends and coworkers have a thorough and accurate impression of you, you realize comfort and predictability in interactions with them. However, when other people have a more negative impression of you than you have of yourself, you sense vulnerability, tension, and unpredictability in interactions with them. The fact that others' beliefs about us are an important source of our own self-understanding poses a problem for stigmatized people. They face chronic inconsistency between their own self-views and the negative views other people have of them. Thus, stigma involves a mismatch of identities—when the *you* reflected in others' behavior does not match the *you* you really are. Also, the discrepancy between actual and virtual identities cannot be felt without some imagined or actual interaction with other people.

Stigma Involves an Attribute–Stereotype Connection

Stigma can also be understood as a connection between an attribute and the stereotype associated with it. We have learned that social categories and stereotypes are useful social information-processing tools. By shifting our focus from the perception to the experience of diversity, we become aware that we can be categorized and stereotyped by other people. Most of us possess attributes that are associated with stereotypic knowledge. Dark skin, physical disability, and extreme overweight are examples of attributes that prompt stereotypic thinking and prejudice in others.

From others' perspective, the associations between attributes and stereotypes make you known and somewhat predictable to other people. However, as we discussed above, the *you* that other people know stereotypically is not likely to match the *you* that you know yourself to be. Others' stereotypic knowledge of us differs in three important ways from our self-knowledge. First, other people see us in more negative terms than we see ourselves. Second, other people explain our behavior more in terms of our inner dispositions and abilities than our situations and circumstances. Third, their understanding of us is more simplistic than is warranted, and if you have ever had the experience of being *reduced to a stereotype*, you know how other people oversimplify who you are. Thus, the experience of stigma involves recognizing that others see us in predominantly negative and characterological terms and that these terms are tied to just one (of your many) attributes.

Stigma Is Situationally Determined

Consistent with conceptualizations of stigma as a discrepancy between personal and social identities and an association between an attribute and a stereotype is an understanding that stigma is situationally determined (Crocker, 1999). That is, to be stigmatized is to be in a situation that calls for a particular skill or attribute with people who (are believed to) hold negative beliefs about what that attribute means. Put another way, people are stigmatized when situations spotlight a particular trait of theirs that others regard negatively. Being overweight, as we learned in Chapter 7, is associated with a negative stereotype that includes the belief that overweight people are unattractive. According to Jennifer Crocker's (1999) analysis, the meanings associated with overweight—in this case, the cultural stereotype of overweight people—would stigmatize people most when they were in situations that focused on looks and attractiveness. Dating situations, for example, would make obesity more burdensome and stigmatizing than other less appearance-oriented situations. For Crocker, stigma is not something that people carry around with them that spoils every interaction in the same way. Rather, the negativity of one's (potentially) stigmatizing mark—say, a facial disfigurement—depends on a range of situational variables like what you're asked to do, whom you're asked to do it with or for, what those people believe about people with disfigured faces, and whether those beliefs are likely to matter in the context.

Thus, a situation is stigmatizing if the situation reveals to others an attribute or part of yourself that is vulnerable to negative evaluation. In that situation, it may be *found out* by others that you are different along some dimension, and they may make assumptions about you based on that difference. For example, I have a friend who enjoys playing games and with whom I have played many games. However, he has always avoided word games. This inconsistency only made sense when I learned that he was dyslexic and did not feel confident or competent in those game-playing situations. For him, the prospect of his reading disability being exposed to others was sufficiently threatening to make him avoid those situations. His stigma was only felt in situations that publicly spotlighted reading and spelling skills. Broadening out from social situations to cultural contexts, the same principle applies. The relationship between an attribute and a stereotype is often embedded in cultural beliefs and norms. For example, being openly gay is more stigmatizing in socially conservative, religious regions of the country than in the northeastern cities because the attribute *gay* is connected to more negative judgments and beliefs in conservative religious cultures. Unlike stigmatizing situations, which often can be strategically avoided, living in a culture that condemns or devalues your attribute cannot be avoided and exerts chronic negative effects on stigmatized individuals' mental health.

In summary, these three conceptualizations of stigma complement each other. To possess an attribute that prompts negative stereotypic beliefs about you in other people is to have a virtual identity that is negative and inaccurate. Moreover, stigma is a potential by-product of a socially constructed identity. Because we look outward to our interactions and social groups for cues about who we are and what we are like, we must sometimes face the troubling prospect that we are not assumed (by others) to be the individual we know ourselves to be. And this negotiation process—who I am and who others believe I am based on a single attribute—depends heavily on how situations may either spotlight or obscure the attribute.

Stigma Involves Being the Object of Ambivalent Attitudes

Finally, as we learned in Chapter 2, many cultural stereotypes are not uniformly negative but feature some positive beliefs mixed in with a larger portion of negative beliefs. Accordingly, negative reactions to stigmatized people are often accompanied by positive feelings. Sympathy, pity, and admiration are also common emotional responses to stigmatized people. Thus, stigmatized individuals must deal with others' ambivalent feelings toward them (Katz, 1981).

Irwin Katz and his colleagues reasoned that **ambivalence** toward stigmatized people is rooted in two traditional and somewhat conflicting American values (Katz & Hass, 1988). The Protestant work ethic emphasizes self-reliance, hard work, and achievement, whereas humanitarianism stresses the equality and worthiness of all people. If people endorse these values equally, then it is possible to both dislike (for not working hard or taking personal responsibility for their lives) *and* support (for the disadvantages they face) the members of a stigmatized group. To test this idea, the researchers developed two questionnaires measuring pro-Black and anti-Black attitudes, respectively, and administered them to students at several northern colleges and universities (Katz & Hass, 1988). The results reflected students' ambivalence toward Blacks. Endorsement of the Protestant work ethic was related to holding anti-Black attitudes, and endorsement of humanitarian values was related to having pro-Black attitudes. This study showed that White people can hold and justify both positive and negative attitudes toward Blacks. To rule out the possibility that this finding was peculiar to people who already espouse both of these values, a second study randomly assigned subjects to think about either Protestant work ethic or humanitarian ideals (Katz & Hass, 1988, Study 2) and found similar effects. Subjects who were primed to think about the Protestant work ethic displayed more anti-Black attitudes, and those forced to think about humanitarianism endorsed pro-Black attitudes.

Together, these studies suggest that social stigma sometimes involves experiencing both positive and negative attitudes from others. As we discussed with benevolent sexism (see Chapter 6), others' sympathy and pity may feel good and obscure the fact that even positive reactions to stigmatized people can spring from, and be experienced as, assumptive and demeaning.

> **?** Think of a situation in which you were stigmatized. (Even middle-class White men, who seem to hold all the majority-group cards, encounter situations where an attribute of theirs becomes, in others' eyes, a shortcoming or a flaw.) What attribute of yours was negatively spotlighted? What assumptions did you think others were making about you? What feelings or thoughts did you have about being socially flawed?

Stigma Can Be Acquired by Association

Erving Goffman (1963) asserted that stigma could be experienced indirectly based on one's association with a stigmatized individual, a phenomenon referred to as **courtesy stigma**. Courtesy stigma is informed by what one's association with a stigmatized person seems to say about you. Courtesy stigma has been observed in children with development disabilities children, gay men, lesbians, people with physical disabilities, and obese individuals (Birenbaum, 1992; Hebl & Mannix, 2003; Swim, Ferguson, & Hyers, 1999).

In one study of courtesy stigma, participants viewed a (staged) conversation between two men after being led to believe either that both of the men were heterosexual or that one was gay and the other was heterosexual (Neuberg, Smith, Hoffman, & Russell, 1994). Participants' perceptions of the heterosexual man were more negative when he was interacting with a gay partner than with a heterosexual partner. In other words, the heterosexual man was stigmatized by his association with the gay interaction partner.

In another study, participants read scenarios about a fictitious male student who was described as either voluntarily rooming with a gay male or being assigned a gay male as a roommate. Compared to the student who did not choose, the student who chose a gay roommate was seen as having gay tendencies of his own and was described in gay stereotypic terms. However, these perceptions were observed only in people who had high levels of intolerance to begin with (Sigelman, Howell, Cornell, Cutright, & Dewey, 1991).

In a study of obesity stigma by association, Michelle Hebl and Laura Mannix (2003) showed participants the résumé of a man, along with a photo of him seated either next to an overweight woman or a thin woman. The participants rated the man as having lower professional qualifications and interpersonal skills when he appeared with an overweight, compared with a thin, woman. A second study tried to determine if this courtesy stigma—disliking a man because he was seen with a heavy woman—was due to assumptions that they had a relationship. Hebl and Mannix found that participants' devaluation of the man who was seen with an overweight woman did not change when the woman was characterized as his girlfriend. Other researchers examined the stigma by association felt by parents of children with autism spectrum disorder (Mak & Kwok, 2010). Courtesy stigma was measured by a questionnaire with items like "Most people look down on families who have a family member with autism spectrum disorder." The researchers found that courtesy stigma predicted poorer psychological well-being: Those who felt more stigmatized by their family member with autism had more anxiety and depression. The study also determined that the effect of courtesy stigma on well-being was due to two primary mechanisms. Parents who felt stigmatized by their child's disorder felt both a lack of control over, and a responsibility for, their child's disorder. In addition, families that had the support of friends and health care professionals coped better with the stigma associated with their child's disorder. Similar findings occurred in a study of courtesy stigma among families with a child with attention deficit disorder (Koro-Ljundberg & Bussing, 2009). A review of the research on courtesy stigma felt by families with relatives with mental illness concluded that parents tend to be blamed for their child's mental illness, and family members are blamed when others perceive that the family members are not providing their mentally ill relative with the proper treatment (Corrigan & Miller, 2004). Such blame may be based on quite unreasonable assumptions—such as the assumption that institutionalized care is always preferable to home care. But trying to correct ignorant assumptions in other people places yet another burden on the family who is already dealing with both the mental illness of a child and the stigma-by-association fallout. Finally, in a study on the effects of Alzheimer's disease on family members and caregivers of a person with Alzheimer's, researchers found no evidence of courtesy stigma (Werner & Heinik, 2008). This could be due to the great sympathy and other positive responses that are generated by a diagnosis of Alzheimer's.

This research suggests that the experience of social stigma is not limited to those who have a discrediting attribute but extends to people who affiliate with the marked individual. The research also has an important implication: If others perceive that associating with a stigmatized (such as a gay, disabled, or obese) individual will affect the way they are treated by others, it will lead to less interaction with stigmatized people. Stigma by association, then, has implications for both those who associate with stigmatized people and the stigmatized themselves in the form of isolation and loss of social opportunity.

> **?**
>
> It is easy to see how a person who hangs out with gay, same-sex friends would be suspected of being gay and that people who were prejudiced against gay people would impute those prejudices to the straight person—*courtesy* of their gay friends. However, it is not as intuitive how someone is stigmatized by associating with overweight friends. What do you think is going through others' minds that leads to courtesy stigmatization from one's heavy friends?
>
> Whom have you tried to avoid being seen with and why? Did that person have an attribute that you would rather not be associated with? What are some implications of avoiding people because they are stigmatized by others: For you? For the stigmatized person?

Implications of Stigma for Identity: Mindfulness and Stereotype Threat

Cognitively, stigmatized individuals are aware that they are known differently to others than they are to themselves, and this has implications for their identity—their overall sense of who they are. The *spoiled identity* (Goffman, 1963) of stigmatized persons refers to their being discredited in others' eyes. This social discrediting has two important implications for one's identity—mindfulness and stereotype threat.

Mindfulness

Recall that the essence of stigma is the knowledge that others know a *you* that is different, more negative, and assumptive than the *you* you know yourself to be. How can two people reach such different conclusions about who you are and what you are like? As behavioral *actors*, our gaze and attention are naturally focused on external factors such as situations and circumstances rather than on our appearance or character. However, when others look at us, they do not see situations or circumstances; they see us—our bodies and personalities. As a result, any distinctive attribute will have more impact on observers' perceptions of an individual than it will on the actor herself, especially if that attribute is associated with stereotypic knowledge. So, stigmatized people must deal with the fact that their attribute—whether it be their skin color, disability, or weight—is more noticeable and meaningful to other people than it is to them. In other words, people with discrediting or stigmatizing attributes are apt to be one-dimensionalized, or reduced to a stereotype, by many of the people with whom they interact.

One of the implications of this perspective differential is that stigmatized individuals may be more motivated than nonstigmatized people to find out what other people see in them or think about them. If being stigmatized is recognizing that others see you more negatively than you see yourself, then stigmatized people should want to reduce or at least understand this discrepancy by taking others' perspective on themselves; this behavior is called **mindfulness**. Deborah Frable and her colleagues tested this idea in a fascinating study (Frable, Blackstone, & Scherbaum, 1990). They had stigmatized people of many types (e.g., obese, Black, and facially scarred people) engage in a conversation with a nonstigmatized partner. These interactions were videotaped and subsequently viewed by each partner, who recorded his or her thoughts and feelings about the interaction. The participants were also asked to recall everything they could about their partner and the room. The results showed that all stigmatized participants, regardless of their stigma type, displayed mindfulness. That is, they took their partner's perspective during the interaction and remembered more details about the interaction than their partner did. This research suggests that, in response to being misunderstood and judged by others, socially stigmatized persons are more vigilant in social situations and adopt the perspective of nonstigmatized interaction partners in viewing the situation and themselves.

Mindfulness has another meaning in the social psychology of stigma—it is the centerpiece of Acceptance and Commitment Therapy (ACT), an approach to psychotherapy that has been applied with success to reduce perceived discrimination and self-stigma (internalizing others' negative assumptions about oneself) among people with stigmatizing qualities such as racial minority status and alcoholism (Hayes, Luoma, Bond, Masuda, & Lillis, 2006; Lillis & Hayes, 2007; Luoma, Kohlenberg, Hayes, Bunting, & Rye, 2007). As a therapy for stigma-related thoughts and feelings, ACT encourages mindfulness as a way of constructively dealing with others' stereotyping and prejudice. The goal is to train stigmatized people to engage and respond to, rather than disengage and try to escape from, their own thoughts about and reactions to their stigma. Much research has demonstrated that practicing mindfulness helps people deal with difficult thoughts and feelings with flexibility and produces more positive outcomes among people with social stigmas.

In one such study, Jason Lillis and his colleagues (2009) tested the impact of mindfulness-based acceptance therapy for reducing the stigma associated with obesity. The participants were 84 overweight or obese people, mostly middle aged, White, and middle-class women, who were enrolled in weight loss programs. The participants were randomly assigned to a 1-day workshop teaching acceptance and mindfulness techniques regarding obesity stigma or to a waiting list control group. Three months later, the participants completed measures of psychological distress, obesity-related quality of life, and weight-related stigma. The results were remarkable: After controlling for initial levels of those outcome variables, the acceptance/mindfulness treatment participants reported much less psychological distress, as well as greater quality of life and less stigma associated with being obese. Additionally, the treatment participants lost more weight in their weight loss program. Were the reductions in weight-related stigma simply the result of weight loss and not the acceptance/mindfulness treatment?

No—when researchers controlled for the amount of weight lost, the treatment benefits for obesity-related quality of life and stigma remained. A similar study found that mindfulness-based attention reduced the stigma associated with HIV/AIDS (Gonzalez, Solomon, Zvolensky & Miller, 2009). In summary, practicing mindfulness addresses some maladaptive patterns (e.g., avoidance) that sustain one's experience of social stigma and helps stigmatized people improve their quality of life and objective life outcomes.

Stereotype Threat

Striving to achieve in areas where other people believe you (or at least people *like* you) will struggle takes a toll on one's motivation and achievement. The awareness that you, as a member of a negatively stereotyped group, are seen through the lens of a stereotype by others is threatening. **Stereotype threat** refers to the doubts that arise in one's mind about one's own competence and worthiness when faced with others' negative beliefs about one's character and ability. It also involves facing the possibility that one's failures may confirm those stereotypic beliefs (Steele, 1992, 1997). Research demonstrates very clearly that for members of some minority groups the threat of negative stereotypes about their intellectual abilities has serious consequences for academic striving and achievement.

Stereotype Threat in Black Students

Beliefs about low intelligence and laziness have been part of the cultural stereotype of Blacks for decades (see Chapter 5). Stereotypes about their *academic deficiencies* undercut Black students' school ambitions and accomplishments (Steele, 1992, 1997). According to Claude Steele, Black students feel anxious and vulnerable in school settings because they sense that teachers' (and the surrounding culture's) assumptions about their ability set them up for failure. To defend against this threat, Black students tend to disidentify with school. That is, they relinquish the belief that education holds promise for them, that they can feel good about themselves as students, and that they can improve their life prospects through schooling. When students disidentify with school, their school performance drops and this confirms stereotypic beliefs about Black students.

In one of the first demonstrations of stereotype threat, Black and White college students took a test composed of difficult questions from the verbal portion of the Graduate Record Examination. The test was described as "able (or not able) to diagnose intellectual ability." The Black students who believed their academic *deficiency* would not be detected by the test scored just as well as the White students. The Black participants who felt vulnerable to the test—that it was somehow able to *find them out*—scored much poorer than the White participants (Steele & Aronson, 1995). A follow-up study revealed that Black participants who experienced stereotype threat were more mindful of the stereotype about their group, wanted to avoid being stereotyped, and distanced themselves from racial categorization and stereotypic associations. Steele and his colleagues' research shows that school performance among Blacks is related to stereotypes about their ability rather than their actual ability, and when the threatening nature of those beliefs is removed, Black and White students perform equally well.

Stereotype Threat in Female Students

The notion that women are illogical and otherwise intellectually ill suited for scientific pursuits is prominent in the stereotype of women, despite a lack of evidence (Hyde et al., 1990). Female students who are aware of this stereotype, even if they disagree with it, carry an extra burden in math or engineering pursuits. In addition to mastering the material, they also run the risk of confirming what people already believe—that women are not good at math. Stereotypes about women's logical and mathematical deficiencies undercut the ambitions and accomplishments of women in math and science fields (Steele, 1997). In the short run, as was the case with Black students in academic domains, women's performance in math and science will suffer. In the long run, women may disidentify with achievement in math and science domains; in other words, they give up the belief that math and science fields hold promise for them and that their accomplishments in those areas will be appreciated. Both outcomes end up contributing to the stereotype that produced them.

Researchers tested this idea by giving men and women students a math test which was described as "able (or not able) to show gender differences." The women who believed their math *deficiency* would not be detected scored just as well as men, but the women who felt vulnerable to the stereotype of *math deficient* scored much worse than men (Spencer, Steele, & Quinn, 1997). This study demonstrates that women's poorer performance in math-related domains is due to their vulnerability to stereotypical beliefs about women's mathematical skills and not to their math ability. When that vulnerability is eliminated, women achieve equally to men.

Stereotype Threat in Economically Disadvantaged Students

Beliefs about the intellectual inferiority and laziness of poor people are widespread in our culture (Cozzarelli et al., 2001). As is the case with members of other stereotyped groups, these stereotypic beliefs burden economically disadvantaged students, lower their academic achievement, and push them to disidentify with school as a domain of promise and self-improvement. In a study similar to those reported earlier, French researchers gave participants who were of low or high socioeconomic status (SES) a test consisting of items taken from the verbal portion of the Graduate Record Examination (Croizet & Claire, 1998). The test was described either as "a test of verbal intelligence" or "an investigative tool for studying lexical processes." The low SES participants who believed the test was diagnostic of their verbal intelligence attempted significantly fewer questions and scored worse than did low SES participants in the nondiagnostic test condition and all high SES participants. But when participants believed the test was not indicative of their intellectual ability, low and high SES participants scored equally well.

In summary, research on stereotype threat makes it clear that Blacks, women, and economically disadvantaged individuals are vulnerable to widely held stereotypic beliefs about their ability. Stereotype threat interferes with intellectual and academic performance and leads students to devalue school and achievement as a basis for self-esteem and self-improvement. It is important to remember that, from minority students' perspectives, disidentification with school achievement is done to preserve psychological well-being from what Claude Steele calls "the burden of suspicion." Sadly, from teachers' (and other observers') perspectives, disidentification leads to the poor academic achievement that was initially expected of minority students, thus strengthening others' stereotypes of Black, female, and economically deprived students. In other words, this research also shows the power of stereotypic beliefs to generate their own fulfillment. Students who are believed to lack ability—due to stereotypes about their group—are not expected to do well by teachers and peers. These negative expectations contribute to a burdensome and unfriendly context for academic accomplishment, a context that brings about the expected behavior.

Claude Steele has characterized stereotype threat as "in the air", suggesting that stereotypes threaten negatively stereotyped group members in every situation where they must demonstrate their competence. Daryl Wout and his colleagues (2009) reasoned that there must be situations where the likelihood of being stereotyped, and therefore having that awareness undermine one's performance, is low. For example, would female math majors feel their math abilities were assumed to be suspect if the math course was taught by a woman? Researchers tested this idea by having Black students take a test that was either diagnostic or nondiagnostic of academic ability in one of two conditions: The test was evaluated by either a White or Black person (Wout, Shih, Jackson, & Sellers, 2009). They reasoned that if stereotype threat is only experienced when the threat is deemed probable or likely, then the participants' performance should be most affected when taking a diagnostic test with the White evaluator, and that is just what happened. In several follow-up studies, Wout et al. (2009) confirmed this basic finding: Members of stereotyped groups contend with stereotype threat, and see their performances suffer accordingly, only when they believe that the threat is plausible and likely. Indeed, the estimated probability that stereotype threat is likely to be an issue in a situation (such as when a woman takes a math course taught by a sexist male professor) mediates the effect of stereotype threat on performance.

Since the original stereotype threat study was published in 1995 (Steele & Aronson, 1995), hundreds of studies investigating this fascinating phenomenon have been published. Recent meta-analyses—studies that synthesize the data across studies—found that intellectual test outcomes (e.g., grades, scores) in school underestimate the true ability of minority students because, for most minority students, testing situations are fraught with negative stereotypes about their ability. Indeed, Gregory Walton and Steven Spencer's (2009) meta-analysis of 39 experiments showed that when stereotype threat is experimentally eliminated, minority students actually perform better on achievement tests. This outcome may reflect a greater motivation to succeed among minority compared to nonminority students that is typically hidden because stereotype threat effects chronically depressed the grades of those students. A second meta-analysis that combined data from three field experiments of stereotype threat found a similar outcome: When stereotype threat was controlled, minority-group participants outperformed majority-group participants. Walton and Spencer (2009) estimate that the Scholastic Assessment Test (SAT) math test underestimates females' true math ability by about 20 points. Given that the average gender difference on the SAT math test is 34 points, stereotype threat explains about two thirds of that gap.

How Does Stereotype Threat Lower Academic Performance?

In sum, stereotypes that include beliefs about inferior intelligence or competence threaten achievement among members of those negatively stereotyped groups. But how do stereotypes interfere with performance? Several answers have been tested.

- *Negative stereotypes reduce memory capacity.* Toni Schmader and Michael Johns (2003) had men and women take a test that involved solving mathematical equations, for example, does $(9 \times 6) - 4 = 50$?. A word was presented after each equation, and after the test, participants were tested on their recall of the words. One half of the participants were led to believe the test tapped their quantitative ability; the other half were told it was a memory test. Because the stereotype of women includes the belief that they're not very good in math, women should be stereotype threatened in the *quantitative ability* condition. What happened? Women recalled fewer words than men but only in the stereotype threat condition. Follow-up studies confirmed the effects of stereotype threat on memory capacity in Hispanic participants and also showed that the link between stereotype threat and test performance was explained by the loss of working memory in the stereotype-threatened participants. Other research trained female participants to associate their gender with excellent math ability, essentially priming a new, more positive stereotype, and then had them do a test of working memory and math ability (Forbes & Schmader, 2010). To instill a new stereotype, the researchers used the Implicit Associations Test to reinforce the association of *female* and *good at math* concepts; other participants did not receive this retraining. The studies found that female participants whose stereotypes were retrained, essentially reducing or eliminating stereotype threat, demonstrated more working memory and higher math test scores than participants who did not receive the retraining.

- *Negative stereotypes cause depression and anxiety.* Researchers had German high school students take a math test with either stereotype threat ("Men and women tend to score differently on this test") or no-threat ("Men and women tend to score the same on this test") instructions (Keller & Dauenheimer, 2003). As you might expect, female students answered fewer questions than males but only in the stereotype threat condition. More importantly, however, is that students' dejection after the test—their ratings of how disappointed, frustrated, and sad they were—explained the effect of stereotype threat on test performance. Similarly, Black students who were tested under stereotype threat conditions displayed more apprehension in the form of self-doubts about their ability, avoidance of Black-stereotypical preferences, and making excuses for their anticipated (poor) performance (Steele & Aronson, 1995). Anxiety in testing situations also produces inflexibility in trying new problem-solving methods and strategies, according to research by Priyanka Carr and Claude Steele (2009). When female participants took a math test that was described as diagnostic of mathematics ability, they persisted in the use of problem-solving strategies that were not appropriate, and this of course lowered their score on the test. In similar work, Robert Rydell and his colleagues (2010) found that stereotype threat interfered with females' learning of the mathematical rules and operations necessary to solve a series of math problems, leading to lower performance.

- *Negative stereotypes increase stress.* Increased blood pressure is a common response to stress. Jim Blascovich and his colleagues (2001) gave Black and White students a cognitive test under stereotype threat ("This test is being used to develop national norms for your group") or no-threat ("This test is being used to develop a culturally unbiased test") conditions concurrent with monitoring their blood pressure. The Black stereotype-threatened participants had higher blood pressure than the other three groups of participants, and this difference increased across the duration of the test. Brenda Major and Laurie O'Brien (2005), in a review of research in this area, concluded that stereotype threat had numerous physiological consequences, including increasing blood pressure, heart rate, and levels of cortisol (a stress hormone) in the blood. In addition, perceived discrimination predicts disability, including pain-related disability and number of sick days.

- *Negative stereotypes decrease self-control and self-regulation.* Stereotype threat interferes with the resources needed to regulate and control our own actions. Researchers demonstrated this by having Black and White students do the Stroop task under stereotype threat or no-threat conditions (Inzlicht, McKay, & Aronson, 2006). The Stroop task presents color words (e.g., blue, yellow) printed in various colors. Participants were asked to name the ink color while ignoring the word meaning. For example, the word *yellow* printed in blue ink requires the response *blue*, but saying *blue* when you're also reading *yellow* is difficult and takes self-control in the form of attention, focus, and inhibiting the incorrect answer. The results showed that Black participants in the stereotype threat condition were slower at the Stroop task than the other participants, indicating that stereotype threat takes resources that would otherwise be available for self-regulation and control. Other research had sexual (gay, lesbian, and bisexual) and racial (Black) minority participants keep a diary in which they recorded their experiences of discrimination, how they dealt with the discrimination, and their psychological distress regarding each event (Hatzenbuehler, Nolen-Hoeksema, & Dovidio, 2009). The analysis revealed that the experience of discrimination prompted more rumination (e.g., "what did I do to deserve this?") and suppression (e.g., "I kept my emotions to myself"). In addition, participants reported feeling more isolated on days they were discriminated against. Together, these strategies for coping with discrimination eat up resources that would otherwise be available for self-control and regulation tasks. Indeed, rumination mediated the effect of discrimination on psychological distress—the experience of discrimination prompted more rumination, which, in turn, caused distress levels to go up.

To sum up, negative stereotypes about the competence and abilities of stigmatized groups are preoccupying and stressful to the members of those groups, and this interferes with performances in those stereotyped domains. Stereotype threat occurs in particular situations—situations in which people are asked to demonstrate their proficiency in a domain that is part of a stereotype held about their group and when the experience of threat is predictable and plausible. Stereotype threat is very much part of the experience of social stigma. In this research, we see again how powerful stereotypes are, as we learned in Chapter 3, to engineer their own fulfillment.

Summary

We live in a socially diverse world. As a result, most of us are acquainted with the experience of being different than others. In this chapter, we learned how social differences can be stigmatizing. We are stigmatized when we have an attribute that prompts negative attitudes and feelings in others. Stigma arises out of social interaction and is experienced as a spoiled identity. When used, social categories and stereotypes are valuable information-processing tools; when experienced, they are often oppressive and demoralizing.

DI Diversity Issue 10.1: Mental Illness Stigma

Mental illness has a long history of being stigmatized (Hinshaw, 2007). Although perceptions of mental illness depend somewhat on the specific illness, in general, mental illness is seen as being largely uncontrollable (the mentally ill individual generally isn't held responsible for it) but also unstable (the mentally ill individual's behavior is unpredictable; Weiner, Perry, & Magnuson, 1988). Stereotypically, mentally ill people are perceived as dangerous, irrational, and capable of violence. Much of the association of mental illness and perceived dangerousness is due to the assumption that mentally ill people are not fully human—that is, researchers have found that stereotypes of the mentally ill incorporate animal traits (e.g., wild, feral, beastly; Martinez, Piff, Mendoza-Denton, & Hinshaw, 2011). Interestingly, when mental illness is described as *in remission*, according to Martinez et al.'s (2011) research, perceptions of humanity improve. This highlights the fear attached to an unremitted mental illness by others.

According to Patrick Corrigan, an expert on mental illness stigma, mentally ill people are discriminated against for a variety of reasons other than the symptoms associated with their illness, including their appearance, poor social skills, and the mere label they have been given by the psychiatric or lay community. Severe mental illness occurs in about 5% of American adults, according to the 2008 National Survey on Drug Use and Health (National Institute of Mental Health, 2008), although less serious forms of mental disturbance are much more common. Of those who are seriously mentally ill, however, only about 58% receive treatment for their illness. The problem of treatment avoidance is greatest among young adults with mental illness, where only 40% receive treatment. The large gap between those who need treatment and those who seek it has been explained by the stigma associated with mental illness (Corrigan, 2004).

Reactions to mentally ill individuals depend somewhat on whether the illness is consistent with other social information about that person. James Wirth and Galen Bodenhausen (2009) tested participants' reactions to a mentally ill male or female that was described as having a gender stereotype–consistent or inconsistent mental illness. Based on prior testing, they determined that alcoholism and depression were seen as stereotypically male and female mental illnesses, respectively. Their study found that gender-inconsistent mental illnesses (e.g., a female alcoholic) prompted more sympathy and inclination to help than gender-consistent illnesses (e.g., male alcoholic). When peoples' mental illnesses deviate from gender stereotypical expectations, the illness is taken more seriously and seen as less under the control of the person with the illness.

How can the stigma associated with mental illness be reduced? Patrick Corrigan and his colleague (see Corrigan, 2004) suggest three avenues: protesting unfair portrayals or treatment of mentally ill people, educating the public about mental illness to encourage more positive and informed attitudes, and creating more contact between mentally ill individuals and the general public.

KEY TERMS

Social stigma   190

Actual identity   190

Virtual identity   190

Ambivalence   192

Courtesy stigma   193

Mindfulness   196

Stereotype threat   197

FOR FURTHER READING

Corrigan, P. (2004). How stigma interferes with mental health care. *American Psychologist, 59*, 614–625. doi: 10.1037/0003-066X.59.7.614

This article covers how people with mental illness experience both public and private forms of stigma and how stigma impacts seeking out and participating in treatment.

ONLINE RESOURCES

Reducing Stereotype Threat

http://reducingstereotypethreat.org/

This site compiles research about stereotype threat in various domains. Look under *Who is most vulnerable to stereotype threat?* and develop a profile of people who are most at risk for having negative stereotypes about their group threaten their achievement.

Psychology Today: Gay and Lesbian Well-Being Blog

http://www.psychologytoday.com/blog/gay-and-lesbian-well-being/201008/parents-gay-children-and-courtesy-stigma

This blog entry discusses courtesy stigma from the perspective of parents of gay and lesbian children.

Psychology Today: Mindfulness

http://www.psychologytoday.com/basics/mindfulness

This resource from *Psychology Today.com* invites exploration of mindfulness and its role in mental and physical health.

Social Work Today: ABCs of Acceptance and Commitment Therapy (ACT)

http://www.socialworktoday.com/archive/090208p36.shtml

This article presents a reader-friendly summary of ACT.

11

Coping With Social Stigma

Stigmatized people have an attribute that makes them a target of stereotyping, prejudice, and discrimination. What consequences does being socially different have on the well-being and adjustment of stigmatized people? The cost of stigma exists on social and psychological levels; stigma affects social interactions and opportunities, as well as how stigmatized people view and evaluate themselves. Each of these domains of influence has important implications for mental health and adjustment. In this chapter, we discuss the social and psychological consequences of stigma and some of the ways of coping with others' prejudice.

Social Consequences of Stigma

Friendships and companionship play a vital role in preserving mental health and adjustment. Our friends listen when we are burdened and provide material and moral support when we are stressed (Cohen & Wills, 1985; Pennebaker, 1990). It is well documented, however, that stigmatized people face rejection and avoidance from others. Indeed, gaining acceptance is regarded as the chief problem for most stigmatized people (Goffman, 1963). Stigmatized people also provoke negative emotional reactions in others, such as tension, uncertainty, or disliking. Social interactions between stigmatized and nonstigmatized people are often marked by tension, awkwardness, and hostility. In general, stigma disrupts both the quality and quantity of the social relationships of stigmatized people, and this should have aversive consequences for the well-being of stigmatized individuals (French, 1984; see also Crocker & Major, 1989, for review).

In a fascinating classic experiment that demonstrates the negative effects of stigma on social interaction between stigmatized and nonstigmatized people, participants had a conversation with an individual—a confederate playing a role for the researchers—who was either physically disabled (a wheelchair-bound amputee) or nondisabled (Kleck, Ono, & Hastorf, 1966). The participants were fitted with electrodes to measure their skin conductance, a physiological indicator of anxiety that lies beyond conscious control. The researchers also measured the duration of the interaction and the extent to which participants misrepresented their true (negative) attitudes about disabled people in the interaction.

Overall, participants exhibited more anxiety in interactions with disabled than with nondisabled partners. The interactions between participants and disabled partners were shorter than those between the able-bodied partners. Participants conversed with nondisabled partners for about 6½ minutes, whereas the interactions with disabled partners averaged about 5 minutes. Also, participants hid their true attitudes about disabled people from their disabled partner, displaying instead *disabled-friendly* sentiments. Interestingly, participants brought up topics in the conversation that were stereotypically positive, such as the belief that disabled individuals are more academically inclined than nondisabled people.

These studies demonstrate some of the major social consequences of stigma. First, stigmatizing marks and conditions cause anxiety in others such that interactions with stigmatized people tend to be avoided or, if necessary, curtailed. Second, people carefully monitor their behavior toward stigmatized persons. This heightened vigilance about one's actions when interacting with stigmatized people may occur because we want to make them feel comfortable or because we do not want to reveal our own prejudice toward them, or both. Regardless of the motive, stigmatized people experience interactions that are strained and superficial. Finally, stigmatized

Table 11.1 The Social Consequences of Being a Member of a Stigmatized Group

General	Specific
Stigma heightens anxiety . . .	. . . in others, leading to fewer and poorer social interactions.
	. . . in oneself, leading to more vigilance about, and less control over, one's behavior.
Stigma heightens stereotyping . . .	. . . from others, leading to more negative assumptions about, and discrimination of, stigmatized individuals.
	. . . of oneself, leading to avoidance of stereotype-confirming situations and defensiveness toward majority group persons.

people are treated stereotypically. The connection between attributes and stereotypic traits and assumptions are often too well learned and automatic to inhibit. Even others' positive, well-intentioned actions toward stigmatized people are likely to reflect stereotypic ideas and to be perceived by stigmatized individuals as ingratiating or patronizing.

Social consequences of stigma also accrue from the awareness that one is singled out by others based on an attribute that is negatively stereotyped; this awareness is called **stigma consciousness** (Pinel, 1999). Elizabeth Pinel (1999) showed that people who are high in stigma consciousness avoid tasks that heighten stigma, such as women avoiding talking about sports with men lest they confirm men's negative assumptions about them. The systematic avoidance of situations or tasks that could confirm others' beliefs about you can have serious consequences, as when Black and Hispanic students who are stigma conscious avoid academic challenges and end up with poorer grades than similar minority students who are not stigma conscious (Brown & Lee, 2005). Stigma consciousness can also lead people to react defensively toward people who (they believe) hold prejudices against them. In one study, female participants who were highly stigma conscious criticized a male partner who they believed held sexist attitudes (Pinel, 2002). This criticism became a self-fulfilling prophecy because it caused the males to respond negatively toward the female participants, thus confirming the participants' suspicions about the *sexist* partner. This interaction dynamic did not occur among participants who were low in stigma consciousness. This research shows that people who are stigma conscious may preempt the rejection that they anticipate from prejudiced others by defensively rejecting them first.

Perceived Controllability Affects Stigma

The social consequences of stigma are not the same for every stigmatized person. Rather, they depend heavily on the underlying dimensions of stigmatizing conditions, one of which is controllability. **Stigma controllability** refers to who caused or is responsible for the stigmatizing attribute, status, or condition or to what extent it could have been prevented. Stigmatizing marks range in their controllability from those that are uncontrollable and assigned, such as race, ethnicity, or a genetically determined physical ailment to those that are highly controllable, such as having a substance abuse problem, a criminal record, or a tattoo.

A great deal of research has established that people with stigmas that are thought to be controllable are treated more negatively than those with uncontrollable conditions. Much research shows that controllable stigmas elicit more blame and anger and less inclination to help or provide support among perceivers than do uncontrollable stigmas. Perceptions of stigma controllability lead to more negative evaluations of people who are developmentally disabled, obese, unemployed or poverty-stricken, diseased, or speech disabled or who are AIDS victims, substance abusers, or amputees (Farina, Holland, & Ring, 1966; Furnham, 1982b; Lewis & Range, 1992; Menec & Perry, 1995; Rodin et al., 1989; Schwarzer & Weiner, 1991; Vann, 1976; Weiner et al., 1988).

In one study, participants read a scenario about a man who had contracted AIDS due to one of four things: an AIDS-infected homosexual partner, an AIDS-infected heterosexual partner, a blood transfusion, or an AIDS-infected intravenous drug needle (Dooley, 1995). Participants' pity and anger toward and willingness to help the AIDS-infected individual were measured. The results indicated that pity was a crucial mediator of helpful intentions toward an individual with AIDS. That is, to offer help toward a person with AIDS, one is likely to first have to feel pity toward him or her. Compassionate feelings such as pity or sympathy, in turn, were produced by beliefs that AIDS was contracted in an uncontrollable manner (e.g., through a blood transfusion). Participants' perceptions that an AIDS infection could have been prevented, such as in the homosexual and drug-use scenarios, produced anger toward the AIDS victim and an unwillingness to help him or her.

> **?** Would you think about and respond differently to someone with lung cancer or skin cancer versus another form of cancer such as stomach or colon cancer? If so, what does the perceived controllability of the condition have to do with your reactions?

In summary, others' perceptions of the controllability of a stigma are a pivotal dimension for understanding the social consequences of stigma. But why is controllability information so important in understanding others' responses to stigma? **Just world theory** argues that we have a general need to see the world—and the people and events in it—as reasonable, orderly, and just. In a just world, people get what they deserve. That people could be unemployed, disabled, or sick through no fault of their own, however, threatens beliefs in a just world in two ways. First, it suggests that *we* could suffer a similar tragedy. Second, it suggests that we are somehow obliged to help such individuals, perhaps giving some of our time and money to make their lives better. Researchers show that these threats are buffered by making the victim responsible for his or her own plight. Thus, perceptions of stigma controllability are in part a defensive response to the threatening implications of stigma. Further, they justify negative attitudes and feelings toward stigmatized people.

Visibility Affects Stigma

The social consequences of stigma also depend on the visibility of the status or condition (Frable, 1993a). **Stigma visibility** refers to how apparent it is to others and how difficult it is to conceal from others. Stigmatizing marks range in their visibility from the completely invisible, such as being gay or a paroled convict, to the completely visible, such as having a physical disability, being obese, or having a racial minority status. Stigma visibility is a key moderator of stigma because those with invisible marks may avoid stigma altogether, provided such individuals can keep their stigmatizing conditions hidden from others. In other words, possessors of invisible but potentially stigmatizing attributes are not socially discredited—they are *discreditable*. As long as invisible or concealable failings go undetected by others, much of the negative experience of stigma is averted. This is perhaps best illustrated by the plight of lesbians and gay men who are aware of widespread prejudice and discrimination they will experience if their sexual orientation becomes public knowledge (Berrill, 1990; Herek, 1991). The concealability of that attribute allows gay individuals to avoid some of those negative reactions by revealing their identity to potentially friendly people and concealing it from those who are potentially hostile.

This does not mean that individuals with invisible stigmas experience no social difficulties. Deborah Frable (1993b) had university students from visible (such as ethnic minority or overweight) and invisible (such as being gay or hearing disabled) stigmatized groups estimate what proportion of their peers shared their attitudes and preferences. The results revealed that students with invisible social flaws perceived more difference between themselves and their peers than did those with visible marks. In a second study, participants viewed *uniqueness* adjectives (such as *different* or *outsider*) and *similarity* adjectives (such as *normal* or *commonplace*) presented by a computer and responded whether each adjective described them or not. Again, compared with people with visible stigmas, those with invisible stigmas described themselves with more *uniqueness* adjectives and were faster, and therefore more certain, in their responses. These studies show that people with hidden social flaws experience more marginality and differentness than do people whose stigma is obvious. Although Frable's studies did not establish this, feeling marginalized is likely to be associated with or cause loneliness and social isolation.

People with invisible social flaws have another concern that affects their social well-being—whether to conceal or reveal their stigma. A concealed discreditable attribute can assume an important position in the stigmatizable person's daily life, determining (and often limiting) his or her social, employment, or recreation options and taxing his or her attentional and cognitive resources. Furthermore, individuals who choose to conceal their invisible stigmas develop friendships on somewhat false pretenses and must reconcile the benefits of those relationships with the social costs of revealing one's discrediting attribute. That is, one's friends may be disillusioned or angry to learn that you are not who they believed you to be or that you did not trust them to enough to confide in them.

Denying or hiding an important aspect of one's identity is associated with decrements to mental health (Pennebaker, 1990). Researchers have studied the well-being and social support of people who were diagnosed with AIDS and who either kept their condition private or revealed it to varying numbers of people (Crandall & Coleman, 1992). The results show that the highest levels of anxiety, depression, and stigma existed among AIDS victims who concealed their disease from everyone and among those for whom the diagnosis became public knowledge. In both of these situations, the prospect of meaningful social support is dim. However, persons with AIDS who revealed their diagnosis to one other or to a few individuals reported higher social support and well-being. This study shows that invisible stigmas that are concealed prevent stigmatizable people from receiving others' support, understanding, and acceptance. In a study to measure the psychological impact of having a concealable stigma, Diane Quinn and Stephanie Chaudoir (2009) surveyed almost 400 students who said they had an aspect of their identity that they kept hidden and, if revealed, it would generate a negative or surprised reaction in others. They measured anticipated stigma, or the extent to which these students felt they would be stigmatized if they revealed their secret to others. Other measures in the study included how important the concealed identity was to their overall self-concept (centrality), how often they thought about their concealed identity (salience), and how negatively valued the identity aspect was in the general population (cultural stigma). Psychological distress (anxiety and depression combined) was the outcome variable. The study found that anticipated stigma and cultural stigma were related but not very much. In other words, the reaction the participants thought people would have to their true identity did not correlate very highly with others' actual attitudes toward that attribute. Anticipated stigma, centrality, and salience all independently predicted psychological distress: The more stigma that was anticipated if they revealed their secret, the more important the attribute was to their identity, and the more they thought about it all predicted greater anxiety and depression. To determine if concealable stigmas have negative effects on health, a second study examined the relationships of these variables to a measure of illness (a checklist of symptoms). Quinn and Chaudoir found that the best predictor of illness was psychological distress. Of the measures associated with participants' concealable stigmas, only anticipated stigma had a direct effect on illness. Apparently, the anxiety over how people will react to one's secret, if you were to reveal it, is enough to directly cause illness. This finding is consistent with the conclusions of a major meta-analysis of studies that measured perceived discrimination and health (Pascoe & Richman, 2009). That review combined the results of 134 studies, including those that measured perceived discrimination based on race, gender, sexual orientation, and other identities; in other words, most of the studies focused on visible rather than concealable stigmas. Pascoe and Richman (2009) concluded that perceived discrimination was negatively associated with mental and physical health outcomes. Furthermore, perceived discrimination predicted both unhealthy stress responses (e.g., anger) and poorer health behavior (e.g., smoking).

On the opposite end of the visibility spectrum are people with completely apparent stigmas. They cannot avoid being identified, labeled, and stereotyped; hence, their social plight is in being judged and rejected by others on sight. Visibly stigmatized people, then, are denied opportunities to interact with others. Aside from the implications for social support discussed previously, disrupted social interactions also affect one's social skills.

Individuals with visible stigmas do not have the luxury of strategically concealing and revealing their stigma to maximize acceptance and social adjustment. Rather, they are caught in a vicious cycle of rejection and limited opportunity. Others' rejection disrupts the social prospects and skills of stigmatized people, which, in turn, contributes to even more avoidance and rejection.

Peril Affects Stigma

A final dimension of the social consequences of stigma is the danger that other people associate with a stigmatizing condition called **stigma peril** (Jones et al., 1984). The more peril that is associated with a stigma, the more negative is its impact on the social prospects of stigmatized people. One aspect of stigma peril is contagiousness. People may be stigmatized by physical ailments that are perceived by others to be contagious, even when such contagion is irrational or highly improbable. The stigma felt by HIV/AIDS victims, for example, combines others' moral disgust with their irrational fear about contracting the disease, and it profoundly affects the social prospects of people with HIV/AIDS (Crawford, 1996; Herek & Glunt, 1988).

In a national telephone survey of American adults, Gregory Herek and John Capitanio (1998) measured whether respondents' attitudes toward people with AIDS were based on upholding cultural or personal values (e.g., "I avoid people with AIDS because homosexuality is morally wrong") or on concerns about peril and personal risk (e.g., "I avoid people with AIDS because I don't want to get AIDS"). The survey results showed that respondents' negative feelings toward AIDS sufferers and their support of policies such as mandatory AIDS testing were related to upholding personal values. However, behavioral intentions toward people with AIDS, such as not wanting to work alongside someone with AIDS, were related to fear of infection.

In sum, the peril associated with a stigmatizing condition contributes to our avoidance and exclusion of some stigmatized people. Another aspect of stigma peril draws on the concept of courtesy stigma (see Chapter 10). Stigmatized individuals are *perilous* if they are perceived to negatively affect nonstigmatized individuals' relations with peers and friends. Thus, our desire to avoid acquiring courtesy-stigmatized status likely adds to the rejection and isolation felt by stigmatized people.

> **?**
> We discussed the courtesy stigma that is imparted to you by associating with obese people in Chapter 10. Some people believe, however, that obesity is (somehow) contagious. Do people's responses toward obese individuals turn on the peril that might be associated with obesity? Discuss this.

Psychological Consequences Of Stigma

Self-Concept

The self-concept is the summary of one's self-knowledge and consists of traits, roles, and abilities. Identity and self-concept are similar terms, with identity referring to the most central or defining elements of the self-concept. Self-conceptions that are realistically positive, clear, and multifaceted promote psychological well-being (Campbell, 1990; Linville, 1985; Wylie, 1979). Many stigmatized people may struggle to maintain these mental health-promoting qualities of the self-concept.

As was discussed in Chapter 10, the discrepancy between your actual self-views and the person you are believed to be by others is the essence of stigma. Accordingly, stigma could be reduced in two ways. First, stigmatized people could bring their virtual identity—who they are assumed to be—in line with their actual self-views. This would require a massive attitude-change campaign among the general public, a practical impossibility for most stigmatized individuals. However, it is this notion that is at the heart of public education campaigns on behalf of stigmatized groups, such as the developmentally disabled or welfare recipients. When stereotypes are broken down in society at large, stigmatized people become less socially discredited and their self-concepts should reflect the more positive views held about them by others. And having a more positive self-concept contributes to well-being. A second route to reducing stigma is to align one's actual identity with one's virtual identity. In other words, stigmatized persons could internalize and fulfill others' beliefs about them, thereby reducing the mismatch between who they really are and who they are in others' eyes. Theoretically, this would reduce or eliminate stigma. Practically, however, it has two negative implications for the self-concept and psychological well-being.

First, we know from research on the self-fulfilling prophecy that stereotypic (and negative) expectations about others can elicit the expected negative behavior. Further, much research shows that one's self-views can be adjusted and rationalized to be consistent with one's actions (Cooper & Fazio, 1984). If, in order to reduce stigma, stigmatized individuals behave in the ways expected of them by others, their self-concepts will inevitably reorganize to reflect those negative qualities and detract from psychological well-being.

Second, in coming to view themselves as others view them, stigmatized people risk elevating their stigmatizing attribute to a master status in the self-concept. In other words, all of a stigmatized person's other abilities and qualities will become subordinate to and colored by the **master status attribute**. For example, imagine an overweight college student who, in an effort to fit in socially and reduce the stigma he experiences, begins to play the stereotypical (and expected) role of "the jolly clown who never met a meal he didn't like." Although this may improve his social prospects, he in effect becomes in others' eyes what he was assumed to be all along—a person with little self-control or dignity. In his efforts to reduce stigma, his weight has become the dominant aspect of his identity, not only to others but now also to him.

One of the consequences of having one's stigmatized status elevated in prominence is that stigmatized people think of themselves in more stereotypical terms. Researchers studied men's and women's self-descriptions when they were in same-sex or mixed-sex groups (Abrams, Thomas, & Hogg, 1990; Hogg & Turner, 1987). It was predicted that females would be aware of their stigmatized status in social situations in which they are in the minority. Indeed, after interacting in mixed-sex compared to same-sex groups, female participants' self-descriptions included more stereotypically female terms and greater acceptance of traditional sex roles. These studies show that stereotyping oneself may be a particular problem for stigmatized people because repeated interactions with nonstigmatized people and the focus those interactions bring to one's stigma may elevate their attribute toward master status.

What are the consequences of master status self-concepts for adjustment? People who have relatively few facets, or sides, to their identities or whose self-views are all closely intertwined are described as having simple self-concepts; that is, their self-views are not diversified but cluster around a small number of identities. Research shows that simple self-concepts are psychologically vulnerable (Linville, 1985). The vulnerability arises when a person experiences criticism or a setback in an area that essentially defines them. If they have no other identities or abilities to turn to as a means to soften the sting, they are vulnerable to depression. In sum, stigmatized people who seek to lessen stigma by playing the expected role run the risk of reorganizing their self-concepts in a way that makes them vulnerable.

The negative consequences of social stigma for stigmatized individuals' self-concepts also extends to their possible self-concepts—the *you* (specifically, the set of some traits or abilities) that is possible or anticipated in some future situation (Brown, 1998). To demonstrate this, Lisa Brown had White, Latino, and Black students watch a videotape of a teaching assistant (TA) supervisor who would be evaluating them either in a future class (short-term interaction) or throughout the next semester (long-term interaction). The ethnicity of the teaching assistant in the videotape was manipulated so as to be either White or of the same group as the participant. The students' views of their possible selves in the future semester—what they would be like as a TA—were affected by both the ethnicity of the supervisor and whether they anticipated a short- or long-term interaction with him or her. Students of color who imagined a long-term rather than a short-term interaction with a White supervisor generated more negative possible self-views than the White students. The findings were reversed when students anticipated having a supervisor of their own ethnic background. Students of color generated more positive possible self-views when they imagined having a long-term rather than a short-term interaction with the minority supervisor than the White students did.

In sum, minority students who anticipated being evaluated by a White supervisor recognized that the supervisor's stereotypes would have a more negative impact as the length of the future interaction increased. Even before the interaction with the White supervisor occurred, then, minority students thought of themselves as less qualified and confident (future) teaching assistants than did White students. This study suggests that the negative implications of stigma for one's self-conceptions are not limited to the effect of present interactions on current self-views but extend to the effects of anticipated interactions on possible self-views.

Self-Esteem

Self-esteem refers to our feelings of personal value, worthiness, and competence. Self-esteem is associated with many mental health outcomes, such as lowered depression, anxiety, and pessimism and healthy reactions to criticism (Kernis, Brockner, & Frankel, 1989). Stigma stands to influence self-esteem in two ways. First, self-esteem is derived partly from the evaluations we receive from and observe in other people when we interact with them (Mead, 1934; Shrauger & Schoeneman, 1979). Over time, these evaluations become part of us. By definition, stigmatized people are aware of others' negative attitudes toward them. It follows that, through repeated interaction with others, stigmatized people will become aware of and internalize others' negative appraisals of them, thus lowering their self-esteem. Second, self-esteem is also developed by demonstrating competence and achieving positive outcomes (White, 1959). Competence is demonstrated to ourselves as we successfully manipulate and control aspects of our environment, and this competency contributes to feelings of worthiness and confidence. Stigmatized people, by virtue of being socially isolated, excluded, or discriminated against, are denied many opportunities to demonstrate personal competence, thus lowering their self-esteem.

This theoretical analysis says that because of others' negative attitudes and the discrimination experienced by stigmatized people, stigmatized individuals should have lower self-esteem than nonstigmatized persons. However, studies that compare the self-esteem levels of stigmatized and nonstigmatized people consistently find no difference between them, and in some cases, stigmatized people have higher self-esteem (Crocker & Major, 1989). According to Jennifer Crocker and Brenda Major, the self-esteem of stigmatized people appears to be equal to or higher than that of nonstigmatized individuals because of the chronic presence and effect of self-esteem defense strategies in stigmatized people. They checked this hunch in several experiments by giving women and Black participants a negative evaluation and, for some participants, preventing them from thinking the kind of thoughts that typically protect against threats to self-esteem (Crocker, Voelkl, Testa, & Major, 1991). These studies showed that when stigmatized as opposed to nonstigmatized people receive a negative outcome and cannot defend against it, their self-esteem goes down. When they were allowed to use a defensive strategy, however, stigmatized and nonstigmatized participants' self-esteem did not differ.

To summarize, the psychological effects of stigma are felt most immediately in threats to self-esteem. However, stigmatized people have adapted ways to defend their self-esteem from the negative attitudes and hurtful actions of others. The profound effects of stigma on the self-concept, however, are more subtle and pervasive; these, as a result, may be more difficult to defend against.

Positive Consequences of Stigma?

Not all of the consequences of stigma are overtly negative. Sympathy, pity, and offers of help are common positive responses to stigmatized individuals. However, research shows that these positive and perhaps well-intentioned reactions toward stigmatized people can have negative effects. In one study, Black and White participants solved anagrams cooperatively with a White partner in the adjacent room (Schneider, Major, Luhtanen, & Crocker, 1996). In half of the conditions, the partner sent a note to the participants containing some helpful tips on solving the next round of anagrams; the other participants received no help. The results showed that unsolicited help damaged the self-esteem of the Black participants but not of the Whites.

In other words, the positive consequences of stigma may not be positive at all. Offers of help and expressions of sympathy can carry a demeaning message that you, as a stigmatized person, are assumed to need help. Often, such positive behaviors reveal the same stereotypic assumptions that underlie the negative consequences of stigma discussed previously. Also, positive reactions to stigmatized people may be motivated more by selfish concerns, such as a need to see oneself, or be seen by others, as helpful rather than by a genuine concern for stigmatized individuals. Finally, according to the competency-based model of self-esteem discussed earlier, stigmatized people who are constantly on the receiving end of sympathy and help may lose some control over their own environments and outcomes and, as a result, lose an important source of self-esteem.

To sum up, the social and psychological costs of being socially different are high. Stigma disrupts the social relationships of stigmatized people, undermining the important stress-buffering and supportive effects of having friends and acquaintances. Spoiled social relationships can also undermine one's social skills, which further contribute to psychological maladjustment. Stigma also has adverse implications for the self-concepts and self-esteem of stigmatized people. These general consequences are reflected in the experience of overweight individuals in our society. Although stigma often elicits positive behavior from others in the form of help or sympathy, the net effect of such experiences is negative for stigmatized people. In the next few pages, let's consider how stigmatized people cope with the stereotyping, prejudice, and discrimination that they face.

Coping With Prejudice: Stigma Management

We have learned that being socially different is often associated with rejection, limited social opportunities, and chronically threatened psychological well-being. What response can be made to this social problem? In this chapter, we explore individual strategies for coping with social stigma—termed **stigma management** (Goffman, 1963). In devoting this chapter to learning about ways stigmatized people manage the rejection and disadvantage they face, we should not assume that redressing the social problem of stigma is best left to stigmatized individuals themselves. Interventions for managing stigma can also come from governing agencies, as in the form of educational campaigns to promote tolerance and reduce stereotypes or programs to promote equal opportunities in school, housing, and work.

In reality, we all have developed strategies for improving the quality of our lives. Socially stigmatized people only differ in that they have more to cope with than do those of us who possess *majority* status or are members of relatively advantaged groups. In the following pages, I describe several stigma management strategies and discuss their implications for social adjustment and psychological well-being. The strategies are organized into those that are primarily aimed at improving interpersonal outcomes, such as acceptance, and those that generally focus on improving psychological outcomes, such as self-esteem.

Strategies for Gaining Social Acceptance

Withdrawal

One strategy by which stigmatized individuals may cope with the negative social implications of stigma—namely, rejection, strained interactions, and loss of opportunity—is to simply avoid people who treat them stereotypically. How can **withdrawal** from the nonstigmatized world increase one's acceptance and social opportunity? There are two possible ways, each requiring that withdrawal from circles populated by nonstigmatized people be associated with increased connection to a circle of similarly stigmatized people.

First, associating with similarly stigmatized people should afford stigmatized individuals greater acceptance and more normal social interaction within those in-groups. Indeed, there is no rule that states that acceptance in nonstigmatized majority groups is a better quality of acceptance than is offered by one's own kind. Associating with in-groups provides friendships, support, and a social context in which one's stigma is a nonissue. Disadvantaged social groups—especially if they have many members—also develop organizations and services that meet the social, educational, and occupational needs of their members, further enhancing the opportunities of stigmatized people.

Second, stigmatized people may realize greater acceptance and social opportunity in the nonstigmatized world through social and political activism. Minority and disadvantaged groups that press for change in society *do* have influence, and stigmatized people can benefit from the social and political power of their in-group. Perhaps more important, participation in the social activism of their group can help redefine their stigmatizing attribute into a positive label. For example, the National Association to Advance Fat Acceptance (NAAFA) is a support and advocacy group for overweight individuals. This organization helps its members deal with prejudice, educates others about the stigma of overweight, and addresses the difficulties of buying clothes, getting and keeping jobs, and buying health insurance among overweight people. Through this group, many overweight people have refused to accept the negative cultural stereotype of obesity and, working together, have encouraged the public to confront and reconsider their beliefs about fatness.

As a stigma management strategy to increase social acceptance, withdrawal has two distinct disadvantages. First, withdrawal is physically and socially isolating from the broader, nonstigmatized culture. Friendships with nonstigmatized people, as well as the opportunities and resources associated with them, become less available. Second, people who are marginalized from the nonstigmatized majority and more socially identified with their stigmatizing attribute risk experiencing *greater* stereotyping and prejudice. Recall that stereotypes guide our social perception when we have little experience or contact with socially different others. Therefore, withdrawal into a group of similarly stigmatized people may heighten the prominence of one's attribute or status to others and prompt ever more stereotyping and discrimination.

Passing

Passing concerns methods and strategies for concealing one's stigmatizing attribute or condition from others. To *pass* is to be known by others as normal, as if you possessed no discrediting or discreditable attribute. All of us have attempted to pass at one time or another, behaving so as not to draw others' attention to something we wanted to conceal. For example, students who are not prepared to discuss a reading in class are vulnerable to being exposed to their professor as a less-than-responsible student. From students' perspectives, to go unrecognized in this situation is desirable, and thus, particular behaviors are enacted (e.g., avoiding eye contact with the professor) in order to pass.

Stigmatized people have considerably more at stake when considering passing. Let's consider some of the advantages and drawbacks. The chief advantage of passing is that you, as a stigmatizable (rather than stigmatized) person, are accepted, known to others as normal, and afforded a full range of social opportunities. This is particularly beneficial in short-term interactions when passing does not require great effort or monitoring. Passing, then, depends on the concealability of one's stigmatizing attribute or status. For example, a deaf individual who could read lips might well pass as a hearing person in many contexts, but a blind individual would not be able to easily conceal his or her cane or guide dog.

There are considerable drawbacks for those who attempt to pass as normal (Goffman, 1963). First, stigmatizable people must invest great energy in concealing their failing, particularly when passing becomes a way of life. The effort consists of two parts: filtering one's own behavior and speech for inadvertent cues or references that might raise suspicion in others and being alive to the *safety* of social situations. For example, consider a lesbian who opts to pass as heterosexual at her workplace. To pass successfully, she must monitor her own speech for references (such as admiring gay writers or gay organizations and events) that might disclose, or raise suspicion about, her identity to her coworkers. Because she has come out to a small group of friends, she must also try to keep her gay social world separate from her straight work-related world. That is, if stigmatized people have revealed their attribute to selected people, *those* people become potential, if unwitting, cover blowers. In short, to pass effectively, nearly all of one's daily activities must be scrutinized from the perspective of others; this is a daunting information-processing burden. As was mentioned in Chapter 10, stigmatized people are mindful in social situations, attending to overt and subtle behaviors of people with whom they interact and noting details of the situation, and this mindfulness is fatiguing and stressful (Frable et al., 1990).

A second drawback associated with passing is that stigmatizable individuals will feel divided loyalties to both the group composed of similarly stigmatized people and the group to which passing gains one's admittance. For example, a lesbian or gay man passing as heterosexual may be privy to the jokes and barbs of other heterosexuals about gay people. At once that person may sense the warmth of inclusion, the guilt of being a party to homophobia, and defensiveness at being the (undiscovered) butt of the joke. Additionally, the undetected gay person must still monitor passing issues and thus may feel obliged to laugh along in order to avoid being suspected as a sort of *gay sympathizer*. And, as if it weren't bad enough, the gay person also faces the possibility of criticism from his or her gay friends for being hypocritical or for not supporting them in their gay identity.

According to Erving Goffman (1963), to pass is to confront the tension between managing information that could lead to one's discovery and managing the restraints that being known (and stigmatized) impose on one's social interactions. The overall effect of passing versus openness on one's psychological and social well-being is therefore difficult to judge. The benefits of being treated and known as a nonstigmatized person must be weighed against the cognitive investments needed to pass, as well as the social costs if one is *discovered*. Furthermore, many scholars argue that disclosure of one's true identity is an important aspect of healthy adjustment (Cass, 1979; Miranda & Storms, 1989). A review of research on passing among gay individuals concluded, however, that disclosing to *oneself*—coming to terms with being gay—was more predictive of self-esteem than revealing one's gay identity to others (Savin-Williams, 1990).

John Pachankis (2007) reviewed research on the consequences of concealing a stigmatizing attribute and summarized that body of research with the following conclusions.

• Concealing a stigma—or passing, in Goffman's terms—makes ambiguous the feedback we get from other people about our self. Concealing one's stigma means that others' feedback about one's ability or effort is given under somewhat false pretenses. The feedback is ambiguous because the stigmatized person never knows if he or she would receive, for example, the same compliment or praise if the other person really knew who they were.

• Concealing one's stigma isolates one from the camaraderie and protection of other people with the same attribute. Whereas revealing one's stigmatizing mark might taint social relationships formed earlier, that loss of social opportunity is potentially compensated by the new in-group that one can be a part of. The prospect of a new source of social and practical support for coping with one's stigma may well be worth the cost of revealing it. Kristin Beals and her colleagues (2009) asked gay men and lesbians to keep a diary for a 2-week period in which they noted when they disclosed their sexual identity to other people and their thoughts and feelings surrounding those stigma-disclosure events. The research found that disclosing one's sexual orientation to other people was associated with higher psychological well-being. The main reason for the positive effects of disclosure was that gay individuals perceived more social support and understanding upon disclosing their identity.

• Compared with those who reveal their stigma, those who conceal it must deal with the fear and anxiety that their secret will be discovered. As a result, they must be vigilant to avoid revealing clues to their true identity and, to the extent that those clues slip out, must contend with suspicions that form in others' minds about the possibility that you are not the person you seem to be. This social information management agenda is preoccupying and is a source of distress independent of the stigma itself.

• Because of the burden of managing the information around one's stigma, for the purposes of keeping it hidden, people with concealable stigmas tend to avoid social situations. In the same way, the burden of guarding one's true identity interferes with the development of close relationships. Thus, social isolation and loneliness constitute yet another source of psychological distress for the person who chooses to conceal his or her stigma.

> **?**
>
> Imagine you have a skeleton in your closet. For example, perhaps you had an abortion you'd like to keep secret, or you carry the herpes virus, or ...
>
> When do you reveal this to the person you're dating, and what are some of the issues that make revealing or concealing this potentially stigmatizing trait a tricky and stressful issue?

Exploiting Stigma

The stigma management strategies discussed previously seek to improve the social reception of stigmatized people by minimizing the focus or impact of their stigmatizing attribute on interactions. Other strategies accomplish the same end by other means. We now consider behaviors in which stigmatized people may strategically exploit their attribute or status to improve their social prospects.

In regard to managing the negative implications of stigma, **self-promotion** refers to demonstrating to other people that you, as a stigmatized person, are multidimensional and competent in several domains. For example, wheelchair athletes who play basketball or race in a marathon show the nonstigmatized world that they are comparable or even superior to nonstigmatized people in abilities or roles that are unrelated to their stigmatizing attribute.

Self-promotion has two primary advantages. First, it proactively changes one's virtual identity. Recall that stigma is the experience of being known by others in a more negative or simplistic way than you know yourself. If stigmatized people show others their *hidden* talents and assets, they help reform the image that other people have of them into something more positive, multifaceted, or both. And, if stigma decreases, acceptance and social opportunity should increase.

Second, self-promotion is a compelling strategy because it allows others to see and evaluate one's competencies in spite of (what others assume are) the hindrances and disadvantages of being stigmatized. That is, others may well augment their positive reactions to a stigmatized individuals' display of talent or skill because they are perceived to have overcome special disadvantages or adversity.

As another form of stigma management, **compensation** involves stigmatized people deliberately presenting to others behavior that contradicts the assumptions held about their abilities or character. This strategy seeks to compensate for an inadequacy assumed (by others) to characterize a stigmatized person by presenting evidence to the contrary. As with self-promotion, compensating for a presumed failing strives to reshape the virtual identity of stigmatized people and reduce stigma. Research suggests not only that compensation is used by stigmatized people but that it also improves their social image.

Amerigo Farina and his colleagues examined compensation in a study that was described as "how personal characteristics affect perceivers' perceptions and attitudes" (Farina, Allen, & Saul, 1968). Participants were told that they (as the *target* individual) would be presented to the real participants (the *perceivers*) as a student who was either mentally disabled or normal, followed by an interaction between the target and the perceiver. The target participants believed, however, that the researchers were interested in the perceiver's behavior, thus reducing their concern about being temporarily stigmatized (in another student's eyes) as mentally disabled. This was done to allow their responses to be as genuine and unself-conscious as possible.

The perceivers studied information about the target person; either the target was described as *mentally disabled* or that label was not mentioned. The students then played a game that involved moving a marble through a maze using two knobs to control the pitch of the maze. This game was chosen because it called on abilities and skills that would be regarded as lacking in mentally disabled people—namely, mental and motor skill. The results were revealing: The targets who believed they were known to their partner as mentally disabled performed better on the maze game than those who believed they weren't labeled. In other words, those participants who were temporarily stigmatized in a peer's eyes compensated for their failing by demonstrating greater proficiency on a test of mental skill than those who were not stigmatized.

A more recent study of stigma compensation asked women to write an essay about what their life would be like in 10 years, offering a monetary reward for essays that received a C grade or better (Kaiser & Miller, 2001). One half of the participants (randomly determined) were notified of the possibility of sexist attitudes in the man who would read and grade the essay; the other participants only learned of the possible prejudiced evaluator after the essay. After independent readers coded the essays for content, the study showed that women who anticipated the sexist evaluator and could compensate for their *flaw* in the evaluator's eyes, presented themselves differently in the essay than the other women. Specifically, those women distanced themselves from female-stereotypic references in their essays like family importance, niceness, and femininity. In other words, the participants who felt they were potential targets for the evaluator's prejudice compensated by presenting themselves in less stereotypic terms.

Together, these studies suggest two things. First, stigmatized people can and do present themselves in ways that compensate for the negative assumptions of others that contribute to their stigma and rejection. Second, when employed, compensatory self-presentation has social benefits; it improves one's virtual identity and prompts greater acceptance in others.

Strategies for Protecting Psychological Well-Being

High self-esteem and a self-concept consisting of positive terms held with certainty are cornerstones of psychological well-being. As was discussed in Chapter 10, stigma has negative implications for self-esteem and self-concept. To counter the general threat to well-being posed by stigma and stigma-related outcomes, stigmatized people may draw on several self-protective strategies. Self-protective strategies are cognitive in nature and involve thinking about one's stigma and the experiences associated with it in ways that are beneficial to self-esteem and well-being (Crocker & Major, 1989). These stigma management strategies and their consequences are explained in this section.

Attributing Negative Outcomes to Prejudice

As objects of prejudice and discrimination, stigmatized individuals chronically experience negative events and receive negative feedback from others. Such outcomes could be due to some inadequacy or incompetency in the stigmatized person or to prejudice in others. The former attribution would threaten and the latter would protect the self-esteem and self-concepts of stigmatized people. Because it is often difficult to determine exactly why something occurred, attributing negative outcomes to prejudice is a plausible and adaptive strategy for stigmatized people.

In a test of this strategy, Jennifer Crocker and her colleagues had Black college students receive a negative evaluation from a (bogus) White evaluator who could either see them or not (Crocker et al., 1991). The researchers reasoned that it would be impossible for participants to attribute negative feedback to prejudice when the evaluator could not see and therefore identify them as Black. The results of the study showed that receiving a negative evaluation from a White evaluator lowered Black participants' self-esteem but only when they could not be seen. In other words, participants who were afforded the opportunity to blame the negative evaluation on prejudice did not have lowered self-esteem. Similar results were obtained when women received negative feedback from a male evaluator (Crocker et al., 1993).

These studies illustrate the benefit to well-being of attributing negative outcomes to prejudice. However, they may have oversimplified the conditions under which stigmatized individuals receive negative feedback from others by having just two conditions: one in which prejudice can be blamed for the outcome and one in which it cannot be blamed for the outcome. Other research has further studied this stigma management strategy by varying the likelihood that a negative experience is due to someone else's prejudice (Ruggiero & Taylor, 1995, 1997). Karen Ruggiero and Donald Taylor (1995) had women university students do a test that was evaluated by a male judge randomly selected from a panel of male judges. The women were told that 100%, 75%, 50%, 25%, or 0% of the judges held sexist attitudes and discriminated against women. Thus, women received negative feedback about their ability along with some probability that it was due to discrimination. They were then asked to rate how much their failure was due to the quality of their answers and how much was due to discrimination. The only women who faulted the prejudice of the male judge for their poor test score were the women in the 100% condition—those who were certain that their evaluator was discriminatory. In the other conditions, women took responsibility for their negative experience by blaming the quality of their work—even in the 75% condition—in which discrimination was very likely! Similar results were observed when the participants were Black and Asian (Ruggiero & Taylor, 1997). Taken together, this research suggests that, although attributing negative outcomes to prejudice protects the self-esteem of stigmatized individuals, the strategy may only be used when it is likely to be a fair and accurate attribution.

Attributing negative experiences to others' prejudice is not, then, a talisman for magically turning negative experiences into positive ones. There are negative implications for overusing this stigma management strategy. If stigmatized people abuse the strategy by overattributing their negative experiences to others' prejudice, they may dismiss constructive (as well as prejudicial) criticism. Further, chronic attributions of negative experiences to prejudice may be perceived by others as defensive and paranoid. Given the burden stigma places on one's social interactions, stigmatized individuals may have learned to moderate their responses to negative and possibly discriminatory outcomes in the interest of better social relations. If so, stigmatized people may be balancing their needs for self-esteem with their needs for acceptance and social opportunity.

Devaluing Negative Outcome Dimensions

A second stigma management strategy for protecting psychological well-being involves devaluing the areas in which stigmatized individuals or members of their group receive negative outcomes. The principle behind this strategy is intuitive: When you receive criticism in an area that is not important to you, it doesn't hurt as much. This is applicable to stigmatized people in two ways. First, they experience more criticism and negative experiences than nonstigmatized people, and second, they are less likely to be able to change the outcome than nonstigmatized people.

For example, overweight individuals would likely receive chronically negative feedback on dimensions related to appearance or physical competence, such as dating or athletics, respectively. Altering the outcomes by losing weight may not be an option if the individual is comfortable with his or her weight or is unable to lose weight. So, rather than suffer recurring blows to their self-esteem, overweight people may devalue the importance of dating or athletics. In sum, if stigmatized people are unable to effect change in the amount or nature of their negative outcomes, devaluing the dimension in which they receive those outcomes is a reasonable self-protective strategy. A similar process occurs when Black students disidentify with school achievement (see Chapter 10).

Although the strategy of devaluing protects stigmatized students against the effects of chronic negative outcomes on the stigma-related dimension, it has a downside. It simplifies one's self-concept, leaving a stigmatized person fewer and more vulnerable dimensions or abilities on which to base his or her self-esteem.

Second, devaluing tends to close off potential avenues of advancement or enrichment that contribute to life satisfaction. Black youth who drop out of school because they see little potential in education for developing their self-esteem have less education as a consequence.

Making In-Group Comparisons

We often evaluate our own outcomes by what is expected or by what most other people are receiving. Even if they are not disadvantaged in absolute terms, stigmatized people realize that they are disadvantaged compared with others. A third self-protective strategy addresses the fact that chronic comparisons with the fortunes of nonstigmatized people have negative implications for the self-esteem of stigmatized individuals. Comparing one's outcomes and opportunities with those of similar others, such as members of one's stigmatized group, are likely to be less threatening and perhaps even beneficial. Hence, making in-group comparisons on dimensions in which stigmatized people experience discrimination is protective of well-being.

There is ample evidence that all of us prefer to compare our abilities and outcomes with those of similar others (Ross, Eyman, & Kishchuk, 1986). We believe that people who are similar to us will give us the best information about our abilities and outcomes. Comparing ourselves with similar others rules out many of the possible reasons why we might be doing worse than someone else. The tendency for stigmatized individuals to compare themselves with other similarly stigmatized persons has been noted in blind people, the elderly, and women (Crosby, 1982; Rosow, 1974; Strauss, 1968).

Comparisons with nonstigmatized people are a constant reminder to stigmatized individuals that their attribute is associated with discrimination. However, things that are associated can, over time, be erroneously assumed to be causally related. Thus, chronic out-group comparisons may damage stigmatized persons' self-esteem in two ways: through the sting of being discriminated against and through the possibility that the discrimination may be deserved. One of the benefits of in-group comparisons for stigmatized people is that such comparisons disassociate negative outcomes from one's stigmatizing attribute or status.

In summary, attributing negative outcomes to prejudice and either devaluing or comparing oneself with in-group members on dimensions on which one (or one's group) fares poorly potentially protects a person's self-esteem and well-being from the negative implications of stigma. Unlike strategies for maximizing acceptance and opportunity, the self-protective strategies do not objectively improve the social circumstances of stigmatized people. Rather, they tend to be used defensively and in response to specific threatening outcomes.

Seeking Social Support

The positive influence of social support—being connected to other people who like you and help you in times of distress—on psychological well-being is well established (Wills, 1991). Other people can provide informational support when giving helpful advice and information, emotional support by empathizing with our hardships, or instrumental support by performing needed tasks on our behalf. Recall the research on well-being and social support among people who were diagnosed with AIDS (Crandall & Coleman, 1992). Compared with those who concealed their illness and received no social support from others, persons with AIDS who revealed their diagnosis to a small number of individuals reported greater levels of social support and well-being.

Karen Ruggiero and her colleagues did a study that examined how stigmatized individuals (in this case women) coped with discrimination when they believed there was social support available (Ruggiero, Taylor, & Lydon, 1997). They had 60 female university students take a test that was then evaluated by a male evaluator selected from a panel of eight male judges. The women were told that half of the judges discriminated against women; this communicated that there was a 50% chance their test would be evaluated by a prejudiced judge. All participants subsequently received a failing (D) grade on the test. After the bogus failure feedback, participants were afforded either informational or social support, both types of social support, or no social support at all. This was done by giving the women an opportunity to know how another participant had done on the test (informational support), to talk to another person about the test (emotional support), or both. The women then rated how much their test failure was due to their ability or to discrimination.

The results revealed that when participants thought *some* type of social support was available, compared with no support at all, they attributed their failure more to discrimination than to themselves. That is, the availability of either informational or emotional support reversed women's tendency to blame their own ability for a negative outcome and thereby discount the effect of discrimination. When both types of support were available, the effect was stronger. Women who could draw on informational and emotional support made the most "it's discrimination" attributions and the fewest "it's my fault" attributions.

Two lessons can be drawn from this study. First, having social support available is empowering to stigmatized people; it makes it less likely that stigmatized individuals will tolerate and rationalize the discrimination they face. Research reviewed earlier indicated that stigmatized people tend to minimize discrimination even when there is a 75% chance that they did experience it (Ruggiero & Taylor, 1995), perhaps because they are reluctant to react to interpersonal outcomes in ways that could alienate others. This research suggests that social support helps stigmatized people object to discrimination even when its likelihood is just 50%. Second, the participants in this study never actually received social support; they merely anticipated receiving it. So, the availability of social support has positive effects even when other people are able and willing but not quite ready to lend support.

Summary

Faced with chronic social rejection and discrimination and their negative effects on psychological well-being, stigmatized people may turn to a variety of stigma management strategies for the purposes of increasing their social opportunities and protecting their self-concepts and self-esteem. Although many stigma management strategies promote specific aspects of well-being and adjustment, their benefits must be reconciled with possible drawbacks in other areas of adjustment. Thus, for many stigmatized people, protecting self-esteem may be associated with losses in social opportunity; likewise, improving acceptance may involve dealing with others' derogatory remarks or insulting actions.

DI Diversity Issue 11.1: Covering

Kenji Yoshino, an attorney who happens to be openly gay, was advised by his professional colleagues as a law student to avoid being a *professional homosexual*—that is, someone whose professional life revolved around gay issues and causes (Yoshino, 2006). In a fascinating story, Yoshino tells of feeling pressure to conform to mainstream straight norms, despite being accepted as gay. His story illustrates a response to stigma called **covering**, and he proposes that the pressure to cover is a new form of discrimination. Whereas passing involves hiding one's stigmatized identity from others, covering involves efforts to minimize the impact of one's stigmatizing attribute on social interactions (Goffman, 1963).

Who covers, and how? Blind people who use a seeing eye dog to get around cover their blindness. Although the individual's disability would be apparent to most people, the dog's appearance as a pet and companion, as well as its skill in guiding the blind person, keeps the blindness from becoming obtrusive and burdensome to others. Heavy people cover by wearing loose or dark-colored clothing, people with missing limbs cover through the use of prosthetic devices, and the hearing disabled cover through the use of hearing assistance devices in the ear. In each of these instances, the person's stigmatizing attribute is not concealed, but it is made less obvious to others. According to our understanding of stigma as occurring in social interactions, efforts to minimize the obtrusiveness of one's stigmatizing attribute should in turn lessen stigma.

? Discuss some other ways that stigmatized people cover.

According to Yoshino, discrimination that was once targeted at whole groups of minority individuals has been replaced by a more focused form of discrimination, which is targeted at subsets of minority groups that *flout their differentness* by refusing to cover. He describes cases in which a Black person was fired for wearing her hair in cornrows and violating a *no cornrows* corporate policy. Similarly, a rabbi and Air Force officer was threatened with court martial for wearing his yarmulke and thus violating military policy regarding appearance. Both sued and lost their cases. According to Yoshino's legal analysis, discrimination based on immutable (e.g., race or gender) group differences is illegal, but courts are not protecting discrimination that is based on differences *within* those groups that is seen as a matter of personal preference. In short, members of many minority groups face pressure to cover distinctive attributes and conform to standards of appearance and behavior that are held about their group.

(Continued)

(Continued)

? How is covering a kind of self-fulfilling prophecy? Think about it: Do White managers reward Black employees who dress and act in keeping with (White) corporate standards? And if they do, what implications might this *rewarded covering* have for how Whites think of Blacks as a group? And how the Black employees think of themselves?

DI Diversity Issue 11.2: Online Support: Virtual Communities for Stigmatized People

The Internet, chat rooms, and newsgroups comprise a new virtual form of social support that is available to stigmatized individuals. Participation in virtual communities may be especially advantageous for stigmatized people, many of whom are denied acceptance in traditional social groups because of their identifiable discrediting mark (such as obesity or physical disability). However, people who have concealed stigmatizing marks (such as gays and lesbians or alcoholics) may also benefit from the support of virtual groups for a different reason. As discussed earlier, although these individuals pass as normal in actual social contexts, the very strategy of passing combined with the difficulty of identifying other similarly stigmatized people may contribute to profound isolation and loneliness.

Researchers examined whether individuals with visible or concealed stigmas would be more likely to turn to virtual social support in the form of newsgroup participation (McKenna & Bargh, 1998). They selected newsgroups representing visible (obese, stutterers, baldness, cerebral palsy) and other concealable stigmatizing marks. Researchers analyzed the content of all the original posts in each newsgroup, as well as any follow-up posts that addressed the original post, for a 3-week period (totaling 1,888 posts). They measured how frequently an original poster reposted to the newsgroup after his or her original contribution and whether this participation in a virtual social group depended on their type of stigma (visible or hidden) and the groups' response to the original post (positive or negative). The results showed that individuals with hidden stigmas posted almost twice as often to the newsgroups as people with conspicuous stigmas (5.5 and 2.8 posts per person, respectively). However, getting a positive, rather than a negative, reply to one's original post did not affect the participation of people with visible stigmas but greatly increased the subsequent posts of individuals with hidden stigmas. In other words, stigmatized people who cannot easily avail themselves of actual support groups (those with hidden marks) turned to virtual groups more often than people with visible stigmas.

In follow-up studies, Katelyn McKenna and John Bargh (1998) looked at whether virtual group participation led to increased self-esteem and decreased social isolation among stigmatized individuals. They surveyed about 150 participants in the three newsgroups related to concealed sexual stigmas (gay, bondage, and spanking). The results indicated that posters placed greater importance on belonging to the group and were significantly less socially isolated than *lurkers* (those who read but did not post to the group). The importance of the virtual group to posters' identity, in turn, predicted greater levels of self-acceptance, less estrangement from the dominant culture, and more instances of *coming out* to friends or family as a result of the newsgroup. Finally, John Bargh and his colleagues (2002) found that people were better able to express their true selves on the Internet than in real face-to-face interactions.

To sum up, virtual communities provide social support to stigmatized people. Virtual social support, however, is more popular among and beneficial to people with hidden stigmas.

? Why might it be easier to reveal your *true self* to someone online than to someone in face-to-face interaction? Are there implications of being a somewhat different person, even if it is your true self, online than in normal interactions?

KEY TERMS

Stigma consciousness   207

Stigma controllability   207

Just world theory   208

Stigma visibility   208

Stigma peril   211

Master status attribute   212

Stigma management   215

Withdrawal   216

Passing   217

Self-promotion   219

Compensation   219

Covering   225

FOR FURTHER READING

Goffman, E. (1963). *Stigma: Notes on the management of spoiled identity.* New York, NY: Simon & Schuster.

This is the classic work on the psychology of stigma and is written in an engaging style and at a level that is suitable for undergraduate students.

ONLINE RESOURCES

Slo the Stigma

http://www.slothestigma.org/

This site raises awareness regarding the stigma associated with mental illness. The video on this site is worth watching for examples of stigma concepts covered in this chapter.

LETS: Let's Erase the Stigma

http://www.letserasethestigma.org/

This site educates the public regarding mental illness in children and adolescents. They encourage advocacy through the setting up of campus clubs (see For Educators, then Start a LETS Club).

HIV/AIDS Stigma

http://www.avert.org/hiv-aids-stigma.htm

http://psychology.ucdavis.edu/rainbow/html/aids.html

Learn about the stigma experienced by people with HIV and AIDS at these sites.

Yale Law School Visual Law Project

http://yalevisuallawproject.org/film/stigma/

Watch the compelling film on stigma, viewed through the lens of racial profiling.

Yale Rudd Center for Food Policy & Obesity

http://www.yaleruddcenter.org/

For resources on obesity-related stigma, go to What We Do, then Weight Bias & Stigma.

12

Responding to Social Inequality: Behavioral and Cognitive Interventions for Reducing Prejudice

TOPICS COVERED IN THIS CHAPTER:

- Intergroup contact and self-regulation
- Stereotype inhibition and substitution
- Cross-categorization and empathy

Throughout this book, we have learned the basic principles and processes that comprise a psychological understanding of diversity, or social difference. If you draw a line under the list of principles we have covered in the last 11 chapters and calculate a sum, the *bottom line* will be: Stereotyping, prejudice, and discrimination create or at least sustain social inequality. **Social inequality** can be defined in comparative or absolute terms. Comparatively speaking, social inequality occurs when people from some social groups have vastly worse life outcomes (e.g., less income, poorer health and health care, poorer quality education) than people from other groups. In absolute terms, social inequality occurs when the members of a group do not have some minimum amount of opportunity and resources to make a decent life (e.g., a living-wage job, safe and affordable housing), regardless of what the richest groups of society have.

Some of the big principles that have emerged from our study of the psychology of diversity are: (a) people oversimplify their social worlds, preferring *us* to *them*; (b) people prefer to have their preexisting social beliefs confirmed and supported rather than challenged; (c) people rely on prejudice and discrimination to meet basic needs for self-integrity and security; and (d) people's well-learned and automatic prejudices often overrule their intentions to be fair-minded. Responses to social inequality must, therefore, overcome human nature to be effective. This chapter will describe specific strategies or interventions in the psychological literature that redress our natural, and largely negative and divisive, responses to diversity.

Behavioral Interventions

We know that prejudice is anchored in cognitive structures such as social categories and stereotypes and is associated with personal needs for self-esteem, security, and social approval. Understanding what factors contribute to prejudice can also inform us about how to reduce prejudice. Below, we consider two approaches for reducing prejudice that involve changing how and how much we interact with members of negatively stereotyped groups.

Personal Contact With Members of Negatively Stereotyped Groups

Social categorization often goes hand in glove with physical segregation. That is, we perceive people as a group not only because they share a distinctive social quality but also because they are physically proximal. In most large cities, there is a remarkable degree of race-based and class-based segregation. That is, members of racial and ethnic minority groups often live in different neighborhoods and frequent different stores, schools, and churches than majority group individuals. Similarly, people who differ based on their income, especially high-income compared to working-poor people, live highly segregated lives. Because physical segregation limits the contact between members of racial and class-based groups, people rely more on cultural stereotypes when dealing with people from different races and economic classes. As we learned in Chapter 2, social categorization enhances the separateness of socially different groups of people. But separateness is not just a mental image; in many cases, we are physically and geographically separated from out-group individuals. If our separation from people who are socially different from ourselves reinforces stereotypes and their associated negative feelings, then contact with those people should help break down stereotypes and prejudicial feelings of uncertainty, fear, or judgment that we often harbor about out-group members. This idea is the essence of the contact hypothesis. Proposed by Gordon Allport (1954), the **contact hypothesis** says that physical contact with a member of a negatively stereotyped group lessens the negative beliefs and feelings we hold about that individual and improves our attitudes and feelings toward the group as a whole.

Is Any Contact Okay?

Research on the contact hypothesis has established that several conditions must occur for contact with an out-group individual to reduce stereotypes and negative feelings. First, this personal interaction should ideally be with an out-group member of equal status—someone who has a similar set of life circumstances as yourself (Brown, 1984). For example, negative beliefs and feelings about Jews would be reduced more effectively by interacting with a Jewish classmate than with a Jewish professor or administrator. Status differences are a convenient excuse for one's stereotypic beliefs, preventing personal contact from having its positive effects when they loom over an interaction.

Second, sustained personal interaction with an out-group member reduces negative beliefs and feelings when that interaction is cooperative—when you and the other person are interested in and working toward a common goal (Dechamps & Brown, 1983). For example, neighborhoods with a mix of opposed racial or religious groups will reduce the suspicion and hostility between them by joining together to fight crime or beautify the streets. Additionally, research has shown that personal, cooperative contact must be sanctioned and supported by authority figures or institutions to effectively reduce prejudice (Cook, 1984).

Finally, although equal-status and cooperative contact are sufficient to reduce stereotypes about an individual from a disliked group, that goodwill does not generalize to the whole group unless the individual is seen as representative of the group (Desforges et al., 1997). We learned that people who don't fit our stereotype for their group are either subtyped or dismissed as *exceptions to the rule*. Social interactions with typical group members that challenge our stereotypes are more difficult to dismiss. Research shows that typicality—seeing an out-group member as typical of his or her group—reduces prejudice best or perhaps only when the individual also self-discloses (Ensari & Miller, 2002). When out-group members, unprompted, reveal personal information about themselves, they are seen as more trustworthy, and when also perceived as a typical member of their group, people develop more positive evaluations of that out-group and its members.

Indirect Contact

The contact hypothesis states that personal and cooperative interaction with people from out-groups will help reduce our negative attitudes and stereotypic beliefs about them, especially if we perceive that the individual is a typical member of his or her group. New research also suggests that the contact hypothesis can have beneficial indirect effects. Stephen Wright and his colleagues had participants take a (bogus) test, which was diagnostic of an important individual difference variable (Wright, Aron, McLaughlin-Volpe, & Ropp, 1997). Allegedly on the basis of the test, participants were assigned membership to a green or blue group and given a correspondingly colored T-shirt to wear throughout the study. Participants then watched an interaction through a one-way mirror between a green group member and a blue group member. The nature of these interactions was manipulated to be either between close friends (who happened to be in the same study by chance), neutral strangers, or disliked strangers (participants who ostensibly had a tense negative relationship outside of the study). After observing the interaction, participants rated their fellow group member and the out-group member of the dyad. The ratings of fellow participants' interactions reflected in-group bias, such that in-group members were rated more positively than out-group members, but only when the interactions were between neutral or disliked strangers. When participants observed an interaction between friends from opposing groups, participants' ratings did not reflect the typical in-group-biased pattern. Rather, they liked both groups equally. In a different test of the effects of indirect contact on intergroup attitudes, Rhiannon Turner and her colleagues (2008) asked White participants to report how many White people they knew who had South Asian friends. Having participants think about this second hand kind of contact with out-group members improved a range of intergroup outcomes, including lowered anxiety regarding, greater liking for, and perceived similarity with South Asians. Richard Crisp and Rhiannon Turner (2009) reviewed the research on indirect forms of intergroup contact and concluded that imagined interactions are effective tools for reducing stereotyping and prejudice. **Imagined intergroup contact** occurs when people mentally simulate contact—ideally imagining a real-life, positive experience—with someone from another social group or category. Take a minute to try it: Focus on a person who is a member of a group with whom you have little interaction and harbor some negative or anxious feelings about. Conjure up an everyday experience with this person as if it were occurring with a same-group acquaintance. Imagine the interaction being casual, friendly, and interesting. According to Crisp and Turner's review, imagined intergroup contact improves attitudes toward out-groups in part because it causes people to project more positive attributes and feelings onto that group. In addition, imagined intergroup contact has been shown to reduce anxiety in subsequent real interactions with members of that group (Turner, Crisp, & Lambert, 2007). Other research has determined that imagined contact also helps people reduce the effects of stereotype threat on their behavior when they encounter people who hold negative stereotypes about them (Crisp & Abrams, 2008).

Two other forms of imagined intergroup contact are worth mentioning. First, when people witness an interracial interaction and then are asked to write about a similar experience happening to them, their interracial attitudes improve. This effect does not happen when people merely witness the interaction, so the prejudice reduction must be related to imagining themselves in that situation. Second, the prejudice-reducing benefits of indirect intergroup contact also occur when our contact with out-group members improves attitudes toward *other* minority or negatively stereotyped groups with whom we have no contact (Tausch et al., 2010). In summary, imagined intergroup contact holds promise for being an effective prejudice-reduction tool, particularly in contexts where majority group members have little contact with out-group individuals and thus, little opportunity to put the contact hypothesis into practice.

In short, the effect of contact with out-group individuals on softening prejudice and stereotypes need not occur firsthand. Merely observing an interaction between members of opposing groups, when those people seemed friendly with each other, led to positive evaluations of both groups. This research has important implications for the role of television in breaking down stereotypes and prejudice. Specifically, cross-group interactions (e.g., interactions between Black and White characters), which are portrayed in a way that implies the individuals have some prior friendly relations, will be beneficial in reducing viewers' negative attitudes toward the out-group character. It is not certain that these attitudes toward TV characters would generalize to the same group members in the real world.

Contact Lessens Our Reliance on Social Categories and Stereotypes

Our beliefs about members of other social groups are based on a single distinction—for example, we are middle-class and they are poor—which, due to its distinctiveness or importance in the culture, masks many dimensions on which *we* and *they* are similar. These similarities tend to go unnoticed and unappreciated unless we have personal contact with an out-group individual in the manner discussed above. Imagine interacting with a classmate who is physically disabled and about whom you believed stereotypical things. During the interaction, however, you might learn that you both have similar difficulties with your parents, have both traveled to Europe, or like the same music groups—subtle groupings that include you both. Discovering your social similarities and shared group memberships causes the initial social distinction (physical disability) and its stereotype to fade in relevance and importance, even if you don't revise that stereotype.

In addition to finding common ground, personal and friendly contact with an out-group member makes individuating information more salient than group-based information and is a more reliable basis for making inferences about out-group individuals. Thus, the distinctiveness of group labels and categories fades when we interact with people from out-groups. This was demonstrated in a study in which fourth grade children were randomly assigned to a classroom integrated with some students with learning disabilities or to a nonintegrated classroom (Maras & Brown, 1996). The nondisabled students' categorizations of the students with disabilities were observed over a 3-month term. At the beginning of the term, both groups used gender and disability to characterize the students in the class. In other words, you were either a boy with disabilities (or without disabilities) or a girl with disabilities (or without disabilities). At the end of the term, students in the nonintegrated (control) class described their classmates in similar categorical terms. In the integrated class, however, students' descriptions were much more idiosyncratic; the ordering of the students in their classroom was not dominated by the *disabled/nondisabled* dimension. This study shows that personal, cooperative contact lessens the importance of social categories in our thinking about members of other groups.

Intergroup contact also lessens automatic or implicit stereotyping, according to a study done by Natalie Shook and Russell Fazio (2008). They studied the racial attitudes of White first-year college students before the term began, when they were randomly assigned a roommate, and at the end of the term after they had spent 10 weeks living with the roommate. The point of the study was to observe the effect of having a different-race compared with same-race roommate on participants' racial implicit attitudes and stereotypes. By the end of the term, White students' attitudes toward Blacks had improved when they had a Black roommate but did not change when they had a White roommate. Their anxiety levels about interracial interactions also declined, and this effect was not observed in the same-race roommate condition. Participants with Black roommates were less satisfied and comfortable with their roommate situation than were participants with White roommates. This study points out that intergroup contact makes extra demands on people, but despite those demands, the benefits of interracial contact help to revise implicit racial biases, not just about one's roommate, but about the group of which one's roommate is a member.

Recall that stereotypes involve assumptions about the character and personality of out-group members and that we tend to explain their behavior in dispositional terms. This tendency is partly due to lack of contact between in-group and out-group members. When we are separated from people who are different then ourselves, we remain ignorant of the life circumstances and situational pressures they face and how their behavior might be as much due to circumstances as is our own. Personal interaction gives us insight into others' situations and circumstances. As a result, we are more socially informed, less judgmental, and more willing to acknowledge that the negative traits we perceive in out-group members (if they are true at all) may be caused by forces over which they have little control.

Applications of the Contact Hypothesis

In 1954, the U.S. Supreme Court declared race segregation in schools unconstitutional. As a result, schools opened their doors to students of all racial groups. This situation provided opportunity for researchers to evaluate the contact hypothesis in an important, real-life setting. In a review of that research, Walter Stephan (1978) reported that only 13% of the studies examining the effect of desegregation on students' racial attitudes actually found support for the contact hypothesis. Worse, half of the studies found the opposite effect: Racial integration in the classroom heightened students' negative stereotypes and feelings about other-race students.

Although this seems disappointing, there are reasons to believe that school systems have not given the contact hypothesis a fair test. First, many school administrators in the 1950s were firmly against desegregation. Their racist attitudes did not foster a friendly or supportive environment for interracial student contacts. More importantly, although White and Black students did (and still do) have personal contact in school-rooms, they have too few opportunities to interact in cooperative tasks. Research shows that it is common for students to compete against rather than cooperate with each other for grades and the teacher's attention (Aronson, Blaney, Stephan, Sikes, & Snapp, 1978). Moreover, the interaction of White and Black students is often overlaid with differences in socioeconomic status. Thus, even if a White and Black student worked cooperatively on a school project, status differences (such as family income or neighborhood affiliation) might preclude any softening of negative stereotypes between them.

Clearer evidence for the contact hypothesis comes from studies that examine how cooperative, equal-status learning groups affect students' stereotypes of socially differ-ent group members. In one study, junior high school students learned English skills over a 10-week period in one of two ethnically mixed settings (determined randomly): a cooperative learning group or a traditional classroom (Slavin, 1979). At the end of the unit, students listed their friends in the class. Compared to the classroom group, the cooperative learning group listed significantly more cross-ethnic friends. In a similar study, students with learning disabilities and normal students learned class-room material in either cooperative groups or in a conventional classroom setting (Armstrong, Johnson, & Balow, 1981). After the 4-week unit, students with learning disabilities were viewed more positively by their nondisabled peers in the cooperative group compared to the classroom condition. These experiments demonstrate that classroom interaction with socially different others, which occurs under the proper conditions, breaks down stereotypic beliefs and engenders positive feelings toward those individuals and their group.

In summary, physical contact provides opportunities for people of different and perhaps disliked social categories to relate and cooperate. Equal-status, cooperative interactions contribute to liking, reveal shared interests, and provide us with individu-ating information about others. However, contact and cooperation with people from negatively stereotyped groups do not come naturally. Contact between members of social groups, especially those separated based on racial and class distinctions, can be fostered and rewarded by concerned agents such as churches, school boards, commu-nity service agencies, and local government.

Self-Regulation of One's Own Prejudiced Behavior

Modern forms of prejudice feature a strong element of personal ambivalence. Ambivalent attitudes also characterize cultural stereotypes of particular groups, such as Asians and Jews. Ambivalence or holding both positive and negative attitudes toward members of an out-group can lead to inconsistencies in one's behavior toward those individuals, which in turn supports prejudice. Another behavioral approach to reducing prejudice, then, consists of making people aware of the inconsistencies in their behavior that support their prejudice and having them learn to regulate their own responses.

It has been shown that when people—particularly those for whom being nonprejudiced is important—become aware that they had responded in a prejudiced manner, they feel guilty and embarrassed (Devine, Monteith, Zuwerink, & Elliot, 1991). In that study, participants wrote how they should and how they *would* interact with Black individuals and gay men in social situations. Researchers then measured participants' negative emotions, such as guilt, regret, and shame, following the writing exercise. The results demonstrated that a discrepancy between how one should act and how one would act toward out-group individuals increased negative feelings toward them. However, this effect was greatest among people who thought of themselves as nonprejudiced.

Can the embarrassment and shame associated with recognizing our own prejudiced behavior motivate us to change? According to research by Margo Monteith (1993), yes, it can. In one study, she had participants read and evaluate the credentials of a hypothetical gay law school applicant. Some of the participants were led to believe that they had evaluated the applicant negatively because of his sexual orientation, thus activating a discrepancy between their nonprejudiced intentions and their *discriminatory* behavior. Other participants received no such information. What happened? The discrepancy-activated participants—especially those who were nonprejudiced to begin with—had more negative feelings about themselves compared to the other participants. More importantly, those participants also thought more about the discrepancy between their values and their actions, spent more time reading an article explaining why people are prejudiced against gays, and recalled more details from the article than all other participants.

This study shows that people with nonprejudiced values who become aware of their own prejudiced behavior are disturbed by their own actions, and they actively try to determine what went wrong and how they can prevent future regretful actions. Moreover, when the negative emotional reactions to such behavior were held constant, participants' self-improvement efforts were weakened. In other words, personal regulation of prejudiced behavior is not likely to occur without first experiencing the embarrassment and shame of unintended, hurtful prejudice.

In a follow-up study, Monteith (1993) again made some participants aware of the discrepancy between their prejudiced responses and their preexisting attitudes. Participants then entered what they believed was an unrelated study in which they rated the funniness of a variety of jokes, some of which involved gay bashing. The homophobic jokes were rated as less funny than the other jokes but only among participants who possessed nonprejudiced values and were aware of the discrepancy between their values and actions. This study suggests that nonprejudiced people who experience the sting of being aware of their prejudice make an effort to become less prejudiced in subsequent situations. Since those early studies, other evidence has accumulated that people can under the proper conditions moderate their implicit prejudice. For example, Brian Lowery and his colleagues (2001) used the Implicit Associates Test to measure racial bias in White participants in the presence of either a White or Black experimenter. In the presence of the Black experimenter, when social pressures to avoid the appearance of prejudice are high, White participants displayed less implicit racism than in the presence of a White experimenter. Similar findings occurred when participants were told to avoid prejudice. Other research, however, finds that people are not able to control their prejudicial attitudes that easily; in fact, attempts to control prejudicial attitudes can have the opposite effect and increase our bias. Why? Intergroup situations—like interacting with out-group members, or even anticipating such an interaction—can raise anxiety levels and that can interfere with our efforts to control our attitudes toward members of that group (Richeson & Trawalter, 2005). David Amodio (2009) tested this by having White participants discuss race issues with either a Black or White experimenter. Prior to and during the interaction, the participants' salivary cortisol (a stress hormone) and anxiety levels were measured. Finally, they completed a measure of automatic racial stereotyping. Participants who interacted with the Black compared with the White experimenter reported more anxiety. And, those participants whose cortisol levels were high after the interaction with the Black but not the White experimenter were much less able to control their race stereotypes. In summary, controlling one's stereotypes is not a simple matter of applying willpower. Although the expression of our implicit prejudices can be reduced with effort, the situations in which we desire to control our own prejudiced impulses are complex and, as we have seen, stressful. The stress of intergroup interactions can leave us unable to control stereotypes and prejudice.

Integrating the Contact and Self-Regulation Approaches to Prejudice Reduction

The research discussed above has important implications for understanding what intergroup contact—as a prejudice-reduction method—can and cannot do. Allport (1954) believed contact between members of antagonistic groups would reduce prejudice in part through revising our stereotypes about that group. Devine's research shows that stereotypes operate on our thinking automatically, even among people who want to be nonprejudiced. Remember, stereotypes are firmly implanted by a socialization process that draws on family, media, and traditional beliefs about out-groups. So while cultural stereotypes tend to be slow to change in the culture, one's personal beliefs about members of other groups can be changed. Therefore, the benefit of intergroup contact is to lessen our reliance on rather than to transform our stereotypes and to help replace the internalized stereotypic beliefs given to us by our culture with more informed and personal beliefs about members of negatively stereotyped groups.

Personal, cooperative contact with people from other social groups and self-regulation of one's prejudiced responses are complementary approaches to reducing prejudice. That is, sustained contact is more likely to cause us to revise our personal beliefs than our stereotypes about out-group members. The automatic influence of cultural stereotypes will cause discrepancies among people whose personal beliefs become more tolerant and egalitarian than the stereotypes with which they are familiar. Therefore, learning to self-regulate one's prejudiced and stereotype-driven responses will be a second step in reducing prejudice in oneself.

Cognitive Interventions

Although intergroup contact can under specific conditions reduce the misunderstanding, suspicion, and conflict people experience with members of negatively stereotyped groups, the engineering of those conditions may be a significant obstacle for using contact as a practical prejudice-reduction intervention. Likewise, the self-regulation of our prejudice requires that we get objective feedback about our behavior toward outgroup individuals; such objectivity is not easily achieved by observing our own actions. Cognitive prejudice-reduction approaches recommend themselves because they require less engineering and planning than interventions based on cooperative intergroup contact. Indeed, the cognitive interventions discussed below are easily understood and implemented as a part of general self-improvement efforts. Just as people diet to achieve weight loss and exercise to improve their health, so also can people practice fair-mindedness for the purposes of correcting their prejudices.

Stereotype Inhibition and Substitution

As we discussed in several previous chapters, well-learned and unquestioned stereotypes automatically guide our thinking and judgments about the members of those groups. The automaticity of social categorization and stereotyping does not mean, however, that such responses are uncontrollable or inevitable. Rather, much research clarifies the conditions surrounding **stereotype inhibition**, which involves deliberate monitoring and suppressing of expressing one's automatic prejudices (Blair, 2002). For example, White participants who were asked to categorize pictures of Black and White faces activated both the portion of the brain (i.e., the amygdala) that controls responses to people who are different than ourselves and automatic racial stereotypes in response to Black but not White faces (Wheeler & Fiske, 2005). However, when the participants were given instructions that discouraged racial categorization of the faces, they did not differentiate between Black and White faces. Apparently, being given a nonracial processing goal helped participants inhibit their racial stereotypes.

Being primed with positive images in the form of rapid, computer-presented pictures or words, especially when the images are associated with members of negatively stereotyped groups, also results in less automatic stereotyping on subsequent tasks (Aarts, Chartrand, & Custers, 2005; Olson & Fazio, 2006). This research shows that mood-improving stimuli cause people to alter their own automatic stereotypical responses. In that same vein, people make fewer stereotypic responses and judgments after they have been affirmed, say, by getting a positive evaluation on a task (Sinclair & Kunda, 1999). Apparently, when we feel good about ourselves, we can and do inhibit automatic stereotypes. Using a measure of automatic stereotyping, Steven Spencer and his colleagues (1998) found that people avoided stereotyping another person when they wanted to project a positive, nonprejudiced public image. In other words, when properly motivated, people seem able to inhibit their automatic stereotypical responses. Similarly, stereotype inhibition also occurs when people are aware of nonprejudiced norms (Sechrist & Stangor, 2001). That is, when participants believed other people did not share their stereotypic beliefs, they successfully prevented them from influencing their behavior. In sum, our needs for self-esteem and social approval motivate stereotype inhibition. Even automatic stereotypes—those cultural beliefs about people from other groups that are socialized into us from an early age—can be inhibited to achieve these important self-related goals. This makes sense when we remember (from Chapter 4) that needs for self-esteem and social approval figure prominently in the development and expression of prejudice. In the absence of a strong motive not to express prejudice, stereotype inhibition can also be achieved through self-instruction and mental imagery. Deliberate instructions to oneself to "avoid stereotypic thinking" or "don't think of him/her as a (insert social category)" leads to less automatic stereotyping compared with the judgments of people who didn't practice such self-instruction (Gollwitzer & Schaal, 1998). Similarly, people who were instructed to imagine a counterstereotypic image—for example, an intelligent poor person, an athletic obese person, or an assertive woman—expressed weaker stereotypes than people who didn't engage in such mental imagery (Blair, Ma, & Lenton, 2001). Deliberately thinking about the members of an out-group in counterstereotypical terms (e.g., men are nurturing) interferes with automatic stereotyping. So, it is possible that reductions in automatic stereotyping could happen by inhibiting stereotypic thoughts or by exhibiting counterstereotypic thoughts. For example, if I want to reduce my bias against old people, will it be more effective to suppress my well-learned stereotype of old people as doddering and dim or instead bring to mind exemplars of physically active, high achieving seniors? Bertram Gawronski and his colleagues (2008) wanted to find out which mental process had the beneficial effect on automatic stereotyping—negating your own stereotype or affirming a counterstereotype? In two studies, they trained participants to do one or the other—negate or affirm—regarding gender stereotypes. They found that refuting one's own stereotypic beliefs increased automatic gender stereotyping, whereas affirming counterstereotypical beliefs reduced automatic gender bias. Similar effects occurred when researchers measured preference for Whites over Blacks in the second study: Those who had tried to inhibit gender stereotypes ended up showing more racial bias, whereas those who affirmed counterstereotypic idea grew less biased.

Stereotype substitution was demonstrated in a study in which participants were exposed to pictures of Black or White people who were either widely liked (Bill Cosby, John F. Kennedy) or disliked (O. J. Simpson, Timothy McVeigh). Participants in the Cosby condition expressed less automatic racial prejudice than those in the other conditions, suggesting that they had replaced their negative beliefs about Blacks with more positive associations (Dasgupta & Greenwald, 2001). The effect of this stereotype substitution was not simply momentary: Tested a day later, participants who were in the Cosby condition were still less racist than the other participants. Finally, even learning about the principles of stereotyping, prejudice, and prejudice reduction in an academic course, as you may be engaged in right now, encourages self-instruction and rehearsal in detecting, avoiding, and replacing one's own stereotypes. Researchers found that students in prejudice or diversity courses expressed less automatic stereotyping at the end of the course than at the beginning

(Rudman, Ashmore, & Gary, 2001). To sum up, stereotypes intrude spontaneously into our thinking about members of other groups, but these stereotypes can be inhibited through self-instruction.

Cross-Categorization

Although social categorization helps us manage the complexity of our social contexts, social categories also impose differences on the world that are exaggerated and overemphasized. Once established, in-groups and out-groups are never equal. Thanks to the pervasive in-group bias, we always attach greater value to our social groups than to others' groups. Thus, prejudice is a direct result of social categorization and our needs for positive in-group feelings.

Imagine that you attend a soccer game between your school, City College, and the cross-town rival, State College. Among some of the fans, there will be a clear and simple social categorization (us versus them) with no love lost between the groups. At the game, however, you run into several old friends from high school who are now students at State College. How will **cross-categorization**, the realization that you share a group membership with people from a disliked out-group, affect your attitudes toward these students? Anthropologists who study primitive societies have observed that crosscutting social ties lessens the prejudice between neighboring tribes and clans (LeVine & Campbell, 1972). The effect of cross-categorization has been demonstrated in controlled research settings too (see Brown, 1995, for review). These studies show a clear pattern: When members of opposing groups share another category membership, their natural feelings about each other (e.g., suspicion, anxiety, hostility) are reduced or eliminated.

Although it is well known that cross-categorization reduces feelings of prejudice, how does it work? Many explanations for the beneficial effects of cross-categorization have been tested and found to have empirical support. To determine which model best explains the effect, researchers summarized a large number of cross-categorization studies through the process of meta-analysis—examining evidence for an idea across many studies rather than within a single study (Migdal, Hewstone, & Mullen, 1997). They concluded that the best explanation for cross-categorization effects is the idea that cross-categorization reduces the perceived differences between one's own and another's social group, while increasing the perceived differences among the members of one's own group. In other words, when we cross-categorize ourselves with a member of a negatively stereotyped group, *they* become (or actually are perceived to be) less different than *us*. Additionally, the act of cross-categorization is a reminder that you and your fellow in-group members share group memberships with other people, and this leads to the perception that *we* are not as similar to each other as once believed. Both outcomes can help explain why cross-categorization undercuts prejudice. Prejudice is more difficult to maintain against people with whom we share some similarity. Likewise, one's in-groups when perceived to be more variable are less of a breeding ground for prejudice because we sense less agreement among the members of our own group about who *they* are and how we should act toward *them*.

Researchers have investigated the effect of having cross-group friendships on prejudice and other forms of intergroup behavior. One study followed Black students at a mostly White university across 3 years of their undergraduate experience to see if having White friends in year 1 predicted more positive attitudes toward Whites at year 3 compared to those who didn't form cross-group friendships (Mendoza-Denton & Page-Gould, 2008). After controlling for background variables, they found that the more majority-group (White) friends participants' had, the more they felt they belonged at their school. In a follow-up study, cross-group friendships were experimentally manipulated by randomly assigning Latino and White participants to a cross-group or same-group friendship induction experience. The experience consisted of several sessions in which participants bonded with other students through self-disclosure exercises and cooperative games. Among the Latino participants, particularly those who were sensitive about race issues, the cross-group friendship experience caused more positive identification with their school. Other researchers asked people to think about a cross-group friend compared with a same-group friend and found they were more likely to identify positively with that friend's ethnicity (Page-Gould, Mendoza-Denton, Alegre, & Siy, 2010).

The principle of cross-categorization illustrates how the contact hypothesis works. Cooperative interaction among typical and equal-status members of opposing groups reduces prejudice between them, but how? Uniting with others under a common goal or identity forms a new crosscutting social category. It is difficult to maintain negative feelings toward people from a once-disliked group when you realize that you share certain interests and affiliations. When people share common features, interests, or goals with people from negatively stereotyped groups, by emphasizing one's commonalities they become fellow in-group members. So, cross-categorization has the potential to lessen prejudice felt toward members of out-groups and, subsequently, the stigma felt by members of those groups. To cross-categorize ourselves and those who populate our social world is not to ignore the ways we are socially different from each other. Nor does cross-categorization require us to give up our social allegiances. In-group pride is an important contributor to psychological well-being. Only when in-group pride is dependent on how we stack up against individuals from another group do we dislike and derogate out-group members. Cross-categorization, then, encourages us to structure our thoughts about people who are socially different from ourselves so that our obvious social differences (e.g., race, class) do not overshadow our not-so-obvious similarities.

Empathy

The eminent psychiatrist and writer Scott Peck (1994) has observed that many of the ills of modern society stem from a general lack of civility among people. The role of empathy in prejudice reduction has received much attention among psychologists; they distinguish between two kinds of empathy (Duan & Hill, 1996). **Cognitive empathy** refers to perspective taking or the act of imagining the circumstances and perspective of someone else. **Emotional empathy** involves trying to share another's feelings or responding emotionally to the plight or circumstances of another person. The empirical connections between empathy and prejudice reduction are many. Let's briefly explore some of the ways empathy works.

Empathy Changes Attributions for Others' Behavior

Many of the outcomes associated with prejudice and stereotyping arise because we make dispositional inferences about others. That is, we attribute others' actions to internal, stable qualities rather than to their circumstances or some interaction of traits and situations. For example, we observed in Chapter 8 that poor people's lack of achievement tends to be seen as due to their laziness and lack of motivation or competence for work rather than, for example, their inability to pay for college or job training. This attribution bias occurs because the situations in which other people behave are notoriously hard to see, and even if we can imagine them, we see others' circumstances primarily from our (rather than their) perspective (Gilbert & Malone, 1995). Cognitive empathy reduces the attribution bias that leads to judgment and blame for out-group members' negative behavior. Researchers have established that when we are asked to imagine and explain the situations in which other people act, we are more evenhanded and accurate about the causes of out-group members' behavior (Krull, 1993). Although the practice of cognitive empathy may seem onerous, it actually demands no more of our attention or memory than our default social perception goal—drawing dispositional inferences for others' behavior.

As we learned in Chapter 7, prejudice against obese people is driven by beliefs about the controllability of weight and the perceived irresponsibility of eating too much or exercising too little (Crandall, 1994). Developing cognitive empathy for an obese person involves considering the idea that weight is largely uncontrollable and being overweight is not a simple matter of gluttony or laziness. Indeed, when Crandall (1994) had his study participants take the perspective of obese people by thinking about the possibility that weight is not as controllable as they assumed, they were more accepting of obese people than were participants who did not engage in perspective taking. Two things may occur while engaging in cognitive empathy. First, empathizing with the circumstances in which people live gives us an opportunity to picture *ourselves* in those circumstances and thus better appreciate the impact of the social context on behavior. Second, cognitive empathy means making some effort to know negatively stereotyped people as multidimensional rather than unidimensional individuals, and this new perspective can lead to a revision and updating of our stereotype about the members of a group.

Empathy Prompts Compassion

Emotional empathy, sharing the emotional experiences of another person, is associated with more positive and forgiving attitudes toward such extremely negatively stereotyped groups as the homeless, people with HIV/AIDS, and death row prisoners (Batson et al., 1997). In one study, Batson and his colleagues instructed participants to either maximize or minimize empathy while reading some scenarios about people who were suffering. Empathy improved participants' attitudes toward the individuals in the scenarios and toward the groups of which those individuals were members. Moreover, the positive, prejudice-reducing effects of empathy endured for at least 2 weeks. A similar study tested the effect of empathy instructions on Whites' attitudes toward Blacks (Finlay & Stephan, 2000). When asked to empathize with the Black victims in various scenarios, participants' in-group bias disappeared. In a subsequent and seemingly unrelated study measuring racial attitudes, empathic participants had equally positive attitudes toward Black and White individuals, whereas the no-empathy participants held more positive attitudes toward Whites. What's more, the empathic participants themselves reported experiencing more of the emotions described as being experienced by the person in the scenario, suggesting that the effect was due more to emotional than to cognitive empathy.

The practical implications of these effects of empathy are obvious: Both cognitive and emotional empathy are easily instilled in both individuals and groups through workshops and training sessions. Numerous studies have tested interventions designed to increase empathy through workshops, online interactions, and media messages (Malhotra & Liyanage, 2005; Paluck, 2009; Stephan & Finlay, 1999). Generally, according to a review by Mina Cikara and her colleagues (2011), these interventions have been successful at instilling greater empathy, and some studies have evidence that the greater empathy actually changes intergroup behavior. However, empathy interventions can also prompt more negative attitudes toward out-group members, particularly when the perspective taking needed for empathy enables us to think about how *they* view *us* (Cikara, Bruneau, & Saxe, 2011).

Summary

Behavioral interventions for prejudice reduction use personal contact with individuals of negatively stereotyped groups, as well as behavioral feedback, to help break down stereotypes and build liking and trust. Cognitive interventions address the same goal by changing how we think about out-group individuals. Although stereotypes can be so well learned and familiar that they operate almost by themselves to shape our behavior, much research shows that even automatic stereotypes and prejudices can be suppressed and changed.

DI **Diversity Issue 12.1: Stereotype Rebound**

Have you ever tried not to think about something? Occasionally we all find ourselves in situations in which prejudiced behavior—a sexist or homophobic remark, for example—would have serious consequences. In these situations, we make an effort to strategically inhibit our stereotypes. Psychologists who study mental control have found that trying

(Continued)

(Continued)

not to think about something actually increases the mental accessibility of the event or object, making it potentially more likely to intrude into our thoughts and behavior than had we not tried to suppress the thing at all. In a fascinating study of what happens when we try not to express a stereotype, Neil Macrae and his colleagues gave British students a photograph of a skinhead (a negatively stereotyped group in the UK) and asked them to write an essay describing the traits and behaviors of the person in the photograph (Macrae, Bodenhausen, Milne, & Jetten, 1994). Some of the participants were asked to avoid stereotypic references in their essay (experimental group); the other participants received no instructions (control group). The essays were then evaluated for skinhead-stereotypic content by independent raters who knew nothing of the instructions given. The stereotype suppression encouraged by the experimental instructions worked: Those who tried to avoid using a stereotype wrote essays with significantly fewer stereotypic references. In the second part of the study, participants again wrote a descriptive essay about a different skinhead target, but this time there were no suppression instructions. The essays that were written by the participants who earlier had suppressed their stereotypes were significantly more prejudiced and stereotypical than those of the participants in the control group. Termed **stereotype rebound**, this effect was shown in a follow-up study in which participants who had suppressed their stereotype on an essay-writing task displayed more automatic prejudice on a subsequent computer task than the control group participants. In short, stereotype suppression was effective—producing less prejudicial behavior—until the participants ceased the active suppression of their beliefs about skinheads. Once stereotype suppression is abandoned or forgotten, the stereotype rebounds into one's behavior with more strength than it had before the suppression effort.

In a more recent demonstration of stereotype rebound effects in behavior, participants were randomly assigned to suppress or not suppress their stereotype of elderly people (Follenfant & Ric, 2010). They were given a photograph of an older woman and asked to write a descriptive essay about the woman. In the experimental condition, however, participants were instructed to avoid using old-age stereotypical terms in their essay. After the writing task, participants' walking speed across the room was unobtrusively timed as they returned the materials to the experimenter. What happened? Participants who suppressed their stereotype walked much slower than those who didn't. This shows that a suppressed age stereotype rebounds to subtly influence behavior in a manner consistent with that stereotype.

? One implication of stereotype rebound is that in trying not to say something prejudiced—say, in a job interview—you might be successful at keeping the stereotype out of your speech but miss its leakage into your behavior, which you are not monitoring. In other words, your nonverbal behavior may reveal the stereotype that you're trying to suppress in your verbal behavior, even more obviously than had you not tried to suppress it at all. Have you ever observed this in yourself or another person?

KEY TERMS

Social inequality   230

Contact hypothesis   231

Imagined intergroup contact   232

Stereotype inhibition   238

Stereotype substitution   239

Cross-categorization   240

Cognitive empathy   241

Emotional empathy   241

Stereotype rebound   244

FOR FURTHER READING

Crisp, R., & Turner, R. (2009). Can imagined interactions produce positive perceptions?: Reducing prejudice through simulated social contact. *American Psychologist, 64*, 231–240. doi: 10.1037/a0014718

This paper reviews research on all forms of imagined intergroup contact and summarizes the benefits associated with this kind of prejudice-reduction intervention.

Online Resources

The Jigsaw Classroom

http://www.jigsaw.org/

The Jigsaw Classroom is a much-tested technique for reducing racial conflict and promoting better learning among students. Read the website material and explain how, in terms of the prejudice-reduction principles discussed in this chapter, the Jigsaw Classroom achieves it effects.

Psychlopedia: Contact Hypothesis
PsychWiki: Cross-Categorization

http://www.psych-it.com.au/Psychlopedia/article.asp?id=197

http://www.psychwiki.com/wiki/Crossed_Categorization

Psycholpedia and PsychWiki are wiki sites with useful descriptions and summaries of psychological concepts and theories, including the contact hypothesis and cross-categorization.

Understanding Prejudice.Org

http://www.understandingprejudice.org/links/reducing.htm

This site provides many useful links for learning about real prejudice-reduction initiatives.

References

Aarts, H., Chartrand, T., & Custers, R. (2005). Social stereotypes and automatic goals pursuit. *Social Cognition, 23,* 465–490.

Aberson, C., Healy, M., & Romero, V. (2000). Ingroup bias and self-esteem: A meta-analysis. *Personality and Social Psychology Review, 4,* 157–173.

Abrams, D., Thomas, J., & Hogg, M. (1990). Numerical distinctiveness, social identity, and gender salience. *British Journal of Social Psychology, 29,* 87–92.

Adams, G., & Beehr, T. (1998). Turnover and retirement: A comparison of their similarities and differences. *Personnel Psychology, 51,* 643–665.

Adolphs, R. (2009). The social brain: Neural basis of social knowledge. *Annual Review of Psychology, 60,* 693–716.

Adorno, T., Frenkel-Brunswik, E., Levinson, D., & Sanford, R. (1950). *The authoritarian personality.* New York, NY: Harper.

Agerstrom, J., & Rooth, D. (2011). The role of automatic obesity stereotypes in real hiring discrimination. *Journal of Applied Psychology, 96,* 780–805.

Akrami, N., Ekehammar, B., & Bergh, R. (2011). Generalized prejudice: Common and specific components. *Psychological Science, 22,* 57–59.

Allen, B., & Niss, J. (1990, April). A chill in the college classroom? *Phi Delta Kappan,* 607–609.

Allon, N. (1982). The stigma of overweight in everyday life. In B. Wolman (Ed.), *Psychological aspects of obesity: A handbook* (pp. 130–174). New York, NY: Van Nostrand Reinhold.

Allport, G. (1954). *The nature of prejudice.* Reading, MA: Addison-Wesley.

Allport, G., & Ross, J. (1967). Personal religious orientation and prejudice. *Journal of Personality and Social Psychology, 5,* 432–443.

Altemeyer, B. (1998). The other "authoritarian personality." In M. P. Zanna (Ed.), *Advances in experimental social psychology* (Vol. 30, pp. 47–92). New York, NY: Academic Press.

Altemeyer, B., & Hunsberger, B. (1992). Authoritarianism, religious fundamentalism, quest, and prejudice. *International Journal for the Psychology of Religion, 2,* 113–133.

Amato, M., & Crocker, J. (1995, August). *The stigma of being overweight and self-esteem: The role of controllability.* Paper presented at the annual meeting of the American Psychological Association, New York.

Amodio, D. (2009). Intergroup anxiety effects on the control of racial stereotypes: A psychoneuroendocrine analysis. *Journal of Experimental Social Psychology, 45,* 60–67.

Anderson, C., Peterson, C., Fletcher, L., Mitchell, J., Thuras, P., & Crow, S. (2001). Weight loss and gender: An examination of physician attitudes. *Obesity Research, 9,* 257–263.

Archer, J. (1996). Sex differences in social behavior: Are the social role and evolutionary explanations compatible? *American Psychologist, 51,* 909–917.

Arias, E. (2011). *United States Life Tables, 2007.* Centers for Disease Control National Vital Statistics Reports. Retrieved from http://www.cdc.gov/nchs/data/nvsr/nvsr59/nvsr59_09.pdf

Armstrong, B., Johnson, D., & Balow, B. (1981). Effects of cooperative vs. individualistic learning experiences on interpersonal attraction between learning-disabled and normal progress elementary school students. *Contemporary Educational Psychology, 6,* 102–109.

Arndt, J., Greenberg, J., Solomon, S., Pyszczynski, T., & Simon, L. (1997). Suppression, accessibility of death-related thoughts, and worldview defense: Exploring the psychodynamics of terror management. *Journal of Personality and Social Psychology, 73*, 5–18.

Aronson, E., Blaney, N., Stephan, C., Sikes, J., & Snapp, M. (1978). *The jig-saw classroom.* Beverly Hills, CA: Sage.

Babad, E., Bernieri, R., & Rosenthal, R. (1991). Students as judges of teachers' verbal and nonverbal behaviors. *American Educational Research Journal, 28*, 211–234.

Bacon, L., Stern, J., Van Loan, M., & Keim, N. (2005). Size acceptance and intuitive eating improve health for obese, female chronic dieters. *Journal of the American Dietetic Association, 105*, 929–936.

Bal, A., Reiss, A., Rudolph, C., & Baltes, B. (2011). Examining positive and negative perceptions of older workers: A meta-analysis. *Journal of Gerontology: Social Sciences, 66*, 687–698.

Banaji, M., & Hardin, C. (1996). Automatic stereotyping. *Psychological Science, 7*, 136–141.

Banaji, M., Hardin, C., & Rothman, A. (1993). Implicit stereotyping in person judgment. *Journal of Personality and Social Psychology, 65*, 272–281.

Banton, M. (1977). *The idea of race.* Boulder, CO: Westview Press.

Barden, J., Maddux, W., Petty, R., & Brewer, M. (2004). Contextual moderation of racial bias: The impact of social roles on controlled and automatically activated attitudes. *Journal of Personality and Social Psychology, 87*, 5–22.

Bargh, J., McKenna, K., & Ritzsimons, G. (2002). Can you see the real me? Activation and expression of the "true self" on the Internet. *Journal of Social Issues, 58*, 33–48.

Baron, R., Albright, L., & Malloy, T. (1995). Effects of behavioral and social class information on social judgment. *Personality and Social Psychology Bulletin, 21*, 308–315.

Barreto, M., Ellemers, N., Piebinga, L., & Moya, M. (2010). How nice of us and how dumb of me: The effect of exposure to benevolent sexism on women's task and relational self-descriptions. *Sex Roles, 62*, 532–544.

Batson, D. (1975). Rational processing or rationalization? The effect of disconfirming information on a stated religious belief. *Journal of Personality and Social Psychology, 32*, 176–184.

Batson, D., Polycarpou, M., Harmon-Hones, E., Imhoff, H., Mitchener, E., Bednar, L., . . . Highberger, L. (1997). Empathy and attitudes: Can feeling for a member of a stigmatized group improve feelings toward the group? *Journal of Personality and Social Psychology, 72*, 105–118.

Batson, D., Sympson, S., Hindman, J., Decruz, P., Todd, R., Jennings, G., & Burris, C. (1996). "I've been there too": Effect on empathy of prior experience with a need. *Personality and Social Psychology Bulletin, 22*, 474–482.

Baum, C., & Ford, T. (2004). The wage effects of obesity: A longitudinal study. *Health Economics, 13*, 885–899.

Beals, K., Peplau, L., & Gable, S. (2009). Stigma management and well-being: The role of perceived social support, emotional processing, and suppression. *Personality and Social Psychology Bulletin, 35*, 867–879.

Becker, J. (2010). Why do women endorse hostile and benevolent sexism? The role of salient female subtypes and internalization of sexist contents. *Sex Roles, 62*, 453–467.

Beckham, E. (1997, January 5). Diversity opens doors to all: A multicultural focus helps stimulate more critical thinking. *New York Times Book Review*, 58.

Belle, D., & Doucet, J. (2003). Poverty, inequality, and discrimination as sources of depression among U.S. women. *Psychology of Women Quarterly, 27*, 101–113.

Berg, C. (1990). Stereotyping in films in general and of the Hispanic in particular. *Howard Journal of Communications, 2*, 286–300.

Berrill, K. (1990). Anti-gay violence and victimization in the United States. *Journal of Interpersonal Violence, 5*, 274–294.

Bessenoff, G., & Sherman, J. (2000). Automatic and controlled components of prejudice toward fat people: Evaluation versus stereotype activation. *Social Cognition, 18,* 329–353.

Bettencourt, B., & Miller, N. (1996). Sex differences in aggression as a function of provocation: A meta-analysis. *Psychological Bulletin, 119,* 422–447.

Beukeboom, C., Finkenauer, C., & Wigboldus, D. (2010). The negation bias: When negations signal stereotypic expectancies. *Journal of Personality and Social Psychology, 99,* 978–992.

Biernat, M., & Dovidio, J. (2000). Stigma and stereotypes. In T. F. Heatherton, R. E. Kleck, M. R. Hebl, & J. G. Hull (Eds.), *The social psychology of stigma* (pp. 88–125). New York, NY: Guilford Press.

Biernat, M., & Kobrynowicz, D. (1997). Gender- and race-based standards of competence: Lower minimum standards but higher ability standards for devalued groups. *Journal of Personality and Social Psychology, 72,* 544–557.

Birenbaum, A. (1992). Courtesy stigma revisited. *Mental Retardation, 5,* 265–268.

Bishop, J., & Krause, D. (1984). Depictions of aging and old age on Saturday morning television. *The Gerontologist, 24,* 91–94.

Bizman, A., & Yinon, Y. (2001). Intergroup and interpersonal threats as determinants of prejudice: The moderating role of in-group identification. *Basic and Applied Social Psychology, 23,* 191–196.

Black, K., Marola, J., Littman, A., Chrisler, J., & Neace, W. (2009). Gender and form of cereal box characters: Different medium, same disparity. *Sex Roles, 60,* 882–889.

Blaine, B., DiBlasi, D., & Connor, J. (2002). The effect of weight loss on perceptions of weight controllability: Implications for prejudice against fat people. *Journal of Applied Biobehavioral Research, 7,* 44–56.

Blair, I. (2002). The malleability of automatic stereotypes and prejudice. *Personality and Social Psychology Review, 6,* 242–261.

Blair, I., Judd, C., & Chapleau, K. (2004). The influence of Afrocentric facial features in criminal sentencing. *Psychological Science, 15,* 674–679.

Blair, I., Ma, J., & Lenton, A. (2001). Imagining stereotypes away: The moderation of implicit stereotypes through mental imagery. *Journal of Personality and Social Psychology, 81,* 828–841.

Blascovich, J., Spencer, S., Quinn, D., & Steele, C. (2001). African Americans and high blood pressure: The role of stereotype threat. *Psychological Science, 12,* 225–229.

Blashill, A., & Powlishta, K. (2009). Gay stereotypes: The use of sexual orientation as a cure for gender-related attributes. *Sex Roles, 61,* 783–793.

Boatright-Horowitz, S. L., & Soeung, S. (2009). Teaching White privilege to White students can mean saying good-bye to positive student evaluations. *American Psychologist, 64*(6), 574–575. doi: 10.1037/a0016593

Bobo, L. (1988). Attitudes toward the Black political movement: Trends, meaning, and effects on racial policy preferences. *Social Psychology Quarterly, 51,* 287–302.

Bodenhausen, G. (1990). Stereotypes as judgmental heuristics: Evidence of circadian variations in discrimination. *Psychological Science, 1,* 319–322.

Bonham, V., Warshauer-Baker, E., & Collins, F. (2005). Race and ethnicity in the genome era: The complexity of the constructs. *American Psychologist, 60,* 9–15.

Bordieri, J., Drehmer, D., & Taylor, D., (1997). Work-life for employees with disabilities: Recommendations for promotion. *Rehabilitation Counseling Bulletin, 40,* 181–191.

Bousfield, C., & Hutchison, P. (2010). Contact, anxiety, and young people's attitudes and behavioral intentions towards the elderly. *Educational Gerontology, 36,* 451–466.

Brandt, M., & Reyna C. (2010). The role of prejudice and the need for closure in religious fundamentalism. *Personality and Social Psychology Bulletin, 36,* 715–725.

Brescoll, V., Dawson, E., & Uhlmann, E. (2010). Hard won and easily lost: The fragile status of leaders in gender-stereotype incongruent occupations. *Psychological Science, 21,* 1640–1642.

Bresnahan, M., Ohashi, R., Nebashi, R., Liu, W., & Shearman, S. (2002). Attitudinal and affective response toward accented English. *Language and Communication, 22,* 171–185.

Brewer, M. (1979). Ingroup bias in the minimal intergroup situation: A cognitive motivation analysis. *Psychological Bulletin, 86,* 307–324.

Brewer, M. (1999). The psychology of prejudice: Ingroup love or outgroup hate? *Journal of Social Issues, 55,* 429–444.

Brewer, M., Dull, V., & Lui, L. (1981). Perceptions of the elderly: Stereotypes as prototypes. *Journal of Personality and Social Psychology, 41,* 656–670.

Brewer, M., & Lui, L. (1989). The primacy of age and sex in the structure of person categories. *Social Cognition, 7,* 262–274.

Brezina, T., & Winder, K. (2003). Economic disadvantage, status generalization, and negative racial stereotyping by White Americans. *Social Psychology Quarterly, 66,* 402–418.

Brigham, J. C. (1974). Views of Black and White children concerning the distribution of personality characteristics. *Journal of Personality, 42,* 144–158.

Brophy, J., & Good, T. (1974). *Teacher-student relationships: Causes and consequences.* New York, NY: Holt, Rinehart & Winston.

Brown, L. (1998). Ethnic stigma as a contextual experience: A possible selves perspective. *Personality and Social Psychology Bulletin, 24,* 163–172.

Brown, R. (1984). The effects of intergroup similarity and cooperative vs. competitive on intergroup discrimination. *British Journal of Social Psychology, 23,* 21–33.

Brown, R. (1995). *Prejudice: Its social psychology.* Oxford, UK: Blackwell.

Brown, R., & Lee, M. (2005). Stigma consciousness and the race gap in college achievement. *Self and Identity, 4,* 149–157.

Bugental, D., & Hehman, J. (2007). Ageism: A review of research and policy implications. *Social Issues and Policy Review, 1,* 173–216.

Bureau of Labor Statistics (2009). *Labor force statistics from the current population survey.* Retrieved from http://www.bls.gov

Buruma, I. (2003, August 31). How to talk about Israel. *New York Times Magazine,* 28–33.

Buss, D. (1995). Psychological sex differences: Origins through sexual selection. *American Psychologist, 50,* 164–168.

Buss, D., & Schmidt, D. (1993). Sexual strategies theory: An evolutionary perspective on human mating. *Psychological Review, 100,* 204–232.

Butler, J., Ryckman, R., Thornton, B., & Bouchard, R. (1993). Assessment of the full content of physique stereotypes with a free-response format. *Journal of Social Psychology, 133,* 147–162.

Butz, D., & Yogeeswaran, K. (2011). A new threat in the air: Macroeconomic threat increases prejudice against Asian Americans. *Journal of Experimental Social Psychology, 47,* 22–27.

Bylsma, W., & Major, B. (1994). Social comparisons and contentment: Exploring the psychological consequences of the gender wage gap. *Psychology of Women Quarterly, 18,* 241–249.

Campbell, J. (1990). Self-esteem and the clarity of the self-concept. *Journal of Personality and Social Psychology, 59,* 538–549.

Canning, H., & Meyer, J. (1966). Obesity—its possible effect on college acceptance. *New England Journal of Medicine, 275,* 1172–1174.

Caporael, L., Lukaszewski, M., & Culbertson, G. (1983). Secondary baby talk: Judgments by institutionalized elderly and their caregivers. *Journal of Personality and Social Psychology, 44,* 746–754.

Carr, P., & Steele, C. (2009). Stereotype threat and inflexible perseverance in problem solving. *Journal of Experimental Social Psychology, 45,* 853–859.

Cass, V. (1979). Homosexual identity formation: A theoretical model. *Journal of Homosexuality, 4,* 219–235.

Cassata, M., Anderson, P., & Skill, T. (1980). The older adult in daytime serial drama. *Journal of Communication, 30,* 48–49.

Ceci, S., & Williams, W. (2010). Sex differences in math-intensive fields. *Psychological Science, 19,* 275–279.

Centers for Disease Control and Prevention. (2008). *Disability and health: Data and statistics.* Retrieved from http://www.cdc.gov/ncbddd/disabilityandhealth/data.html

Centers for Disease Control and Prevention. (2012). Defining overweight and obesity. Retrieved from http://www.cdc.gov/obesity/defining.html

Chafel, J. (1997). Societal images of poverty: Child and adult beliefs. *Youth and Society, 28,* 432–463.

Chalabaev, A., Sarrazin, P., Trouilloud, D., & Jussim, L. (2009). Can sex-undifferentiated teacher expectations mask an influence of sex stereotypes? Alternative forms of sex bias in teacher expectations. *Journal of Applied Social Psychology, 39,* 2469–2498.

Chang, D., & Sue, S. (2003). The effects of race and problem type on teachers' assessments of student behavior. *Journal of Consulting and Clinical Psychology, 71,* 235–242.

Chen, E. (2005). Why socioeconomic status affects the health of children: A psychosocial perspective. *Current Directions in Psychological Science, 13,* 112–115.

Cheryan, S., & Bodenhausen, G. (2000). When positive stereotypes threaten intellectual performance: The psychological hazards of "model minority" status. *Psychological Science, 11,* 399–402.

Cheung, F., & Halpern, D. (2010). Women at the top: Powerful leaders define success as work + family in a culture of gender. *American Psychologist, 65,* 182–193.

Cialdini, R., Borden, R., Thorne, A., Walker, M., Freeman, S., & Sloan, L. (1976). Basking in reflected glory: Three (football) field studies. *Journal of Personality and Social Psychology, 34,* 366–374.

Cikara, M., Bruneau, E., & Saxe, R. (2011). Us and them: Intergroup failures of empathy. *Current Directions in Psychological Science, 20,* 149–153.

Clark, K., & Clark, M. (1940). Skin color as a factor in racial identification of Negro preschool children. *The Journal of Social Psychology, 11,* 159–169.

Clark, R. (2000). Perceptions of inter-ethnic group racism predict increased blood pressure responses to a laboratory challenge in college women. *Annals of Behavioral Medicine, 22,* 214–222.

Clark, R. (2006). Perceived racism and vascular reactivity in Black college women: Moderating effects of seeking social support. *Health Psychology, 25,* 20–25.

Clark, R., Anderson, N., Clark, V., & Williams, D. (1999). Racism as a stressor for African Americans: A biopsychosocial model. *American Psychologist, 54,* 805–816.

Clausell, E., & Fiske, S. (2005). When do subgroup parts add up to the stereotypic whole? Mixed stereotype content for gay male subgroups explains overall ratings. *Social Cognition, 23,* 161–181.

Clayton, S. (1992). Remedies for discrimination: Race, sex, and affirmative action. *Behavioral Sciences and the Law, 10,* 245–257.

Clayton, S. (1996). Reactions to social categorization: Evaluating one argument against affirmative action. *Journal of Applied Social Psychology, 26,* 1472–1493.

Cohen, S. (1996). Psychological stress, immunity, and upper respiratory infections. *Current Directions in Psychological Science, 5,* 86–89.

Cohen, S., & Wills, T. (1985). Stress, social support, and the buffering hypothesis. *Psychological Bulletin, 98,* 310–357.

Columb, C., & Plant, E. A. (2011). Revisiting the Obama Effect: Exposure to Obama reduces implicit prejudice. *Journal of Experimental Social Psychology, 47,* 499–501.

Cook, S. (1984). Cooperative interaction in multiethnic contexts. In N. Miller & M. Brewer (Eds.), *Groups in contact: The psychology of desegregation* (pp. 291–302). New York, NY: Academic Press.

Cooley, C. (1902). *Human nature and the social order.* New York, NY: Scribner.

Cooper, H., & Tom, D. (1984). Teacher expectation research: A review with implications for classroom instruction. *Elementary School Journal, 85,* 77–89.

Cooper, J., & Fazio, R. (1984). A new look at dissonance theory. In L. Berkowitz (Ed.), *Advances in experimental social psychology* (Vol. 17, pp. 229–266). New York, NY: Academic Press.

Correll, J., Park, B., Judd, C., & Wittenbrink, B. (2002). The police officer's dilemma: Using ethnicity to disambiguate potentially threatening individuals. *Journal of Personality and Social Psychology, 83,* 1314–1329.

Corrigan, P. (2004). How stigma interferes with mental health care. *American Psychologist, 59,* 614–625.

Corrigan, P., & Miller, F. (2004). Shame, blame, and contamination: A review of the impact of mental illness stigma on family members. *Journal of Mental Health, 13,* 537–548.

Costa, P., & McCrae, R. (1992). *The NEO Personality Inventory (Rev.).* Odessa, FL: Psychological Assessment Resources.

Cowan, G., & Hodge, C. (1996). Judgments of hate speech: The effects of target group, publicness, and behavioral responses of the target. *Journal of Applied Social Psychology, 26,* 355–374.

Cozzarelli, C., Tagler, M., & Wilkinson, A. (2002). Do middle-class students perceive poor women and poor men differently? *Sex Roles, 47,* 519–529.

Cozzarelli, C., Wilkinson, A., & Tagler, M. (2001). Attitudes towards the poor and attributions for poverty. *Journal of Social Issues, 57,* 207–227.

Crandall, C. (1991). Do heavy-weight students have more difficulty paying for college? *Personality and Social Psychology Bulletin, 17,* 606–611.

Crandall, C. (1994). Prejudice against fat people: Ideology and self-interest. *Journal of Personality and Social Psychology, 66,* 882–894.

Crandall, C. (1995). Do parents discriminate against their heavyweight daughters? *Personality and Social Psychology Bulletin, 21,* 724–735.

Crandall, C., & Biernat, M. (1990). The ideology of anti-fat attitudes. *Journal of Applied Social Psychology, 20,* 227–243.

Crandall, C., & Coleman, R. (1992). AIDS-related stigmatization and the disruption of social relationships. *Journal of Social and Personal Relationships, 9,* 163–177.

Crandall, C., D'Anello, S., Sakalli, N., Lazarus, E., Wieczorkowska, G., & Feather, N. T. (2001). An attribution-value model of prejudice: Anti-fat attitudes in six nations. *Personality and Social Psychology Bulletin, 27,* 30–37.

Crandall, C., & Eshleman, A. (2003). A justification-suppression model of the expression and experience of prejudice. *Psychological Bulletin, 129,* 414–446.

Crandall, C., & Martinez, R. (1996). Culture, ideology, and antifat attitudes. *Personality and Social Psychology Bulletin, 22,* 1165–1176.

Crawford, A. (1996). Stigma associated with AIDS: A meta-analysis. *Journal of Applied Social Psychology, 26,* 398–416.

Crisp, R. J., & Abrams, D. (2008). Improving intergroup attitudes and reducing stereotype threat: An integrated contact model. In W. Stroebe M. & Hewstone (Eds.), *European review of social psychology* (Vol. 19, pp. 242–284). Hove, England: Psychology Press.

Crisp, R. J., & Turner, R. (2009). Can imagined interactions produce positive perceptions?: Reducing prejudice through simulated social contact. *American Psychologist, 64,* 231–240.

Crissey, S. (2009). *Educational attainment in the United States: 2007.* U.S. Census Bureau Current Population Reports. Retrieved from http://www.census.gov/prod/2009pubs/p20-560.pdf

Crocker, J. (1999). Social stigma and self-esteem: Situational construction of self-worth. *Journal of Experimental Social Psychology, 35,* 89–107.

Crocker, J., Cornwell, B., & Major, B. (1993). The affective consequences of attributional ambiguity: The case of overweight women. *Journal of Personality and Social Psychology, 64,* 60–70.

Crocker, J., & Major, B. (1989). Social stigma and self-esteem: The self-protective properties of stigma. *Psychological Review, 96,* 608–630.

Crocker, J., Voelkl, K., Testa, M., & Major, B. (1991). Social stigma: The affective consequences of attributional ambiguity. *Journal of Personality and Social Psychology, 60,* 218–228.

Croizet, J., & Claire, T. (1998). Extending the concept of stereotype threat to social class: The intellectual underperformance of students from low socioeconomic backgrounds. *Personality and Social Psychology Bulletin, 24,* 588–594.

Crosby, R. (1982). *Relative deprivation and the working woman.* New York, NY: Oxford University Press.

Crosby, R., & Cordova, D. (1996). Words worth of wisdom: Toward an understanding of affirmative action. *Journal of Social Issues, 52,* 33–49.

Crosnoe, R. (2007). Gender, obesity, and education. *Sociology of Education, 80,* 241–260.

Cross, S., & Madsen, L. (1997). Models of the self: Self-construals and gender. *Psychological Bulletin, 122,* 5–37.

Cuddy, A., & Fiske, S. (2002). Doddering but dear: Process, content, and function in stereotyping of older persons. In T. D. Nelson (Ed.), *Ageism: Stereotyping and prejudice against older persons* (pp. 3–26). Cambridge, MA: MIT Press.

Cuddy, A., Fiske, S., & Glick, P. (2004). When professionals become mothers, warmth doesn't cut the ice. *Journal of Social Issues, 60,* 701–718.

Cuddy, A., Norton, M., & Fiske, S. (2005). This old stereotype: The pervasiveness and persistence of the elderly stereotype. *Journal of Social Issues, 61,* 267–285.

Dail, P. (1988). Prime-time television portrayals of older adults in the context of family life. *The Gerontologist, 28,* 700–706.

Darley, J., & Gross, P. (1983). A hypothesis-confirming bias in labeling effects. *Journal of Personality and Social Psychology, 44,* 20–33.

Dasgupta, N., & Greenwald, A. (2001). On the malleability of automatic attitudes: Combating automatic prejudice with images of admired and disliked individuals. *Journal of Personality and Social Psychology, 81,* 800–814.

Davies, P., Spencer, S., & Steele, C. (2005). Clearing the air: Identity safety moderates the effects of stereotype threat on women's leadership aspirations. *Journal of Personality and Social Psychology, 88,* 276–287.

Davis, L., & Hagen, J. (1996). Stereotypes and stigma: What's changed for welfare mothers. *Affilia, 11,* 319–337.

Deaux, K., & Emswiller, T. (1974). Explanations of successful performance on sex-linked tasks: What is skill for the male is luck for the female. *Journal of Personality and Social Psychology, 29,* 80–85.

Deaux, K., & Major, B. (1987). Putting gender into context: An interactive model of gender-related behavior. *Psychological Review, 94,* 369–389.

Dechamps, J., & Brown, R. (1983). Superordinate goals and intergroup conflict. *British Journal of Social Psychology, 22,* 189–195.

Degner, J., & Wentura, D. (2010). Automatic prejudice in childhood and early adolescence. *Journal of Personality and Social Psychology, 98,* 356–374.

DeJong, W. (1993). Obesity as a characterological stigma: The issue of responsibility and judgments of task performance. *Psychological Reports, 73,* 963–970.

DeNavas-Walt, C., Proctor, B., & Smith, J. (2010, September). *Income, poverty, and health insurance coverage in the U.S.: 2009* (Current Population Reports). Washington, DC: U.S. Census Bureau. U.S. Department of Commerce.

Desforges, D., Lord, C., Pugh, M., Sia, T., Scarberry, N., & Ratcliff, C. (1997). Role of group representativeness in the generalization part of the contact hypothesis. *Basic and Applied Social Psychology, 19,* 183–204.

Desmarais, S., & Curtis, J. (2001). Gender and perceived income entitlement among fulltime workers: Analyses for Canadian national samples, 1984 and 1994. *Basic and Applied Social Psychology, 23,* 157–168.

Desmond, R., & Danilewicz, A. (2010). Women are on, but not in, the news: Gender roles in local television news. *Sex Roles, 62,* 822–829.

DeSteno, D., Dasgupta, N., Bartlett, M., & Cajdric, A. (2004). Prejudice from thin air: The effect of emotion on automatic intergroup attitudes. *Psychological Science, 15,* 319–324.

Devine, P. (1989). Stereotypes and prejudice: Their automatic and controlled components. *Journal of Personality and Social Psychology, 56,* 5–18.

Devine, P., & Baker, S. (1991). Measurement of racial stereotype subtyping. *Personality and Social Psychology Bulletin, 17,* 44–50.

Devine, P., & Elliot, A. (1995). Are racial stereotypes really-fading? The Princeton trilogy revisited. *Personality and Social Psychology Bulletin, 21,* 1139–1150.

Devine, P., Monteith, M., Zuwerink, J., & Elliot, A. (1991). Prejudice with and without compunction. *Journal of Personality and Social Psychology, 60,* 817–830.

Devine, P., & Sharp, L. (2009). Automaticity and control in stereotyping and prejudice. In T. Nelson (Ed.), *Handbook of prejudice, stereotyping, and discrimination* (pp. 61–87). New York, NY: Psychology Press.

Dixon, T., & Maddox, K. (2005). Skin tone, crime news, and social reality judgments: Priming the stereotype of the dark and dangerous black criminal. *Journal of Applied Social Psychology, 35,* 1555–1570.

Doise, W., Deschamps, J. C., & Meyer, G. (1978). The accentuation of intracategory similarities. In H. Tajfel (Ed.), *Differentiation between social groups: Studies in the social psychology of intergroup relations* (pp. 159–168). London, England: Academic Press.

Donlan, M., Ashman, O., & Levy, B. (2005). Re-vision of older television characters: A stereotype-awareness intervention. *Journal of Social Issues, 61,* 307–319.

Dooley, P. (1995). Perceptions of the onset controllability of AIDS and helping judgments: An attributional analysis. *Journal of Applied Social Psychology, 25,* 858–869.

Dovidio, J., & Gaertner, S. (1986). Prejudice, discrimination, and racism: Historical trends and contemporary approaches. In J. F. Dovidio & S. L. Gaertner (Eds.), *Prejudice, discrimination, and racism* (pp. 1–34). New York, NY: Academic Press.

Dovidio, J., Smith, J., Donnella, A., & Gaertner, S. (1997). Racial attitudes and the death penalty. *Journal of Applied Social Psychology, 27,* 1468–1487.

Downs, E., & Smith, S. (2010). Keeping abreast of hypersexuality: A video game character content analysis. *Sex Roles, 62,* 721–733.

Duan, C., & Hill, C. (1996). The current state of empathy research. *Journal of Counseling Psychology, 43,* 261–274.

Duckitt, J. (2001). A dual process cognitive-motivational theory of ideology and prejudice. In M. P. Zanna (Ed.), *Advances in experimental social psychology* (Vol. 33, pp. 41–113). New York, NY: Academic Press.

Dumont, M., Sarlet, M., & Dardenne, B. (2010). Be too kind to a woman, she'll feel incompetent: Benevolent sexism shifts self-construal and autobiographical memories toward incompetence. *Sex Roles, 62,* 545–553.

Duncan, L., & Schaller, M. (2009). Prejudicial attitudes toward older adults may be exaggerated when people feel vulnerable to infectious disease: Evidence and implications. *Analyses of Social Issues and Public Policy, 9,* 97–115.

Duval, L., & Ruscher, J. (1994). *Men use more detail to explain a gender-neutral task to women.* Paper presented at the American Psychological Society meeting, Washington, DC.

Eagly, A. (1987). *Sex differences in social behavior: A social role interpretation.* Hillsdale, NJ: Erlbaum.

Eagly, A., Ashmore, R., Makhijani, M., & Longo, L. (1991). What is beautiful is good, but . . . A meta-analytic review of research on the physical attractiveness stereotype. *Psychological Bulletin, 110,* 107–128.

Eagly, A., & Carli, L. (1981). Sex of researchers and sex-typed communications as determinants of sex differences in influenceability: A meta-analysis of social influence studies. *Psychological Bulletin, 90,* 1–20.

Eagly, A., & Crowley, M. (1986). Gender and helping behavior: A meta-analytic review of the social psychological literature. *Psychological Bulletin, 100,* 283–308.

Eagly, A., & Karau, S. (2002). Role congruity theory of prejudice toward female leaders. *Psychological Review, 109,* 573–598.

Eagly, A., & Mladinic, A. (1989). Gender stereotypes and attitudes toward women and men. *Personality and Social Psychology Bulletin, 15,* 543–558.

Eagly, A., & Steffen, V. J. (1984). Gender stereotypes stem from the distribution of women and men into social roles. *Journal of Personality and Social Psychology, 46,* 735–754.

Eagly, A., & Steffen, V. (1986). Gender and aggressive behavior: A meta-analytic review of the social psychological literature. *Psychological Bulletin, 100,* 309–330.

Eckes, T. (2002). Paternalistic and envious gender stereotypes: Testing predictions from the stereotype content model. *Sex Roles, 47,* 99–114.

Eibach, R., Mock, S., & Courtney, E. (2010). Having a "senior moment": Induced aging phenomenology, subjective age, and susceptibility to ageist stereotypes. *Journal of Experimental Social Psychology, 46,* 643–649.

Eisenberg, N., & Lennon, R. (1983). Sex differences in empathy and related capacties. *Psychological Bulletin, 94,* 100–131.

Ensari, N., & Miller, N. (2002). The out-group must not be so bad after all: The effects of disclosure, typicality, and salience on intergroup bias. *Journal of Personality and Social Psychology, 83,* 313–329.

Erber, J., Szuchman, L., & Rothberg, S. (1990). Everyday memory failure: Age differences in appraisal and attribution. *Psychology and Aging, 5,* 236–241.

Ernsberger, P., & Koletsky, R. (1999). Biomedical rationale for a wellness approach to obesity: An alternative to a focus on weight loss. *Journal of Social Issues, 55,* 221–260.

Fairchild, H., & Cozens, J. (1981). Chicano, Hispanic, or Mexican-American: What's in a name? *Hispanic Journal of Behavioral Sciences, 3,* 191–198.

Farina, A., Allen, J., & Saul, B. (1968). The role of the stigmatized person in affecting social relationships. *Journal of Personality, 36,* 169–182.

Farina, A., Holland, C., & Ring, K. (1966). The role of stigma and set in interpersonal interaction. *Journal of Abnormal Psychology, 71,* 421–428.

Farina, A., Sherman, M., & Allen, J. G. (1968). The role of physical abnormalities in interpersonal perception and behavior. *Journal of Abnormal Psychology, 73,* 590–593.

Feather, N., & Simon, J. (1975). Reactions to male and female success and failure in sex-linked occupations: Impressions of personality, causal attributions, and perceived likelihood of different consequences. *Journal of Personality and Social Psychology, 31,* 20–31.

Federal Bureau of Investigations. (2004). *Uniform crime reporting.* Retrieved from http://www.fbi.gov/nucr/cius_04/

Fein, S., & Spencer, S. (1997). Prejudice as self-image maintenance: Affirming the self through derogating others. *Journal of Personality and Social Psychology, 73*, 31–44.

Feingold, A. (1988). Cognitive gender differences are disappearing. *American Psychologist, 43*, 95–103.

Feingold, A. (1992). Good-looking people are not what we think. *Psychological Bulletin, 111*, 304–341.

Feitosa, M., Borecki, I., Hunt, S., Arnett, D., Rao, D., & Province, M. (2000). Inheritance of the waist-to-hip ratio in the National Heart, Lung, and Book Institute Family Heart Study. *Obesity Research, 8*, 294–301.

Festinger, L., Reicken, H., & Schachter, S. (1956). *When prophecy fails.* Minneapolis: University of Minnesota Press.

Finlay, K., & Stephan, W. (2000). Reducing prejudice: The effects of empathy on intergroup attitudes. *Journal of Applied Social Psychology, 30*, 1720–1737.

Fiscella, K., Franks, P., Doescher, M., & Saver, B. (2002). Disparities in health care by race, ethnicity, and language among the insured: Findings from a national sample. *Medical Care, 40*, 52–59.

Fiske, S. (2010). Venus and Mars or down to Earth: Stereotypes and realities of gender differences. *Perspectives on Psychological Science, 5*, 688–692.

Fiske, S., Cuddy, A., & Glick, P. (2007). Universal dimensions of social cognition: Warmth and competence. *Trends in Cognitive Sciences, 11*, 77–83.

Fiske, S., Cuddy, A., Glick, P., & Xu, J. (2002). A model of (often mixed) stereotype content: Competence and warmth respectively follow from perceived status and competition. *Journal of Personality and Social Psychology, 82*, 878–902.

Fitzgibbon, M., Blackman, L., & Avellone, M. (2000). The relationship between body image discrepancy and body mass index across ethnic groups. *Obesity Research, 8*, 582–589.

Fitzpatrick, M., & McPherson, B. (2010). Coloring within the lines: gender stereotypes in contemporary coloring books. *Sex Roles, 62*, 127–137.

Flegel, K., Carroll, M., Ogden, C., & Curtin, L. (2010). Prevalence and trends in obesity among US adults, 1999-2008. *Journal of the American Medical Association, 303*, 235–241.

Follenfant, A., & Ric, F. (2010). Behavioral rebound following stereotype suppression. *European Journal of Social Psychology, 40*, 774–782.

Forbes, C., & Schmader, T. (2010). Retraining attitudes and stereotypes to affect motivation and cognitive capacity under stereotype threat. *Journal of Personality and Social Psychology, 99*, 740–754.

Ford, E., & Cooper, R. (1995). Implications of race/ethnicity for health and health care use. *Health Services Research, 30*, 237–252.

Foschi, M. (1996). Double standards in the evaluation of men and women. *Social Psychology Quarterly, 59*, 237–254.

Fouts, G., & Burggraf, K. (1999). Television situation comedies: Female body images and verbal reinforcements. *Sex Roles, 40*, 473–481.

Fouts, G., & Burggraf, K. (2000). Television situation comedies: Female weight, male negative comments, and audience reactions. *Sex Roles, 42*, 925–932.

Fouts, G., & Vaughan, K. (2002). Television situation comedies: Male weight, negative references, and audience reactions. *Sex Roles, 46*, 439–442.

Fox, J., & Bailenson, J. (2009). Virtual virgins and vamps: The effects of exposure to female characters' sexualized appearance and gaze in an immersive virtual environment. *Sex Roles, 61*, 147–157.

Frable, D. (1993a). Dimensions of marginality: Distinctions among those who are different. *Personality and Social Psychology Bulletin, 19*, 370–380.

Frable, D. (1993b). Being and feeling unique: Statistical deviance and psychological marginality. *Journal of Personality, 61,* 85–109.

Frable, D., Blackstone, T., & Scherbaum, C. (1990). Marginal and mindful: Deviants in social interactions. *Journal of Personality and Social Psychology, 59,* 140–149.

France, D. (2007, June 17). The science of gaydar. *New York Magazine.* Retrieved from http://nymag.com/news/features/33520/

Frasure-Smith, N., & Lesperance, R. (2005). Depression and coronary heart disease: Complex synergism of mind, body, and environment. *Current Directions in Psychological Science, 14,* 39–43.

Freeman, H. (2004). Poverty, culture, and social injustice: Determinants of cancer disparities. *CA: A Cancer Journal for Clinicians, 54,* 72–77.

French, R. (1984). The long-term relationships of marked people. In E. Jones, A. Rarina, A. Hastorf, H. Markus, D. Miller, & R. Scott (Eds.), *Social stigma: The psychology of marked relationships* (pp. 254–294). New York, NY: Freeman.

Freudinger, P., & Almquist, E. (1978). Male and female roles in the lyrics of three genres of contemporary music. *Sex Roles, 4,* 51–65.

Friedman, M., & Brownell, K. (1995). Psychological correlates of obesity: Moving to the next research generation. *Psychological Bulletin, 117,* 3–20.

Fulton, A., Gorsuch, R., & Maynard, E. (1999). Religious orientation, antihomosexual sentiment, and fundamentalism among Christians. *Journal for the Scientific Study of Religion, 38,* 14–22.

Furnham, A. (1982a). The Protestant work ethic and attitudes toward unemployment. *Journal of Occupational Psychology, 55,* 277–286.

Furnham, A. (1982b). Explanations for unemployment in Britain. *European Journal of Social Psychology, 12,* 335–352.

Furnham, A., & Gunter, B. (1984). Just world beliefs and attitudes toward the poor. *British Journal of Social Psychology, 23,* 265–269.

Gaertner, S., & Dovidio, J. (1986). The aversive form of racism. In J. F. Dovidio & S. L. Gaertner (Eds.), *Prejudice, discrimination, and racism* (pp. 61–89). Orlando, FL: Academic Press.

Gaertner, S., & McLaughlin, J. (1983). Racial stereotypes: Associations and ascriptions of positive and negative characteristics. *Social Psychology Quarterly, 46,* 23–30.

Gailliot, M., & Baumeister, R. (2007). The physiology of willpower: Linking blood glucose to self-control. *Personality and Social Psychology Review, 11,* 303–327.

Gailliot, M., Peruche, B. M., Plant, E. A., & Baumeister, R. (2009). Stereotypes and prejudice in the blood: Sucrose drinks reduce prejudice and stereotyping. *Journal of Experimental Social Psychology, 45,* 288–290.

Gallo, L., Espinosa de los Monteros, K., & Shivpuri, S. (2009). Socioeconomic status and health: What is the role of reserve capacity? *Current Directions in Psychological Science, 18,* 269–274.

Gawronski, B., Deutsch, R., Mbirkou, S., Seibt, B., & Strack, F. (2008). When "just say no" is not enough: Affirmation versus negation training and the reduction of automatic stereotype activation. *Journal of Experimental Social Psychology, 44,* 370–377.

General Social Survey. (1990). *General social survey.* Chicago, IL: National Opinion Research Center.

Gerbner, G. (1997). Gender and age in prime-time television. In S. Kirschner & D. A. Kirschner (Eds.), *Perspectives on psychology and the media* (pp. 69–94). Washington, DC: American Psychological Association.

Gerbner, G., Gross, L., Morgan, M., & Signorielli, N. (1986). Living with television: The dynamics of the cultivation process. In J. Bryant & D. Zillman (Eds.), *Perspectives on media effects* (pp. 17–40). Hillsdale, NJ: Erlbaum.

Gerbner, G., Gross, L., Signorielli, N., & Morgan, M. (1980). Aging with television: Images on television drama and conceptions of social reality. *Journal of Communication, 30,* 37–48.

Gerbner, G., & Ozyegin, N. (1997). Proportional representation of diversity index. Cultural indicators project. In *Diversity in film and television,* Issue Brief Series. Studio City, CA: Mediascope Press.

Gibbons, F. X., Gerrard, M., Cleveland, M., Wills, T., & Brody, G. (2004). Perceived discrimination and substance use in African-American parents and their children: A panel study. *Journal of Personality and Social Psychology, 86,* 517–529.

Gibbons, F. X., Sawin, L. S., & Gibbons, B. N. (1979). Evaluations of mentally retarded persons: "Sympathy" or patronization? *American Journal of Mental Deficiency, 84,* 124–131.

Gilbert, D., & Hixon, T. (1991). The trouble of thinking: Activation and application of stereotypic beliefs. *Journal of Personality and Social Psychology, 60,* 509–517.

Gilbert, D., & Malone, P. (1995). The correspondence bias. *Psychological Bulletin, 117,* 21–38.

Gilbert, G. (1951). Stereotype persistence and change among college students. *Journal of Abnormal and Social Psychology, 46,* 245–254.

Gilens, M. (1996). Race and poverty in America: Public misperceptions and the American news media. *Public Opinion Quarterly, 60,* 515–541.

Glick, P., & Fiske, S. (1997). Hostile and benevolent sexism: Measuring ambivalent sexist attitudes toward women. *Psychology of Women Quarterly, 21,* 119–135.

Glick, P., & Fiske, S. (2001). An ambivalent alliance: Hostile and benevolent sexism as complementary justifications for gender inequality. *American Psychologist, 56,* 109–118.

Glick, P., Fiske, S., Mladinic, A., Saiz, J., Abrams, D., Masser, B., . . . Lopez, W. (2000). Beyond prejudice as simple antipathy: Hostile and benevolent sexism across cultures. *Journal of Personality and Social Psychology, 79,* 763–775.

Gluszek, A., & Dovidio, J. (2010). The way *they* speak: A social psychological perspective on the stigma of nonnative accents in communication. *Personality and Social Psychology Review, 14,* 214–237.

Goff, P., Steele, C., & Davies, P. (2008). The space between us: Stereotype threat and distance in interracial contexts. *Journal of Personality and Social Psychology, 94,* 91–107.

Goffman, E. (1963). *Stigma: Notes on the management of spoiled identity.* New York, NY: Simon & Schuster.

Goldberg, P. (1968). Are women prejudiced against women? *Transaction, 5,* 28–30.

Gollwitzer, P., & Schaal, B. (1998). Metacognition in action: The importance of implementation intentions. *Personality and Social Psychology Review, 2,* 124–136.

Gonzalez, A., Solomon, S., Zvolensky, M., & Miller, C. (2009). The interaction of mindful-based attention and awareness and disengagement coping with HIV/AIDS-related stigma in regard to concurrent anxiety and depressive symptoms among adults with HIV/AIDS. *Journal of Health Psychology, 14,* 403–413.

Good, J., & Rudman, L. (2010). When female applicants meet sexist interviewers: The costs of being a target of benevolent sexism. *Sex Roles, 62,* 481–493.

Gray, J. (1992). *Men are from Mars, women are from Venus.* New York, NY: HarperCollins.

Green, A., Carney, D., Pallin, D., Ngo, L., Raymond, K., Iezzoni, L., & Banaji, M. (2007). Implicit bias among physicians and its prediction of thrombolysis decisions for Black and White patients. *Journal of General Internal Medicine, 22,* 1231–1238.

Greenberg, B., Eastin, M., Hofshire, L., Lachlan, K., & Brownell, K. (2003). The portrayal of overweight and obese persons in commercial television. *American Journal of Public Health, 93,* 1342–1348.

Greenberg, J., & Pyszczynski, T. (1985). The effects of an overheard ethnic slur on evaluations of the target: How to spread a social disease. *Journal of Experimental Social Psychology, 21,* 61–72.

Greenberg, J., Pyszczynski, T., & Solomon, S. (1986). The causes and consequences of the need for self-esteem: A terror management theory. In R. F. Baumeister (Ed.), *Public self and private self* (pp. 189–212). New York, NY: Springer-Verlag.

Greenberg, J., Pyszczynski, T., Solomon, S., Rosenblatt, A., Veeder, M., Kirkland, S., & Lyon, D. (1990). Evidence for terror management theory II: The effects of mortality salience on reactions to those who threaten or bolster the cultural worldview. *Journal of Personality and Social Psychology, 58,* 308–318.

Greenberg, J., Schimel, J., & Martens, A. (2002). Ageism: Denying the face of the future. In T. D. Nelson (Ed.), *Ageism: Stereotyping and prejudice against older persons* (pp. 27–48). Cambridge, MA: MIT Press.

Greenwald, A., Oakes, M., & Hoffman, H. (2003). Targets of discrimination: Effects of race on responses to weapons holders. *Journal of Experimental Social Psychology, 39,* 399–405.

Gungor, G., & Biernat, M. (2009). Gender bias or motherhood disadvantage? Judgments of blue collar mothers and fathers in the workplace. *Sex Roles, 60,* 232–246.

Gupta, A., Szymanski, D., & Leong, F. (2011). The "Model minority myth:" Internalized racialism of positive stereotypes as correlates of psychological distress and attitudes towards help-seeking. *Asian American Journal of Psychology, 2,* 101–114.

Gutierrez, A., & Unzueta, M. (2010). The effect of interethnic ideologies on the likability of stereotypic vs. counterstereotypic minority targets. *Journal of Experimental Social Psychology, 46,* 775–784.

Haldeman, D. (1994). The practice and ethics of sexual orientation conversion therapy. *Journal of Consulting and Clinical Psychology, 62,* 221–227.

Hall, J. (1978). Gender effects in decoding nonverbal cues. *Psychological Bulletin, 85,* 845–875.

Halpert, J., Wilson, M., & Hickman, J. (1993). Pregnancy as a source of bias in performance appraisals. *Journal of Organizational Behavior, 14,* 649–663.

Hamilton, D. L., & Gifford, R. K. (1976). Illusory correlation in interpersonal perception: A cognitive basis of stereotypic judgments. *Journal of Experimental Social Psychology, 12,* 392–407.

Hamilton, D. L., & Sherman, J. (1994). Stereotypes. In R. S. Wyer & T. K. Srull (Eds.), *Handbook of social cognition* (pp. 1–68). Hillsdale, NJ: Lawrence Erlbaum.

Harris, M. (1990). Is love seen as different for the obese? *Journal of Applied Social Psychology, 20,* 1209–1224.

Harris, M., Harris, R., & Bochner, S. (1982). Fat, four-eyed and female: Stereotypes of obesity, glasses and gender. *Journal of Applied Social Psychology, 6,* 503–516.

Harris, M., Moniz, A., Sowards, B., & Krane, K. (1994). Mediation of interpersonal expectancy effects: Expectancies about the elderly. *Social Psychology Quarterly, 57,* 36–48.

Harrison, K. (2000). Television viewing, fat stereotyping, body shape standards, and eating disorder symptomatology in grade school children. *Communication Research, 27,* 614–640.

Harrison, M., & Thomas, K. (2009). The hidden prejudice in selection: A research investigation on skin color bias. *Journal of Applied Social Psychology, 39,* 134–168.

Harwood, J. (1995). *Viewing age: The age distribution of television characters across the viewer lifespan.* Electronic manuscript. Retrieved from http://falcon.cc.ukans.edu/~harwood/crr.htm# table4r

Haslam, N., & Levy, S. (2006). Essentialist beliefs about homosexuality: Structure and implications for prejudice. *Personality and Social Psychology Bulletin, 32,* 471–485.

Hatzenbuehler, M. (2009). How does sexual minority stigma "get under the skin"? A psychological mediation framework. *Psychological Bulletin, 135,* 707–730.

Hatzenbuehler, M., Nolen-Hoeksema, S., & Dovidio, J. (2009). How does stigma "get under the skin"? The mediating role of emotion regulation. *Psychological Science, 20,* 1282–1289.

Hayes, J., Luoma, J., Bond, F., Masuda, A., & Lillis, J. (2006). Acceptance and commitment therapy: Model, processes, and outcomes. *Behavioral Research and Therapy, 44*, 1–25.

Hayes, J., Schimel, J., & Williams, T. (2008). Fighting death with death: The buffering effects of learning that worldview violators have died. *Psychological Science, 19*, 501–507.

Hebl, M., Foster, J., Mannix, L., & Dovidio, J. (2002). Formal and interpersonal discrimination: A field study of bias toward homosexual applicants. *Personality and Social Psychology Bulletin, 28*, 815–825.

Hebl, M., & Heatherton, T. (1998). The stigma of obesity in women: The difference is Black and White. *Personality and Social Psychology Bulletin, 24*, 417–426.

Hebl, M., King, E., & Perkins, A. (2009). Ethnic differences in the stigma of obesity: Identification and engagement with a thin ideal. *Journal of Experimental Social Psychology, 45*, 1165–1172.

Hebl, M., & Mannix, L. (2003). The weight of obesity in evaluating others: A mere proximity effect. *Personality and Social Psychology Bulletin, 29*, 28–38.

Hegarty, P., & Buechel, C. (2006). Androcentric reporting of gender differences in APA journals: 1965-2004. *Review of General Psychology, 10*, 377–389.

Hegarty, P., Lemieux, A., & McQueen, G. (2010). Graphing the order of the sexes: Constructing, recalling, interpreting, and putting the self in gender difference graphs. *Journal of Personality and Social Psychology, 98*, 375–391.

Hegewisch, A., Williams, C., & Henderson, A. (2011, April). *The gender wage gap: 2010.* Retrieved from http://www.iwpr.org/publications/pubs/the-gender-wage-gap-2010-up dated-march-2011

Hehman, E., Gaertner, S., & Dovidio, J. (2011). Evaluations of presidential performance: Race, prejudice, and perceptions of Americanism. *Journal of Experimental Social Psychology, 47*, 430–435.

Heilman, M., Block, C., & Lucas, A. (1992). Presumed innocent? Stigmatization and affirmative action efforts. *Journal of Applied Psychology, 77*, 536–544.

Heilman, M., Block, C., & Stathatos, P. (1997). The affirmative action stigma of incompetence: Effects of performance information ambiguity. *Academy of Management Journal, 40*, 603–625.

Heilman, M., & Wallen, A. (2010). Wimpy and undeserving of respect: Penalties for men's gender-inconsistent success. *Journal of Experimental Social Psychology, 46*, 664–667.

Helms, J., Jernigan, M., & Mascher, J. (2005). The meaning of race in psychology and how to change it: A methodological perspective. *American Psychologist, 60*, 27–36.

Hendrick, S., Hendrick, C., Slapion-Foote, J., & Foote, F. (1985). Gender differences in sexual attitudes. *Journal of Personality and Social Psychology, 48*, 1630–1642.

Herbenick, D., Reese, M., Schick, V., Sanders, S., Dodge, B., & Fortenberry, J. D. (2010). Sexual behavior in the United States: Results from a national probability sample of men and women ages 14-94. *Journal of Sexual Medicine, 7*, 255–265.

Herek, G. (1984). Attitudes toward lesbians and gay men: A factor-analytic study. *Journal of Homosexuality, 10*, 39–51.

Herek, G. (1991). Stigma, prejudice, and violence against lesbians and gay men. In J. C. Gonsiorek & J. D. Weinrich (Eds.), *Homosexuality: Research implications for public policy* (pp. 60–80). Newbury Park, CA: Sage.

Herek, G. (1999). *"Reparative therapy" and other attempts to alter sexual orientation: A background paper.* Retrieved from http://psychology.uc.davis.edu/rainbow/html/facts_changing.html

Herek, G. (2000). The psychology of sexual prejudice. *Current Directions in Psychological Science, 9*, 19–22.

Herek, G. (2005). When sex equals AIDS: Symbolic stigma and heterosexual adults' inaccurate beliefs about sexual transmission of AIDS. *Social Forces, 52*, 15–37.

Herek, G. (2006). *Facts about homosexuality and child molestation.* Retrieved from http://psychology .ucdavis.edu/rainbow/html/facts_molestation.html

Herek, G., & Capitanio, J. (1998). Symbolic prejudice or fear of infection? A functional analysis of AIDS-related stigma among heterosexual adults. *Basic and Applied Social Psychology, 20,* 230–241.

Herek, G., Gillis, J., & Cogan, J. (1999). Psychological sequelae of hate-crime victimization among lesbian, gay, and bisexual adults. *Journal of Consulting and Clinical Psychology, 67,* 945–951.

Herek, G., & Glunt, E. (1988). An epidemic of stigma: Public reaction to AIDS. *American Psychologist, 43,* 886–891.

Herrnstein, R., & Murray, C. (1994). *The bell curve: Intelligence and class structure in American life.* New York, NY: Free Press.

Hess, T., Hinson, J., & Hodges, E. (2009). Moderators of and mechanisms underlying stereotype threat effects on older adults' memory performance. *Experimental Aging Research, 35,* 153–177.

Heuer, C., McClure, K., & Puhl, R. (2011). Obesity stigma in on line news: A visual content analysis. *Journal of Health Communication: International Perspectives, 16,* 1–12.

Heumann, M., & Church, T. (1997). *Hate speech on campus: Cases, case studies, and commentary.* Boston, MA: Northeastern University Press.

Hewitt, N., & Seymour, E. (1991). *Factors contributing to high attrition rates among science and engineering undergraduate majors.* Unpublished report to the Alfred P. Sloan Foundation.

Hickman, C. (1997). The devil and the one drop rule: Racial categories, African Americans, and the U.S. Census. *Michigan Law Review, 95,* 1161–1265.

Hiller, D. (1981). The salience of overweight in personality characterization. *Journal of Psychology, 108,* 233–240.

Hilton, J. L., & von Hippel, W. (1990). The role of consistency in the judgment of stereotype-relevant behaviors. *Personality and Social Psychology Bulletin, 16,* 430–448.

Hinshaw, S. (2007). *The mark of shame: Stigma of mental illness and an agenda for change.* New York, NY: Oxford University Press.

Ho, A., Sidanius, J., Levin, D., & Banji, M. (2011). Evidence for hypodescent and racial hierarchy in the categorization and perception of biracial individuals. *Journal of Personality and Social Psychology, 100,* 492–506.

Hodgins, H., Liebeskind, E., & Schwartz, W. (1996). Getting out of hot water: Facework in social predicaments. *Journal of Personality and Social Psychology, 71,* 300–314.

Hogg, M., & Turner, J. (1987). Intergroup behavior, self-stereotyping and the salience of social categories. *British Journal of Social Psychology, 26,* 325–340.

Horton, R. (2003). Medical journals: Evidence of bias against the diseases of poverty. *The Lancet, 361,* 712–713.

Howden, L., & Meyer, J. (2011). *Age and sex composition: 2010* (2010 Census Briefs). Washington, DC: U.S. Census Bureau. U.S. Department of Commerce. Retrieved from http://www.census .gov/prod/cen2010/briefs/c2010br-03.pdf

Hoyt, S. (1999). Mentoring with class: Connections between social class and developmental relationships in the academy. In A. J. Murrell & F. J. Crosby (Eds.), *Mentoring dilemmas: Developmental relationships within multicultural organizations* (pp. 189–210). Mahwah, NJ: Erlbaum.

Hughes, M., & Hertel, B. (1990). The significance of color remains: A study of life chances, mate selection, and ethnic consciousness among Black Americans. *Social Forces, 68,* 1105–1120.

Humes, K., Jones, N., & Ramirez, R. (2011). *Overview of Race and Hispanic Origin: 2010* (2010 Census Briefs). Washington, DC: U.S. Census Bureau. U.S. Department of Commerce. Retrieved from www.census.gov/prod/cen2010/briefs /c2010br-02.pdf

Hummert, M., Garstka, T., O'Brien, L., Greenwald, A., & Mellott, D. (2002). Using the Implicit Association Test to measure age differences in implicit social cognitions. *Psychology and Aging, 17,* 482–495.

Hummert, M. L., Garstka, T. A., Shaner, J. L., & Strahm, S. (1994). Stereotypes of the elderly held by young, middle-aged and elderly adults. *Journal of Gerontology: Psychological Sciences, 49,* 240–249.

Hunsberger, B. (1996). Religious fundamentalism, right-wing authoritarianism, and hostility toward homosexuals in non-Christian religious groups. *International Journal for the Psychology of Religion, 6,* 39–49.

Hunt, M. (1996). The individual, society or both? A comparison of Black, Latino and White beliefs about the causes of poverty. *Social Forces, 75,* 293–322.

Hunt, S. (2000). "Winning ways:" Globalization and the impact of the health and wealth gospel. *Journal of Contemporary Religion, 15,* 331–347.

Hunter, M. (2002). "If you're light you're alright": Light skin color as social capital for women of color. *Gender and Society, 16,* 175–193.

Hutchings, P., & Haddock, G. (2008). Look Black in anger: The role of implicit prejudice in the categorization and perceived emotional intensity of racially ambiguous faces. *Journal of Experimental Social Psychology, 44,* 1418–1420.

Hyde, J. (1984). How large are gender differences in aggression? A developmental meta-analysis. *Developmental Psychology, 20,* 722–736.

Hyde, J., Fennema, E., & Lamon, S. (1990). Gender differences in mathematics performance: A meta-analysis. *Psychological Bulletin, 107,* 139–155.

Hyde, J., & Linn, M. (1988). Gender differences in verbal ability: A meta-analysis. *Psychological Bulletin, 104,* 53–69.

Imhoff, R., & Banse, R. (2009). Ongoing victim suffering increases prejudice: The case of secondary anti-Semitism. *Psychological Science, 20,* 1443–1447.

Institute for Social Research. (2000). *Economic penalty of extra pounds to middle-aged women* [news release]. Retrieved from http://www.umich.edu/~newsinfo/Releases/2000/Nov00/r111700c.html

Institute of Medicine of the National Academies. (2003). *Unequal treatment: Confronting racial and ethnic disparities in healthcare.* Washington, DC: National Academies Press.

International Association of Chiefs of Police. Retrieved from http://www.theiacp.org

Inzlicht, M., McKay, L., & Aronson, J. (2006). Stigma as ego depletion: How being the target of prejudice affects self-control. *Psychological Science, 17,* 262–269.

Iyer, A., Leach, C., & Crosby, F. (2002). White guilt and racial compensation: The benefits and limits of self-focus. *Personality and Social Psychology Bulletin, 29,* 117–129.

Jackson, L., Sullivan, L., & Hodge, C. (1995). Physical attractiveness and intellectual competence: A meta-analytic review. *Social Psychology Quarterly, 58,* 108–122.

Jamieson, D., Lydon, J., Stewart, G., & Zanna, M. (1987). Pygmalion revisited: New evidence for student expectancy effects in the classroom. *Journal of Educational Psychology, 79,* 461–466.

Jeffery, R., Epstein, L., & Wilson, G. T. (2000). Long-term maintenance of weight loss: Current status. *Health Psychology, 19(1S),* 5–16.

Johannesen-Schmidt, M., & Eagly, A. (2002). Diminishing returns: The effects of income on the content of stereotypes of wage earners. *Personality and Social Psychology Bulletin, 28,* 1538–1545.

Johnson, C., & Mullen, B. (1994). Evidence for the accessibility of paired distinctiveness in distinctiveness-based illusory correlation in stereotyping. *Personality and Social Psychology Bulletin, 20,* 65–70.

Johnson, J., Olivo, N., Gibson, N., Reed, W., & Ashburn-Nardo, L. (2009). Priming media stereotypes reduces support for social welfare policies: The mediating role of empathy. *Personality and Social Psychology Bulletin, 35,* 463–476.

Johnson, J., Whitestone, E., Jackson, L., & Gatto, L. (1995). Justice is still not colorblind: Differential racial effects of exposure to inadmissible evidence. *Personality and Social Psychology Bulletin, 21,* 893–898.

Jones, C., & Kaplan, M. (2003). The effects of racially stereotypical crimes on juror decision-making and information-processing strategies. *Basic and Applied Social Psychology, 25,* 1–13.

Jones, E. (1986). Interpreting interpersonal behavior: The effects of expectancies. *Science, 234,* 41–46.

Jones, E., Farina, A., Hastorf, A., Markus, H., Miller, D., & Scott, R. (1984). *Social stigma: The psychology of marked relationships.* New York, NY: Freeman.

Jones, J. (1994). Our similarities are different: Toward a psychology of affirmative diversity. In E. Trickett, R. Watts, & D. Birman (Eds.), *Human diversity: Perspectives on people in context* (pp. 27–45). San Francisco, CA: Jossey-Bass.

Jones, J. (1997). *Prejudice and racism* (2nd ed.). New York, NY: McGraw-Hill.

Josephs, R., Markus, H., & Tafarodi, R. (1992). Gender and self-esteem. *Journal of Personality and Social Psychology, 63,* 391–402.

Judd, C., & Park, B. (1993). Definition and assessment of accuracy in social stereotypes. *Psychological Review, 100,* 109–128.

Jussim, L. (1989). Teacher expectations: Self-fulfilling prophecies, perceptual biases, and accuracy. *Journal of Personality and Social Psychology, 57,* 469–480.

Jussim, L. (1991). Social perception and social reality: A reflection-construction model. *Psychological Review, 98,* 54–73.

Jussim, L., Cain, T., Crawford, J., Harber, K., & Cohen, F. (2009). The unbearable accuracy of stereotypes. In T. Nelson (Ed.), *Handbook of prejudice, stereotyping, and discrimination* (pp. 199–227). New York, NY: Psychology Press.

Jussim, L., & Eccles, J. (1992). Teacher expectations II: Construction and reflection of student achievement. *Journal of Personality and Social Psychology, 63,* 947–961.

Jussim, L., Eccles, J., & Madon, S. (1996). Social perception, social stereotypes, and teacher expectations: Accuracy and the quest for the powerful self-fulfilling prophecy. *Advances in Experimental Social Psychology, 28,* 281–388.

Jussim, L., & Harber, K. (2005). Teacher expectations and self-fulfilling prophecies: Knowns and unknowns, resolved and unresolved controversies. *Personality and Social Psychology Review, 9,* 131–155.

Kaiser, C., & Miller, C. (2001). Reacting to impending discrimination: Compensation for prejudice and attributions to discrimination. *Personality and Social Psychology Bulletin, 27,* 1357–1367.

Kao, G. (1995). Asian Americans as model minorities? A look at their academic performance. *American Journal of Education, 103,* 121–159.

Karlins, M., Coffman, T., & Walters, G. (1969). On the fading of social stereotypes: Studies in three generations of college students. *Journal of Personality and Social Psychology, 13,* 1–16.

Kashima, Y. (2000). Maintaining cultural stereotypes in the serial reproduction of narratives. *Personality and Social Psychology Bulletin, 26,* 594–604.

Katz, I. (1981). *Stigma: A social psychological analysis.* Hillsdale, NJ: Erlbaum.

Katz, D., & Braly, K. (1933). Racial prejudice and racial stereotypes. *Journal of Abnormal and Social Psychology, 30,* 175–193.

Katz, I., & Hass, R. G. (1988). Racial ambivalence and American value conflict: Correlational and priming studies of dual cognitive structures. *Journal of Personality and Social Psychology, 55,* 893–905.

Kawai, Y. (2005). Stereotyping Asian Americans: The dialectic of the model minority and the yellow peril. *Howard Journal of Communications, 16,* 109–130.

Keller, J., & Dauenheimer, D. (2003). Stereotype threat in the classroom: Dejection mediates the disrupting threat effect on women's math performance. *Personality and Social Psychology Bulletin, 29,* 371–381.

Kelly, C. (1988). Intergroup differentiation in a political context. *British Journal of Social Psychology, 27,* 314–322.

Kemper, S. (1994). Elderspeak: Speech accommodations to older adults. *Aging and Cognition, 1,* 17–28.

Kemper, S., Othick, M., Gerhing, H., Gubarchuk, J., & Billington, C. (1998). The effects of practicing speech accommodations to older adults. *Applied Psycholinguistics, 19,* 175–192.

Kernis, M., Brockner, J., & Frankel, B. (1989). Self-esteem and reactions to failure: The mediating role of overgeneralization. *Journal of Personality and Social Psychology, 57,* 707–714.

Kim, B. S., & Park, Y. S. (2008). East and Southeast Asian Americans. In G. Mcauliffe (Ed.), *Culturally alert counseling: A comprehensive introduction* (pp. 189–219). Thousand Oaks, CA: Sage.

Kinder, D., & Sears, D. (1981). Prejudice and politics: Symbolic racism versus racial threats to the good life. *Journal of Personality and Social Psychology, 40,* 414–431.

Kinzler, K., Shutts, K., DeJesus, J., & Spelke, E. (2009). Accent trumps race in guiding children's social preferences. *Social Cognition, 27,* 623–634.

Kirkland, S., Greenberg, J., & Pyszczynski, T. (1987). Further evidence of the deleterious effects of overheard derogatory ethnic labels: Derogation beyond the target. *Personality and Social Psychology Bulletin, 13,* 216–227.

Kirkpatrick, L. (1993). Fundamentalism, Christian orthodoxy, and intrinsic religious orientation as predictors of discriminatory attitudes. *Journal for the Scientific Study of Religion, 32,* 256–268.

Kirkpatrick, L., Hood, R., & Hartz, G. (1991). Fundamentalist religion conceptualized in terms of Rekeach's theory of the open and closed mind: New perspectives on some old ideas. In M. Lynn & D. Moberg (Eds.), *Research in the social scientific study of religion* (Vol. 3, pp. 157–179). Greenwich, CT: JAI Press.

Kleck, R., Ono, H., & Hastorf, A. (1966). The effects of physical deviance on face-to-face interaction. *Human Relations, 19,* 425–436.

Klein, H., & Shiffman, K. (2005). Thin is "in" and stout is "out": what animated cartoons tell viewers about body weight. *Eating and Weight Disorders, 10,* 107–116.

Klein, O., Clark, A., & Lyons, A. (2010). When the social becomes personal: Exploring the role of common ground in stereotype communication. *Social Cognition, 28,* 329–352.

Kluegel, J., & Smith, E. (1986). *Beliefs about inequality: Americans' views of what is and what ought to be.* New York, NY: Aldine de Gruyter.

Knowles, E., Lowery, B., & Schaumberg, R. (2010). Racial prejudice predicts opposition to Obama and his health care reform plan. *Journal of Experimental Social Psychology, 46,* 420–423.

Ko, S., Judd, C., & Stapel, D. (2009). Stereotyping based on voice in the presence of individuating information: Vocal femininity affects perceived competence but not warmth. *Personality and Social Psychology Bulletin, 35,* 198–211.

Kornadt, A., & Rothermund, K. (2011). Contexts of aging: Assessing evaluative age stereotypes in different life domains. *Journal of Gerontology: Social Sciences, 66,* 547–556.

Koro-Ljungberg, M., & Bussing, R. (2009). The management of courtesy stigma in the lives of families with teenagers with ADHD. *Journal of Family Issues, 30,* 1175–1200.

Kravitz, D., & Platania, J. (1993). Attitudes and beliefs about affirmative actions: Effects of target and of respondent sex and ethnicity. *Journal of Applied Psychology, 78,* 928–938.

Krings, F., Sczesny, S., & Kluge, A. (2011). Stereotypical inferences as mediators of age discrimination: The role of competence and warmth. *British Journal of Management, 22,* 187–201.

Krull, D. (1993). Does the grist change the mill? The effect of the perceiver's inferential goal on the process of social inference. *Personality and Social Psychology Bulletin, 19,* 340–348.

Kuo, H., & Hauser, R. (1995). Trends in family effects on the education of Black and White brothers. *Sociology of Education, 68,* 136–160.

Kurz, T., & Lyons, A. (2009). Intergroup influences on the stereotype consistency bias in communication: Does it matter who we are communicating about and to whom we are communicating? *Social Cognition, 27,* 893–904.

Lambert, A., Payne, B., Jacoby, L., Shaffer, L., Chasteen, A., & Khan, S. (2003). Stereotypes as dominant responses: On the "social facilitation" of prejudice in anticipated public contexts. *Journal of Personality and Social Psychology, 84,* 277–295.

Larson, E. (1994). Exclusion of certain groups from clinical research. *Image Journal of Nursing Scholarship, 26,* 185–190.

Lathan, C., Neville, B., & Earle, C. (2006). The effect of race on invasive staging and surgery in non-small-cell lung cancer. *Journal of Clinical Oncology, 24,* 413–418.

Latner, M., & Stunkard, A. (2003). Getting worse: The stigmatization of obese children. *Obesity Research, 11,* 452–456.

Lau, G., Kay, A., & Spencer, S. (2008). Loving those who justify inequality. *Psychological Science, 19,* 20–21.

Lemyre, L., & Smith, P. (1985). Intergroup discrimination and self-esteem in the minimal group paradigm. *Journal of Personality and Social Psychology, 49,* 660–670.

Lerner, M. J. (1980). *The belief in a just world: A fundamental delusion.* New York, NY: Plenum.

LeVine, R., & Campbell, D. (1972). *Ethnocentrism: Theories of conflict, ethnic attitudes and group behavior.* New York, NY: John Wiley.

Levinson, R. (1975). Sex discrimination and employment practices: An experiment with unconventional job inquiries. *Social Problems, 22,* 533–543.

Levy, B. (2003). Mind matters: Cognitive and physical effects of aging self-stereotypes. *Journal of Gerontology: Social Sciences, 58B,* 203–211.

Levy, B. (2009). Stereotype embodiment: A psychosocial approach to aging. *Current Directions in Psychological Science, 18,* 332–336.

Lewis, R., Derlega, V., Clarke, E., & Kuang, J. (2006). Stigma consciousness, social constraints, and lesbian well-being. *Journal of Counseling Psychology, 53,* 48–56.

Lewis, S., & Range, L. (1992). Do means of transmission, risk knowledge, and gender affect AIDS stigma and social interactions? *Journal of Social Behavior and Personality, 7,* 211–216.

Lillie-Blanton, M., Brodie, M., Rowland, D., Altman, D., & McIntosh, M. (2000). Race, ethnicity and the health care system: Public perceptions and experiences. *Medical Care Research and Review, 57,* 218–235.

Lillis, J., & Hayes, S. (2007). Applying acceptance, mindfulness, and values to the reduction of prejudice. *Behavior Modification, 31,* 389–411.

Lillis, J., Hayes, S., Bunting, K., & Masuda, A. (2009). Teaching acceptance and mindfulness to improve the lives of the obese: A preliminary test of a theoretical model. *Annals of Behavioral Medicine, 37,* 58–69.

Lin, M., Kwan, V., Cheung, A., & Fiske, S. (2005). Stereotype content model explains prejudice for an envied outgroup: Scale of anti-Asian American stereotypes. *Personality and Social Psychology Bulletin, 31,* 34–47.

Lind, A. (2004). Legislating the family: Heterosexist bias in social welfare policy. *Journal of Social Policy and Welfare, 31,* 21–35.

Lindberg, S., Hyde, J. S., Petersen, J., & Linn, M. (2010). New trends in gender and mathematics performance: A meta-analysis. *Psychological Bulletin, 136,* 1123–1135.

Linville, P. (1985). Self-complexity and affective extremity: Don't put all your eggs in one cognitive basket. *Social Cognition, 3,* 94–120.

Linville, P., & Jones, E. (1980). Polarized appraisals of outgroup members. *Journal of Personality and Social Psychology, 38,* 689–703.

Lippi-Green, R. (1997). *English with accents: Language, ideology, and discrimination in the United States.* New York, NY: Routledge.

Lips, H. (2003). The gender pay gap: Concrete indicator of women's progress toward equality. *Analyses of Social Issues and Public Policy, 3,* 87–109.

Livingston, R., & Pearce, N. (2009). The teddy-bear effect: Does having a baby face benefit Black chief executive officers? *Psychological Science, 20,* 1229–1236.

Loehlin, J., Lindzey, G., & Spuhler, J. (1975). *Race differences in intelligence.* San Francisco, CA: W. H. Freeman.

Loh, E. (1993). The economic effects of physical appearance. *Social Science Quarterly, 74,* 420–437.

Lott, B. (2002). Cognitive and behavioral distancing from the poor. *American Psychologist, 57,* 100–110.

Lott, B., & Saxon, S. (2002). The influence of ethnicity, social class, and context on judgments about U.S. women. *Journal of Social Psychology, 142,* 481–499.

Lowery, B., Hardin, C., & Sinclair, S. (2001). Social influence effects on automatic racial prejudice. *Journal of Personality and Social Psychology, 81,* 842–855.

Luhtanen, R., & Crocker, J. (1992). A collective self-esteem scale: Self-evaluation of one's social identity. *Personality and Social Psychology Bulletin, 18,* 302–318.

Luoma, J., Kohlenberg, B., Hayes, S., Bunting, K., & Rye, A. (2007). Reducing self-stigma in substance abuse through acceptance and commitment therapy: Model, manual development, and pilot outcomes. *Addiction Research and Therapy, 16,* 149–165.

Lybarger, J., & Monteith, M. (2011). The effect of Obama saliency on individual-level racial bias: Silver bullet or smokescreen. *Journal of Experimental Social Psychology, 47,* 647–652.

Lyons, A., & Kashima, Y. (2003). How are stereotypes maintained through communication? The influence of stereotype sharedness. *Journal of Personality and Social Psychology, 85,* 989–1005.

Maass, A., Ceccarelli, R., & Rudin, S. (1996). Linguistic intergroup bias: Evidence for ingroup-protective motivation. *Journal of Personality and Social Psychology, 71,* 512–526.

Maass, A., Milesi, A., Zabbini, S., & Stahlberg, D. (1995). Linguistic intergroup bias: Differential expectancies or in-group protection? *Journal of Personality and Social Psychology, 68,* 116–126.

Maccoby, E. (1990). Gender and relationships: A developmental account. *American Psychologist, 45,* 513–520.

Macnicol, J. (2006). *Age discrimination: An historical and contemporary analysis.* Cambridge, UK: Cambridge University Press.

Macrae, C., Bodenhausen, G., & Milne, A. (1995). The dissection of selection in person perception: Inhibitory processes in social stereotyping. *Journal of Personality and Social Psychology, 69,* 397–407.

Macrae, C., Milne, A., & Bodenhausen, G. (1994). Stereotypes as energy-saving devices: A peek inside the cognitive toolbox. *Journal of Personality and Social Psychology, 66,* 37–47.

Macrae, N., Bodenhausen, G., Milne, A., & Jetten, J. (1994). Out of mind but back in sight: Stereotypes on the rebound. *Journal of Personality and Social Psychology, 67,* 808–817.

Maddox, G., Back, K., & Liederman, V. (1968). Overweight as social deviance and disability. *Journal of Health and Social Behavior, 9,* 287–298.

Maddux, W., Galinsky, A., Cuddy, A., & Polifroni, M. (2008). When being a model minority is good . . . and bad: Realistic threat explains negativity toward Asian Americans. *Personality and Social Psychology Bulletin, 34,* 74–89.

Madey, S., & Ondrus, S. (1999). Illusory correlations in perceptions of obese and hypertensive patients' noncooperative behaviors. *Journal of Applied Social Psychology, 29,* 1200–1217.

Madon, S. (1997). What do people believe about gay males? A study of stereotype content and strength. *Sex Roles, 37,* 663–685.

Madon, S., Guyll, M., Aboufadel, K., Montiel, E., Smith, A., Palumbo, P., & Jussim, L. (2001). Ethnic and national stereotypes: The Princeton Triology revisited and revised. *Personality and Social Psychology Bulletin, 27,* 996–1010.

Madon, S., Guyll, M., Spoth, R., & Willard, J. (2004). Self-fulfilling prophecies: The synergistic accumulative effect of parents' beliefs on children's drinking behavior. *Psychological Science, 15,* 837–845.

Madon, S., Jussim, L., & Eccles, J. (1997). In search of the powerful self-fulfilling prophecy. *Journal of Personality and Social Psychology, 72,* 791–809.

Madon, S., Jussim, L., Keiper, S., Eccles, J., Smith, A., & Palumbo, P. (1998). The accuracy and power of sex, social class, and ethnic stereotypes: A naturalistic study of person perception. *Personality and Social Psychology Bulletin, 24,* 1304–1318.

Mahaffey, A., Bryan, A., & Hutchison, K. (2005). Using startle eye blink to measure the affective component of antigay bias. *Basic and Applied Social Psychology, 27,* 37–45.

Maio, G., & Esses, V. (1998). The social consequences of affirmative action: Deleterious effects on perceptions of groups. *Personality and Social Psychology Bulletin, 24,* 65–74.

Major, B. (1994). From disadvantage to deserving: Comparisons, justification and the psychology of entitlement. In M. P. Zanna (Ed.), *Advances in experimental social psychology* (Vol. 26, pp. 124–148). Thousand Oaks, CA: Sage.

Major, B., McFarlin, D., & Gagnon, D. (1984). Overworked and underpaid: On the nature of gender differences in personal entitlement. *Journal of Personality and Social Psychology, 47,* 1399–1412.

Major, B., & O'Brien, L. (2005). The social psychology of stigma. *Annual Review of Psychology, 56,* 393–421.

Mak, W., & Kwok, Y. (2010). Internalization of stigma for parents of children with autism spectrum disorder in Hong Kong. *Social Science & Medicine, 70,* 2045–2051.

Malhotra, D., & Liyanage, S. (2005). Long-term effects of peace workshops in protracted conflicts. *Journal of Conflict Resolution, 49,* 908–924.

Manor, J., Kenrick, D., Becker, D. V., Delton, A., Hofer, B., Wilbur, C., & Neuberg, S. (2005). Sexually selective cognition: Beauty captures the mind of the beholder. *Journal of Personality and Social Psychology, 85,* 1107–1120.

Maras, P., & Brown, R. (1996). Effects of contact on children's attitudes toward disability: A longitudinal study. *Journal of Applied Social Psychology, 26,* 2113–2134.

Marin, G. (1984). Stereotyping Hispanics: The differential effect of research method, label, and degree of contact. *International Journal of Intercultural Relations, 8,* 17–27.

Markus, H., & Kitayama, S. (1991). Culture and the self: Implications for cognition, emotion, and motivation. *Psychological Review, 98,* 224–253.

Maroney, D., & Golub, S. (1992). Nurses' attitudes toward obese persons and certain ethnic groups. *Perceptual and Motor Skills, 75,* 387–391.

Martinez, A., Piff, P., Mendoza-Denton, R., & Hinshaw, S. (2011). The power of a label: Mental illness diagnoses, ascribed humanity, and social rejection. *Journal of Social and Clinical Psychology, 30,* 1–23.

Mays, V., & Cochran, S. (2001). Mental health correlates of perceived discrimination among lesbian, gay, and bisexual adults in the United States. *American Journal of Public Health, 91,* 1869–1876.

McFarland, S. (1989). Religious orientation and targets of discrimination. *Journal for the Scientific Study of Religion, 28,* 324–336.

McGregor, H., Leiberman, J., Greenberg, J., Solomon, S., Arndt, J., Simon, L., & Pyszczynski, T. (1998). Terror management and aggression: Evidence that mortality salience promotes aggression against worldview threatening individuals. *Journal of Personality and Social Psychology, 74,* 590–605.

McIntosh, P. (1989, July/August). White privilege: Unpacking the invisible knapsack. *Peace and Freedom,* 8–10.

McKenna, K., & Bargh, J. (1998). Coming out in the age of the Internet: Identity "demarginalization" through virtual group participation. *Journal of Personality and Social Psychology, 75,* 681–694.

McLaughlin, S., Connell, C., Heeringa, S., Li, L., & Roberts, J. S. (2010). Successful aging in the United States: Prevalence estimates from a national sample of older adults. *Journal of Gerontology: Social Sciences, 65B,* 216–226.

Mead, G. (1913). The social self. *Journal of Philosophy, 10,* 374–380.

Mead, G. (1934). *Mind, self, and society.* Chicago, IL: University of Chicago Press.

Meisner, B. (2010). A meta-analysis of positive and negative age stereotype priming effects on behavior among older adults. *Journal of Gerontology: Social Sciences, 66.* doi: 10.1093/geronb/gbr062. First published online: July 11, 2011.

Mendoza-Denton, R., & Page-Gould, E. (2008). Can cross-group friendships influence minority students' well-being at historically White universities? *Psychological Science, 19,* 933–939.

Menec, V., & Perry, R. (1995). Reactions to stigmas: The effect of targets' age and controllability of stigmas. *Journal of Aging and Health, 7,* 365–383.

Merton, R. (1948). The self-fulfilling prophecy. *Antioch Review, 8,* 193–210.

Meyer, I. (2003). Prejudice, social stress, and mental health in lesbian, gay, and bisexual populations: Conceptual issues and research evidence. *Psychological Bulletin, 129,* 647–697.

Migdal, M., Hewstone, M., & Mullen, B. (1997). The effects of crossed categorizations on intergroup evaluations: A meta-analysis. *British Journal of Social Psychology, 37,* 303–324.

Miller, C., & Downey, K. (1999). A meta-analysis of heavyweight and self-esteem. *Personality and Social Psychology Review, 3,* 68–84.

Miller, C., & Myers, A. (1998). Compensating for prejudice: How heavyweight people (and others) control outcomes despite prejudice. In J. Swim & C. Stangor (Eds.), *Prejudice: The target's perspective* (pp. 191–218). San Diego, CA: Academic Press.

Miller, C., Rothblum, E., Felicio, D., & Brand, P. (1995). Compensating for stigma: Obese and nonobese women's reactions to being visible. *Personality and Social Psychology Bulletin, 21,* 1093–1106.

Miller, D., Leyell, T., & Mazachek, J. (2004). Stereotypes of the elderly in US television commercials from the 1950s to the 1990s. *International Journal of Aging and Human Development, 58,* 315–340.

Miller, S., Maner, J., & Becker, D. V. (2010). Self-protective biases in group categorization: Threat cures shape the psychological boundary between "us" and "them". *Journal of Personality and Social Psychology, 99,* 62–77.

Miranda, J., & Storms, M. (1989). Psychological adjustment of lesbians and gay men. *Journal of Counseling and Development, 68,* 41–45.

Monteith, M. (1993). Self-regulation of prejudiced responses: Implications for progress in prejudice-reduction efforts. *Journal of Personality and Social Psychology, 65,* 469–485.

Monteith, M., Zuwerink, J., & Devine, P. (1994). Prejudice and prejudice reduction: Classic challenges, contemporary approaches. *Social cognition: Impact on social psychology* (pp. 323–346). New York, NY: Academic Press.

Montepare, J., & Zebrowitz, L. (2002). A social-developmental view of ageism. In T. D. Nelson (Ed.), *Ageism: Stereotyping and prejudice against older persons* (pp. 77–125). Cambridge, MA: MIT Press.

Moradi, B., van den Berg, J., & Epting, F. (2006). Intrapersonal and interpersonal manifestations of antilesbian and gay prejudice: An application of personal construct theory. *Journal of Counseling Psychology, 53,* 57–66.

Morgeson, F., Reider, M., Campion, M., & Bull, R. (2008). Review of research on age discrimination in the employment interview. *Journal of Business Psychology, 22,* 223–232.

Morrison, K., Plaut, V., & Ybarra, O. (2010). Predicting whether multiculturalism positively or negatively influences White Americans' intergroup attitudes: The role of ethnic identification. *Personality and Social Psychology Bulletin, 36,* 1648–1661.

Moskovitz, G., Salomon, A., & Taylor, C. (2000). Preconsciously controlling stereotyping: Implicitly activated egalitarian goals prevent the activation of stereotypes. *Social Cognition, 18,* 151–177.

Mullen, B., Brown, R., & Smith, C. (1992). Ingroup bias as a function of salience, relevance, and status: An integration. *European Journal of Social Psychology, 22,* 103–122.

Mullen, B. (2001). Ethnophaulisms for ethnic immigrant groups. *Journal of Social Issues, 57,* 457–475.

Mullen, B., & Rice, D. (2003). Ethnophaulisms and exclusion: The behavioral consequences of cognitive representation of ethnic immigrant groups. *Personality and Social Psychology Bulletin, 29,* 1056–1067.

Murrell, A., Dietz-Uhler, B., Dovidio, J., Gaertner, S., & Drout, C. (1994). Aversive racism and resistance to affirmative action: Perceptions of justice are not necessarily color blind. *Basic and Applied Social Psychology, 15,* 71–86.

Myers, A., & Rosen, J. (1999). Obesity stigmatization and coping: Relation to mental health symptoms, body image, and self-esteem. *International Journal of Obesity 23,* 221–230.

Myers, D., & Bishop, G. (1970). Discussion effects on racial attitudes. *Science, 169,* 778–779.

Nasser, R., Singhal, S., & Abouchedid, K. (2005). Causal attributions for poverty among Indian youth. *Current Research in Social Psychology, 11,* 1–13.

National Assessment of Educational Progress. (1996). *Data book.* Retrieved from http://www.nces.ed.gov/naep

National Center for Educational Statistics. (2008). *Digest of education statistics.* Retrieved from http://nces.ed.gov/programs/digest/d09/tables/dt09_226.asp

National Council of State Legislatures. (2011). Retrieved from http://www.ncsl.org/legislatures-elections/elections-campaigns/same-sex-marriage-on-the-ballot.aspx

National Institute of Mental Health. (2008). *Prevalence of serious illness among U.S. adults by age, sex, and race.* Retrieved from http://www.nimh.nih.gov/statistics/SMI_AASR.shtml

Neuberg, S., Smith, D., Hoffman, J., & Russell, F. (1994). When we observe stigmatized and "normal" individuals interacting: Stigma by association. *Personality and Social Psychology Bulletin, 20,* 196–209.

Neumark-Sztainer, D., Story, M., & Faibisch, L. (1998). Perceived stigmatization among overweight African-American and Caucasian adolescent girls. *Journal of Adolescent Health, 23,* 264–270.

Newman, L., Caldwell, T., Chamberlin, B., & Griffin, T. (2005). Thought suppression, projection, and the development of stereotypes. *Basic and Applied Social Psychology, 27,* 259–266.

Nosworthy, G., Lea, J., & Lindsay, R. (1995). Opposition to affirmative action: Racial affect and traditional value predictors across four programs. *Journal of Applied Social Psychology, 25,* 314–337.

Oakes, P., & Turner, J. (1980). Social categorization and intergroup behaviour: Does minimal intergroup discrimination make social identity more positive? *European Journal of Social Psychology, 10,* 295–301.

Obama, B. (2004). *Dreams of my father: A story of race and inheritance.* New York, NY: Random House.

O'Brien, L., Crandall, C., Horstman-Reser, A., Warner, R., Alsbrooks, A., & Blodorn, A. (2010). But I'm no bigot: How prejudiced White Americans maintain unprejudiced self-images. *Journal of Applied Social Psychology, 40,* 917–946.

O'Connor, B., & St. Pierre, E. (2004). Older persons' perceptions of the frequency and meaning of elderspeak from family, friends, and service workers. *International Journal of Aging and Human Development, 58,* 197–221.

Oliver, M., & Hyde, J. (1993). Gender differences in sexuality: A meta-analysis. *Psychological Bulletin, 114,* 29–51.

Olson, M., & Fazio, R. (2006). Reducing automatically activated racial prejudice through implicit evaluative conditioning. *Personality and Social Psychology Bulletin, 32,* 421–433.

Osajima, K. (1988). Asian Americans as the model minority: An analysis of the popular press image of the 1960s and 1980s. In G. Okihiro, S. Hune, A. Hansen, & J. Liu (Eds.), *Reflections on shattered windows* (pp. 165–174). Pullman: Washington State University Press.

Osterman, K., Bjorkqvist, K., Lagerspetz, K., Kauklainen, A., Landau, S., Rraczek, A., & Caprara, G. (1998). Cross-cultural evidence of female indirect aggression. *Aggressive Behavior, 24,* 1–8.

Ostrov, J., & Keating, C. (2004). Gender differences in preschool aggression during free play and structured interactions: An observational study. *Social Development, 13,* 255–274.

Pachankis, J. (2007). The psychological implications of concealing a stigma: A cognitive-affective-behavioral model. *Psychological Bulletin, 133,* 328–345.

Pack, H., & Shah, H. (2003). Racial ideology, model minorities, and the "not-so-silent partner": Stereotyping of Asian Americans in US magazine advertising. *The Howard Journal of Communications, 14,* 225–243.

Page-Gould, E., Mendoza-Denton, R., Alegre, J., & Siy, J. (2010). Understanding the impact of cross-group friendship on interactions with novel outgroup members. *Journal of Personality and Social Psychology, 98,* 775–793.

Paluck, E. (2009). Reducing intergroup prejudice and conflict using the media: A field experiment in Rwanda. *Journal of Personality and Social Psychology, 96,* 574–587.

Park, B., Ryan, C., & Judd, C. (1992). Role of meaningful subgroups in explaining differences in perceived variability for in-groups and out-groups. *Journal of Personality and Social Psychology, 63,* 553–567.

Park, J., Schaller, M., & Crandall, C. (2007). Pathogen-avoidance mechanisms and the stigmatization of obese people. *Evolution and Human Behavior, 28,* 410–414.

Pascoe, E., & Richman, L. (2009). Perceived discrimination and health: A meta-analytic review. *Psychological Bulletin, 135,* 531–554.

Pearson, J., Crissey, S., & Riegle-Crumb, C. (2009). Gendered fields: Sports and advanced course taking in high school. *Sex Roles, 61,* 519–535.

Peck, M. S. (1994). *A world waiting to be reborn: Civility rediscovered.* New York, NY: Bantam Books.

Peery, D., & Bodenhausen, G. (2008). Black + White = Black. *Psychological Science, 19,* 973–977.

Pennebaker, J. (1990). *Opening up: The healing power of confiding in others.* New York, NY: William Morrow.

Penner, L., Dovidio, J., West, T., Gaertner, S., Albrecht, T., Dailey, R., & Markova, T. (2010). Aversive racism and medical interactions with Black patients: A field study. *Journal of Experimental Social Psychology, 46,* 436–440.

Pettigrew, T. F. (1979). The ultimate attribution error: Extending Allport's cognitive analysis of prejudice. *Personality and Social Psychology Bulletin, 5,* 461–476.

Pew Forum on Religion and Public Life. (2009). *A religious portrait of African-Americans.* Retrieved from http://www.pewforum.org/A-Religious-Portrait-of-African-Americans.aspx#2

Pew Forum on Religion and Public Life. (2011). *The future of the global Muslim population: Projections for 2010-2030.* Retrieved from http://www.pewforum.org/The-Future-of-the-Global-Muslim-Population.aspx

Phelan, J., & Rudman, L. (2010). Reactions to ethnic deviance: The role of backlash in racial stereotype maintenance. *Journal of Personality and Social Psychology, 99,* 265–281.

Phelps, E., O'Connor, K., Cunningham, W., Funayama, S., Gatenby, C., Gore, J., & Banaji, M. (2000). Performance on indirect measures of race evaluation predicts amygdala activation. *Journal of Cognitive Neuroscience, 12,* 729–738.

Phinney, J. (1996). When we talk about American ethnic groups, what do we mean? *American Psychologist, 51,* 918–927.

Pinel, E. (1999). Stigma consciousness: The psychological legacy of social stereotypes. *Journal of Personality and Social Psychology, 76,* 114–128.

Pinel, E. (2002). Stigma consciousness in intergroup contexts: The power of conviction. *Journal of Experimental Social Psychology, 38,* 178–185.

Plant, E. A., Devine, P., Cox, W., Columb, C., Miller, S., Goplen, J., & Peruche, M. (2009). The Obama effect: Decreasing implicit prejudice and stereotyping. *Journal of Experimental Social Psychology, 45,* 961–964.

Plant, E. A., Peruche, M., & Butz, D. (2005). Eliminating automatic racial bias: Making race non-diagnostic for responses to criminal suspects. *Journal of Experimental Social Psychology, 41,* 141–156.

Plaut, V., Garnett, G., Buffardi, L., & Sanchez-Burks, J. (2011). "What about me?" Perceptions of exclusion and Whites' reactions to multiculturalism. *Journal of Personality and Social Psychology, 101,* 337–353.

Plaut, V., Thomas, K., & Goren, M. (2009). Is multiculturalism or color blindness better for minorities? *Psychological Science, 20,* 444–446.

Posthuma, R., & Campion, M. (2009). Age stereotypes in the workplace: Common stereotypes, moderators, and future research directions. *Journal of Management, 35,* 158–188.

Puhl, R., & Heuer, C. (2009). The stigma of obesity: A review and update. *Obesity, 17,* 941–964.

Puhl, R., & Luedicke, J. (2012). Weight-based victimization among adolescents in the school setting: Emotional reactions and coping behaviors. *Journal of Youth and Adolescence, 41,* 27–40.

Puhl, R., Luedicke, J., & Heuer, C. (2011). Weight-based victimization toward overweight adolescents: Observations and reactions of peers. *Journal of School Health, 81,* 696–703.

Quick, H., & Moen, P. (1998). Gender, employment, and retirement quality: A life course approach to the differential experiences of men and women. *Journal of Occupational Health Psychology, 3,* 44–64.

Quinley, H., & Glock, C. (1979). *Anti-Semitism in America.* New York, NY: Free Press.

Quinn, D., & Chaudoir, S. (2009). Living with a concealable stigmatized identity: The impact of anticipated stigma, centrality, salience, and cultural stigma on psychological distress and health. *Journal of Personality and Social Psychology, 97,* 634–651.

Quist, R., & Resendez, M. (2002). Social dominance threat: Examining social dominance theory's explanation of prejudice as legitimizing myths. *Basic and Applied Social Psychology, 24,* 287–293.

Register, C., & Williams, D. (1990). Wage effects of obesity among young workers. *Social Science Quarterly, 71,* 130–141.

Richardson, S., Goodman, N., Hastorf, A., & Dornbusch, S. (1961). Cultural uniformity in reaction to physical disabilities. *American Sociological Review, 26,* 241–247.

Richeson, J., & Ambady, N. (2001). When roles reverse: stigma, status, and self-evaluation. *Journal of Applied Social Psychology, 31,* 1350–1378.

Richeson, J., & Ambady, N. (2003). Effects of situational power on automatic racial prejudice. *Journal of Experimental Social Psychology, 39,* 177–183.

Richeson, J., & Trawalter, S. (2005). Why do interracial interactions impair executive function? A resource depletion account. *Journal of Personality and Social Psychology, 88,* 934–947.

Risman, B. (1987). Intimate relationships from a microstructural perspective: Men who mother. *Gender and Society, 1,* 6–32.

Robinson, T., Callister, M., & Jankoski, T. (2008). Portrayal of body weight on children's television sitcoms: A content analysis. *Body Image, 5,* 141–151.

Rodin, J., & Langer, E. (1980). Aging labels: The decline of control and the fall of self-esteem. *Journal of Social Issues, 36,* 12–29.

Rodin, J., & Slochower, J. (1974). Fat chance for a favor: Obese-normal differences in compliance and incidental learning. *Journal of Personality and Social Psychology, 29,* 557–565.

Rodin, M., Price, J., Sanchez, F., & McElligot, S. (1989). Derogation, exclusion, and unfair treatment of persons with social flaws: Controllability of stigma and the attribution of prejudice. *Personality and Social Psychology Bulletin, 15,* 439–451.

Roehling, M. (1999). Weight-based discrimination in employment: Psychological and legal aspects. *Personnel Psychology, 52,* 969–1017.

Roehling, M., Roehling, P., & Pichler, S. (2007). The relationship between body weight and perceived weight-related employment discrimination: The role of sex and race. *Journal of Vocational Behavior, 71,* 300–318.

Roehling, P., Roehling, M., Vandlen, J., Blazek, J., & Guy, W. (2009). Weight discrimination and the glass ceiling effect among top US CEOs. *Equal Opportunities International, 28,* 179–196.

Roscigno, V. (2010). Ageism in the American workplace. *Contexts, 9,* 16–21.

Roscigno, V., Mong, S., Byron, R., & Tester, G. (2007). Age discrimination, social closure, and employment. *Social Forces, 86,* 313–334.

Rosen, B., & Jerdee, T. (1978). Perceived sex differences in managerially relevant characteristics. *Sex Roles, 4,* 837–843.

Rosenthal, R. (1974). *On the social psychology of the self-fulfilling prophecy: Further evidence for Pygmalion effects and their mediating mechanisms.* New York, NY: MSS Modular Publications.

Rosenthal, R., & Jacobson, L. (1968). *Pygmalion in the classroom: Teacher expectations and student intellectual development.* New York, NY: Holt, Rinehart & Winston.

Rosenthal, R., & Lawson, R. (1964). A longitudinal study of the effect of experimenter bias on the operant learning of laboratory rats. *Journal of Psychiatric Research, 2,* 61–72.

Rosow, I. (1974). *Socialization to old age.* Berkeley: University of California Press.

Ross, M., Eyman, A., & Kishchuk, N. (1986). Determinants of subjective well-being. In J. Olsen, C. Herman, & M. Zanna (Eds.), *Relative deprivation and social comparison: The Ontario symposium* (pp. 217–242). Hillsdale, NJ: Erlbaum.

Rotenberg, K., Gruman, J., & Ariganello, M. (2002). Behavioral confirmation of the loneliness stereotype. *Basic and Applied Social Psychology, 24,* 81–89.

Rothbart, M., Dawes, R., & Park, B. (1984). Stereotyping and sampling biases in intergroup perception. In J. R. Eiser (Ed.), *Attitudinal judgment* (pp. 109–134). New York, NY: Springer-Verlag.

Rothbart, M., Evans, M., & Fulero, S. (1979). Recall for confirming events: Memory processes and the maintenance of social stereotyping. *Journal of Experimental Social Psychology, 15,* 343–355.

Rothbart, M., Fulero, S., Jensen, C., Howard, J., & Birrel, P. (1978). From individual to group impressions: Availability heuristics in stereotype formation. *Journal of Experimental Social Psychology, 14,* 237–255.

Rothblum, E., Brand, P., Miller, C., & Oetjen, H. (1990). The relationship between obesity, employment discrimination, and employment-related victimization. *Journal of Vocational Behavior, 37,* 251–266.

Rubin, K., & Brown, D. (1975). A life-span look at person perception and its relationship to communicative interaction. *Journal of Gerontology, 30,* 461–468.

Rudman, L. (1998). Self-promotion as a risk factor for women: The costs and benefits of counter stereotypical impression management. *Journal of Personality and Social Psychology, 74,* 629–645.

Rudman, L., Ashmore, R., & Gary, M. (2001). "Unlearning" automatic biases: The malleability of implicit prejudice and stereotypes. *Journal of Personality and Social Psychology, 81,* 856–868.

Rudman, L., & Fairchild, K. (2004). Reactions to counter stereotypic behavior: The role of backlash in cultural stereotype maintenance. *Journal of Personality and Social Psychology, 87,* 157–176.

Rudman, L., & Glick, P. (1999). Feminized management and backlash toward agentic women: The hidden costs to women of a kinder, gentler image of middle managers. *Journal of Personality and Social Psychology, 77,* 1004–1010.

Rudman, L., & Glick, P. (2001). Prescriptive gender stereotypes and backlash toward agentic women. *Journal of Social Issues, 57,* 743–762.

Ruggiero, K., & Taylor, D. (1995). Coping with discrimination. How disadvantaged group members perceive the discrimination that confronts them. *Journal of Personality and Social Psychology, 68,* 826–838.

Ruggiero, K., & Taylor, D. (1997). Why minority group members perceive or do not perceive the discrimination that confronts them: The role of self-esteem and perceived control. *Journal of Personality and Social Psychology, 72,* 373–389.

Ruggiero, K., Taylor, D., & Lydon, J. (1997). How disadvantaged group members cope with discrimination when they perceive that social support is available. *Journal of Applied Social Psychology, 27,* 1581–1600.

Rule, N., & Ambady, N. (2008). Brief exposures: Male sexual orientation is accurately perceived at 50 ms. *Journal of Experimental Social Psychology, 44,* 1100–1105.

Ruppel, S., Jenkins, W., Griffin, J., & Kizer, J. (2010). Are they depressed or just old? A study of perceptions about the elderly suffering from depression. *North American Journal of Psychology, 12,* Source issue 1. ISSN: 1527-7143.

Ruscher, J. (1998). Prejudice and stereotyping in everyday communication. *Advances in Experimental Social Psychology, 30,* 241–307.

Ruscher, J. (2001). *Prejudiced communication: A social psychological perspective.* New York, NY: Guilford Press.

Ruscher, J., & Duval, L. (1998). Multiple communicators with unique target information transmit less stereotypical impressions. *Personality and Social Psychology, 74,* 329–344.

Ruscher, J., & Hammer, E. D. (1994). Revising disrupted impressions through conversation. *Journal of Personality and Social Psychology, 66,* 530–541.

Ryan, C. (1996). Accuracy of Black and White college students' in-group and out-group stereotypes. *Personality and Social Psychology Bulletin, 22,* 1114–1127.

Ryan, E., Bourhis, R., & Knops, U. (1991). Evaluative perceptions of patronizing speech addressed to elders. *Psychology and Aging, 6,* 442–450.

Rydell, R., Rydell, M., & Boucher, K. (2010). The effect of negative performance stereotypes on learning. *Journal of Personality and Social Psychology, 99,* 883–896.

Sachdev, I., & Bourhis, R. (1978). Status differentials and intergroup behaviour. *European Journal of Social Psychology, 17,* 277–293.

Sack, K. (2008, June 5). Research finds wide disparities in healthcare by race and region. *New York Times.* Retrieved from http://www.nytimes.com/2008/06/05/health/research/05disparities.html

Savin-Williams, R. (1990). *Gay and lesbian youth: Expressions of identity*. New York, NY: Hemisphere.

Schafer, M., & Ferraro, K. (2011). Distal and variably proximal causes: Education, obesity, and health. *Social Science & Medicine, 73*, 1340–1348.

Schimel, J., Simon, L., Greenberg, J., Pyszczynski, T., Solomon, S., Waxmonsky, J., & Arndt, J. (1999). Stereotypes and terror management: Evidence that mortality salience enhances stereotypic thinking and preferences. *Journal of Personality and Social Psychology, 77*, 905–926.

Schmader, T., & Johns, M. (2003). Converging evidence that stereotype threat reduces working memory capacity. *Journal of Personality and Social Psychology, 85*, 440–452.

Schmader, T., Major, B., & Gramzow, R. (2001). Coping with ethnic stereotypes in the academic domain: Perceived injustice and psychological disengagement. *Journal of Social Issues, 57*, 93–111.

Schmidt, D., & Boland, S. (1986). Structure of perceptions of older adults: Evidence for multiple stereotypes. *Psychology and Aging, 1*, 255–260.

Schmidt, K., & Nosek, B. (2010). Implicit (and explicit) racial attitudes barely changed during Barack Obama's presidential campaign and early presidency. *Journal of Experimental Social Psychology, 46*, 308–314.

Schneider, D. (2004). *The psychology of stereotyping*. New York, NY: Guilford Press.

Schneider, M., Major, B., Luhtanen, R., & Crocker, J. (1996). Social stigma and the potential costs of assumptive help. *Personality and Social Psychology Bulletin, 22*, 201–209.

Schulman, K., Berlin, J., Harless, W., Kerner, J., Sisrunk, S., Gersh, . . . Ayers, W. (1999). The effect of race and sex on physicians' recommendations for cardiac catheterization. *New England Journal of Medicine, 340*, 618–626.

Schultz, R., Martire, L., Beach, S., & Scheier, M. (2000). Depression and mortality in the elderly. *Current Directions in Psychological Science, 9*, 204–208.

Schulz, K., & Wang, M. (2011). Psychological perspectives on the changing nature of retirement. *American Psychologist, 66*, 170–179.

Schwartz, M., Chambliss, H., Brownell, K., Blair, S., & Billington, C. (2003). Weight bias among health professionals specializing in obesity. *Obesity Research, 11*, 1033–1039.

Schwarzer, R., & Weiner, B. (1991). Stigma controllability and coping as predictors of emotions and social support. *Journal of Social and Personal Relationships, 8*, 133–140.

Sears, D. (1988). Symbolic racism. In P. A. Katz & D. M. Taylor (Eds.), *Eliminating racism: Profiles in controversy* (pp. 53–84). New York, NY: Plenum.

Seccombe, K., James, D., & Walters, K. (1998). "They think you ain't much of nothing": The social construction of the welfare mother. *Journal of Marriage and Family, 60*, 849–865.

Sechrist, G., & Stangor, C. (2001). Perceived consensus influences intergroup behavior and stereotype accessibility. *Journal of Personality and Social Psychology, 80*, 645–654.

Seta, J., Seta, C., & McElroy, T. (2003). Attributional biases in the service of stereotype maintenance: A schema-maintenance through compensation analysis. *Personality and Social Psychology Bulletin, 29*, 151–163.

Sherif, M. (1966). *Group conflict and cooperation: Their social psychology*. London, England: Routledge & Kegan Paul.

Sheldon, W. H., Stevens, S. S., & Tucker, W. B. (1940). *The varieties of human physique*. New York, NY: Harper & Row.

Sherman, G., & Clore, G. (2009). The color of sin: White and Black are perceptual symbols of moral purity and pollution. *Psychological Science, 20*, 1019–1025.

Shih, M., Pittinsky, T., & Ambady, N. (1999). Stereotype susceptibility: Identity salience and shifts in quantitative performance. *Psychological Science, 10*, 80–83.

Shook, N., & Fazio, R. (2008). Interracial roommate relationships: An experimental field test of the contact hypothesis. *Psychological Science, 19*, 717–723.

Shrauger, S., & Schoeneman, T. (1979). Symbolic interactionist views of self-concept: Through the looking glass darkly. *Psychological Bulletin, 86,* 549–573.

Sibley, C., & Duckitt, J. (2008). Personality and prejudice: A meta-analysis and theoretical review. *Personality and Social Psychology Review, 12,* 248–279.

Sidanius, J. (1993). The psychology of group conflict and the dynamics of oppression: A social dominance perspective. In S. Iyengar & W. McGuire (Eds.), *Explorations in political psychology* (pp. 183–219). Durham, NC: Duke University Press.

Sidanius, J., & Pratto, F. (1999). *Social dominance: An intergroup theory of social hierarchy and oppression.* Cambridge, UK: Cambridge University Press.

Sigall, H., & Page, R. (1971). Current stereotypes: A little fading, a little faking. *Journal of Personality and Social Psychology, 18,* 247–255.

Sigelman, C., Howell, J., Cornell, D., Cutright, J., & Dewey, J. (1991). Courtesy stigma: The social implications of associating with a gay person. *The Journal of Social Psychology, 131,* 45–56.

Silverschanz, P., Cortina, L., Konik, J., & Magley, V. (2008). Slurs, snubs, and queer jokes: Incidence and impact of heterosexist harassment in academia. *Sex Roles, 58,* 179–191.

Sinclair, L., & Kunda. Z. (1999). Reactions to a Black professional: Motivated inhibition and activation of conflicting stereotypes. *Journal of Personality and Social Psychology, 77,* 885–904.

Sitton, S., & Blanchard, S. (1995). Men's preferences in romantic partners: Obesity versus addiction. *Psychological Reports, 77,* 1185–86.

Slavin, R. (1979). Effects of biracial learning teams on cross-racial friendships. *Journal of Educational Psychology, 71,* 381–387.

Smith, E., & Zarate, M. (1992). Exemplar-based model of social judgment. *Psychological Review, 99,* 3–21.

Smith, S., Pieper, K., Granados, A., & Choueiti, M. (2010). Assessing gender-related portrayals in top-grossing G-rated films. *Sex Roles, 62,* 774–786.

Smith, T. (1993). Actual trends or measurement artifacts? A review of three studies of anti-Semitism. *Public Opinion Quarterly, 57,* 380–393.

Snodgrass, S. (1985). Women's intuition: The effect of subordinate role on interpersonal sensitivity. *Journal of Personality and Social Psychology, 49,* 146–155.

Snyder, M., & Cantor, N. (1979). Testing hypotheses about other people: The use of historical knowledge. *Journal of Experimental Social Psychology, 15,* 330–343.

Snyder, M., & Haugen, J. (1995). Why does behavioral confirmation occur? A functional perspective on the role of the target. *Personality and Social Psychology Bulletin, 21,* 963–974.

Snyder, M., Tanke, E., & Berscheid, E. (1977). Social perception and interpersonal behavior: On the self-fulfilling nature of social stereotypes. *Journal of Personality and Social Psychology, 35,* 656–666.

Sommers, S., & Norton, M. (2008). Race and jury selection. *American Psychologist, 63,* 527–539.

Spence, J., Helmreich, R., & Holohan, C. (1979). Negative and positive components of psychological masculinity and femininity and their relationships to self-reports of neurotic and acting-out behaviors. *Journal of Personality and Social Psychology, 37,* 1673–1682.

Spencer, S., Rein, S., Wolfe, C., Fong, C., & Dunn, M. (1998). Automatic activation of stereotypes: The role of self-image threat. *Personality and Social Psychology Bulletin, 24,* 1139–1152.

Spencer, S., Steele, C., & Quinn, D. (1997). *Under suspicion of inability: Stereotype threat and women's math performance.* Manuscript submitted for publication.

Spencer, S., Steele, C., & Quinn, D. (1999). Stereotype threat and women's math performance. *Journal of Experimental Social Psychology, 35,* 4–28.

Stangor, C., & Schaller, M. (1996). Stereotypes as individual and collective representations. In C. Macrae, C. Stangor, & M. Hewstone (Eds.), *Stereotypes and stereotyping* (pp. 3–40). New York, NY: Guilford Press.

Steele, C. (1992, April). Race and the schooling of the Black Americans. *The Atlantic Monthly,* 68–78.

Steele, C. (1997). A threat in the air: How stereotypes shape intellectual identity and performance. *American Psychologist, 52,* 613–629.

Steele, C., & Aronson, J. (1995). Stereotype threat and the intellectual test performance of African Americans. *Journal of Personality and Social Psychology, 69,* 797–811.

Stephan, W. (1978). School desegregation: An evaluation of predictions made in *Brown vs. Board of Education. Psychological Bulletin, 85,* 217–238.

Stephan, W., & Finlay, K. (1999). The role of empathy in improving intergroup relations. *Journal of Social Issues, 55,* 729–743.

Sternberg, R., Grigorenko, E., & Kidd, K. (2005). Intelligence, race, and genetics. *American Psychologist, 60,* 46–59.

Stone, J., Perry, Z., & Darley, J. (1997). "White men can't jump": Evidence for the perceptual confirmation of racial stereotypes following a basketball game. *Basic and Applied Social Psychology, 19,* 291–306.

Strauss, H. (1968). Reference group and social comparison among the totally blind. In H. H. Hyman & E. Singer (Eds.), *Readings in reference group theory and research* (pp. 222–237). New York, NY: Free Press.

Sunnafrank, M., & Fontes, N. (1983). General and crime related stereotypes and influence on juridic decisions. *Cornell Journal of Social Relations, 17,* 1–15.

Suzuki, B. (1989, November-December). Asian Americans as the "model minority": Outdoing Whites? Or media hype? *Change,* 13–19.

Swann, W. (1985). The self as an architect of social reality. In B. Schlenker (Ed.), *The self and social life* (pp. 100–125). New York, NY: McGraw-Hill.

Swann, W., Hixon, J., & De La Ronde, C. (1992). Embracing the bitter "truth": Negative self-concepts and marital commitment. *Psychological Science, 3,* 118–121.

Swim, J. (1994). Perceived versus meta-analytic effect sizes: An assessment of the accuracy of gender stereotypes. *Journal of Personality and Social Psychology, 66,* 21–36.

Swim, J., Borgida, E., Maruyama, G., & Myers, D. (1989). Joan McKay vs. John McKay: Do gender stereotypes bias evaluations? *Psychological Bulletin, 105,* 409–429.

Swim, J., Ferguson, M., & Hyers, L. (1999). Avoiding stigma by association: Subtle prejudice against lesbians in the form of social distancing. *Basic and Applied Social Psychology, 21,* 61–68.

Swim, J., & Miller, D. (1999). White guilt: Its antecedents and consequences for attitudes toward affirmative action. *Personality and Social Psychology Bulletin, 25,* 500–514.

Tausch, N., Hewstone, M., Kenworthy, J., Psaltis, C., Schmid, K., Popan, J., . . . Hughes, J. (2010). Secondary transfer effects of intergroup contact: Alternative accounts and underlying processes. *Journal of Personality and Social Psychology, 99,* 282–302.

Tavris, C. (1992). *The mismeasure of woman.* New York, NY: Simon & Schuster.

Taylor, S., & Fiske, S. (1978). Salience, attention, and attribution: Top of the head phenomena. In L. Berkowitz (Ed.), *Advances in experimental social psychology* (Vol. 11, pp. 249–288). New York, NY: Academic Press.

Taylor, S. E., Fiske, S. T., Etcoff, N. L., & Ruderman, A. J. (1978). Categorical and contextual bases of person memory and stereotyping. *Journal of Personality and Social Psychology, 36,* 778–793.

Teachman, B., & Brownell, K. (2001). Implicit anti-fat bias among health professionals: Is anyone immune? *International Journal of Obesity, 25,* 1525–1531.

Thomas, K. (2011, April 26). College teams, relying on deception, undermine gender equity. *New York Times,140,* A1, 16.

Thorne, B. (1986). Girls and boys together . . . but mostly apart: Gender arrangements in elementary school. In W. Hartup & Z. Rubin (Eds.), *Relationships and development* (pp. 167–184). Hillsdale, NJ: Erlbaum.

Thuan, J. F., & Avignon, A. (2005). Obesity management: Attitudes and practices of French general practitioners in a region of France. *International Journal of Obesity, 25,* 1100–1106.

Tiggemann, M., & Anesbury, T. (2000). Negative stereotyping of obesity in children: The role of controllability beliefs. *Journal of Applied Social Psychology, 30,* 1977–1993.

Tomkiewicz, J., & Adeyemi-Bello, T. (1997). Perceptual differences in racial descriptions of Euro-Americans and Hispanic persons. *Psychological Reports, 80,* 1339–1343.

Trawalter, S., Todd, A., Baird, A., & Richeson, J. (2008). Attending to threat: Race-based patterns of selective attention. *Journal of Experimental Social Psychology, 44,* 1322–1327.

Truman, J., & Rand, M. (2010). *Criminal victimization, 2009.* Bureau of Justice Statistics National Crime Victimization Survey. Retrieved from http://bjs.ojp.usdoj.gov/content/pub/pdf/cv09.pdf

Turner, R. N., Crisp, R., & Lambert, E. (2007). Imagining intergroup contact can improve intergroup attitudes. *Group Processes & Intergroup Relations, 10,* 427–441.

Turner, R. N., Hewstone, M., Voci, A., & Vonofakou, C. (2008). A test of the extended intergroup contact hypothesis: The mediating role of intergroup anxiety, perceived ingroup and outgroup norms, and inclusion of the outgroup in the self. *Journal of Personality and Social Psychology, 95,* 843–860.

U.S. Census Bureau. (2002). *Poverty in the United States.* Washington, DC: Author.

U.S. Census Bureau. (2010). http://www.census.gov/

U.S. Department of Justice. (1997). *Bureau of Justice statistics.* Retrieved from http://www.ojp.usdoj.gov/bjs

Van Houtven, C., Voils, C., Oddone, E., Weinfurt, K., Rriedman, J., Schulman, K., & Bosworth, H. (2005). Perceived discrimination and reported delay of pharmacy prescriptions and medical tests. *Journal of General Internal Medicine, 20,* 578–583.

Vann, D. (1976). *Personal responsibility, authoritarianism, and treatment of the obese* (Unpublished doctoral dissertation). New York University, New York.

Vanneman, R., & Pettigrew, T. (1972). Race and relative deprivation in the urban United States. *Race, 13,* 461–486.

Volz, K., Kessler, T., & von Cramon, D. Y. (2009). In-group as part of the self: In-group favoritism is mediated by medial prefrontal cortex activation. *Social Neuroscience, 4,* 244–260.

Walton, G., & Spencer, S. (2009). Latent ability: Grades and test scores systematically underestimate the intellectual ability of negatively stereotyped students. *Psychological Science, 20,* 1132–1139.

Weaver, C. (2005). The changing image of Hispanic Americans. *Hispanic Journal of Behavioral Sciences, 27,* 337–354.

Weber, M. (1958). *The Protestant ethic and the spirit of capitalism.* New York, NY: Scribner.

Weinberg, G. (1972). *Society and the healthy homosexual.* New York, NY: St. Martin's Press.

Weiner, B., Perry, R., & Magnusson, J. (1988). An attributional analysis of reactions to stigmas. *Journal of Personality and Social Psychology, 55,* 738–748.

Werner, P., & Heinik, J. (2008). Stigma by association and Alzheimer's disease. *Aging & Mental Health, 12,* 92–99.

Weyant, J. (2005). Implicit stereotyping of Hispanics: Development and validity of a Hispanic version of the Implicit Association Test. *Hispanic Journal of Behavioral Sciences, 27,* 355–363.

Wheeler, M., & Fiske, S. (2005). Controlling racial prejudice: Social-cognitive goals affect amygdala and stereotype activation. *Psychological Science, 16,* 56–63.

White, J., & Kowalski, R. (1994). Deconstructing the myth of the nonaggressive women. *Psychology of Women Quarterly, 18,* 487–508.

White, R. (1959). Motivation reconsidered: The concept of competence. *Psychological Review, 36,* 953–962.

Wilkinson, W. (2004). Religiosity, authoritarianism, and homophobia: A multidimensional approach. *International Journal for the Psychology of Religion, 14,* 55–67.

Williams, J. (2004, November-December). Hitting the maternal wall. *Academe,* 16–20.

Williams, K., Kemper, S., & Hummert, M. (2003). Improving nursing home communication: An intervention to reduce elderspeak. *Gerontologist, 43,* 242–247.

Willoughby, B. (2003, February 11). *Considering the N-word.* Retrieved from http://www.tolerance .org/news/article_tol.jsp?id=703

Wills, T. (1991). Social support and interpersonal relationships. In M. S. Clark (Ed.), *Prosocial behavior* (pp. 265–289). Newbury Park, CA: Sage.

Wilson, T. (1996). Compliments will get you nowhere: Benign stereotypes, prejudice, and anti-Semitism. *The Sociological Quarterly, 37,* 465–479.

Wineburg, S. (1987). The self-fulfillment of the self-fulfilling prophecy. *Educational Researcher, 16,* 28–37.

Wirth, J., & Bodenhausen, G. (2009). The role of gender in mental-illness stigma. *Psychological Science, 20,* 169–173.

Wittenbrink, B., Judd, C., & Park, B. (1997). Evidence for racial prejudice at the implicit level and its relationship with questionnaire measures. *Journal of Personality and Social Psychology, 72,* 262–274.

Wolsko, C., Park, B., & Judd, C. M. (2006). Considering the tower of Babel: Correlations of assimilation and multiculturalism among ethnic minority and majority groups in the United States. *Social Justice Research, 19,* 277–306.

Wout, D., Shih, M., Jackson, J., & Sellers, R. (2009). Targets as perceivers: How people determine when they will be negatively stereotyped. *Journal of Personality and Social Psychology, 96,* 349–362.

Wright, S., Aron, A., McLaughlin-Volpe, T., & Ropp, S. (1997). The extended contact effect: Knowledge of cross-group friendships and prejudice. *Journal of Personality and Social Psychology, 73,* 73–90.

Wylie, R. (1979). *The self-concept* (Vol. 2). Lincoln: University of Nebraska Press.

Yang, A. (1997). Poll trends: Attitudes toward homosexuality. *Public Opinion Quarterly, 61,* 477–507.

Yee, A. (1992). Asians as stereotypes and students: Misperceptions that persist. *Educational Psychology Review, 4,* 95–132.

Yood, M., Johnson, C., Blount, A., Abrams, J., Wolman, E., McCarthy, B., . . . Wolman, S. (1999). Race and differences in breast cancer survival in a managed care population. *Journal of the National Cancer Institute, 91,* 1487–1491.

Yoshino, K. (2006, January 15). The pressure to cover. *New York Times Magazine,* 32–37.

Zanna, M., & Pack, S. (1975). On the self-fulfilling nature of apparent sex differences in behavior. *Journal of Experimental Social Psychology, 11,* 583–591.

Zucker, G., & Weiner, B. (1993). Conservatism and perceptions of poverty: An attributional analysis. *Journal of Applied Social Psychology, 23,* 925–943.

Zuckerman, M. (1990). Some dubious premises in research and theory on racial differences. *American Psychologist, 45,* 1297–1303.

Zur, O. (1989). War myths: Exploration of the dominant collective beliefs about warfare. *Journal of Humanistic Psychology, 29,* 297–327.

Author Index

Subject Index

About the Author

Bruce E. Blaine (PhD, State University of New York at Buffalo) is a professor of psychology and director of the statistics program at St. John Fisher College in Rochester, New York. He is widely published in social and health psychology. His other research interests include obesity treatment effectiveness and meta-analytic research methods.

⑤SAGE research**methods**

The essential online tool for researchers from the world's leading methods publisher

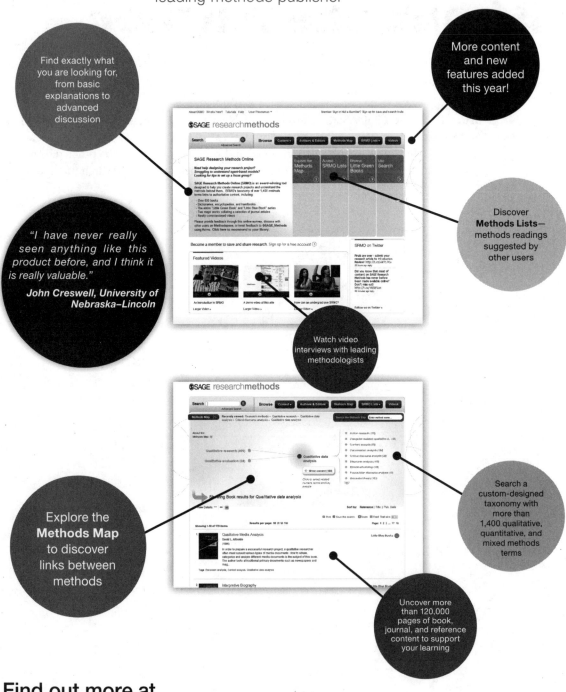

Find exactly what you are looking for, from basic explanations to advanced discussion

More content and new features added this year!

"I have never really seen anything like this product before, and I think it is really valuable."
John Creswell, University of Nebraska–Lincoln

Discover Methods Lists—methods readings suggested by other users

Watch video interviews with leading methodologists

Explore the Methods Map to discover links between methods

Search a custom-designed taxonomy with more than 1,400 qualitative, quantitative, and mixed methods terms

Uncover more than 120,000 pages of book, journal, and reference content to support your learning

Find out more at
www.sageresearchmethods.com